Power and Authority in Afghanistan

Power and Authority in Afghanistan

Rethinking Politics, Intervention and Rule

Edited by Anna Larson, Dipali Mukhopadhyay
and Omar Sharifi

I.B. TAURIS
LONDON · NEW YORK · OXFORD · NEW DELHI · SYDNEY

I.B. TAURIS
Bloomsbury Publishing Plc
50 Bedford Square, London, WC1B 3DP, UK
1385 Broadway, New York, NY 10018, USA
29 Earlsfort Terrace, Dublin 2, Ireland

BLOOMSBURY, I.B. TAURIS and the I.B. Tauris logo are trademarks
of Bloomsbury Publishing Plc

First published in Great Britain 2025

Copyright © Anna Larson, Dipali Mukhopadhyay and Omar Sharifi, 2025

Anna Larson, Dipali Mukhopadhyay and Omar Sharifi and Contributors have
asserted their rights under the Copyright, Designs and Patents Act, 1988,
to be identified as authors of this work.

For legal purposes the Acknowledgements on p. xv constitute
an extension of this copyright page.

Series design by Adriana Brioso
Cover image: Laila and Majnun at school from *Khamsa (Five Poems)* by Nizami, Herat,
1494–1495. Or. 6810, f.106v. From the British Library archive

All rights reserved. No part of this publication may be reproduced or
transmitted in any form or by any means, electronic or mechanical,
including photocopying, recording, or any information storage or
retrieval system, without prior permission in writing from the publishers.

Bloomsbury Publishing Plc does not have any control over, or responsibility for,
any third-party websites referred to or in this book. All internet addresses given
in this book were correct at the time of going to press. The author and publisher
regret any inconvenience caused if addresses have changed or sites have
ceased to exist, but can accept no responsibility for any such changes.

A catalogue record for this book is available from the British Library.

A catalog record for this book is available from the Library of Congress.

ISBN: HB: 978-0-7556-4748-4
ePDF: 978-0-7556-4749-1
eBook: 978-0-7556-4750-7

Typeset by Integra Software Services Pvt. Ltd.

To find out more about our authors and books visit www.bloomsbury.com
and sign up for our newsletters.

This volume is dedicated to the Afghan scholars from whom we have learned so much, and from whom we look forward to learning more.

Contents

List of Figures	ix
List of Contributors	x
Acknowledgements	xv
List of Abbreviations	xvi
General Maps	xix

Introduction: Rethinking Power and Authority in Afghanistan *Anna Larson*		1

Part 1 Logics of Rule and Institutional (Dis-)Continuities

1	Stability as Strength in the Musahiban Era *Thomas Barfield*	17
2	The Taliban, Women and the Hegelian Private Sphere *Juan Cole*	25
3	Legitimizing Power in Afghanistan *Haroun Rahimi*	49
4	Unlocking the Taliban Puzzle: Traditions and Fundamentalisms *Mujib Abid*	55
5	Neopatrimonial Perspectives on Political Structures in Afghanistan *Zinab Attai, Maryam Jami and Boshra Moheb*	71
6	Civil–Military Relations, Battlefield Performance and the Disintegration of Afghanistan's Security Forces *Abdul Basir Yosufi*	81

Part 2 Intervention and Its Legacies

7	Ghost Schools: Imperial Debris and the Erasure of Educated Women *Marya Hannun*	101
8	Peace Building and State Building in Afghanistan: Constructing Sovereignty for Whose Security? *Barnett R. Rubin*	106
9	Afghan Subjectivities and US Foreign Policy: Postcolonial Perspectives *Nasema Zeerak*	117

10	Leased Power and Vague Authority: The Political Culture and Economy of Rule in Afghanistan *M. Nazif Shahrani*	139
11	Legitimacy by Design *Astri Suhrke*	145
12	Brokerage, Business and the Continuities in Power *Noah Coburn and Arsalan Noori*	149
13	Power, Ideas and the 'Taliban 2.0' Myth *William Maley*	163

Part 3 The Politics of Recognition and Resistance

14	The State, the Clergy and British Imperial Policy in Afghanistan during the Nineteenth and Early Twentieth Centuries *Senzil Nawid*	171
15	The Pushback against the Hazara Rise in Afghanistan *Ali Yarwar Adili*	199
16	Minority Games: Intergroup Power Imbalances in a Nation of Competing Identities *Annika Schmeding*	209
17	Inheriting Hegemonic Nobility: Urban Elite Lineage and Legitimacy *Adam H. Dehsabzi*	231
18	Failed Democracy in Afghanistan: Rethinking Deliberation and Pluralism *Omar Sadr*	250
19	Mujahidin Memory and the Legacies of Wartime Governance in Afghanistan *Munazza Ebtikar*	271

Afterword *Dipali Mukhopadhyay*	286
Index	290

Figures

	Map of Afghanistan	xix
1.1	Zahir Shah banknote	19
1.2	Soviet-made BTR-60 armoured personal carrier parked at Charahi Ansari, Shahr-e Naw, Kabul, in July 1973	20
1.3	Daoud Khan banknote	22
6.1	Ethnic composition of Ministry of Interior leadership between February and June 2021	89
18.1	The Islamist-secularist spectrum	261
18.2	Online Anti-Nawroz campaign picture 1	264
18.3	Online Anti-Nawroz campaign picture 2	265

Contributors

Mujib Abid is Postdoctoral Research Fellow at the University of Melbourne's Initiative for Peacebuilding. Mujib is an Afghan scholar of modern Afghan history, peace studies and political theory. He researches the social and cultural dimensions of post-2001 Australian involvement in the 'war on terror' and statebuilding regimes in Afghanistan. Mujib is a co-founder of the Salaam Center for Dialogue (SCD), a Virginia-based non-profit organization that specializes in dialogue facilitation, peace research and advocacy. He holds a PhD from the University of Queensland, a master's degree in Peace and Conflict Studies from the University of Sydney and a BA from the American University of Afghanistan.

Ali Yarwar Adili is an independent researcher. Previously, he worked as a researcher and Country Director with the Afghanistan Analysts Network. There, his research focused on elections, political parties, state institutions, ethnic politics and security dynamics for ethnic minorities. He has also worked with New America, United Nations Development Program (UNDP), United Nations High Commissioner for Refugees (UNHCR) in Iraq, the National Democratic Institute for International Affairs and the Afghanistan Independent Human Rights Commission (AIHRC). Ali holds a master's degree in International Affairs from Columbia University, where he majored in International Security Policy and specialized in international conflict resolution.

Zinab Attai is a PhD student in Cornell University's Department of Government with research interests in state building, rebel governance and gender in conflict-affected areas. Her recent work investigates the institutional legacies of the US and Soviet intervention in Afghanistan and its consequences on social service provision under the Taliban. Her research has received support from the National Science Foundation and the Judith Reppy Institute for Peace and Conflict Studies. Before starting her PhD, Zinab worked as an international survey researcher and project manager at the Afghan Center for Socioeconomic Opinion Research (ACSOR).

Thomas Barfield is Professor of Anthropology at Boston University. He is a social anthropologist who conducted extensive ethnographic fieldwork among pastoral nomads in northern Afghanistan in the mid-1970s and shorter periods of research in Xinjiang, China, and post-Soviet Central Asia. He is the author of *The Central Asian Arabs of Afghanistan* (1981), *The Perilous Frontier: Nomadic Empires and China* (1989), *Afghanistan: An Atlas of Indigenous Domestic Architecture* (1991) and *Afghanistan: A Cultural and Political History* (2010).

Noah Coburn is a socio-cultural anthropologist and interdisciplinary scholar currently serving as Provost at Evergreen State College. He is the author of *Bazaar Politics: Pottery and Power in an Afghan Market Town* (2011), among other works.

Juan Cole is Richard P. Mitchell Collegiate Professor of History at the University of Michigan. He is an American academic and scholar on the modern Middle East and South Asia.

Adam H. Dehsabzi is Australian Graduate Researcher at the University of Chicago's Committee for International Relations. His research primarily focuses on self-determination, state formation, borderlands, identity conflicts and nationalism in the Middle East, and the region's relationship with the West. Prior to the political sciences, Adam had a seven-year career in architecture and urban development. He holds an undergraduate degree from the UTS School of Architecture and a master's degree from Macquarie University.

Munazza Ebtikar is a doctoral candidate at St John's College, University of Oxford. She is completing her thesis on war and memory in Afghanistan. Munazza is a recipient of numerous grants and awards and works as an international consultant for various research and policy institutions.

Marya Hannun is a historian currently based at the University of Exeter's Institute of Arab and Islamic Studies. She is researching Afghanistan's first women's movement and legal reform in the early twentieth century, examining its relationship to a wider transregional nexus.

Maryam Jami is an LLM student at Columbia University, New York, where she focuses her studies on sustainability, climate change and corporate governance. She also has another LLM degree in International and Comparative Law from the University of Pittsburgh in Pennsylvania. Maryam has written on various topics including human rights, international relations, security and peace building. Her research papers have been published by the *Oxford Human Rights Hub Journal*, *International Review of Human Rights Law*, *Groningen Journal of International Law*, *India Quarterly* (Taylor & Francis) and *The Diplomat*.

Anna Larson is an independent analyst and writer. She has worked in and on Afghanistan since 2004, writing and teaching at SOAS, University of London and Tufts University. Her PhD (2013) explored concepts and forms of democratization in Afghanistan. She has published widely, and her work includes *Derailing Democracy in Afghanistan: Elections in an Unstable Political Landscape* (Columbia, 2014), co-authored with Noah Coburn.

William Maley is Emeritus Professor of Diplomacy at The Australian National University. He is the author of *Rescuing Afghanistan* (2006), *What Is a Refugee?* (2016), *Transition in Afghanistan: Hope, Despair and the Limits of Statebuilding* (2018), *Diplomacy, Communication and Peace: Selected Essays* (2021) and *The Afghanistan Wars* (2021), and co-author (with Ahmad Shuja Jamal) of *The Decline and Fall of Republican Afghanistan* (2023).

Boshra Moheb is a graduate of Herat University's School of Law and Political Science. As the former head of the university's scientific and research committees, she has a strong background in academic research and legal studies. She has actively participated in, mentored and judged national and international legal debates and moot courts. Specializing in constitutional law and history, her research has been recognized in the Monash University Journal and presented at the 2nd Asian Legal Story Conference.

Dipali Mukhopadhyay is Associate Professor at the School of Advanced International Studies at Johns Hopkins University. Mukhopadhyay is the author of *Warlords, Strongman Governors, and the State in Afghanistan* (2014) and, with Kimberly Howe, of *Good Rebel Governance: Revolutionary Politics and Western Intervention in Syria* (2023). She was appointed to the Afghanistan War Commission as a Commissioner in 2024 and also currently serves as Vice President for the American Institute of Afghanistan Studies.

Senzil Nawid is Research Affiliate at the Southwest Institute for Research on Women, University of Arizona. She is the author of multiple works on Afghanistan, including *Religious Response to Social Change in Afghanistan: King Aman-Allah and the Afghan Ulama, 1919–1929* (1999).

Arsalan Noori (a pseudonym) is an Afghan scholar and social science researcher. He has worked with the international community for over fifteen years. He is co-author of *The Last Days of the Afghan Republic: A Doomed Evacuation Twenty Years in the Making* (2023), as well as numerous articles and reports.

Haroun Rahimi is Associate Professor and the Chair of the Law Department at the American University of Afghanistan. Rahimi is also a research fellow at the Raoul Wallenberg Institute of Human Rights and Humanitarian Law. His research focuses on religious education, religious authority, the rule of law, Islamic finance, economic laws and institutional reform. He obtained his BA in Law from Herat University, his LLM in Global Business Law and his PhD from the University of Washington.

Barnett R. Rubin is Distinguished Fellow with the China Program at the Stimson Center. He is Non-Resident Senior Fellow at the Quincy Institute for Responsible Statecraft and at New York University's Center on International Cooperation, where he was Senior Fellow and Director of the Afghanistan Regional Program from 2000 to 2020. He has taught at Columbia and Yale Universities. Rubin is the author of multiple books on Afghanistan including *Afghanistan from the Cold War through the War on Terror* (2013) and *The Fragmentation of Afghanistan: State Formation and Collapse in the International System* (Yale, 2002: first edition 1995).

Omar Sadr is a senior research scholar at the University of Pittsburgh's Center for Governance and Markets (CGM), United States. Previously, he taught political science at the American University of Afghanistan (AUAF). His primary research interests include pluralism and democracy in diverse societies, political Islam and secularism. He is the author of *Negotiating Cultural Diversity in Afghanistan,* which won a 2022 book prize for Best Book in Social Science from the Central Eurasian Studies Society. The book examines the challenges of peaceful coexistence in a fragile pluralistic society and develops a theory of governance of diversity.

Annika Schmeding is Lecturer at the University of Amsterdam. She is also Senior Researcher at NIOD – Institute for War, Holocaust and Genocide Studies, where she works on the Dutch parliamentary inquiry of the NATO war in Afghanistan. She has researched in Afghanistan since 2011 and her PhD (2020) explored Afghanistan's Sufi communities as both centres of spiritual learning as well as nodes for social action. As a cultural anthropologist and former Harvard Society Fellow, Schmeding is the author of *Sufi Civilities: Religious Authority and Political Change in Afghanistan* (2023) and *Frontier Ethnographies: Deconstructing Research Experiences in Afghanistan and Pakistan*, co-edited with Nafay Choudhury (2024).

M. Nazif Shahrani is Professor Emeritus of Anthropology, Central Asian Studies, and Middle Eastern Studies at Indiana University, Bloomington. He is a sociocultural anthropologist with extensive field research in Afghanistan and has studied Afghan refugee communities in Pakistan and Turkey. Since 1992 he has also conducted field research in post-Soviet Muslim republics of Uzbekistan, Kazakhstan and Kyrgyzstan. He specializes in political anthropology with a focus on state-society relations and an anthropological approach to the study of religion with a focus on Islam. Some of his publications include *Modern Afghanistan: The Impact of 40 Years of War*. Editor and contributor, Indiana University Press (2018); *Revolutions and Rebellions in Afghanistan: Anthropological Perspectives*, with Robert L. Canfield, eds. (1984) re-published with a new 'Preface' by Indiana University Press (2022); *The Kirghiz and Wakhi of Afghanistan: Adaptation to Close Frontiers and War,* University of Washington Press (1979 and an expanded edition in 2002).

Omar Sharifi is President's Postdoctoral Fellow at the Humphrey School of Public Affairs. In addition, he is Assistant Professor at the American University of Afghanistan, Senior Research Fellow and Kabul Director of the American Institute of Afghanistan Studies.

Astri Suhrke has been Professor of International Relations at the American University in Washington, DC, a journalist writing for Norwegian newspapers, and a senior researcher at the Chr. Michelsen Institute in Bergen, Norway, where she is now Associated Research Professor.

Abdul Basir Yosufi is a PhD candidate at Norman Paterson School of International Affairs, Carleton University. He worked at Afghanistan's Ministry of Interior as the Director-General for International Cooperation from 2015 to 2018 and as Senior Policy Advisor from 2010 to 2015, advising five ministers. Basir has received several awards and fellowships, including a Fulbright Scholarship and a Rumsfeld Fellowship for leaders from Central Asia, Magnolia, Caucuses and Afghanistan (CAMCA). His academic research focuses on the role of political institutions in state building, ethnic conflict and counterinsurgency.

Nasema Zeerak is a doctoral student in International Policy at the Humphrey School of Public Affairs, University of Minnesota. Her educational background includes an MSc in Conflict Management and Resolution from the Joan B. Kroc School of Peace Studies at the University of San Diego (2021), as well as a Master of Public Administration from the Middlebury Institute of International Studies at Monterey (2018). Her intellectual inquiries encompass anti-colonial and anti-imperial thought, international relations theory, the politics of knowledge production and political violence.

Acknowledgements

In putting together this volume, we have had the great privilege of working with scholars whose writings and research we believe contribute greatly to understandings of power and authority in Afghanistan. We hope that bringing their work together will allow current and future scholars of Afghanistan to access these in one compilation and believe that the contributions, read together, provide value greater than the sum of the individual chapters. To this end we are indebted to all the authors in this volume for their insightful contributions.

We are very grateful also to the editorial team at Bloomsbury, and in particular Sophie Rudland, Nayiri Kendir and Faiza Zakaria for their invaluable assistance throughout the process of compiling the volume.

In brainstorming the potential format for this book, we were very keen to incorporate works that we had found seminal to our own research, writing and teaching. We are grateful to Juan Cole, Senzil Nawid and Barnett Rubin for giving us kind permission to reprint their impactful work in the volume. We also thank *Social Research*, *Third World Quarterly* and *The International Journal of Middle East Studies* for their permissions on this front. We acknowledge with appreciation the grant given to us by the American Institute for Afghanistan Studies (AIAS) that allowed us to realize this vision in the purchase of copyright permissions, with special thanks to Andi Kokkinos for her support in facilitating this.

We thank those who provided anonymous peer reviews of the whole manuscript – your suggestions and encouragements proved most valuable.

Finally, as long-time scholars of Afghanistan who have greatly benefited from the kindness and hospitality of its people over the years, we are not indifferent observers to the plight of the country. On the contrary, we fervently hope that this volume demonstrates the creative possibilities that emerge when questions of power and authority are visited anew with particular attention to those voices and perspectives that too often remain at the margins or unheard.

Abbreviations

ACSOR	Afghan Center for Socioeconomic Opinion Research
AIAS	American Institute for Afghanistan Studies
AIHRC	Afghanistan Independent Human Rights Commission
AKF	Aga Khan Foundation
ANA	Afghan National Army
ANCOP	Afghan National Civil Order Police
ANDSF	Afghan National Defense and Security Forces
ANP	Afghan National Police
AREU	Afghanistan Research and Evaluation Unit
ARTF	Afghanistan Reconstruction Trust Fund
AUAF	American University of Afghanistan
AWWP	Afghan Women's Writing Project
BBC	British Broadcasting Company
CEO	Chief Executive Officer
CIA	Central Intelligence Agency
CPAU	Cooperation for Peace and Unity
DAD	Donor Assistance Database
DDR	Demobilization, Disarmament and Reintegration
DFID	Department for International Development
DOD	Department of Defense
FGD	Focus Group Discussion
GDP	Gross Domestic Product
GIROA	Government of the Islamic Republic of Afghanistan
HRW	Human Rights Watch
IDKA	Independent Directorate for Kuchi Affairs
IDMC	Internal Displacement Monitoring Centre

IDP	Internally Displaced Person
IEC	Independent Election Commission
IR	International Relations
IROA	Islamic Republic of Afghanistan
ISAF	International Security Assistance Force
ISI	Inter-Service Intelligence Agency
ISIS	Islamic State of Iraq and Syria
ISKP	Islamic State of Khorasan Province
KIS	Kabul Informal Settlement
LOTFA	Law and Order Trust Fund for Afghanistan
MAIL	Ministry of Agriculture, Irrigation and Livelihoods
MMCC	Mobile Mini Circus for Children
MP	Member of Parliament
MRRD	Ministry of Rural Rehabilitation and Development
NATO	North Atlantic Treaty Organization
NCO	Non-Commissioned Officer
NDI	National Democratic Institute for International Affairs
NDS	National Directorate of Security
NGO	Non-Governmental Organization
NIOD	Netherlands Institute for War, Holocaust and Genocide Studies
NRAP	National Rural Access Program
NRF	National Resistance Front
NUG	National Unity Government
ONSC	Office of the National Security Council
PDPA	People's Democratic Party of Afghanistan
PEACE	Pastoral Engagement, Adaption and Capacity Enhancement Programme
PIN	People in Need (NGO)
PLO	Palestine Liberation Organisation
RAMP	Rebuilding Agricultural Markets Program
RAWA	Revolutionary Association of Afghan Women

RS	Resolute Support
RTA	National Radio and Television of Afghanistan
SCD	Salaam Center for Dialogue
SIGAR	Special Inspector General for Afghanistan Reconstruction
SNTV	Single Non-Transferable Vote
SRSG	Special Representative of the Secretary-General
SSR	Security Sector Reform
TLO	Tribal Liaison Office
UAE	United Arab Emirates
UCLA	University of California in Los Angeles
UIF	National United Islamic Front for the Salvation of Afghanistan
UNDP	United Nations Development Program
UNHCR	United Nations High Commission for Refugees
UNICEF	United Nations Fund for Children
USAID	United States Agency for International Development
USIP	United States Institute for Peace
USSR	Union of Soviet Socialist Republics

General Maps

Map of Afghanistan.

Introduction: Rethinking Power and Authority in Afghanistan

Anna Larson

To the casual observer, Afghanistan in 2024 is a country ruled by an authoritarian regime that derives much of its internal authority from having ousted a global superpower. This narrative, continually emphasized by Taliban leaders, draws on multiple logics of legitimation: a nationalist, anti-colonial sentiment that flourished across parts of Afghanistan in the later years of the international intervention; a conservative religious xenophobia that linked the interference of foreigners to the desecration of Islam; the longevity of the Taliban's domestic campaign for recognition and influence; and a historical record of some local-level service delivery and administration. Do these strands, combined, constitute a recipe for power and authority in the longer term? Are they needed in equal measure? Was it the failure of internationally backed service delivery and administration alone that led to the downfall of the Islamic Republic? Or was the intervention always doomed to fail simply *because* it was internationally backed? We hope that this volume, as a detailed multidisciplinary examination of power and authority in Afghanistan, might offer some new answers to these questions.

International attention has turned resolutely away from Afghanistan since the withdrawal of troops in August 2021. One might ask, then, why these questions are important, and why they are important now. We ground their salience in the withdrawal itself: now that this chapter of intervention has ended, it is critical to consider the twenty-year period in retrospect, both as its own era and in relation to other chapters of Afghanistan's history. Even the most generous of observers looking back at the last two decades would conclude that mistakes were made by a great number of actors: to simply move on and refrain from an analysis of these mistakes, as international policy makers and the media are wont to do, would preclude the urgent responsibility of learning from them. To learn from, or at least acknowledge them, might also offer insights into what comes next for Afghanistan and its people going forward.

Much has been written on the shortcomings of international and Afghan actors during the intervention (see, for example, Smith 2010; Suhrke 2011; Fishstein and Wilder 2012; Rubin 2013; Coburn and Larson 2014; and Coburn 2016). Indeed, as a result of the twenty-year war, Afghanistan has been at the centre of global academic and policy debates on intervention and state building in conflict contexts more generally. Yet these debates have often been piecemeal, ahistorical and West-oriented. This volume addresses this gap with its emphasis on new scholarly contributions from emerging Afghan and international scholars, whose research has been conducted since 2001. Confronting the deep colonial roots of ethnography, geography and anthropology as disciplines, it attempts a shift away from West-centric analyses by relocating attention to inquiries more rooted in Afghan contexts and understandings.

The volume targets a new generation of students of Afghanistan – a generation looking critically and *retrospectively* at the longest military intervention in American history. This is a generation attuned to the complexities of the Afghan context and the dilemmas of international engagement more broadly. Its members are not satisfied with many of the reductionist categories and logics of 'fragile statehood', 'post-conflict politics' or 'good governance' that marked the discourses of the early 2000s. Beyond criticism of a failed intervention and the simplistic analytical tools that have been used to measure it, the chapters in this book illuminate novel epistemological approaches to power and authority in Afghanistan that offer a new generation of scholars the opportunity to speak with (and back to) those who have come before.

Structure of the Volume

The questions we raise above about the nature of power and authority in Afghanistan are central to current attempts by many scholars, practitioners and long-time observers (including ourselves) to understand what is currently taking place in the country. In the past, similar attempts have been limited by the use of prescribed frameworks that have hindered a deeper understanding of political dynamics. In early discussions about the format of this volume, we decided that a more organic approach – allowing contributing authors to define power and authority on their own terms – would facilitate a more thoughtful set of analyses. Our call for contributions yielded scholarship on a variety of topics ranging from civil-military relations and women's education to Islamic jurisprudence and the (geo)political narratives of intervention. These submissions quite naturally gave rise to three overlapping but distinct subcategories of power and authority by which we organize the book: logics of rule and institutional (dis)continuities; intervention and its legacies; and the politics of recognition and resistance.

Each of the three parts comprises a mixture of longer chapters outlining new research, much of it by emerging scholars, and shorter reflections, many written by eminent scholars looking both back and forward after decades spent observing Afghanistan. Each part also includes one previously published article that we feel offers a seminal contribution to the conversation. This combination of chapters, reflections and articles has resulted in a unique, readable volume that provides a far-reaching but accessible tool for scholars looking to explore these themes more deeply. It helps to contextualize and link together a wide array of perspectives and taps into over fifty years of collective knowledge production.

The volume does not claim to cover all of the ways in which power and authority might be conceptualized, either in general or in Afghanistan in particular. It does not prescribe any specific lens of analysis. Many contributors use theoretical frameworks from their own disciplines; others rely more heavily on their own primary data and yet others speak largely from lived experience. Far from a limitation, we feel that this plural approach strengthens the volume: the combination of theory, empirical data and experience provides a grounded, interdisciplinary and original way by which to facilitate social enquiry and analysis.

Historical Overview

The volume draws on a rich canon of literature that offers deep insight into Afghanistan's history – not least, the writings of Mir Ghulam Mohammad Ghubar (1967), Vartan Gregorian (1969) Louis Dupree (1980), Thomas Barfield (1981), Whitney Azoy (1982) M. Nazif Shahrani and Robert Canfield (1984), Olivier Roy (1986), Barnett Rubin (1995), David Edwards (1996), M. Hassan Kakar (1997), Senzil Nawid (1999), Ahmed Rashid (2000) and Amin Saikal (2006). More recently, volumes by Barfield (2010), Asti Suhrke (2011), Noah Coburn (2011), Dipali Mukhopadhyay (2014), Noah Coburn and Anna Larson (2014), Robert Crews (2015), Martin Bayly (2016), David Mansfield (2016), Jennifer Murtazashvili (2016), Jonathan Lee (2018), Romain Malejacq (2020), Nivi Manchanda (2020), Omar Sadr (2020) and Sonia Ahsan-Tirmizi (2021) have contributed to deeper understandings of power and authority through a broad range of disciplinary lenses. Many of this volume's chapters provide detailed historical accounts of different periods in Afghanistan's history (see, for example, those by Senzil Nawid, Haroun Rahimi, Juan Cole, Thomas Barfield and Adam H. Dehsabzi). There is little need to pre-empt the content of those chapters here – and yet, for the reader who may not be intimately familiar with it, the following is a short overview of elements of Afghanistan's history that we believe are critical to the analysis of power and authority as they are manifest (or indeed missing) in 2024.

Most contemporary accounts of Afghan history begin with the coming together of different tribal leaders in 1747 to select Ahmad Shah Abdali (later known as Ahmad Shah Durrani) as the 'first among equals', or overall ruler of tribes (Nawid 1997; Saikal 2006). Indeed, much of the historical significance of regimes before this time is often overlooked, and yet, as detailed by Hamid Kashmiri (2022 [1846]), Mir Ghulam Mohammad Ghubar (1967) and later Louis Dupree (1980) and Thomas Barfield (2010), there is much value in understanding the ways in which earlier regional empires established structures of governance across different parts of what is now the territory of Afghanistan. Examples include the ways in which succession lines were (or were not) established, the ways in which local revenue was generated and justified, and the role of art, poetry and religion in articulating and disseminating narratives of legitimate rule. A look back before 1747 also demonstrates the extent to which non-European/non-western empires conducted imperial operations in the region and highlights how the convenient narrative of Afghanistan as a 'graveyard of empires'– a frequently invoked justification for the failure of western attempts at conquest – is connected to the use of 1747 as a 'start point'.

Nevertheless, it is true that 1747 represents what might be called a 'critical juncture' in Afghanistan's history, to use the language of historical institutionalism; this was the point at which Ahmad Shah Durrani essentially claimed and secured the authority – in essence, the recognition and acquiescence of other tribal leaders – in his effort to begin consolidating the geographical territory of Afghanistan (and indeed beyond its current borders) under one rule. After his death in 1772, however, a period of instability and infighting between his offspring followed. The Sadozai dynasty continued until Dost Muhammad of the Barakzais claimed the throne in 1826 even as the governing apparatus of the central state weakened, and the influence of regional strongmen and tribes grew (Nawid 1997). Indeed, between 1772 and 1880, a century passed in which, to a greater or lesser degree, central rulers were forced to negotiate their authority and influence with tribal leaders and members of the clergy – a model which, at times, and especially under the later years of Dost Muhammad's rule, resulted in relatively stable governance and set precedents for the relationships between the central government and the people groups in its writ. These precedents of negotiation and compromise, with limited central intervention in countryside and tribal affairs, while crushed under the violent central consolidation of Abdur Rahman Khan (r. 1880–1901) would resurface once again during the era of the Musahiban dynasty (1929–78). During this time, once again, a period of relative stability returned *without* an especially intrusive central government (Barfield, this volume).

Even these meagre observations might lead a curious scholar to question the links between power, authority and stability. Where it seems, for example, as discussed below – that contemporary models of state capacity are linked uncritically to *power*, and military power most particularly in the establishment and maintenance of a monopoly of violent force – periods of stability in Afghanistan's history would suggest that *authority* and stability are more closely intertwined. This is not to say that military strength and centralized state control were not important, but rather that the successive regimes that attempted to establish these *without* corresponding authority – most dramatically, communist rule (1978–92) and the Taliban Emirate (1995–2001) – have failed. This point is one that the ruling Taliban in Afghanistan in 2024 appear uninterested in heeding even as they seek to consolidate control in the longer term.

Scholars of Afghanistan, including those in this volume, have also noted that the Musahiban era (1929–78) was a period of sustained stability characterized neither by effective service provision nor much by way of institutionalized downward accountability to Afghan subjects. Royalty and the courts were very much isolated from the rest of the country. Elections for the legislature took place in the 1930s and onwards but participation was very limited, even after 1964 when universal suffrage was adopted into the new constitution. In other words, liberal democratic logics that make direct connections between election-centred accountability on the one hand and stability on the other are inadequate, in and of themselves, to explain what in fact has generated stability in Afghanistan in the past. Musahiban kings presided over a period of stability for reasons largely unconnected to the occurrence of elections during their reigns.

Evidently, stability in and of itself is not the sole indicator of authoritative governance. The Taliban may succeed in establishing some form of stability now relative to the violent insurgency they conducted prior to taking control. But longer-term, substantive stability relies not only on brute force or military strength but rather on authority that is recognized and reinforced by those on the ground and those prepared to lend support from the outside. As one of my co-editors has argued in *Foreign Affairs*, if the Taliban neglect to prioritize this over their apparent distractions with beauty salons and musical instruments, their second foray as leaders of Afghanistan will likely be as short-lived as the first (Mukhopadhyay 2022).

A number of the chapters in this volume (see, for example, Rubin, Suhrke, Yosufi, Zeerak and Sadr) address the failings of the intervention years (2001–21) from different angles. Together, they highlight the greatest challenge to power and authority for the government of the Republic: the way in which the United States and its allies imposed their own agendas and restricted state autonomy during this period. The twenty-year intervention could be divided into three parts: military retribution for 9/11 combined with a great naïveté and optimism on the part of many from 2001 to 2007; a period from 2008 to 2014 of denial and mission creep stemming from a set of American policies marked by the 'sunk-cost fallacy', with spikes in spending and military activity given the huge investments in blood and treasure already made; and an acute decline into civil war from 2015 to 2021. Neatly reflecting these three sub-eras was the way in which elections – my own field of study – played out against the backdrop of international interference in the electoral process: in 2005, a veritable mix of strongmen, established elite political family representatives, NGO workers and teachers were elected to parliament, signalling that while money, influence and a violent past could buy a place in the 249-seat *wolesi jirga* (lower house), so too could hard work, service provision and honest concern for real people and their struggles. In 2010, the finances required to run a campaign for a parliamentary seat essentially excluded most 'ordinary' candidates; and by 2015, legislative elections did not even take place, deferred for a further three years due to security concerns and a lack of international investment, among other things.[1] In this sense, the swift demise of electoral politics in and of itself demonstrates the precarious platform on which power without authority rests.

Defining Power and Authority

Both power and authority are terms that, most simply put, describe a relationship: the relationship between ruler and ruled. In choosing these terms as the guiding framework for this volume, we made a conscious decision to allow contributing authors to define them as they considered most appropriate and helpful to the study of Afghanistan. For us, the two terms are separate but interrelated: *Power* can be 'hard' or 'soft': it is often connected to military strength and the imposition of rule by violence or fear but is also a product of coercion and/or diplomacy, following Nietsche and Foucault. It can be decision-making, non-decision-making (in the sense of behind-the-scenes influence) or ideological (Lukes 2005). *Authority*, by contrast, relies on some form of power but implies recognition and acquiescence by both those being ruled and outside actors also. As Juan Cole writes, referring to Taliban rule in the 1990s, '[t]he … Taliban took and kept *power* by military means, instituting rule by militia, but their *authority* was enhanced by their religious charisma as holy men' (2003: 777, emphasis added). This way of looking at authority can be connected to notions of legitimacy – a term we avoided on account of its normative implications and measurement challenges but one that a number of the authors in this volume use to their own ends.[2]

State Capacity and Fragility

Much work on Afghanistan in the past two decades has tried to define and assess power and authority based on notions of state capacity (Paris 2004; Barakat et al. 2008; Ghani and Lockhart 2009). This approach, part and parcel of a positivist perspective dominant across much of the International Relations and Political Science literature, especially in the United States, considers the state to be a discrete unit of analysis that can be compared internationally and that functions or *should* function in roughly the same way across contexts (Nicholson 2003; Krasner 2009). As post-positivist and constructivist critiques of this view suggest, most notably those of the feminist tradition, while the ontological basis of positivism implies a connection with the 'hard sciences' and the analysis of real 'things' that exist in the world, there is yet a normative bias underpinning much of this analysis that is seldom acknowledged (Tickner 2001; Enloe 2014).

Analyses of power and authority through a state capacity lens attempt to assess the bureaucratic capabilities and reach of the state, and, following Weber, the degree to which a state holds a monopoly of violence within a given territory: in other words, the extent to which the state is seen by citizens and would-be dissident or competing leaders as the sole arbiter of violent force (Weber 1919). The challenges to its authority can serve as an indication of the state's lack of capacity to assert itself as the primary authority in its territory. Accordingly, these challenges also become an indicator of instability, with multiple sources of authority within a territory competing for resources and the loyalty of its inhabitants.

Weber's concept of the state underpins the majority of western scholarship on the subject, with more recent scholars and development practitioners applying it globally (Collier et al. 2003; Stewart and Brown 2010; DFID 2010). Yet, as analysts of many a non-western state have observed (Migdal 1988; Herbst 2000; Centeno 2002; North 2007), the experience of European state making was not a universal one and, instead, depended on a very particular set of circumstances including (but not limited to) the convergence of continental warfare and the revenues that this required (Tilly 1985), emerging market economies, technological innovation, religious animosity, an evolving relationship between church and state, and imperial pursuits. The creation and strengthening of the European state, along with increased competition between states, then had its own impact elsewhere. In what is often termed 'the developing world', the consecutive trajectories of an industrialized slave trade, colonial expansion and extraction, independence movements and the aid economies that followed became inseparable from state formation, development and capacity. As such, these processes unfolded on very different terms than had their counterparts in Europe.

In addition, before and indeed in parallel to European developments, alternative models of statehood existed that defy Weber's parameters. Olivier Roy describes a historical relationship between ruler and ruled in Afghanistan, for example, that is based on 'externality and compromise': not absolute, overbearing state capacity that is intent on eliminating all competing sources of authority, but a continually negotiated compromise between leaders at the centre and social groups in the countryside (Roy 1998: 181). While these groups did not usually aim to seize control of the state in its entirety, their regular demands for recognition, favour and/or alimony were given weight by the extent of the loyalty of their members and their willingness to take up arms against central rulers if necessary. In and of themselves, these demands became a mechanism through which stability and accountability were sought and established. Competing sources of legitimate leadership across the country thus became a vehicle that promoted (rather than undermined) stability, provided state capture was not an objective.

In the early 2000s, the term 'Fragile States' became lingua franca among development practitioners and bilateral aid agencies attempting to categorize states with limited capacity and identify particular forms of assistance tailored to such contexts (Stewart and Brown 2010; DFID 2010). An overarching goal of this approach was to quantify and, then, ameliorate the 'fragility' of conflict-affected countries. The more services a government was able to provide (which in turn related to its territorial reach, monopoly over the means of violent force and authority within that territory), the more legitimate it would ostensibly be perceived by its citizens. From this basis, then, aid and development programmes in the 2000s were tailored towards strengthening state capacity to provide services, and to the support and/or establishment of electoral processes that would allow citizens to reward government service provision with re-election. This approach rested on the assumption that citizens of a given state would see the source of those services as the state itself, and not simply redirected from a foreign power with an alternate agenda. It also presumed a materialist logic of legitimation.

As a number of scholars have pointed out, however, there were considerable flaws in the logics underpinning the 'fragile states' concept and the institutional approach to state building it prescribed (Lemay-Hébert 2009; Barakat and Larson 2013). In Afghanistan, all living memory (alongside many long-standing stories from the nineteenth century) associates aid with foreign political influence (Fishstein and Wilder 2012; Beath et al. 2015), and thus any services provided with the assistance of foreign aid have long been tainted with suspicion, producing a perverse effect to the one ostensibly intended. Compounding this phenomenon has been the sheer extent to which various governments in Afghanistan have been reliant on foreign aid: As Astri Suhrke notes in this volume, in 2019 75 per cent of Afghan public expenditure was financed by foreign aid (Suhrke, this volume) – but then as M. Nazif Shahrani reminds us in his reflection, this was not unprecedented, with foreign aid comprising approximately 70 per cent of the government's budget throughout the 1960s and 1970s, itself reflecting a much longer history of foreign subsidies and rents (Shahrani, this volume; Bizhan 2018). Afghanistan has in effect carried the traits of an aid-reliant rentier state for at least sixty years.[3]

Recently, scholarship has refined and nuanced the 'fragile state' framework to move beyond questions of state capacity and legitimacy, to include resilience against economic shocks and state–society relations more broadly (Bizhan 2023). This shift away from simplistic concepts and measurements towards holistic political economy analysis is exemplified by many of the articles, chapters and reflections in this volume. In the composition of this volume, we push further, arguing that any attempt to understand trajectories of power and authority in Afghanistan needs to consider the intersections of three critical areas of focus: logics of rule (the strategies and intentions of successive regimes and the institutions in which they invest); intervention and its legacies (the ongoing impact of external interference from a postcolonial perspective); and the politics of recognition and resistance (the ways in which authority is established in the dialectics between state and society).

Logics of Rule and Institutional (Dis-)Continuities

Looking back at Afghanistan's modern history, it is possible to compare regimes (and indeed distinguish them from one another) by analysing choices that ruling elites made over *how* to establish power and authority. In other words, regimes and their leaders can be scrutinized according to strategies or 'logics' of rule. When (and through what means) leaders have decided to use violence and extraction to solidify power, to give one example, are decisions that have varied across and within regimes. How they have chosen to build support in provincial areas, to give another, has also differed from one ruler to the next. These kinds of decisions themselves shed light on the political landscapes in which they were made.

Logics of rule and the choices they involve also give rise to different sets of institutional arrangements – some of which involve continuities with previous regimes, and some of which (ostensibly at least) involve a direct and intentional breakage with existing institutions and norms. In some cases, institutional continuities can lead to stability over time, encouraging a sense of security within the population, which grows accustomed to 'how things are done' and what to expect in their interactions with the state. On the other hand, institutional continuities can also produce dissent if the state is seen to be overreaching in its role, intolerant of opposition, or indeed, both. In this way, institutional (dis)continuities and the extent to which they are made manifest reflect the level of a regime's power and the depth and breadth of its authority.

This first part of the book opens with a personal and historical reflection by Thomas Barfield on how the Musahiban leaders managed to maintain stability from 1929 to 1973 – in stark contrast to the turbulence that followed. Next, we include Juan Cole's seminal 2003 article on the Taliban's first tenure, in which he details the regime's reliance on the performance of a stark departure from the politics of its predecessors, employing violent spectacle as a critical component of its instantiation of rule in the 1990s. Some important parallels exist to the ways in which the Taliban have attempted to reassert authority since their return in 2021. Haroun Rahimi then analyses historical continuities with respect to political legitimation in Afghanistan over time. Mujib Abid, in turn, seeks to explain Taliban approaches to Islamic practice and principles in analysing the internal evolution (and, in fact, discontinuities) in their modes of presentation and governance. As an insurgent force, the Taliban were keen to emphasize their connection to traditional Afghan and Islamic values, incorporating local norms and leaders into their politics; but now as a state, they appear to be reneging on these connections in favour of a fundamentalist approach to Islam and government that may prove more authoritarian and uncompromising. Next, Zinab Attai, Boshra Moheb and Maryam Jami contend that the vagaries of power and authority in Afghanistan cannot be understood fully without the use of a neopatrimonial framework – one that intimately connects patronage with externally imposed structures of governance. Their work emphasizes logics of rule that have prioritized institutional continuities as a way to promote the personal power and influence of different leaders over time. Finally, Basir Yosufi analyses Ashraf Ghani's approach to the Afghan National Defense and Security Forces (ANDSF) and, in particular, his attempts at 'coup-proofing' his own position of leadership that ultimately rendered them incapable of defending against the Taliban's return.

Intervention and Its Legacies

Different periods of Afghan history have seen many forms of outside influence. From that of the Mongols and Timurids in the thirteenth and fourteenth centuries to the East India Company in the mid-nineteenth century; the Cold War rivalry between the United States and the Soviet Union and the regional interferences of that era, and the US-led intervention (2001–21): all have held enormous sway over the actions and longevity of different leaders and groups. These outside influences and interventions have also impacted the nature of these leaders' relationships with the Afghan people (Nawid 1997; Kandiyoti 2005; Dalrymple 2014). Scholars have characterized different moments of this influence in varying ways – as 'quasi-colonial' (Manchanda 2020), 'neocolonial', 'crypto-colonial' (Hannun, this volume) – but common to all of these characterizations is the contention that the very concepts of power and authority in Afghanistan cannot be easily separated from the legacies of intervention. A leader's fate has been intimately connected to their ability to maintain autonomy over internal affairs while courting foreign sources of funding, given a distinct lack of internal industry and a limited history of reliable taxation.

It is for these reasons that we consider intervention and its legacies to be a critical component of any analysis of power and authority in Afghanistan – not because historical paths and the policies, decisions and approaches of leaders and groups were *determined* by outside forces but because they were often formed in dialogue with them. In this second part of the volume, we bring together contributions that are connected by their critique of the most recent intervention in Afghanistan's history – that of the United States and its allies from 2001 to 2021. We begin with a reflection by Marya Hannun, who describes the way in which women's education in the twentieth and twenty-first centuries has been weaponized successively by the 'crypto-colonial' Afghan state, the international coalition forces and the Taliban government, affecting a kind of erasure of substance. 'Ghost schools' are a literal and metaphorical reminder of this outcome. We then include Barnett R. Rubin's seminal 2006 article, 'Peace building and State-building in Afghanistan: Constructing Sovereignty for Whose Security?', which captures the way in which international military objectives profoundly undermined state building and peace building initiatives in the country as they were often employed at cross purposes. Nasema Zeerak then employs discourse analysis to reconsider the US engagement with Afghanistan with a focus on the justification for war and the justification for withdrawal two decades later. She highlights the importance of the discursive construction of Afghan identities by imperial powers that seek to define the relationship between colonizers and colonized on their own terms. M. Nazif Shahrani follows by summarizing the impact of colonial legacies with his use of the term 'leased power' – detailing how Afghanistan's rentier economy and its leaders' reliance on foreign backing undermined any substantive authority they might have gained over time. Astri Suhrke reflects on the way in which the Afghan state's dependence on foreign subsidies and the performances that its leaders put on for the benefit of foreign powers fed into a legitimacy deficit. Noah Coburn and Arsalan Noori drop down into the local political economy of aid and reconstruction, exploring the strategies of Afghan interlocutors who rose to prominence as powerbrokers on the back of international contracts and funds and continued to thrive in spite of an abrupt regime change in 2021. Finally, William Maley reflects on narratives of a 'whitewashed' Taliban generated in US policy-making circles in the lead-up to the takeover of 2021. For Maley, this reflects a 'power of ideas' that should not be dismissed as a significant contributing factor in the decisive American move to withdraw all troops from Afghanistan, and the collapse of the government that followed.

The Politics of Recognition and Resistance

In response to both regime politics and the intrusions of outsiders, groups of ordinary Afghans have pushed back against overbearing rule in often legendary terms. This dialectical relationship between state (or ruling elite) and society is where the essence of authority lies. Authority rests on the recognition of rule: *securing* authority involves ensuring that ordinary people acquiesce to and accept the terms of governance. Resistance occurs when they do not – and thus, an examination of the politics of both recognition and resistance is critical to understanding the character and extent of authority.

In this two-way conversation, a ruling power demands recognition from those it governs (and those outside its borders), while, at the same time, different groups within society demand recognition from the state (and one another) in order to wield influence therein.

An exploration of this dynamic push and pull, the third part of the volume begins with a 1999 article by Senzil Nawid that details the nature of the relationship between the Afghan clergy and the state vis-à-vis British imperial policy in the nineteenth and twentieth centuries. Ali Yarwar Adili then offers a reflection on the extraordinary trajectory of Hazara politics, from exclusion to empowerment and, tragically, back again, an arc that captures the group's struggle for state recognition and its sustained confrontation with discriminatory subjugation. Next, Annika Schmeding makes a related observation on the importance of state recognition, this time from the perspective of peripatetic groups and their exclusion from the post-2001 category of 'Kuchi'. Her exposition of the power of labels highlights the divergent paths of status and national-level influence that Kuchi and other nomadic communities have experienced on account of the strategic narratives generated by and about them. Adam H. Dehsabzi's chapter then draws scholarly attention to the understudied notion of an urban elite in Afghanistan, and its relationship to those who have ruled the country, undermining the common trope that ethnic identity politics trump all else. Omar Sadr critiques the post-2001 design and modalities of liberal democracy as introduced, arguing that they precluded possibilities for a peaceful politics of difference and even disagreement. Finally, Munazza Ebtikar provides a gendered analysis of how Panjshiri collective memory has shaped and sustained modes of resistance and rebel governance for many decades, a poignant reminder that the institutions, practices and norms that sustain contentious politics can outlive their armed protagonists.

Notes

1. For more on post-2001 legislative elections and the changes they reflected, see Wordsworth (2007); Larson (2009); Coburn and Larson (2011, 2014); and Larson (2021).
2. For further reference, see Lisa Wedeen's *Ambiguities of Domination* (1999) in which she describes the problems with legitimacy as a social scientific outcome.
3. As Nematullah Bizhan (2018) points out, however, there are key differences in the way in which resource-based rentier economies and aid-based rentier economies function, not least when – as in Afghanistan post-2001, aid is tied to international state-building initiatives and/or military intervention that themselves have far-reaching political-economic impacts.

References

Ahsan-Tirmizi, S. (2021), *Pious Peripheries: Runaway Women in Post-Taliban Afghanistan*. Stanford: Stanford University Press.
Azoy, G. W. (2012) [1982], *Buzkashi: Game and Power in Afghanistan*. 3rd ed. Long Grove, Illinois: Waveland Press.
Barakat, S., Strand, A., Murphy, M., Giustozzi, A., Langton, C. and Sedra, M. (2008), *A Strategic Conflict Assessment of Afghanistan*. London: Department for International Development.
Barakat, S. and Larson, A. (2013), 'Fragile States: A Donor-Serving Concept? Issues with Interpretations of Fragile Statehood in Afghanistan'. *Journal of Intervention and Statebuilding*, 8(1): 21–41.
Barfield, T. (1981), *Central Asian Arabs in Afghanistan*. Austin, Texas: University of Texas.
Barfield, T. (2010), *Afghanistan: A Cultural and Political History*. Princeton: Princeton University Press.

Bayly, M. J. (2016), *Taming the Imperial Imagination: Colonial Knowledge, International Relations and the Anglo-Afghan Encounter 1808–1878*. Cambridge: Cambridge University Press.

Beath, A., Christia, F. and Enikolopov, R. (2015), 'The National Solidarity Programme: Assessing the Effects of Community-Driven Development in Afghanistan'. *International Peacekeeping*, 22(4): 302–20.

Bizhan, N. (2018), *Aid Paradoxes in Afghanistan: Building and Undermining the State*. Oxford and New York: Routledge.

Bihzan, N. (2023), *State Fragility: Cases and Comparisons*. Oxford and New York: Routledge.

Centeno, M. A. (2002), *Blood and Debt: War and the Nation State in Latin America*. University Park, PA: Penn State University Press.

Coburn, N. (2011), *Bazaar Politics: Power and Pottery in an Afghan Market Town*. Stanford: Stanford University Press.

Coburn, N. (2016), *Losing Afghanistan: An Obituary for the Intervention*. Stanford: Stanford University Press.

Coburn, N. and Larson, A. (2014), *Derailing Democracy in Afghanistan: Elections in an Unstable Political Landscape*. New York: Columbia University Press.

Coburn, N. and Larson, A. (2011), 'Undermining Representative Governance: Afghanistan's 2010 Parliamentary Election and Its Alienating Impact'. Kabul: AREU. https://www.refworld.org/reference/countryrep/areu/2011/en/77246.

Cole, J. R. I. (2003), 'The Taliban, Women, and the Hegelian Private Sphere'. *Social Research*, 70(3): 771–808.

Collier, P., Elliott, L., Hegre, H., Hoeffler, A., Reynal-Querol, M. and Sambanis, N. (2003), *Breaking the Conflict Trap: Civil War and Development Policy*. World Bank Policy Research Report: 56793. Washington, DC: World Bank.

Crews, R. D. (2015), *Afghan Modern: The History of a Global Nation*. Cambridge, MA: Harvard University Press.

Dalrymple, W. (2014), *The Return of a King: The Battle for Afghanistan*. London: Bloomsbury.

Department for International Development (DFID) (2010), *The Politics of Poverty: Elites, Citizens and States – Findings from Ten Years of DFID-Funded Research on Governance and Fragile States 2001–2010. A Synthesis Paper*. London: Department for International Development. Available at: https://www.oecd.org/derec/unitedkingdom/48688822.pdf

Dupree, L. (2002) [1980], *Afghanistan*. Oxford: Oxford University Press.

Edwards, D. B. (1996), *Heroes of the Age: Moral Faultlines on the Afghan Frontier*. Berkeley: University of California Press.

Enloe, C. (2014), *Bananas, Beaches and Bases: Making Feminist Sense of International Politics*. Berkeley: University of California Press.

Fishstein, P. and Wilder, A. (2012), 'Winning Hearts and Minds? Examining the Relationship between Aid and Security in Afghanistan'. Medford, MA: Feinstein International Center.

Ghani, A. and Lockhart, C. (2009), *Fixing Failed States: A Framework for Rebuilding a Fractured World*. Oxford: Oxford University Press.

Ghubar, M. G. M. (2001) [1967], *Afghanistan in the Course of History* (Volume 2, English Translation). Hashmat Ghobar Publishing.

Gregorian, Vartan (1969), *The Emergence of Modern Afghanistan: Politics of Reform and Modernization 1880–1946*. Stanford: Stanford University Press.

Herbst, J. (2000), *States and Power in Africa: Comparative Lessons in Authority and Control*. Princeton: Princeton University Press.

Johnson, T. H. (2017), *Taliban Narratives: The Use and Power of Stories in the Afghanistan Conflict*. London: Hurst & Co.

Hassan, M. (1997), *Afghanistan: The Soviet Invasion and the Afghan Response 1979–1982*. Berkeley: University of California Press.

Kandiyoti, D. (2005), 'The Politics of Gender and Reconstruction in Afghanistan'. UNRISD. Available at: http://www.unrisd.org/publications/opgp4

Kashmiri, H. H. (2022 [1846]), *Akbar Nama, An Epic Poetry by Hameed-i-Kashmiri* (کشمیری حمید حمیدالله ملا از حماسی ی سروده ،اکبرنامه). Kabul: Shah M Book Co.

Krasner, S. D. (2009), *Power, the State and Sovereignty: Essays on International Relations*. London and New York: Routledge.

Larson, A. (2009), *Toward an Afghan Democracy? Exploring Perceptions of Democratisation in Afghanistan*, September 2009. Kabul: Afghanistan Research and Evaluation Unit.

Larson, A. (2021), *Democracy in Afghanistan: Amid and beyond Conflict*. USIP Special Report 497, July 2021. Washington, DC: USIP.

Lee, J. L. (2018), *Afghanistan: A History from 1260 to the Present*. Chicago: University of Chicago Press.

Lemay-Hébert, N. (2009). 'Statebuilding without Nation-building? Legitimacy, State Failure and the Limits of the Institutionalist Approach'. *Journal of Intervention and Statebuilding*, 3(1): 21–45.

Lukes, S. (2005), *Power: A Radical View* (Second Edition). Basingstoke: Palgrave Macmillan.

Malejacq, R. (2020), *Warlord Survival: The Delusion of State Building in Afghanistan*. Ithaca and London: Cornell University Press.

Manchanda, N. (2020), *Imagining Afghanistan: The History and Politics of Imperial Knowledge*. Cambridge: Cambridge University Press.

Mansfield, D. (2016), *A State Built on Sand: How Opium Undermined Afghanistan*. London: Hurst.

Migdal, J. S. (1988), *Strong Societies and Weak States: State-society Relations and State Capabilities in the Third World*. Princeton: Princeton University Press.

Mukhopadhyay, D. (2014), *Warlords, Strongman Governors and the State in Afghanistan*. New York: Cambridge University Press.

Mukhopadhyay, D. (2022), 'The Taliban Have Not Moderated: An Extremist Regime Is Pushing Afghanistan to the Brink'. *Foreign Affairs*, 28 March 2022. Available online: https://www.foreignaffairs.com/afghanistan/taliban-have-not-moderated

Murtazashvili, J. (2016), *Informal Order and the State in Afghanistan*. Cambridge: Cambridge University Press.

Nawid, S. (1997), 'The State, the Clergy, and British Imperial Policy in Afghanistan during the 19th and Early 20th Centuries'. *International Journal of Middle East Studies*, 29(4): 581–605.

Nawid, S. (1999), *Religious Response to Social Change in Afghanistan, 1919–1929: King Aman-Allah and the Afghan Ulama*. Costa Mesa, CA: Mazda Publishers.

Nicholson, M. (2003), *International Relations: A Concise Introduction*. New York: New York University Press.

North, D. C. (2007), *Institutions, Institutional Change and Economic Performance*. Cambridge: Cambridge University Press.

Paris, R. (2004), *At War's End: Building Peace after Civil Conflict*. Cambridge and New York: Cambridge University Press.

Rashid, A. (2000), *Taliban: Militant Islam, Oil and Fundamentalism in Central Asia*. New Haven: Yale University Press.

Roy, O. (1986), *Islam and Resistance in Afghanistan*. Cambridge: Cambridge University Press.

Roy, O. (1998), *The Failure of Political Islam*. Cambridge, MA: Harvard University Press.

Rubin, B. R. (1995), *The Search for Peace in Afghanistan: From Buffer State to Failed State*. New Haven: Yale University Press.

Rubin, B. R. (2013), *Afghanistan from the Cold War through the War on Terror*. Oxford and New York: Oxford University Press.

Sadr, O. (2020), *Negotiating Cultural Diversity in Afghanistan*. Delhi: Routledge India.

Saikal, A. (2006), *Modern Afghanistan: A History of Struggle and Survival*. London and New York: I.B. Tauris.

Shahrani M. N. and Canfield, R. (eds.) (1984), *Revolutions and Rebellions in Afghanistan: Anthropological Perspectives*. Bloomington: Indiana University Press.

Smith, S. S. (2010), *Afghanistan's Troubled Transition: Politics, Peacekeeping and the 2004 Presidential Election*. Boulder, CO: Lynne Rienner.

Stewart, F. and Brown, G. (2010), *Fragile States: An Overview*. Oxford: CRISE. Available online: https://assets.publishing.service.gov.uk/media/57a08b17ed915d3cfd000b1c/CRISE-Overview-3.pdf

Suhrke, A. (2011), *When More Is Less. The International Project in Afghanistan*. London: Hurst.

Tickner, A. (2001), *Gendering World Politics*. New York: Columbia University Press.

Tilly, C. (1985), 'War Making and State Making as Organized Crime', in Evans, P., Rueschemeyer, D. and Skocpol, T. (eds.), *Bringing the State Back In*. Cambridge: Cambridge University Press.

Weber, M. (1919) [2004], 'Politics as a Vocation', in Owen, D. and Strong, T. B. (eds.), trans. Livingstone R. *The Vocation Lectures*. Indianapolis: Hackett Company.

Wedeen, L. (1999), *Ambiguities of Domination: Politics, Rhetoric and Symbols in Contemporary Syria. Chicago*: Chicago University Press.

Wordsworth, A. (2007), *A Matter of Interests: Gender and the Politics of Presence in Afghanistan's Wolesi Jirga*. Kabul: AREU.

Part One

Logics of Rule and Institutional (Dis-)Continuities

1

Stability as Strength in the Musahiban Era

Thomas Barfield

Ashraf Ghani fled the presidential palace for exile abroad as Taliban forces entered Kabul slightly less than two years after he commemorated Afghanistan's centenary of independence on 19 August 2019. It was the fourth time in four decades that an Afghan government was driven out of Kabul in defeat, leading many to conclude that the country was ungovernable. Yet, between 1929 and 1978, Afghanistan experienced an even longer half century of peace that was not disrupted despite the assassination of Nader Khan in 1933 and the ouster of his son, Zahir Shah, by a cousin Daoud Khan in 1973. As an academic old enough to have had personal experience in Afghanistan before that period ended, I have given some thought as to why its seemingly weak government maintained a peace throughout the country that eluded the regimes that replaced it. Although far from being a perfectly tranquil time, as some nostalgically recall it today, it was a period when a country wracked by civil war recovered its balance and maintained it. What explains this long-lasting stability that began so inauspiciously in 1929?

During the first nine months of 1929, Afghanistan was a failed state, divided by an ideological conflict that emerged in reaction to Amanullah Khan's ambitious modernizing programme to transform Afghan society and governance. His initial effort had provoked a backlash in the more conservative parts of the country and was dialled back after the 1923 Khost Rebellion in eastern Afghanistan proved difficult to suppress. Amanullah's renewal and expansion of these policies in 1928 triggered a more widespread rebellion that forced his abdication in January 1929. The reactionary regime that replaced him was led by Amir Habibullah Kalakani, a populist Tajik bandit championing traditional cultural values, who immediately abolished all of Amanullah's reforms.

Kalakani's success, however, alienated those conservative Pashtuns who had sought to end Amanullah's policies but not at the cost of putting a non-Pashtun on the throne. They shifted their support back to Amanullah Khan only to experience a series of battlefield losses that allowed Kalakani to extend his rule over most of the country. Amanullah Khan left Afghanistan in May for what would prove a lifetime of exile in Europe. His former war minister, Nader Khan, took command of the anti-Kalakani forces. He and his brothers raised fresh troops among the Pashtun tribes on the British

Indian side of the frontier and finally succeeded in capturing Kabul in October. They then executed Kalakani and a *Loya Jirga* (great assembly) composed of his followers proclaimed and renamed Nader Shah the king of Afghanistan.

Nader Shah and his brothers (collectively known as the Musahiban) had good reason to be concerned about their ability to wield power in the aftermath of their victory. The treasury was empty and their trans-frontier tribal troops looted Kabul before they departed the city since the new government had no money to pay them for their services. Nader Shah himself was labelled a usurper by Amanullah's supporters who believed that he was still Afghanistan's rightful king. They also objected to the new government's retention of Kalakani's reactionary laws and the appointment of religious conservatives to the justice system that enforced them. But pandering to the most reactionary ideological elements in Afghanistan proved ineffective in winning the support of former allies who now had other reasons to oppose the regime.

A series of pro-Amanullah Khan revolts broke out in the early 1930s among the Tajiks north of Kabul and a variety of Pashtun tribes in the east and south, all areas that had bitterly opposed Amanullah's reform policies but now used his ouster to legitimize their opposition to the new Musahiban government. A sense of paranoia gripped the Musahibans, who regularly accused the British of fomenting revolts against them in the east. The Soviets, who had been supportive of Amanullah Khan, were also crossing the country's northern border at will to attack Basmachi rebels based there. These fears led the Musahibans to arrest and execute many prominent Amanullah Khan supporters in Kabul. The purge expanded when Nader Shah was assassinated in 1933 by a high school student taking revenge for the killing of Ghulam Nabi Charkhi, a high-ranking Amanullah Khan supporter, and most of his family.

However, nothing demonstrated the unified familial base of Musahiban rule better than the continued smooth governance of Afghanistan in the wake of Nader Shah's assassination. His brothers immediately appointed their nephew, a nineteen-year-old Zahir Shah, as king but continued to rule the country as prime ministers until 1953. Completing Nader Shah's plans, they put their emphasis on rebuilding the army that numbered 40,000 troops in the 1930s, constructing new roads that better linked the country's regions together, and engaging in diplomatic outreach to secure development and military aid from foreign governments. Despite its pro-Axis inclinations, Afghanistan stayed neutral during the Second World War and thereafter took advantage of the post-war rivalry between the United States and the Soviet Union to finance its infrastructure projects and military modernization. An era of more liberal reforms followed as a new Musahiban generation came to power, beginning with Daoud Khan as prime minister (1953–63) and more expansively after Zahir Shah ratified the 1964 constitution that established a parliamentary democracy.

Hallmarks of this dynasty's approach to social change included their piecemeal application of policy and a high degree of voluntarism therein. For example, Daoud Khan protected women in Kabul who appeared unveiled in public after he ended the enforcement of mandatory veiling in 1959. But he did not champion that policy nationwide. And although the Kabul government sought to avoid provocations, it now believed it had the capacity to quickly end any armed uprisings with its soviet-supplied tanks and jets. The central government had crushed the last serious revolt against it in

Kunar province in 1946 and the receipt of these new assets appeared to be an effective deterrent against those who might be considering mounting new uprisings. A more lightly armed gendarmerie within the Interior Ministry replaced the army as the main instrument for projecting the power of the Afghan state in its rural hinterland.

By the 1970s, only the oldest living generation could recall a period when the Musahiban dynasty did not rule or even a time when their grip on power was less than complete. But within Afghanistan's small but expanding military officer corps and educational institutions, the ideological splits that generated so much controversy during Amanullah's reign were re-emerging in more radical forms. Their proponents sought to replace the Musahiban dynasty with more ideological regimes, assuming that Afghanistan's legacy of stability would continue without them. On the right was the Jamiat-e Islami (The Islamic Society) that sought the creation of an Islamic state based on the ideas of the Egyptian Muslim Brotherhood; on the left were two communist party factions, Khalq (Masses) and Parcham (Banner), that took their inspiration from the Soviet Union. Both were largely Kabul-based and small in membership, but then so was the Musahiban governing elite they opposed.

I was unaware of any of this history when I first travelled to Afghanistan in the summer of 1971 as an undergraduate student. I knew Zahir Shah was king only because his balding head stared out at me on the country's banknotes (Figure 1.1). Afghanistan had been largely closed to outsiders until the late 1960s but was now a popular transit route for young and poorly financed westerners travelling overland between Istanbul and Kathmandu. While others moved on quickly, I saw no reason to leave Afghanistan, a place of immense natural beauty with its own distinctive culture so different from my own. I hiked ten days up the Alingar River in western Nuristan and after that travelled to Mazar over the impressive Salang Pass to view the city's Timurid-era tiled shrine.

Catching rides on the painted trucks that traversed Afghanistan's unpaved backroads, I found myself in Bamiyan where I sat on the head of its famous Buddha before taking the mountainous southern route through Yakawlang and Panjao to Kabul. It took three days to cover the 300 kilometres sitting atop a truck on the bed of poplar poles with a dozen goats below me for the last leg of the journey. The contrast

Figure 1.1 Zahir Shah banknote.

between that journey and my departure from Afghanistan a few days later using the country's new ring road was immense. Travelling more than 1000 kilometres on a Mercedes coach bus, I had breakfast in Kabul, dinner in Herat and was well into Iran by the next day. Although I had trained as an archaeologist, my encounter with Afghanistan convinced me that living people were more interesting than dead ones, and I shifted my planned graduate research plans accordingly.

When I began a doctoral programme in anthropology at Harvard the next year, I had the good luck of encountering the Afghan historian Hassan Kakar who was a postdoctoral fellow there. He tore apart a paper for which I had received an A but absolved me of blame by explaining that my error was in relying on the publications I assumed were authoritative. 'Most everything published on Afghanistan is wrong,' he warned me and said I should dig deeper into the country's history and culture myself. I kept that in mind when I returned to Kabul in the summer of 1973 and met with some of the contacts he had given me. But only weeks after I arrived, the forty-year reign of Zahir Shah ended abruptly when Daoud Khan seized power in an almost bloodless coup on 17 July (Figure 1.2). He declared the monarchy abolished and named himself president of a new republic without any public opposition. Zahir Shah was in Italy for medical treatment at the time and did not attempt to return. His ubiquitous portraits immediately disappeared from shops and government offices, replaced by those of President Daoud in a matter of days.

There was nervousness in Kabul, but that quickly subsided. The armoured vehicles parked at the city's roundabouts were soon empty of their crews who sought shade under the awnings of nearby shops where they could get cold drinks. Concerned

Figure 1.2 Soviet-made BTR-60 armoured personal carrier parked at Charahi Ansari, Shahr-e Naw, Kabul, in July 1973 (author's photograph).

about what might happen in the countryside, the Foreign Ministry confined me and other internationals to Kabul. But nothing happened, so about a month later I was told that my permission to travel to Kunduz, Takhar and Badakhshan provinces had been approved. On that trip I encountered a young electrical engineer working for the Spinzar Cotton Company who became my best friend and made my future research possible. Afghanistan was and still is a land that runs on personal relationships rather than formal institutions.

Although today the era of Zahir Shah is portrayed as a kind of Afghan golden age, it was certainly not viewed that way at the time. A series of failed prime ministers (five in ten years) had come and gone, in part because Zahir Shah refused to ratify many important laws the parliament passed that would have improved their effectiveness. Corruption was pervasive. When I assisted a friend in airfreighting his collection of antiques and carpets out of the country, a Lufthansa agent accompanied us as a guide and told us how much to pay each of the officials at the airport whose stamps or signatures were required. When at last all the signatures and stamps were obtained, a poorly dressed man with no evident authority grabbed the paper and put it in a closed cigar box resting on a small rickety table. The Lufthansa agent told us to give him 10 *afghanis* (US 7¢ at the time) to open the box and he handed us the signed forms.

Much more serious were the mismanagement and corruption that plagued the international famine relief effort during the 1970 to 1971 drought. That drought decimated the county's livestock economy and plunged parts of central and northwestern Afghanistan into starvation. Many Afghans put the blame directly on Zahir Shah, whom they now claimed had been a feckless and incapable ruler. These people saw Daoud Khan as a safe solution to that problem. He was the king's stern cousin and brother-in-law, a well-known if somewhat feared quantity from his time as prime minister. His abolition of the monarchy and assumption of the presidential title did not, however, mark the end of the Musahiban dynasty but rather another rotation in its leadership. Fears that Daoud Khan would establish a communist government because some prominent Parcham members were his allies faded after he sidelined them in the new administration. Within a year it was clear that his political model was the nationalist one-party state of the Shah's Iran with which he established good relations. Soon Daoud Khan's bald head graced Afghanistan's new banknotes (Figure 1.3).

It was not that Daoud lacked political opposition: his immediate crackdown on the Islamist Muslim Youth Organization forced many of its members to flee to Pakistan. There they received military training and attempted a coordinated attack in some northern provinces during July and August of 1975. But it generated no local support. I was in the roadless mountains of Badakhshan at that time when I arrived at a village where my host exclaimed that I just missed meeting two *yagi* (rebels). They had attacked a government police station in remote Darwaz and passed through fleeing south the day before. He told me that one of them was armed with a shotgun. Upon arriving at the shepherd camps located in the highest elevations of southern Darwaz, I witnessed a troop of mounted cavalry with carbines strapped on their backs passing by on the trail below us.

Figure 1.3 Daoud Khan banknote.

These Interior Ministry gendarmes had been flown into Darwaz's tiny airstrip at Nusay and were in hot pursuit of the two Islamist rebels I had just missed. Unable to catch up with them, an announcement of a substantial award for their capture was broadcast over the radio that soon led to their apprehension. The mounted troops then returned to Darwaz where I got a close look at them: our dogs had chased after their horses and they entered the shepherd camp to complain. After checking my papers and deciding not to arrest me, their commander invited me to visit the police station in Nusay. I politely declined with the excuse that I was travelling in the opposite direction. Similar attempted uprisings in the Panjshir Valley, Kapisa, Ghorband and Laghman also collapsed after the local population refused to support its organizers.

The failure of the 1975 revolt only burnished Daoud Khan's image as a strongman and he turned his already suspicious eye on the members of every Islamic political group whose participation in the premature revolt had exposed them. Those who did not escape the country found themselves jailed in large numbers and many were executed. The dynasty had cultivated relationships with the country's conservative Islamic religious leaders in 1929, but none of them had sought to rule the country (and none had ever done so historically). On those occasions when clerics did enter the political realm, they did so as supporters of the state or rebel leaders, not as contenders for power themselves. By contrast, these new Muslim Brotherhood-inspired groups championed a radical political Islam that sought to capture the state and were therefore seen as dangerously subversive. For this reason, their persecution was deemed political rather than religious by most members of Afghanistan's *ulema* (clerics) who sought to preserve their good relations with the government.

The communist ideological rivals of the Islamists also drew a lesson from Daoud Khan's success in dousing the sparks of a rural insurgency. In their view, the more secure path to power would be through a coup similar to the one Daoud Khan had employed against the king. Preparation for that required allies in the military and a low profile. That low profile was blown in April 1978 when the Parchami communist faction leader, Mir Akbar Khyber, was assassinated (by whom is still disputed). His funeral drew more than 10,000 supporters to the streets of Kabul. Daoud's subsequent arrest of top communist party leaders panicked their allies in the military, who mounted a coup that resulted in the murder of Daoud and his extended family. The coup's bloody success was a close-run thing, so the new regime began a series of mass arrests and executions of those it deemed enemies. Within eighteen months of the communist ascendancy, a nationwide insurgency against the new People's Democratic Party of Afghanistan (PDPA) ended Afghanistan's half century of peace and opened the door to instability that no one has yet managed to close.

In reflecting on the exceptional, sustained stability of the relatively weak Musahibans, two sources seem germane. The first, paradoxically, stemmed from the feeble Musahiban political and military position in 1929, one of which they were well aware. They understood the imperative to compromise in the service of preserving power and rarely asserted themselves unilaterally. Although their government was highly centralized, in practice it allowed for considerable *de facto* local autonomy. Second, their emergence out of a period of intense ideological struggle informed a strategy that avoided the pursuit of potentially controversial policies. They were excoriated by both sides of the ideological spectrum for having no fixed opinions other than that they continue on as the rulers of Afghanistan.

The Musahiban path to stability and legitimacy thus followed the well-worn path described by the British political philosopher David Hume in 1752. He wrote that when 'a new government is established, by whatever means, the people are commonly dissatisfied with it and pay obedience more from fear and necessity than from any idea of allegiance or of moral obligation'. The passage of time 'removes all these difficulties and accustoms the nation to regard as their lawful or native princes that family which at first they considered as usurpers or foreign conquerors' (Hume 2018 [1752]: 214).

Successor regimes did the opposite. Each presumed its new government was all powerful and could rule by fiat after successfully seizing power in Kabul. And, in turn, each only discovered too late that, in Afghanistan, the threat of military force was most effective when it remained unused. This maxim proved particularly true for governments that relied on foreign troops to maintain their authority. Once conflict became widespread, attempts to become more politically inclusive failed because the basis for cooperation had disappeared. More significantly, each of the post-Musahiban governments attempted to impose its own immoderate cultural vision on the entire population, whether that was the radical socialism of the PDPA or the radical Islam of the Taliban.

This included the American-backed Islamic Republic of Afghanistan that, although democratic in structure, was keen to impose Amanullah's abandoned agenda rather than persuade people of its virtues in due time. What they all shared with the Musahibans were highly centralized governments vulnerable to instantaneous collapse if the centre failed. The Musahibans avoided this fate by never demanding anything from the Afghan people that would put their regime at risk. Their successors, keen to impose their own ideologies, did and paid the price for doing so. Say what you will about the many defects of Musahiban rule, but ordinary people had little to fear from them and lived in peace: no golden age to be sure but something that in retrospect deserves more appreciation than it received at the time.

References

Hume, D. (2018 [1752]), 'Of the Original Contract', in *David Hume on Morals, Politics, and Society*. New Haven: Yale University Press.

2

The Taliban, Women and the Hegelian Private Sphere

Juan Cole

Social Research 70:3 (2003), 771–808 © The New School. Reprinted with permission of John Hopkins University Press.

The society created by the Taliban in Afghanistan between 1996 and 2001 constantly evoked outrage and reactions of open-mouthed disbelief in the western press. Even the ayatollahs in Tehran issued a statement condemning the Taliban for defaming Islam by confusing it with medieval obscurantism. Since the Islamic Republic of Iran had long been called 'medieval' itself by political opponents, this criticism of the Afghan government has a delicious irony. One key to comprehending the somewhat strident bewilderment that the Taliban provoked in many observers is their reconfiguration of the public and the private in their quest for a pure Islamic countermodernity. I use the term 'countermodernity' rather than 'antimodernism' because the Taliban adopted some key motifs from high modernism and depended on modern techniques for their power (the state, radio, mass spectacle, tank corps and machine guns mounted on Toyotas). They put these tools, however, to purposes very different from the goals of the industrialized democracies, especially with regard to the private sphere. The public–private divide as drawn by modern liberalism affects everything from how power is attained and exercised to how women are treated. Did the Taliban strike outsiders as bizarre in part because they drew those lines very differently than most other contemporary societies?

The German sociologist Jürgen Habermas argues that the divide between public and private is a feature of modernity. He reports that the word *privat*, derived from the Latin, can only be found in Germany from the late sixteenth century, and that it initially referred to someone who was not an officer of the state. He says that institutionally, 'a public sphere in the sense of a separate realm distinguished from the private sphere cannot be shown to have existed in the feudal society of the High Middle Ages'. The power of the kings and aristocrats was 'public', not in the sense of a sphere of society but in that of a status position. The lord 'displayed himself, presented himself as an

---

Many thanks to Jamil Hanifi, Shah Hanifi, Najeeb Jan, Rob Gleave and Jon Anderson for comments that much improved the final draft.

embodiment of some sort of "higher" power'. The arena in which power was represented to a wide audience was public, but was not characterized by public participation – it was public the way a stage play is, for a passive audience. The church was likewise 'public' in this sense of open display of ritual and authority until proponents of the Enlightenment increasingly coded it as private from the eighteenth century forward (Habermas 1993: 7, 11). Joan Landes draws attention to Habermas' emphasis on 'features of visibility, display and embodiment, that is, an "aura" that surrounded and endowed the lord's concrete existence'. She argues that 'staged publicity' was fundamental to absolutist society in the early modern nation-states. This re-presentative performance of kingly authority by a royal subject before an audience was not dependent on having a permanent location or on the development of a public sphere of communication (Landes 1998: 138).

Habermas' use of a binary opposition between the 'medieval' and 'modernity' and his concentration on select areas of Western Europe create a teleological natural history of the public sphere that remains highly Eurocentric. His account obscures the ways in which power as representation, and religion as public, continued to characterize many societies in modernity. Rather than being conceived of as medieval throwbacks, such societies must be viewed as forms of alternative modernity. Even in the Soviet Union and the People's Republic of China, Lenin's vanguard theory allowed power to be exercised in the twentieth century by unelected bureaucrats, in part through massive military parades and other spectacles. In Bolivia and Greece, religion remained public, even as it was privatized in Turkey and Mexico.

What of the private sphere? Seyla Benhabib notes three meanings of the private sphere in modern political thought. She says, 'first and foremost, privacy has been understood as the sphere of moral and religious conscience', referring to the separation of religion and state and the granting to the individual of autonomy in deciding such matters, which are 'rationally irresolvable'. The second is private enterprise, or the 'non-interference by the state in the free flow of commodity relations'. The third, she says, is the 'intimate sphere' – 'meeting the daily needs of life, of sexuality and reproduction, of care for the young, the sick and the elderly' – which she says are typically recognized by modern thinkers as belonging to the domain of the household. She points out that for many modern thinkers, a tension exists between their vision of a patriarchal domestic realm and the values of equality and consent in the political sphere (Benhabib 1998: 86). I will argue below that the Taliban stance on the first and the last of these three meanings of the private was the precise opposite of those Benhabib attributes to modern political thought.

As Landes and others have noted, Habermas did his early work on the public sphere before the wide impact of 1970s feminist theory, and he neglects the issue of gender. In retrospect, this lacuna is the most problematic, since all societies imbue the public and the private with overtones of male and female. Even a modern thinker such as Hegel could write:

> The ethical dissolution of the family consists in this, that once the children have been educated to freedom of personality, and have come of age, they become recognized as persons in the eyes of the law and as capable of holding free property

of their own and founding families of their own, the sons as heads of new families, the daughters as wives. ... [T]he natural dissolution of the family by the death of the parents, particularly the father, has inheritance as its consequence so far as the family capital is concerned.

(Hegel 1942: 118–19, para. 172)

The sons hold free property and enter the public sphere on the dissolution of the old family, whereas the daughters remain domestic, as wives. Hegel writes, 'Woman, on the other had, has her substantive destiny in the family, and to be imbued with family piety is her ethical frame of mind' (Hegel 1942: 114, para. 168). As Dorothy Rogers has argued, Hegel sees children as initially closer to the spiritual and feeling-oriented sensibility of women, but through education they gain a sense of objectivity and rationality and are prepared to enter the public sphere. She notes, 'as anyone with even a hint of gender awareness can see, this leaves women conspicuously absent from public life, because as creatures ruled by feeling, they are unable to make this step from family life into civil society' (Rogers 2000: 6). Hegel's was incontrovertibly a modern vision, but he expressed a patriarchal version of modernity.

In Islamdom, as in Europe, the gendering of the public and private was never complete either in theory or practice. An idea of the private, as an inviolable domestic realm, existed in Islamic jurisprudence (Jindi 1993). Moreover, since Muslim women, unlike European women until the mid-nineteenth century, most often owned property, their property transactions and endowments had a somewhat public character, though these tended to be executed by male agents. As for social reality, it should be remembered that the vast majority of Muslim women have never veiled or been excluded from appearing in public. Peasant and tribal women worked outside their domiciles. In the twentieth century millions of Muslim women have become physicians, attorneys, journalists and members of other public professions. It is often not appreciated with what alacrity urban societies in countries such as Egypt, Tunisia, Iraq, Pahlevi Iran and Pakistan adopted key elements of modernity, including changes in the status of women. Afghanistan, much more rural and pastoralist and less urban than most of the Muslim world, had a far more limited and sectoral experience of modernity, mainly among the small urban upper middle and upper classes.[1] Early reformist measures taken by Amanullah Khan in the 1920s, such as improving the position of women, contributed to a popular backlash against that monarch (Moghadam 1993: 218–20). The country was thrown into long-term upheaval by the 1978 Marxist coup and the Soviet invasion and occupation from 1979 to 1989, during which, again, the question of women's position in the public sphere was broached in a major way. A conservative approach to women was taken up by the Islamic guerrilla movement and implemented during the period of warlord infighting between 1992 and 1996. A vast Afghan diaspora in desperately poor refugee camps grew throughout this period, ultimately with some three million expatriates in Pakistan and two million in Iran. In the midst of imposed totalitarian utopias, war, upheaval and squalid camp life, the ideals of personal autonomy and privacy so dear to the liberal tradition could have meant very little, though they continued to have a purchase among the small urban middle classes that remained.[2]

Radical Islamism is a response both to what its adherents see as the 'incomplete' project of Islamization and to the inroads of liberal modernity. Although it draws on 'medieval' motifs and imagines the medieval as a golden age, it is in many ways quite different from anything that actually existed in the medieval period. (Conceiving of Islamization as an incomplete process that now requires the technologies of the state to bring it to fruition is itself a form of high modernism; see Cole 2002.) Radical fundamentalism in any religion challenges the emergence of a reasoned public sphere, favouring forms of authoritarian rule, patriarchy and religious control. Power and faith are reworked as imposed spectacle rather than as discursive give and take. Like Hegel, radical Muslim fundamentalists code women as essentially subjective and private, and therefore excluded from the public sphere. They advocate a neopatriarchal countermodernity in which they actively combat those elements of the modern condition that contribute to the entry of women into the public sphere, including mass coeducation, mixed-sex factory and office work, women's entry into many professions, and consumerism and the consequent desire for a second income within the family. In Afghanistan, the Taliban feared the advent of such developments, given that few actually existed on the ground. By what techniques did they seek to accomplish the publicization of power and the male body, and the almost complete privatization of women? I will attend in particular to the few female Afghan voices we have for the Taliban period, referring to two memoirs and to material published in Persian on the internet by the Revolutionary Association of the Women of Afghanistan (RAWA), a Maoist feminist Afghan group.

The Public Nature of Power

Let us begin with the question of the nature of the Taliban public realm.[3] As in medieval society, there was little in the way of a public sphere in Afghanistan under their rule. The 'public' was coterminous with the power of the state and the somewhat personalistic and arbitrary implementation of its law. Although they advertised themselves as offering a strict interpretation of Sharia (Islamic law), in fact they often practised it in a highly idiosyncratic manner that astonished mainstream Muslims. Habermas depicts two forms of political modernity in his work on the public sphere. In his ideal liberal democracies of the eighteenth and nineteenth centuries, power is exercised through public, reasoned discourse and by the ballot box. He admits that in post-Second World War mass societies, however, corporate media have increasingly made power instead a matter of representation again (through political advertising and the monopoly over opinion mongering in the mass media by a relatively small number of talking heads). In mass society, democratic communicative procedures still exist, but are powerfully subverted by the large corporations. Habermas thus posits two forms of possible political modernity, one liberal and the other employing modern technology to replicate the medieval sense of power as spectacle.

I would argue that the Taliban represent yet a third possibility, also visible in Khomeinist Iran in the 1980s: medieval motifs applied to the modern re-creation of power as representation (and employing some mass media, such as radio, to this end). The Taliban had no elections, public debates or even much of a press. The few newspapers published under their rule were heavily censored and appeared only intermittently, and since 90 per cent of women and 60 per cent of men were illiterate, could have had only a superficial impact in any case. Radio was the major manner by which the Afghan public was reduced to a mass, receiving instructions rather than engaging in democratic consultation. It was supplemented for smaller villages by the network of pro-Taliban clerics throughout the Pashtun regions. Afghanistan had conducted relatively few elections in the twentieth century, so the authoritarian character of Taliban rule was not new. The severity and extreme character of their clampdown, however, surpassed most pre-1979 Afghan regimes.

The overwhelmingly Pashtun Taliban took and kept power by military means, instituting rule by militia, but their authority was enhanced by their religious charisma as holy men. (Pashtuns comprise about 40 per cent of the Afghan population.) In some ways their rule was analogous to that of the urban *lutis* or ruffians in the nineteenth century, when Muslim clerics, seminary students and street gangs often took over cities in the area from Baghdad to Bukhara (Cole 2002). They ruled in part through power spectacle, through the use of captured Soviet tanks and artillery against other ethnic militias. The incessant Taliban warfare and feuding with other ethnic groups such as the Shiite Hazaras and the Tajiks and Uzbeks (who formed the opposition Northern Alliance) demonstrated their power, as did events like the massacres of defeated populations in the towns of Mazar-i Sharif and Bamiyan. The Taliban asserted control over the Hazara region, which had long resisted them and was inhabited by Shiite Muslims, whom they despised. They committed substantial massacres of Hazara civilians. In part, these conflicts and massacres driven by religious ideology reflected a breakdown in barriers to communication and transportation that had enabled heterodox groups like Imami Shiites and Ismailis to flourish in rural areas (Canfield 1973). Modernity brought the highly disparate citizens of Afghanistan together, and the immediate result was not more but less freedom of conscience. Turkic Uzbeks fared little better. Some 8,000 non-combatants are said to have been killed in Mazar in 1998 alone, when the Taliban reconquered it (Goodson 2001: 79).

The Taliban's titular head, Mullah Muhammad Omar, claimed charismatic authority, and eventually the Islamic caliphate itself. Mullah Omar came in many ways to be beholden to and threatened or manipulated by his Saudi guest, Osama bin Laden, the head of Al Qaeda and commander of the Taliban's 55th Brigade (its most effective fighting force, mainly Arab). Mullah Omar was reclusive and staged few public spectacles. His power circulated to the public through his representatives, the Taliban themselves, who were omnipresent in the streets and over Radio Sharia. He did, however, engage in one momentous piece of 'staged publicity', just before his conquest of Kabul in 1996. Kandahar is the site of a mosque complex centred on a relic, the supposed cloak of the Prophet Mohammad, said to have been brought there by Ahmad Shah Durrani, who Afghans believe founded the modern Afghan state in 1747. Amanullah Khan had once also appealed to the charisma of the cloak in his failed bid to avoid being overthrown in the late 1920s. According to *New York Times* reporter Norimitsu Onishi, the shrine keeper said the cloak itself had only been offered for viewing twice before 1996: once to the country's former monarch,

Zahir Shah, who is said to have averted his eyes at the last minute, and once to his cousin, the political leader Pir Sayyid Gailani. In the spring of 1996 Mullah Omar requested permission to see it.

He not only viewed the relic, said to produce miracles, but insisted on bringing it out of the shrine for a public showing. This unprecedented public ritual produced a large crowd. Onishi writes:

> With the cloak in his possession, Mullah Omar went to an old mosque in the center of the city and climbed onto its roof. For the next 30 minutes, he held the cloak aloft, his palms inserted in its sleeves. According to residents of Kandahar who were present, the crowds cheered. Many lost consciousness. Many threw their hats and other items of clothes in the air, in the hope that they would make contact with the cloak. Most importantly, as other mullahs shouted, '*Amir-ul momineen!*' Mullah Omar gained the legitimacy he needed to pursue his conquest of the rest of Afghanistan.
>
> (Onishi 2001)[4]

The cries of *Amir al-Mu'minin* (prince of the believers) served as an affirmation that Mullah Omar had revived the caliphate, which had been abolished several times in Islamic history and then revived, most recently by Ottoman Sultan Abdülhamid II, around 1880. It was abolished by Mustafa Kemal Atatürk in 1924.

It was because of Mullah Omar's status as caliph or prince of the believers that Afghanistan under the Taliban was declared the Emirate of Afghanistan. Apparently bin Laden and Al Qaeda hoped to use this caliphal revivalism as a rallying point for Muslims throughout the world. Mullah Omar took his charge seriously, likening himself to the second caliph, also called Omar, and sneaking out in street clothes as his namesake had done to gauge the problems of the common person. (This sort of story was also told of some Afghan kings, and goes back to the depiction of Harun al-Rashid in the *Thousand and One Nights*.) He also began wearing a perfume said to be based on the same recipe as the one worn by the Prophet Mohammad. Despite his reputation as a recluse, Mullah Omar did circulate, virtually making his SUV into a sort of mobile office. Another press report quotes Mullah Omar's chauffeur.

> After a time, he had so many supplicants that he could no longer maintain an office. 'Everywhere is my office,' he told Saheb [his driver]. 'I can issue orders from anywhere.' Saheb spent hours driving Omar around; after a time the car began to reek of a kind of perfume (probably camphor) which, Omar claimed, had been worn by the Prophet Muhammad himself.
>
> ('Architect,' 2002)

Mullah Omar projected his personal authority through these forms of public display – the famed showing of the prophet's mande, symbolizing Mullah Omar's claiming to be his vicar, the circulating SUV office, the careful olfactory marking of himself as having divine authority through the prophet's perfume (in Afghan folklore, the corpses of holy men in their tombs are widely thought to resist disintegration and to give off a sweet odour). But he more often marked his power by disappearing from public view and rationing access to himself.

The Taliban as a group, in contrast, were far from reclusive, and from the beginning employed public spectacle to rule. They announced their advent in Kabul in September of 1996 from the minarets of mosques (Pahlavan 1998: 218). Like the eighteenth-century French monarchs who inscribed their justice on the criminal by drawing and quartering him, so the Taliban revived public executions as spectacle, as part of their implementation of power as public performance (Foucault 1979). Even the tapes from music and videocassettes were torn from their casings and displayed on the goalposts of the stadium where executions were held. The mined 'bodies' of the offending magnetic tape media were made a spectacle, just as were the bodies of those human beings deemed criminal.

Journalist Jan Goodwin witnessed a Taliban spectacle early in 1998:

> Thirty-thousand men and boys poured into the dilapidated Olympic sports stadium in Kabul, capital of Afghanistan. Street hawkers peddled nuts, biscuits and tea to the waiting crowd. The scheduled entertainment? They were there to see a young woman, Sohaila, receive 100 lashes, and to watch two thieves have their right hands amputated. Sohaila had been arrested walking with a man who was not a relative, a sufficient crime for her to be found guilty of adultery. Since she was single, it was punishable by flogging; had she been married, she would have been publicly stoned to death. ... As Sohaila, completely covered in the shroud-like *burqa* veil, was forced to kneel and then flogged, Taliban 'cheerleaders' had the stadium ringing with the chants of onlookers. Among those present there were just three women: the young Afghan, and two female relatives who had accompanied her. The crowd fell silent only when the luckless thieves were driven into the arena and pushed to the ground. Physicians using surgical scalpels promptly carried out the amputations. Holding the severed hands aloft by the index fingers, a grinning Taliban fighter warned the huge crowd, 'These are the chopped-off hands of thieves, the punishment for any of you caught stealing.' Then, to restore the party atmosphere, the thieves were driven in a jeep once around the stadium, a flourish that brought the crowd to their feet, as was intended. These Friday circuses, at which Rome's Caligula would doubtless have felt at home, are to become weekly fixtures for the entertainment-starved male residents of Kabul.
>
> (Goodwin 1998)

As in Foucault's old regime, these public punishments of miscreants inscribed the power of the state on the body of the offender. Afghan's twentieth-century monarchy had also staged such spectacles, including the gruesome trampling of adulteresses by an elephant. Unlike in absolute monarchy, however, the criminals here were considered to have sinned not against the king, but against the holy law.

Mullah Omar and the Taliban claimed legitimacy as the guarantors of Sharia, and said that it was their duty to conform the bodies of Afghans to its strictures. Thus, the back of the veiled fornicator was scourged by the whip (surely an erotically charged performance), and the hands of the thieves were detached, all before an audience of thousands. Sharia does not require, and perhaps even discourages, punishment as spectacle. The Taliban were not merely affirming their piety or their implementation of Islamic law as they saw it by their weekly show at the stadium; they were engaged in 'staged publicity' that ritually affirmed their power and legitimacy. For this reason, watching the spectacles of punishment was not voluntary, and was even a family affair that exposed young children to the brutality. A young woman memoirist, Zoya, reports, 'Near the stadium, we saw their patrols ordering shopkeepers to close down and go watch the ritual. I was surprised to see women taking their children with them, but [my friend] Zeba explained, "They want their children to realize what will happen to them if they ever steal anything. They think scaring them is a good way to educate them"' (Zoya 2002: 150).

Despite Taliban claims, the public exercise of violence by the Taliban had more to do with power than with piety. Punishments were applied quite apart from the requirements of Islamic law. Latifa, a young Afghan woman, saw a group of women in long black veils being beaten bloody by the Taliban in the street. Bewildered, she later made inquiries. 'They were beaten because they were wearing white socks. ... That is the color of the Taliban flag, and women do not have the right to wear white. It means they are defiling the flag' (Latifa 2001: 65). This public thrashing, delivered to a group of hapless women in the street, upheld the castelike privileges of the Taliban and the sanctity of their flag (a modern instrument for the representation of the power of the state). Like the amputations and whippings in the stadium, it claimed a monopoly of symbolic power in the public sphere for the Taliban. Jan Goodwin reported another such state-related assertion of public power through violence. 'After another man, a saboteur, was hanged, his corpse was driven around the city, swinging from a crane. Clearly, there is nothing covert about the regime's punitive measures. In fact, the Taliban insure they are as widely publicized as possible' (Goodwin 1998). Sabotage against the state required not merely a quiet death sentence in a prison, but a public hanging. Even a hanging in one, stationary site, like the stadium, was insufficiently public in this instance. Rather, the corpse of the miscreant needed to be even further publicized by having it swung from a crane mounted on a Toyota truck and driven around the city. The modernity of such a procedure should be underlined, since it is the combustion engine that makes practical the rapid touring of the saboteur's swinging cadaver. Likewise the bodies of former communist dictator Najibullah and his brother were left dangling from a traffic platform in bustling downtown Kabul for three days in 1996. Goodwin alleges that they had been castrated, not a Sharia punishment but very much an expression of Taliban power in their highly masculine public sphere.

The highly publicized destruction by the Taliban (apparently at the insistence of bin Laden and Al Qaeda) of the mammoth Buddhas of Bamiyan in the spring of 2001 was not merely a statement of religious iconoclasm (graven idols are forbidden in the Taliban version of Islam). It also functioned as a further assertion of power by spectacle. The Taliban clearly enjoyed defying the outrage of the international community. Insofar as the Buddhas had been in the past and might have at some future point again been tourist destinations, the Taliban permanently destroyed this beacon for infidels. The Taliban were not the first Muslim iconoclasts to wreak damage on pre-Islamic art and monuments in Afghanistan, but they were the first to do it in so spectacular and systematic manner.

The Deprivatization of Religion and Conscience

Benhabib's three forms of modern privacy begin with 'moral and religious conscience' and the autonomy granted the individual over these metaphysical matters, which are considered private because they are not amenable to public, rational resolution. That this issue comes first in her listing is no accident. She introduces the paragraph by saying that 'first and foremost' privacy has been thus understood by modern political thinkers. Benhabib serves here as rapporteur for the modem, but of course each form of modernity has its own subtraditions. Raised in Kemalist Turkey with its militant governmental devotion to a sort of Jacobin tradition of forcibly divorcing religion from the state, it may be that Benhabib was influenced by her background to make this sort of privacy her keystone. (Most Americans would probably agree.) It is not clear that autonomy of moral and religious conscience would be quite as thoroughgoing or as central to modernity in the UK, for instance, where there is a blasphemy law on the books, or in Ireland or Greece.

Still, the centrality to 'modern political thinkers' of this privatization of religion may certainly be conceded. The Taliban, in contrast, sought to de-privatize religion. This publicization of the sacred required that all men worship in public, and so it was decreed. 'The decree saw scores of Taliban fighters armed with machine guns, lengths of hosepipe, and sticks forcing passersby into mosques for prayers on the first Friday after the Taliban arrived here' ('Taliban Repeat Warning' 1996). The insistence that the five daily prayers be performed at the mosque had the effect of making the performance or non-performance of worship a matter of public knowledge and concern. (In fact, by 1998 the pressure for universal male mosque worship had weakened considerably in Kabul, and the road blockades initially employed to require it had been given up.) (Huwaydi 2001: 68)

Men were given six weeks to grow their beards to a hand's length and to trim their moustaches in accordance with a literal reading of sayings about the Prophet Muhammad's appearance. The young female memoirist of life in Taliban Kabul, Latifa, reported that her middle-class father complied with the new rule, grumbling, 'My beard belongs to the Taliban, not to me!' (Latifa 2001: 55). The religious state owned the beard of Latifa's father, which was thereby alienated from him insofar as he lost the autonomy to decide its trim. In Taliban terminology, what was *zahir* or public had to conform to their understanding of Sharia as interpreted by medieval jurists. The beard was public, could be seen and so required conformity.

Men's bodies became an arena of contention between globalizing consumer culture and Taliban localization. The popularity of bootleg copies of the film *Titanic* caused many young urban Afghans to lionize Hollywood actor Leonardo DiCaprio. 'The *Titanic* fashion wrought ravages, notably among the barbers,' Latifa tells us. 'Radio Sharia announced that 28 of them were arrested and condemned for having given young men a Leonardo DiCaprio haircut' (Latifa 2001: 204–5). Zoya also recounts the *Titanic* craze, noting that young men wearing the '*Titanic* cut' also risked harassment and beatings in the street. The Taliban issued a *fatwa* or decree of death against Leonardo DiCaprio and his co-star in the movie, Kate Winslet, should they ever come to Afghanistan, since the film celebrated love out of wedlock (Zoya 2002: 161–2).

Privacy as Free Enterprise

The Taliban had a mixed record with regard to Benhabib's second notion of privacy as economic free enterprise. Under their rule private trade between Afghanistan and Pakistan burgeoned. Pakistani journalist Imtiaz Gul reported that 'the biggest supporters of the Taliban rule are the traders' and truckers, because the Taliban had abolished the multitude of illegal checkpoints once run by the warlords. Truck drivers had been forced to pay bribes at each of the forty warlord checkpoints between Kandahar and the Pakistani border town of Chaman, whereas under the Taliban there were only two checkpoints, both legal, and the traders paid only official government taxes (Gul 2000).

Yet the Taliban strictly forbade the taking of interest on loans, the bedrock of the modern banking system. It had been a practice common even in the Muslim bazaar and among money-changers, justified by various legal workarounds (*hiyal*). Islamic modernists such as the Egyptian jurist Muhammad ʿAbduh (d. 1905) had allowed modern banking interest, but the Taliban rejected such modernist interpretations of Islam.

The Taliban sought to forestall the development in Afghanistan of a mass consumer culture and its publicization of the domestic and private spheres. Their policies produced what seem to be contradictions, insofar as they insisted both on an extreme demarcation between private and public but at the same time attempted to extend the power of the state into the bedroom through their insistence on the ubiquity of Islamic law. In some ways, they conducted a vast reprivatization of domesticity, a realm to which they even more inexorably than Hegel assigned to women. Windows had to be painted black so that they did not reveal the private domesticity, especially unveiled women, within. In essence, the window had served as a potential hole in the dike of the public–private divide, and painting windows black served to patch the hole. Latifa complained bitterly of being thus deprived of a ground-level view of the street, but admitted that repairing this breach did have some advantages. It made it more difficult for the Taliban religious police to see the glow of the television screen within when her brother clandestinely set up a showing of Indian films on the family videocassette recorder (Latifa 2001: 56). Street-level windows were not traditional in Afghan buildings, and were largely limited to fairly new upper-middle-class neighbourhoods, so that it was mainly families of Latifa's and Zoya's social class who were affected by this decree (Hanifi 2002).

The Egyptian journalist Fahmi Huwaydi pressed the head of the Ministry for the Promotion of Virtue and the Prevention of Vice about the nature of his work in 1998. This powerful agency had its own extensive funding from Wahhabi sources in the Gulf and was modelled on the similar Saudi corps of religious enforcers.[5] The minister, Mawlavi Qalamuddin, replied:

> We do not spy on people. That is a matter forbidden by the divine law. Likewise, we do not enter anyone's house. Everyone is free (*hurr*) in his home. God will punish him for any vice he commits there. What concerns us is open vice (*al-munkarat al-zahirah*) in the streets or public places (*al-amakin al-ʿammah*). We see it as our

responsibility to combat these vices because they harm the Islamic society we are seeking. In addition, our silence about them would be tantamount to encouraging the spread of vice.

(Huwaydi 2001: 81)[6]

In accordance with classical Islamic law, Mawlavi Qalamuddin acknowledged a sphere of domesticity as properly private. The privacy of domesticity was not entirely sacrosanct, however, because the divine law applied to all human behaviour at all times. In actual fact, the public nature of Sharia, and the application of Sharia to even private acts, extended the reach of the Taliban state even into homes. Latifa notes that her neighbour's telephone went silent for a while, giving no dial tone. When the line was established, however, Latifa's father hesitated to use it. 'We know well that the Taliban listen to everything, monitor everything' (Latifa 2001: 62). The lived reality of life under the Taliban contradicted Mawlavi Qalamuddin's insistence that the Taliban did not spy on private homes. Their de-privatization of society led to a panopticon where, whether justifiably or not, the populace felt under constant scrutiny and dared not commit speech crimes over telephone lines that may have become public. The Taliban employed the technique of circulation to impose this scrutiny, with the armed *talibs* constantly moving about the city in their Toyotas.

Huwaydi reports the text of a decree by the Ministry for the Promotion of Virtue and the Prevention of Vice issued 17 December 1996, at the order of Mullah Omar, banning sixteen activities:

1. Temptation (*fitnah*) likely to cause public disturbance and the baring of women's faces in public was forbidden. Taxi drivers were not to accept as fares women who wore a *burqa* but did not completely cover their faces, on pain of imprisonment. Women were not to walk in the street without a close male relative (*mahram*).
2. Music was forbidden in shops, hotels and automobiles, on pain of imprisonment and the closing of the offending establishment.
3. Shaving a beard was forbidden. A month and a half after this decree, anyone not bearded was to be imprisoned until his beard grew out.
4. Daily prayers were to be said in mosques. Shops had to be closed at prayer time and vehicles had to cease circulating in the streets fifteen minutes before prayer time. Shopkeepers open at prayer time would be jailed for ten days.
5. Training pigeons and playing with birds were forbidden.
6. Drug trafficking was forbidden, along with the use of drugs.
7. Kite flying and betting on it were forbidden.
8. No image of persons could be displayed in shops, hotels or taxis, since this was a form of idolatry.
9. Gambling was forbidden.
10. Letting one's hair grow out in the American or British fashion was forbidden. The agents of the Ministry for the Promotion of Virtue and the Prevention of Vice were to apprehend violators and cut their hair.
11. Taking interest on loans was forbidden, on pain of a long prison term.

12. Women were not to wash clothes on the banks of rivers. If found doing so they would be remanded to the custody of a male guardian and severely punished.
13. Music and dancing were forbidden at wedding ceremonies.
14. Drum music was forbidden. The *ulema* (body of clerics) would decide on the punishment for it.
15. Men were forbidden to tailor women's clothing or to take their measurements. If found doing so they would face a prison term.
16. Practising astrology was forbidden. Astrologers would be imprisoned until they repented. Their books would be burned. (Huwaydi 2001: 66–8)

I would argue that this list signals to us that we are in the presence of a way of thinking, an 'episteme', that differs significantly from that of liberal modernity (Foucault 1973). The premises of the list are not immediately apparent, even to academics trained in Islamics. What logic drove Mullah Omar to issue these instructions in the first place? Many of these decrees forbade activities (music, dancing, pigeon flying, kite flying, gambling, the representation of the human form and astrology) that struck the Taliban as frivolous or impudent. The influence on them of the Wahhabi tradition is important here, since that branch of Islam views frivolity with the utmost disfavour. The public display of soberness is felt to indicate a private, inner piety, whereas public frivolity suggests iniquity in one's inner moral life. Soberness of mien was also a mark of authority for ruling cliques in Afghanistan, as the unsmiling portraits of most past Afghan monarchs suggest (Hanifi 2002). Pigeon flying and kite flying were both occasions for gambling (forbidden in Islam) and were probably banned in part for this reason. Other decrees, however, sought to close any connection between the public and the private. Thus, the baring of women's faces in public, the display of images of women (for instance, posters in shops hawking the charms of Bollywood actresses such as Neema and Madhuri), the male tailoring of women's clothes and the public washing of the family's laundry, including unmentionables, by women, were all banned. In some cases the Taliban were simply implementing again older statutes. Women washing clothes in the river was banned by the Kabul municipality in the 1950s, and tailors have for some time been under suspicion because of their mixing with and easy access to women (Hanifi 2002). I will return later to this concern with the extreme privatization of women. As Huwaydi notes, many of these decrees proved impractical to implement, or were so widely resisted as to remain only partially in force if at all.

The Taliban ban on dancing at weddings extended public, state concerns into a sphere that might be considered private or at least semi-private (Latifa 2001: 203). In Afghanistan, there was almost never mixed-sex dancing at weddings (unlike among the more secular middle-class Pakistani families, where cousins might dance together). Women would dance at their parts of the celebrations, and men at theirs. Even this sort of same-sex display of secular joy was banned, however, along with any playing of music.

In 1997, Latifa heard a woman wailing in the street below. She looked out her upper-storey window to see the mother of Aimal lamenting as a group of three Taliban beat her son with the butts of their Kalashnikov rifles. Aimal had set up a showing for five friends of an Indian movie on videocassette recorder at his home;

somehow the Taliban had learned of it. They broke in, caught the boys in the act and strung out the cassette tape. This 'execution' of magnetic tape media seemed to give the Taliban special pleasure, perhaps because it restored what they saw as a breach in the wall of public and private, real and unreal. Inside its cassette, the tape was capable of illicitly displaying, in private, virtual human images and voice that ought only to exist in a real public sphere. Strung out in the street, the tape was pushed out of the private sphere permanently and inverted so as to be itself lifeless and public. The Taliban took the boys out in the street and made them beat one another in public, a humiliation for an Afghan youth. When Aimal was insufficiently zealous in beating his friend, the Taliban pulled him over and said they would show him how it was done. He died an hour later (Latifa 2001: 70–1).

Zoya tells a similar story as farce rather than tragedy. In her anecdote once the offending family is pulled out of their home for viewing an Indian film and given a public lashing, the Taliban go inside. 'When the family dared to return, they found the Taliban sitting around the television set watching and commenting on the film, which was still playing. The Taliban took a bribe from the family and did not arrest them' (Zoya 2002: 148). These stories by middle-class urban women are about not the harshness of the law but its arbitrariness and unevenness of application. The Taliban regime opened all homes to invasion, it is being said, and could transform minor infractions into capital crimes or could elicit hypocrisy and bribe taking on the part of the young *talibs*.

The sense of being constantly under surveillance was reinforced by the ban on most media, which urban people continued surreptitiously to enjoy. 'Zeba told me that the only time she could listen to her music tapes was before going to sleep, and she would keep the volume as low as possible out of fear that the neighbors would inform on her if they heard the offending sound' (Zoya 2002: 148). She says that although photographs and television were formally forbidden, some families had illegal televisions sets (just as others had illegal videocassette recorders) and even satellite dishes with which they pirated signals (presumably they also had illegal signal decoders and were thus breaking international law as well as the Taliban version of Sharia).

As in Anglo-Saxon law (and unlike the general continental European legal tradition), the Taliban interpretation of Sharia did not recognize a right of privacy where law breaking is concerned. Thus, in 1986, the US Supreme Court upheld Georgia's sodomy law by a 5 to 4 vote, insisting that consenting adults have no constitutional right to private homosexual conduct. Goodwin reported of Afghanistan, 'Earlier that same week, three men accused of "buggery" had been sentenced to death by being partially buried in the ground and then having a wall pushed over on them by a bulldozer, a bizarre and labour-intensive form of execution dreamed up by the supreme leader of the Taliban, the 36-year-old Mullah Muhammad Omar' (Goodwin 1998). This execution was another example of grand spectacle aimed at making public the power of the Taliban state. But Goodwin is wrong that it was thought up by Mullah Omar. Rather, throwing a wall down on gay people is recommended in some very obscure sayings fathered in the medieval period on the Prophet Mohammad. The Taliban delighted in finding the more extreme and unlikely such sayings and then attempting to put them into force (most often for the first time in Islamic history, underlining again that they were engaged in a form of countermodernity rather than in reviving medieval forms). The execution also had the effect, however, of reinforcing the extension of Sharia into the realm of even private behaviour.

Women

The Taliban not only attempted to push (law-abiding) domesticity relentlessly into the private realm, but also coded the female body as inherently private. The neoprivatization of women formed a key goal of Taliban policy, as is clear in the autobiographical accounts of Latifa and Zoya. Their insistence on gender segregation was hardly new in Afghan, and especially in Pashtun society. Because they imposed this norm on urban societies such as Mazar and Kabul, however, and because of the extremes to which they took it there, it seemed more draconian to city dwellers than in the past. Interestingly, this plank of their platform seems not to have stood out for some male Afghan observers. Of the nineteen goals that `Abd al-Hamid Mubariz attributes to the Taliban with regard to establishing a religious state, only one concerns women, and that is the imposition of full public veiling (Mubariz 1997: 194–5). It is precisely because women are so little noticed in Persian and Urdu accounts of the Taliban by men that it is important to look at the little autobiographical material we have from Afghan women in order to grasp some subjective implications of this re-privatization programme. In male conversations, such as those Huwaydi conducted with Taliban officials, the reality of women's life under the Taliban is often obscured by talk about ideals.

Taliban policy towards women reversed that of the Communist government of the 1980s. Val Moghadam has discussed the improvements in the lives of (mainly urban) women during the communist period in the 1980s. Women fought in the Revolutionary Defense Group Militias and even served as commanders. A few served as delegates to the *loya jirga*, the national assembly. She saw women working in factories, including as supervisors of men and as union activists. Women were employed in the national airline, as unveiled newscasters, and in youth and peace organizations. It should be remembered, however, that most rural women's lives were little touched by the changing regimes, except insofar as they got caught up in the fighting. In 1979, according to International Labor Organization statistics, only 313,000 out of 6.2 million Afghan women were counted as economically active, and only 13,000 worked as professional and technical workers. In 1975 the enrolment rate among girls for primary and secondary school was only about 10 per cent. The literacy campaign of the Communist government in the 1980s led, by 1988, to 233,000 girls studying in schools and about 7,000 in colleges and universities. In contrast, few girls among the millions of refugees in Pakistan were provided with any education (Moghadam 1993: 223–5, 232–3, 240–7). When the Islamist government of Burhanuddin Rabbani came to power in 1992, it began the process of rolling back women's rights, and immediately forbade women to drive. The Taliban were even more repressive of women. The urban and small-town women who remained in Afghanistan, working in textiles or professional positions, bore the brunt of Taliban neopatriarchy.

The Taliban announced a policy of closing girls' schools and of immuring women in their homes. Mawlavi Saʽid Shahidkhayl, the Taliban undersecretary of education in 1998, explained the regime's policy towards women to Huwaydi thusly:

> The education of girls requires a jurisprudential ruling *(fatwa)* that would fix its path and its limits. As for women working outside the house, the text concerning that is clear and the matter is incontrovertible. For when the Koran says 'stay in your houses' [33:33; the feminine imperative is used], the issue requires no further discussion and we have nothing to do but obey.
>
> (Huwaydi 2001: 69)

The undersecretary insisted that the formal ban on girls' education was not a fixed policy, but rather a temporary measure. The insistence that women remain within the four walls of their homes, however, was not only rigid policy, he said, but the divine law and so beyond discussion. Huwaydi pointed out that the verse about women staying in their homes concerned only the prophet's wives and had to do with specific social arrangements in the prophet's Medina, and that the Egyptian *ulema* held that it could not be generalized to all Muslim women. Indeed, it is preceded (33:32) by the clear statement to the wives that 'you are not like any other women'. Mawlavi Saʽid insisted that the generalized import of the verse was upheld by all the prominent Afghan *ulema* (he meant those of the neo-Deobandi school, influenced by Wahhabi ideas from Saudi Arabia, who supported the Taliban) (Huwaydi 2001: 72–5).

When Huwaydi quoted to him a saying of the Prophet Mohammad that seeking knowledge is a duty for every Muslim, Mawlavi Saʽid said that there were two possible responses to this point. One was that the saying specified only 'Muslims', using the male form of the word, and not mentioning any female Muslim (*muslimah*). He acknowledged that in Arabic grammar the male was most often considered to encompass the female, but he acknowledged that some among the Taliban took the failure to mention the *muslimah* specifically as an indication that she was not intended by the saying. He insisted that he himself did not belong to that school, and favoured some form of women's education if it could be accomplished properly. He expressed dismay at the state in which the Taliban had found girls' education when they took Kabul, which could not have been pleasing to God. 'Some classes were coeducational, and the curricula were the furthest thing possible from the Sharia of God.' He said the girls knew nothing of their religion and 'had no interest in their roles as wives, mothers and mistresses of the family'. He said the appearance of the girls, the nature of the teaching staff and the condition of the buildings all required extensive review (Huwaydi 2001: 72).

When Huwaydi pressed him as to whether there was any scriptural basis for forbidding men to teach women, Mawlavi Saʽid said the Taliban were opposed to the mixing of the sexes in principle. 'Anyone who is assailed by doubt concerning our stance on this matter has only to follow what the newspapers have published about the story of President Clinton and Monica Lewinsky. I have no doubt that it is repeated in one form or another in every government office where women and men mix.' Huwaydi says that the mischievous mullah fell silent for a moment, then said, laughing, 'I do not say that it is repeated exactly. But note that I used the phrase "in one form or another"' (Huwaydi 2001: 73).

Mawlavi Sa`id gave two examples of the way in which the Taliban had improved women's position and restored for them their human rights. He described the decree of Mullah Omar issued in September 1998 regarding a tribal custom. It was customary, he said, that when one Afghan man killed another, the clan of the offender would present a woman or several women to the clan of the victim as compensation, so as to avoid a blood feud. Mullah Omar ordered this practice halted because it 'was contrary to the teachings of Islam, which bestows respect on women. It is therefore impermissible that they be given away or used as compensation.' Likewise, there was another tribal custom, concerning widows. When a woman's husband died, the clansmen of her late husband would marry her off to another of their men, willy nilly. Mullah Omar insisted that widows had the right to choose their own husbands, from another family or tribe if they so desired (Huwaydi 2001: 70–1). The Taliban saw themselves as recognizing the personhood and private autonomy of women in a far more thoroughgoing manner than was the case in Afghan tribal custom. They saw themselves as Islamic modernizers in an oppressive tribal environment (and it is true that the Taliban discouraged tribalism, at least in their formal discourse).

What Mawlavi Sa`id neglected to say was that the reform allowing widows to remarry outside their husbands' clan had been passed by Abdur Rahman Khan in 1880, and was not a new step at all, though it did partake of a history of modernist reformism (Skaine 2002: 13–14). Even the decrees passed by Amanullah Khan in the 1920s went much further. That such decrees had to be reissued by various governments over a century suggests the resilience of Pashtun tribal practice with regard to widow remarriage and the unstable character of modernity in this setting. Mawlavi Sa`id's justifications for the Taliban highlighted how anti-tribal their more universal, Islamic, ideology was, and denied that they were misogynists. Numerous eyewitness accounts of actual Taliban behaviour on the ground, however, show that hatred of women informed many policies and incidents. Many Taliban were orphans, brought up in all-male radical Islamist seminaries, and so they grew up without much knowledge of or respect for women. Many had been refugees or displaced persons, deprived of the usual male sources of self-esteem, and perhaps they needed to feel superior to, and even to practice sadism on women for that reason. Denied an ordinary private life in the camps and seminaries, and now in the ranks of their militia, many had scant respect for the privacy of others.

Mawlavi Sa`id insisted that, given how the Taliban actually 'improved' women's conditions, there could be only one reason the western press so excoriated their policies towards women. It was not that they really cared about women, he opined, but rather that they hated Islam. 'The Koran informed us fourteen centuries ago that they will never be pleased with us until we follow their religious community (*millatahum*), even in the pattern of life and the manner of living it' (Huwaydi 2001: 71). The Taliban policies on the privatization of women, then, were seen by some officials as a form of Islamic nativism, a refusal to adopt a globalizing western 'pattern of life'.

Despite Mawlavi Sa`id's equivocations, the first step the Taliban took once they captured Kabul was to close the girls' schools (Pahlavan 1998: 218; Skaine 2002).

Within three months, the Taliban had closed sixty-three schools, affecting 103,000 girls and somewhat more boys (Rashid 2000: 108). Soon after the fall of Kabul there were reports of women being sentenced to beating in public at the bazaar for not completely veiling their faces (Pahlavan 1998: 219–20). Zoya reports:

> [Women] were banned from appearing on the balconies of their houses. They could go outside only if they were accompanied at all times by a *mahram*, a close relative. They were banned from working. At certain times during the Ramadan month of fasting, they were simply not allowed on the streets. Women who were sick could only be treated by women doctors. Girls could not go to school – according to the Taliban, schools were a gateway to Hell, the first step on the road to prostitution. Women were not allowed to laugh or even speak loudly, because this risked sexually exciting males. High heels were banned because their sound was also declared provocative. Makeup and nail varnish were banned. Women who failed to respect such edicts would be beaten, whipped, or stoned to death.
> (Zoya 2002: 128)

In the week after the Taliban took Kabul, thousands of women doctors were confined to their houses and denied permission to go out (Latifa's mother was among them) (Pahlavan 1998: 226). Zoya points out that women patients suffered as a result, since they could not be seen by male physicians, and she says that a religious rationale was given for women being a sort of martyr if they died from lack of treatment.

> The women suffered more than the men, because the Taliban would not allow them to be treated by male doctors. For the Taliban, if a woman was sick, it was better for her to die than to be treated by a man. If she refused to let a male doctor touch her, she would be certain of going to Heaven. If she let herself be treated by him, she would be condemned to Hell.
> (Zoya 2002: 144–5)

She described a woman at the hospital she visited who said she could not afford medicine because she was not allowed to work, and had waited days to see one of the few female physicians on staff.

The Taliban rules hit working-class women, especially single women, orphans and war widows, especially hard. The twenty-year-long war had left as many as 30,000 of them without male relatives able and willing to support them. Zoya complained, 'I could only think that for many war widows the rule that they could not go out without a *mahram was* a tragedy. It meant that they could not leave their houses and had no way of earning a living apart from begging in the streets and risking a lashing from the Taliban, or turning to prostitution' (Zoya 2002: 150).

The accounts by Latifa and Zoya, despite their value in giving us a private, insider's view of the impact of these policies on educated urban women, often neglect to distinguish between social reality and stated Taliban policy. By 1999, for instance, CARE had convinced the Taliban to allow Afghan women to distribute food aid on its behalf to the war widows. Thus, not all of them were left to starve or sell themselves, although no doubt some were. Likewise, there were at least some female physicians in government clinics to see women (far too few for the need, and the official ban on female education impeded the training of a new generation). By 1999 some 30,000 girls were being quietly home-schooled or taught in segregated mosque school classes. The numbers are small and the classes were rudimentary and technically illicit (and could bring punishments), but it is important to stress that Taliban policies were not applied consistently and that they did not have the manpower to implement every policy they announced (Rubin 1999).

For middle-class urban women with male providers, the strictures had less dire economic consequences but they still came as a shock. Latifa says she tried on what in Pakistan is called the 'shuttlecock' *burqa* for the tiny mesh that covers the face even as the rest of the body is completely enveloped in black cloth. She found she could barely breathe and was rendered clumsy. 'I left there humiliated and furious. My face belongs to me. And the Koran says that a woman may be veiled, but has to remain recognizable' (Latifa 2001: 60). To Latifa's dismay, around the spring of 1998, Mullah Omar decreed that the mesh of the *burqas* then in use was too large, and must be made finer, even further constraining the women's ability to see their surroundings when outside (Latifa 2001: 87–8). The new confinement to a small interior space, and the end of school and socializing, drove Latifa into ennui and depression. 'My head is empty of projects. Sometimes, I make a tour of the cell' (Latifa 2001: 57). She ultimately fell physically ill with pleurisy and had to be taken to Pakistan for treatment, where she was diagnosed with depression. She also saw her mother, a physician, decline into deep depression from being confined.

RAWA insists that suicide among women rose significantly under the Taliban as a result of depression induced by cabin fever. They cite not only being kept within four walls but also the various assaults on women's honour and feeling of helplessness as driving this phenomenon, which often took the form of self-immolation. They give the example of Lida 'Umid', aged twenty, who, in April 2000, doused herself with gasoline and set herself on fire out of depression under Taliban rule. They report that she was unable to get medical care in her home city of Herat because no female physician was available. The family rushed her to neighbouring Iran but she died of her self-inflicted injuries (Afghanistan 2000). RAWA's anecdotal information is confirmed by the results of a health survey of Afghan women conducted in 1998. The report on the survey explains:

> Participants in the health and human rights survey also reported extraordinarily high levels of mental stress and depression. 81% of participants reported a decline in their mental condition. A large percentage of respondents met the diagnostic criteria for post-traumatic stress disorder (PTSD) (42%) (based on the *Diagnostical and Statistical Manual of Mental Disorders,* Fourth Edition) and major depression (97%), and also demonstrated significant symptoms of anxiety (86%). Twenty-one percent of the participants indicated that they had suicidal thoughts 'extremely often' or 'quite often.' It is clear from PHR's forty interviews with Afghan women that the general climate of cruelty, abuse, and tyranny that characterizes Taliban rule has had a profound affect on women's mental health.

Ninety-five percent of women interviewed described a decline in their mental condition over the past two years.

(Physicians for Human Rights 1999)

The educated middle class in the cities appears to have experienced the extreme privatization of the female body as alienating and productive of serious ennui. Rather than achieving a new, pure Islamic society, these women saw the policy as unreasonably restrictive and as stunting their sense of personhood, even driving them to consider or commit suicide.

Latifa freely admits that fear of the Taliban drove her to stay inside and risk this depression, while some of her friends were more adventurous. Fahmi Huwaydi, the Egyptian journalist, was surprised to see gaggles of unaccompanied women on Kabul streets in 1998, and this sight is reported by western journalists, as well (Huwaydi 2001: 68). Presumably these were working-class women who had no choice but to go out to beg or engage in illicit labour.

Latifa had good reason, even ghoulish reason, for caution, however. Goodwin tells us that Radio Sharia announced that '225 women had been rounded up and sentenced to a lashing for violating the dress code. One woman had the top of her thumb amputated for the crime of wearing nail polish.' Zoya reports that she was whipped on the hand in the streets of Kabul by an elderly *talib* because her hand had inadvertently come out from under the veil while she was walking 'When I turned I saw a Taliban [*sic*] with a lash in his hand. "Prostitute!" he shouted at me, the spittle spraying his greasy beard. "Cover yourself and go from here! Go to your house!"' (Zoya 2002: 142–3).

The strict privatization of the female body made women's presence in public always problematic for the *talibs*. Zoya tells of finding a woman distressed in the street. She tried to comfort her and inquired into the source of her distress. She said her mother had an asthma attack and rushed to the hospital. While there her condition worsened because of her *burqa,* which she removed to fight for breath in the ward. A *talib* 'had burst into the ward and given her mother forty lashes while the daughter watched, helpless to intervene. The nurses had done nothing to stop the beating' (Zoya 2002: 146). Zoya implies that once even a hospital waiting room was coded as 'public' by the Taliban, they were led inexorably to forbid the open appearance of the female body and face there, and thence to beating an asthmatic when she unveiled. The complete privatization of women's bodies aimed at in Taliban ideology, she suggests, inevitably leads to irrational injustices and to the disorientation of women.

As with other forms of illicit behaviour, the Taliban dealt with the problem of women who contravened their laws in part by the use of spectacle. Spanish journalist Ana Tortajada was shown a video by women activists of a staged punishment of a woman, this time an execution. She says that a woman, Zarmena, was accused of having murdered her husband, though there was no real proof that she was the murderer. Once she was brought to the soccer stadium in Kabul and it became clear that she would be executed by the Taliban's summary justice, the family of the deceased exercised their right in Islamic law to pardon the accused in return for a Danegeld. The Taliban officials, however, discussed the matter in the middle of the stadium and announced that, in spite of everything, they would proceed with the execution, for which they had forcibly assembled a large crowd, including children:

> They bring Zarmena to the arena, sitting in the rear of a van they had found, escorted by two other women. Taliban women. All three were covered in blue burqas. They lead her to the site of the execution, on the green of the soccer field. They order her to crouch. Zarmena turns her head back and through the burqa, which at that moment covers her entire body, says something to her executioner, who is leaning against a large cannon. Her head bends again and they shoot her in the nape of the neck. Her body collapses. The lower part of the burqa parts and displays her legs openly, covered in wide printed trousers. The Taliban women hasten to cover back up the lifeless cadaver with the burqa. Zarmena's seven sons attended her execution. The surround-sound of the recording preserves the reaction of the public: weeping and lamentation.
>
> (Tortajada 2001: 152–3)

This particular spectacle underlines the extreme patriarchy of the Taliban interpretation of the law. Tortajada's account implies that they were unreasonable in disregarding the willingness of the murdered husband's family to accept blood money in lieu of the execution. The effrontery of a wife who allegedly kills her husband drives them to make an object lesson of her. The spectacle is daring, insofar as in disciplining the rebellious female body the Taliban also risk exposing it. The pistol shot disorients the executed body, throwing off the *burqa* from her legs and displaying her forbidden pantaloons. Even in death, she must immediately be covered, the privacy of her body restored since it remains female even if a corpse.

The radical Islamist regime of the Taliban affords an extensive view of the logic of Muslim fundamentalism regarding the public and private spheres. I have argued that the Taliban de-privatized several life-worlds, 'publicizing' power, religion and the male body. The Taliban's techniques were spectacle, circularization, corporeal punishment, and informing and surveillance.

The Taliban, like Afghan leaders before them, employed exhibition to project their power. Mullah Omar's display of the prophet's cloak is an example of such staged spectacles. The forcible rounding up of thousands to serve as an audience for executions of gays, thieves, adulteresses and other offenders against the Taliban moral order underlined the public nature of power and the manner in which even private acts could constitute public offences. Another repertoire of power consisted of circulation – the constant movement in the street of Taliban seeking evidence of public infractions or of private indiscretions. As in the state of Georgia in the United States, so among the Taliban, there was no guarantee of privacy within one's own home – despite official Taliban denials of domestic spying. The circulation of a Toyota truck with a corpse swinging from its winch through the streets of Kabul served as an alternative to the stadium, but was equally public, and it also exemplified the technique of circulation.

Religion, too, was to be completely public, as Habermas argues it was in Europe before the eighteenth century. As soon as they took Kabul, the Taliban insisted that all residents had to say their five daily prayers, the men in mosques. Likewise, men were given six weeks to grow out their beards to a hand's length and to trim their moustaches. The rendering public of religion made common property of every religious act, including a man's pious beard and his ritual worship. In both instances, his body had a choice, of being conformed to the movements and shaping of religion, or of being tortured because of lack of compliance. This publicization of the male believer's body resulted in an alienation from individuals of parts of themselves, as with Latifa's father, who lamented that even his beard no longer belonged to him. It was *zahir,* open and apparent, and therefore public property.

Likewise, the gendered character of the public and private spheres, with women confined to the private, is even more developed in Taliban thinking than in Hegel. The expansion of the public realm of power, religion and morality by the Taliban had the effect, in addition, of shrinking the private sphere and so constraining women further. Some fundamentalists accomplish this project through thoroughgoing veiling, which is aimed at disguising women's presence in public. In essence, full veiling allows the private character of women to be made portable. Like scuba divers who bring oxygen from a land-based style of life along with them when invading the underwater sphere, veiled women transport their privacy along with them when they go out onto the street. Some radical fundamentalists are not satisfied with this solution, since it still allows a certain kind of trespass by the feminine into the male public sphere. Thus, the Taliban largely excluded women from going to school, and for the most part from working outside the home. The 40 per cent of women who had worked for a living in Kabul before the Taliban took control of the city in 1996 were at best thrown on the mercy of the international aid agencies and at worst cast into unemployment and penury, sometimes even reduced to begging or prostitution by the Taliban, who professed the ideal of a complete exclusion of women from the public sphere. Many fell into depression from being immobilized in their small apartments, and some committed suicide. Even literacy in modern societies had allowed women to trespass in the public sphere. Women journalists and editorialists attained a public voice through literacy and print. The Taliban solution to this further trespass was to deprive women of the little literacy they had attained. Of course, there was not much of a press for women to publish in under the Taliban, even had they been able to do so. The press was too much a part of the secular public sphere of reasoned communicative action, and was itself largely abandoned, along with most television and videocassettes. The only mass medium regularly allowed was the Voice of the Sharia, carefully controlled by the Taliban, on which no female voice was ever heard. Radio, along with the sermons of pro-Taliban clerics, constituted the Afghan populace as a mass receiving instructions rather than as a public engaged in debate.

The Taliban project was tinged with medieval romanticism, in which supposedly traditional practices were exalted over the West of independent women like Monica Lewinsky and Kate Winslet. It was above all, however, a form of countermodernity. It envisaged itself as a pure form of Islam capable of overcoming the tribal faction fighting and the tribal devaluing of women as persons who had plagued Afghanistan in the past. As a nativist countermodernity it rejected both major foreign forms of cultural imperialism, Marxism and liberalism. It represented itself as at once authentically Afghan and universal in its aspirations, as witnessed by Mullah Omar's claim to the caliphate. At the centre of the project was an alternative conception of how to draw the line between the public and the private.

The Taliban regime fell in late fall of 2001 to American special forces and air raids, which were aided by the forces of their equally Islamist foes, the Northern Alliance. Some journalistic observers assumed that everything therefore changed in Afghanistan. They were puzzled over time that many women continued to wear the *burqa,* unaware that veiling is a highly classed and regional practice, and that for some women its guarantee of privacy was welcome or too familiar to abandon.

On 11 November 2002, the new Hamid Karzai government announced that twenty women were being released from prison because the facility did not meet international standards. Most of these women had been jailed under the new regime. Some of them were imprisoned for 'violations of Shariat laws'. One had been jailed for having eloped with a man her family did not want her to marry; another had been turned over to the police summarily by a son-in-law who accused her of theft. In the Herat province of warlord Ismail Khan, moreover, Taliban-like practices of gender segregation had largely returned after the Americans' war ended. In January 2003, Afghanistan's chief justice ordered the closure of five cable television stations in Kabul and insisted on an end to coeducation for girls and boys. Not everything had changed, after all.

Notes

1 For Afghanistan's recent history, see Hanifi (2001), Gregorian (1969), Dupree (1973), Ghani (1982), Edwards (1996) and Rubin (2002).
2 For the condition of women in the refugee camps around Peshawar, see Tortajada (2001).
3 On the Taliban, see, *inter alia,* Goodson (2001), Rashid (2000), Pahlavan (1998) and Huwaydi (2001).
4 For the founding of the shrine to the prophet's cloak, see Ghani (1982).
5 Wahhabism is a sect of Islam that predominates in Saudi Arabia. Unusually puritanical and iconoclastic, it was begun in the eighteenth century. It has tended to condemn non-Wahhabi Muslims as infidels.
6 Huwaydi calls him Kamal al-Din, but this appears to be a simple transposition, since Qalamuddin or the 'pen of the religion' is a name unknown in Egypt, and we know that Qalamuddin was the head of this ministry in 1998.

References

Afghanistan, Jami`at-i Inqilabi-i Zanan-i. (April 2000), 'Qayd u bandha-yi Talibi-yi Zanan ra bih khudkushi mikashanad'. *Guzarish-ha-yi Sarzamin-i Faji`ih-ha,* http://rawa.fancymarketing.net/lyda.htm
'Architect Who Built Omar's Complex Says Omar Did Not Marry Bin Laden's Daughter'. *PBNewswire,* 13 January 2002.

Benhabib, Seyla. (1998), 'Models of Public Space: Hannah Arendt, the Liberal Tradition, and Jürgen Habermas,' in Landes, Joan B. (ed.), *Feminism, the Public and the Private*. Oxford: Oxford University Press.

Canfield, Robert L. (Oct., 1973), 'The Ecology of Rural Ethnic Groups and the Spatial Dimensions of Power'. *American Anthropologist*, 75(5): 1511–28.

Cole, Juan. (2002), 'Modernity of Theocracy', in *Sacred Space and Holy War: The Politics, Culture and History of Shi'ite Islam*. London: I.B. Tauris.

Dupree, Louis. (1973), *Afghanistan*. Princeton: Princeton University Press.

Edwards, David B. (1996), *Heroes of the Age: Moral Fault Lines on the Afghan Frontier*. Berkeley: University of California Press.

Foucault Michel. (1973), The Order of Things: An Archeology of the Human Sciences. New York: Vintage Books.

Foucault Michel. (1979), Discipline and Punish. New York: Vintage Books.

Ghani, Ashraf. (1982), 'Production and Domination in Afghanistan, 1747–1901'. Diss. Columbia University.

Goodson, Larry P. (2001), *Afghanistan's Endless War*. Seattle: University of Washington Press.

Goodwin, Jan. (Summer 1998), 'Buried Alive: Afghan Women under the Taliban'. *On the Issues*. 7(3). http://www.echonyc.com/~onissues/su98goodwin.html.

Gregorian, Vartan. (1969). *The Emergence of Modem Afghanistan*. Stanford: Stanford University Press.

Gul, Imtiaz. (2000). 'From Chaani'. *The Friday Times*, 22 September 2000.

Habermas, Jürgen. (1993), *The Structural Transformation of the Public Sphere*. Trans. Thomas Burger with Frederick Lawrence. Cambridge: MIT Press.

Hanifi, Jamil. 'Private Communication'. 24 December 2002.

Hanifi, Shah Mahmoud. 'Inter-Regional Trade and Colonial State Formation in Afghanistan'. Diss. University of Michigan, 2001.

Hegel, Georg Wilhelm Friedrich. (1942), *Hegel's Philosophy of Right*. Trans. T. M. Knox. Oxford: Clarendon Press.

Huwaydi, Fahmi. (2001), *Taliban: fund Allah fi al-Ma`rikah al-Ghalat!*. Cairo: Dar al-Shuruq (Arabic).

Jindi, Husni. (1993), *Damanat hurmat al-hayah al-khususah fi al-Islam*. Cairo: Dar al-Nahdah al-Arabiyah.

Landes, Joan B. (1998), 'The Public and the Private Sphere: A Feminist Reconsideration', in Landes, Joan B. (ed.), *Feminism, The Public and the Private*. Oxford: Oxford University Press.

Latifa. (2001), Visage Volé: Avoir vingt ans à Kaboul. Paris: Anne Carrièrre.

Moghadam Valentine M. (1993), Modernizing Women: Gender and Social Change in the Middle East. Boulder, CO: Lynne Rienner.

Mubariz, `Abd al-Hamid. Haqayiq va tahlil va vaqayi`-i siyasi-yi Afghanistan, 1973–1997: Az suqut-i saltanat ta zuhur-i Taliban. Pishavar: Hamid Nur, A.H. 1376 [1997].

Onishi, Norimitsu. 'A Tale of the Mullah and Muhammad's Amazing Cloak'. *New York Times*, 19 December 2001.

Pahlavan, Changiz (1998), *Afghanistan: `Asr-i Mujahidin va baramadan-i Taliban*. Tihran: Nashr-i Qatrah (Persian).

Physicians for Human Rights. '1999 Report: The Taliban's War on Women – A Health and Human Rights Crisis in Afghanistan'. http://www.phrusa.org/research/health_effects/exec.html.

Rashid, Ahmed. 2000, *Taliban*. New Haven: Yale University Press.
Rogers, Dorothy. 'Hegel and His "Victims": On Women and the Private Sphere', in Rogers, Dorothy, et al. (ed.), *Topics in Feminism, History and Philosophy*. Vienna: IWM, 2000.
Rubin, Barnett R. (2002), *The Fragmentation of Afghanistan*. 2d ed. New Haven: Yale University Press.
Rubin, Trudy. 'Visit with Afghan Women Reveals a Picture That Isn't Quite So Hopeless'. *Philadelphia Inquirer*, 19 December 1999.
Skaine, Rosemarie (2002), *The Women of Afghanistan under the Taliban*. Jefferson, NC: McFarland and Co., Inc.
'Taliban Repeat Warning of Punishment for Prayer Shirkers'. Agence France Presse, 31 October 1996.
Tortajada, Ana. (2001), *El Grito Silenciado*. Barcelona: Mondadori.
Zoya, with Follain, John, and Rita Cristofari. (2002), *Zoya's Story*. New York: William Morrow.

3

Legitimizing Power in Afghanistan

Haroun Rahimi

Royalty, tribes and Islam provided the moral foundations of the Afghan polity in the first century of its existence (Edwards 1996). The interaction between Afghan nationalism and communism in the twentieth century provided the first fundamental rupture in the moral sources of Afghan political community. Daoud Khan, a forceful member of the royal family, rode the wave of Afghan-Pashtun nationalism to power. Daoud Khan centred the question of Pashtuns left on the Pakistani side of the colonially imposed Durand Line. In the context of Cold War rivalry, the United States sided with Pakistan on the question of 'Pashtunistan', while the Soviet Union supported the Afghan nationalists, increasing its influence in the country as a result, especially in the military circles (Nunan 2019). The Soviet-trained Afghan military cadre eventually staged a coup replacing Daoud Khan's Republic with a communist regime. Thus, Afghan nationalism ended the Afghan royalty and helped bring the communist ideology to power. Of the three legitimizing sources of power, royalty was terminated, the Islamic character of the state was under unprecedented attack and tribes were sidelined by a foreign-backed force committed to a modernizing ideology that not only condemned tribalism but also attacked the political economy of landed tribal elites.

These fundamental shifts, originating from the Afghan capital and reverberating across the country, ushered in a protracted period of conflict that ended with the collapse of communist rule and the Islamist rise to power. Islamism was also a new idea in Afghanistan. It diverged from the conservative form of Islam practised across the country. In its recent history, Afghanistan never had the urban centres of religious learning necessary to produce a class of sophisticated *ulema* (clerics) who could play a determining role in the politics of the country (Hopkins 2008). The popular Islam of Afghanistan was represented by a large group of poorly educated rural *mullās* who played a generally insignificant role in politics alongside Sufi figures mostly based in the urban centres, where they exercised political influence.

Islamists were of a different type. Fleeing Afghanistan for Pakistan after they clashed with the Daoud regime and later the communists, the Afghan Islamists set up political parties in Pakistan, intermediating between an anti-communist international alliance and the Afghan mujahidin on the ground. Once the communist regime was defeated, they attempted to erect an Islamic state in Afghanistan. An alliance of new jihadi leaders who drew intellectually on the Muslim Brotherhood of Egypt and Jamiat-e Ulama of Pakistan would lead this state, leaving the traditional *ulema* at the margins (Rahimi 2021).

The mujahidin's vision did not materialize as these forces started fighting each other. The country descended into an unprecedented depth of brutality. In the ruins of civil war, members of the traditional *ulema* and tribal forces of southern Afghanistan united under the leadership of a relatively unknown veteran of the Afghan jihad to end the civil war and return the country to its conservative roots. This nominally restorative mission was to come from the rural south and under the leadership of the *mullās*, not from the urban centres and not under the leadership of modernizing royals. The movement was successful. It went on to become the first iteration of the Taliban regime in Afghanistan. While imagining itself as a restorative force, the Taliban absorbed the Islamizing ethos of the failed mujahidin government. But the substantive content of the group's Islamizing mission came from the ultraconservative ethos of religious madrasas on the Afghan-Pakistan border (Rahimi 2021).

Even as non-Pashtuns have always been part of the political calculations for Afghanistan's rulers, the Taliban had to contend with these communities on new terms. They had been politically active and militarily organized and had gained *de facto* autonomy during their anti-Soviet war. And they resisted the Taliban's centralizing advances even though many of them were Sunni Muslims. They perceived the regime as a return to the hegemony of Pashtuns. The Shia Muslims of Afghanistan had additional reason to resist the Taliban whose mission was to unify the country under a strict interpretation of Sunni Islam.

The first Taliban regime was never able to solve its issues with resisting forces. The US intervention following the tragedy of 9/11 changed everything in favour of its opponents with its so-called war on terror that sought to legitimize a new political order, at least ostensibly, through the liberal peace building model. The proposal for the restoration of royalty to regain the moral foundation of Afghan rule was denied by the mujahidin parties and the United States (Dobbins 2008: 90). The will of the people expressed through open and fair elections was to legitimize political power. However, this pronounced democratic ethos clashed with the reality of the US presence in Afghanistan (Murtazashvili 2021). Hamid Karzai, the first post-2001 Afghan ruler, was selected by an American-brokered intra-elite agreement even though a non-Pashtun religious scholar who was minister of justice during the reign of Afghanistan's last monarch, Abdul Satar Sirat, received more votes (Dobbins 2008: 90).

The reasons for the American decision to veto this selection were manifold and set the tone for the US role in the future of the country. The top US diplomat at the conference argued that Sirat could not unify different Afghan factions (Dobbins 2008). The idea that Afghanistan must have a Pashtun ruler – an idea that goes back to the first British encounter with Afghanistan – played a role. The post-Cold War liberal paradigm also militated against the selection of a religious scholar from the era of monarchy in a country that was to be the first object of liberal transformation through the war on terror. This heavy-handed approach set a precedent whereby the outcome of virtually every presidential election was determined by the direct or indirect intervention of the United States, often with the determinative purpose of aligning the result of elections with American preferences. Thus, elections increasingly lost their legitimizing function (Murtazashvili 2021).

In addition to their delegitimizing effect on foreign intervention, some have argued that post-2001 electoral politics may have worsened the ethnic cleavages in the country (Mobasher 2018). The bad memories of Islamist and communist parties as well as the institutional setup of the 2004 constitution hindered the formation of political parties that could mobilize people around an ideology or policy platform. What filled the gap was a group of leaders who claimed to represent ethnic constituencies promoting an ethnic form of identity politics. The rise of mass media, fast urbanization, expansion of education and political awareness provided a fertile ground for a populist form of identity politics.

In the midst of these failed electoral and party politics, a new fault line emerged within the Afghan polity, that between the mujahidin and the technocrats. The mujahidin consisted of prominent figures in Afghan fights against the communists and later the Taliban. They considered themselves on the winning side in the Afghan conflict because they were able to defeat the Taliban albeit with American help. Some members of the mujahidin occupied high government positions, and some assimilated into the liberal politics of post-2001 Afghanistan (Mukhopadhyay 2014), but the majority remained outside the government and aligned with the traditional forces. Mujahidin figures, inside and outside government, initially had great influence over the government since they possessed a great level of *de facto* power across the country. Unconvinced by the liberal democratic paradigm, the majority of them considered themselves the true representative of Afghans and believed the government should govern with their consent. The liberal democratic framework of post-2001 Afghanistan worked against mujahidin because their values were deemed incongruent with liberal values of human rights and democracy. In this context, mujahidin leaders represented guardians of the religious and conservative cultural values of Afghans. They supported conservative social policies when it came to issues like human rights and women's rights. They also favoured a less intervening central government which would have allowed them more space to operate in areas of their influence (Giustozzi 2004; Mukhopadhyay 2009; Malejacq 2020).

After 2001, in the early years of the Afghan Republic, the mujahidin's rival force was that represented by Afghan technocrats. Technocrats tended to be western-educated experts whose claim to power rested on their technical knowledge of governance and their alignment with the internationally sponsored liberal shift in Afghan politics. Most technocrats had lived and studied outside of Afghanistan, typically in western countries, during Afghanistan's recent period of acute conflict. The most influential technocrats were Pashtun since a large group of their co-ethnic strongmen was excluded from post-2001 politics on account of their affiliations with the Taliban and Hizb-e Islami.[1] Technocrats influenced policies through their work in the government, NGOs and INGOs, and their partnership with the international community. Technocrats supported progressive social policies when it came to issues like human rights and women's rights. They invoked a Weberian view of the state to justify their claim to power. They tended to be in favour of government policies that expanded the power of the central government against traditional institutions of power as well as the mujahidin.[2]

Karzai maintained the balance of power between the two camps but facilitated the rise of technocrats as he perceived the mujahidin as a constraint on the power of the central government. Karzai's successor, Ashraf Ghani, sped up the process of sidelining the mujahidin under the banner of meritocracy. Ashraf Ghani also had a cadre of post-2001 highly educated Afghan youth that he could draw upon to staff his government. The Pashtun technocrats who gathered around Ghani also revitalized a narrative around Afghan nationalism, connecting it to the modernizing efforts of Amanullah Khan, whom they considered the first progressive Afghan ruler, while casting both the Taliban and mujahidin as reactionary forces whose predecessors had similarly subverted progressive efforts a century ago.[3]

These technocrats, like their forebears, hoped that Afghan nationalism could unify the country and give them the legitimacy they needed to lead. They also used the issue of Pashtunistan to the same effect, hoping to discredit what was by then a raging Taliban insurgency given its ties to Pakistan.[4] However, the new-found political power of non-Pashtun ethnic groups meant that the Pashtun technocrats' push for Afghan nationalism – rooted in an official reading of Afghan history developed by the first generation of Afghan-Pashtun nationalists[5] – was challenged by an alternative reading of history that centred on the poor treatment of non-Pashtuns by Pashtuns. This alternative reading of history cast the Taliban as an extension of the historical oppression of non-Pashtuns.[6]

Ghani's open fight with the mujahidin drew a wedge between his government and the conservative forces of Afghan politics, giving space for the Taliban to exploit the apathy if not enmity on the part of more traditional social groups towards his version of the Republic. The push for nationalism also backfired, leading the non-Pashtun intellectuals to blur the distinction between the Ghani-controlled Republic and the Taliban. Meanwhile, the traditional rural *ulema* of Afghanistan, the *mullās*, were more aligned with the mujahidin than technocrats but they had lost their capacity to organize politically after the first round of Taliban rule. Nor would the internationally sponsored liberal paradigm of post-2001 Afghanistan accommodate their political activation. *Mullās* remained critical of the Islamic Republic both for its progressive policies and its foreign backing. They grew sympathetic to the Taliban call as the failures of the Republic compounded (Dorronsoro 2009).

Since their takeover in 2021, the Taliban have continued to legitimize their right to rule based on a commitment to the implementation of Sharia. While they remain markedly conservative and reactionary, they have absorbed the statist politics of other Islamists (Rahimi 2021). The Taliban have also increasingly incorporated a nationalist rhetoric, even though their version of Afghan nationalism does not look back to modernizing or progressive rulers such as Amanullah Khan but constitutes a more conservative vision that draws on rural Pashtun sensibilities (Rahimi 2023).

At the turn of the twentieth century, the 'moral fault lines' that marked the Afghan polity were royalty, tribes and Islam (Edwards 1996). Two decades into the twenty-first century, royalty is long gone; tribal politics remains relevant, but it is now layered with a form of nationalism that positions the Pashtuns against the non-Pashtuns. Traditional Islam remains politically powerful. But the Taliban and their self-proclaimed restorative nationalist and Islamist project can only be understood if we keep in mind how different legitimizing forces of Afghan polity were deconstructed over the course of a century through violent encounters with three different imperial forces.

In this process, traditional Islam assumed an ambition for direct rule through the state as other competing moral forces of Afghan polity increasingly lost legitimacy. The Taliban's Islamic Emirate is the vehicle for that. The question of what makes power moral in Afghanistan is far from resolved. Democracy, autonomy-demanding tribal politics, non-Pashtun demands for communal self-rule, and localized traditional Islam all provide moral sources of resistance as they challenge the Taliban's Emirate and its claim to exclusive legitimacy. The question of how power can be legitimized in Afghanistan appears, in other words, to be as relevant and as vexing in the twenty-first century as it was 100 years ago.

Notes

1   Many Pashtun technocrats were, in fact, affiliated with the wing of Hizb-e Islami that joined the Republic. During the years of jihad, Hizb-e Islami had attracted many modernist Pashtuns. For a closer look at the internal dynamics of Hizb-e Islami and its charismatic leader, see Sands and Qazizai (2019).
2   The distinction between the technocrats and the mujahidin was far less clear in practice. However, since I am tracing the evolution of a moral foundation of political power in Afghanistan, I am focusing on the normative positions of different political factions. For a detailed analysis of how both technocrats and mujahidin engaged in patronage and corruption, see Sharan (2023).
3   Ashraf Ghani delivered his remark on the occasion of 100th anniversary of Afghanistan's independence at the renovated Darulaman Palace and in the presence of Amanullah Khan's daughter. See https://www.youtube.com/watch?v=NQnHN1oyJbU andab_channel=ARG1880.
4   Towards the end of the Republic, Hamdullah Moheb, the country's national security advisor and a close ally of President Ghani, delivered a fiery speech on the issue of Pashtunistan and the Taliban's ties to Pakistan in the border province of Nangarhar. See https://www.youtube.com/watch?v=ERsr2kpxwvs andab_channel=NSCAfghanistan.
5   I am hyphenating Afghan-Pashtun to acknowledge the murky and contested nature of the relationship between these two terms vis-à-vis the question of what it means to be a citizen of the Afghan nation-state. For an analysis of how the core narratives of Afghan nationalism were formed in the early twentieth century, see Gregorian and colleagues (1967).
6   For an example of this, see an editorial piece by Khadim Hossain Karimi published in Farsi by the influential *Etilaat Roz* newspaper: 'Afghanistan and the failure of nation building; should we deny or admit?' [translated title] (12 February 2020), https://www.etilaatroz.com/92818/afghanistan-and-failure-of-nation-building-conceal-or-confess/.

References

Brick Murtazashvili, J. (2021), 'Democracy Denied: the False Promise of Afghanistan's Constitutional Order'. Available at: https://aiss.af/assets/aiss_publication/Democracy_Denied-Eng.pdf.

Dobbins, J. (2008), *After the Taliban: Nation-Building in Afghanistan*. Lincoln, Nebraska: University of Nebraska Press (Potomac Books).

Dorronsoro, G. (2009), 'The Taliban's Winning Strategy in Afghanistan'. Available at: https://carnegieendowment.org/files/taliban_winning_strategy.pdf.

Edwards, D. B. (1996), *Heroes of the Age: Moral Fault Lines on the Afghan Frontier*. Berkeley: University of California Press.

Giustozzi, A. (2004), *'Good' State vs. 'Bad' Warlords? A Critique of State Building Strategies in Afghanistan*, Working Paper no. 51. London: London School of Economics Crisis States Research Centre.

Gopal, A. (2016), 'The Combined and Uneven Development of Afghan Nationalism'. *Studies in Ethnicity and Nationalism*, 16(3): 478–92.

Gregorian, V. (1967), 'Mahmud Tarzi and Saraj-ol-Akhbar: Ideology of Nationalism and Modernization in Afghanistan'. *Middle East Journal*, 21(3): 345–68.

Hopkins, B. D. (2008), *The Making of Modern Afghanistan*. Basingstoke: Palgrave Macmillan.

Karimi, K. H. (2020), 'Afghanistan and the Failure of Nation Building; Should We Deny or Admit?' [translated title] (12 February 2020), *Etilaat Roz Newspaper*. Available at: https://www.etilaatroz.com/92818/afghanistan-and-failure-of-nation-building-conceal-or-confess/.

Malejacq, R. (2020), *Warlord Survival: The Delusion of State Building in Afghanistan*. Ithaca, NY: Cornell University Press.

Mobasher, M. B. (2018), 'Understanding Ethnic-Electoral Dynamics: How Ethnic Politics Affect Electoral Laws and Election Outcomes in Afghanistan'. Available at: https://www.researchgate.net/publication/323254551_UNDERSTANDING_ETHNIC-ELECTORAL_DYNAMICS_HOW_ETHNIC_POLITICS_AFFECT_ELECTORAL_LAWS_AND_ELECTION_OUTCOMES_IN_AFGHANISTAN.

Mukhopadhyay, D. (2014), *Warlords, Strongman Governors, and the State in Afghanistan*. Cambridge: Cambridge University Press.

Mukhopadhyay, D. (2009), 'Warlords as Bureaucrats: The Afghan Experience'. Available at: https://carnegieendowment.org/files/warlords_as_bureaucrats.pdf.

Nunan, T. (2019), 'The Soviet Elphinstone: Colonial Histories, Postcolonial Presents, and Socialist Futures in the Soviet Receptions of British Orientalism', in Hanifi, S. M. (ed.), *Mountstuart Elphinstone in South Asia*. Oxford: Oxford University Press, 275–97.

Rahimi, H. (2023), 'Islamic Law, the Taliban, and the Modern State' (31 March 2023). Available at: https://islamiclaw.blog/2023/03/31/islamic-law-the-taliban-and-the-modern-state/.

Rahimi, H. (2021), 'A Constitutional Reckoning with the Taliban's Brand of Islamist Politics: The Hard Path Ahead'. Available at: https://www.aiss.af/assets/aiss_publication/Reckoning_with_Islamist_Politics.pdf.

Sands, C. and Qazizai, F. (2019), *Night Letters: Gulbuddin Hekmatyar and the Afghan Islamists Who Changed the World*. London: Hurst & Co.

Sharan, T. (2023), *Inside Afghanistan: Political Networks, Informal Order, and State Disruption*. Oxford and New York: Routledge.

4

Unlocking the Taliban Puzzle: Traditions and Fundamentalisms

Mujib Abid

Throughout its history and then, since its return to power in August 2021, the Taliban movement has rather dizzyingly demonstrated a tendency for hegemonizing power, for building a hierarchical nation state, and for cultivating some degree of political inclusion – seemingly all at once. Taliban politics is often lost in the chaos of war, under the weight of western propaganda and the movement's own reckoning through its disruptive and transformative encounter with modern politics and the West. The movement is often dismissed as an aberration, an inexplicable departure from Afghanistan's postcolonial chronologies, one that requires urgent course correction rather than critical unpacking.

Yet, it is of real importance, for both the present and the futures of (a 'course-corrected') Afghanistan, to understand the Taliban as a theoretical phenomenon. It is under the long shadow of (violent) ideological contestations where the Taliban's politics and worldviews could be brought into sharper focus and its logics and contradictions laid bare. Producing a theoretical account of the Taliban is not, however, a straightforward undertaking. How should one categorize a movement that challenges conventional approaches to theorization? Is it a terrorist organization or an (legitimate) insurgency? A Salafist/Wahabist transnational jihadist organization or a local Islamic organization? Does it subscribe to a Deobandi or a neo-Deobandi creed? Is it a rural, peasant movement or a student movement? While these are critical questions, in large part beyond the scope of this chapter, I believe a more productive query for this moment is an exploration of whether the Taliban is a modernist movement or a traditional one.

The answer lies somewhere in the middle. Neither its traditional underpinnings nor its fundamentalist leanings exclusively define the politics and policy positions of the Taliban. The regime's day-to-day reality, instead, lies in the middle, a tug of war between opposites coexisting in the same seemingly united movement, confounding attempts at predicting future trajectories. Owing to this oppositional tension, within the Taliban there is an impetus for hegemony as well as the potential for coexistence. In this chapter, I argue that an ideological dilemma lies at the heart of the Taliban movement. If the language of 'political Islam' can be organized into three traditions – modernist, fundamentalist and traditional – the Taliban's dilemma is its concurrent embrace of more than one of these traditions.

Throughout the movement's own trajectory and then, in the context of the broader ideological experimentations in Afghanistan, the Taliban has disavowed modernist Islam while embracing traditional and 'fundamentalist' Islam simultaneously. While its proximity to each tradition can be erratic and unstable, bifurcating the movement into an insurgency and a 'state custodianship' phase can serve as a helpful analytical tool to map the group's fluctuating politics. As an insurgency, the Taliban tends to privilege consensus and cooperation, whereas as a state, the group is more prone to closing ranks and concentrating power. Consequently, once in power, rather paradoxically, the Taliban abandons the commitment to native priorities for an exclusionary nativism.

Background: Islam and the State in Afghanistan

Academic treatments of Afghanistan tend to suffer from a certain historical amnesia. Shah M. Hanifi has pointed out how pre-2001 writings on Afghanistan tend 'to view the country as somehow removed from its surroundings', a place 'fundamentally if not naturally isolated, even xenophobic, with only episodic engagements' with local and regional forces (Hanifi 2016: 386). This isolation is extended to representations of Afghan village life, as 'separated from one another' and then to the cities, representations of which, similarly, fixate on disconnection (Hanifi 2016: 386). The post-2001 literature, owing to the cultural and material encroachment of the 'war on terror', has not fared any better. Here too, in the words of Afghan feminist scholar Wazhmah Osman, the 'Afghan culture is interpellated as static, unchanging, and bound by problematic archaic traditions' (Osman 2017: 355), a people 'existing in a vacuum, intrinsically confusing and barbaric, a political "problem" and cultural "conundrum" that needs to be "managed" and "solved" more effectively' (Zeweri 2022: 7). Beyond this civilizational narrative, this corpus neglects, for example, a study of Islam, paying little attention to the role of the clergy in Afghan politics (Nawid 1997: 581), or to the many coexisting and conflictual postcolonial trajectories that have emerged on the question of modernity and modernization. This is a particularly egregious oversight, because, in Afghanistan, though debates on ideological constructs can be fluid, internally fragmented, and 'differentiated', ideological contestations tend to be primarily concerned with the role of Islam.

Historically, modernizing Afghan ruling elites have sought to bind Islam to the state by employing the *ulema* (clergy) both as high-ranking and lower-ranking religious functionaries (i.e. in the justice and education systems). While this served the state, to a certain extent, another class of *ulema* tended to evade attempts at placation: the *ulema* 'affiliated with Sufi orders, who were independent of state control' (Nawid 1997: 583). This evasion was significant because, as Senzil Nawid has demonstrated, on the eve of decolonization in 1919:

> the clergy had established for itself a compelling historical role as the defender of Islam against foreign invasion and as a bulwark of the rural civil society, a role it has traditionally asserted in times of political upheaval. Because of their affiliation with the militant Pashtun tribes along the border with British

India, and their connection with the Qadiri and Naqshbandi orders, religious leaders in the Eastern and Southern provinces emerged as a compelling political force, posing a challenge not only to the British in India but also to the central government at home.

(Nawid 1997: 602)

Afghan nationalism has been marked by periods of intense modernization, chief among them Amir Sher Ali Khan's second rule (1868–79), Amanullah Khan's reign (1919–29) and the 'Decade of Democracy' associated with the Musahiban (1963–73). Culturally, in a genealogical chain, the Young Afghans of the early twentieth century would live on in *pashto tolona* (Pashto society) and, in turn, would give birth to the *wishi zilmiyan* (Awakened Youth) by the mid-twentieth century. The nationalist project gave birth to radical politics on both the left and right in the 1960s and beyond, including the socialist, Islamist and liberal state building periods, each supported by an (invading) superpower. Though not uniform in their approach to problematizing their 'backward', stagnant and archaic society, Afghan nationalist critiques, paradoxically, tended to harbour a contradictory view of the modern West. Like many other postcolonial movements in the Global South, Afghan nationalists professed faith in the humanist ideals of Europe even as they were committed to opposing colonial rule. Mahmud Tarzi, for example, through Quranic exegesis and in reference to the pan-Islamism of his day, argued that Islam should not be conflated with superstition and tradition, proclaiming to his Afghan readers: 'Times of poetry are bygone. It is now the time of action and effort. The era is that of motor, rail, and electricity' (quoted in Gregorian 1967: 356).

This split was possible and indeed desirable, for the colonized to have a chance at saving themselves; to deploy on their own terms the cultural priorities that they also contested as having been employed to legitimize their subjugation. For the nationalist, this 'seduction' of modernity, Anibal Quijano argues, 'became a constitutive part of the conditions of reproduction of those societies and cultures that were pushed into Europeanisation of everything or in part' (Quijano 2007: 170). The Afghan nationalist intellectual was a tormented subject suffering from a psychosocial complex best captured in Ali Shariati's and Syed Hussain Alatas's respective concepts of the 'homeless intellectual' and the 'captive mind'. They operated in 'alienation, or even in some instances "hatred" from "self"' (Shariati 1971: 35), and, as intellectuals, remained 'unconscious of [their] own captivity and the conditioning factors making it what it is' (Alatas 1974: 691).

To organize thought around Islam and political ideology in the Afghan context, including ontologies that transcend state-centrism, I find Syed Hussein Nasr's work instructive. The crisis of the Muslim world, according to Nasr, can be explained along three inter-related and overlapping axis: modernism, 'fundamentalism' and tradition. The western approach largely splits 'political Islam' between a favoured 'Islamic modernism' (repackaged in the language of 'moderate Islam') and a detested 'Islamic fundamentalism' (read, for example, in Sayed Qutb, Abul Ala Maududi, Khomeini) (indicatively, see Moaddel and Talattof 2002: 16–20). Critiquing this colonial binary, Nasr argues that 'fundamentalist' Islam is mischaracterized as the antithesis of modernity. Of both the earlier Wahhabi and later 'counter-traditional' currents (both classified as 'fundamentalist'), Nasr wrote:

> [they] share in common a disdain for the West, a distrust of foreign elements, a strong activist tendency and usually opposition or indifference to all the inward aspects of Islam and the civilization and culture which it created, aspects such as Sufism, Islamic philosophy, Islamic art, etc. They are all outwardly oriented in the sense that they wish to reconstruct Islamic society through the re-establishment of external legal and social norms rather than by means of the revival of Islam through inner purification or by removing the philosophical and intellectual impediments which have been obstacles on the path of many contemporary Muslims.
> (Nasr 1990: 84)

In its structuralism and revolutionary zeal, 'fundamentalist' expressions of political Islam, far from being violent aberrations of modernity are an extension of the encounter with European modernity. Islamic 'fundamentalisms', Nasr points out, 'possess a violent and revolutionary political nature and in some of these the most fanatical and volcanic elements of western republicanism and Marxist revolutionary theory and practice have been set in what the followers of these groups consider to be an Islamic context' (Nasr 1990: 84).

Furthermore, Nasr's critique points to the absence of 'traditionalists' in this colonial binary, a majority of the Muslim faithful around the world. Islamic tradition is located in the esoteric facets of life, where through *philosophia perennis*, it is understood that reality and consciousness cannot be limited to the psychosocial everyday experiences of people and, thus, religion should not be reduced to its manifestation (Nasr and Chittick 2007: 21–2). Nasr presents Islamic tradition as the central cornerstone of Muslim identity, the 'beating heart' of Islam serving as the genuine Other of European and Islamic 'fundamentalisms' (Nasr and Chittick 2007: xiii):

> They [those associated with traditional Islam] stand at the center of Islamic orthodoxy and consider all violent movements which incorporate the worst elements of western civilization in order to combat that civilization to be a disservice to Islam and below the dignity of God's last revelation.
> (Nasr 1990: 92)

In the Afghan geohistorical context, Islamic modernism originated in the form of a pan-Islamism that travelled through the Levant, Ottoman Empire and the Subcontinent to Afghanistan in the works, for example, of Syed Jamaluddin al-Afghani and, later, through the activities of Mahmud Tarzi and multiple generations of *mashrotakhwahan* (Young Afghans). From the 1960s, a number of modernist political parties emerged, with different ideologies: from Maoist Shola-e Javid, to Pashtun nationalist Afghan Mellat and to non-Pashtun nationalists in Sitam-e Mili (Edwards 2002: 205–19). Whether it was these movements, the Marxist-Leninist Khalq or Parcham, or the post-2001 liberal and 'illiberal' allies of the West, upon closer inspection, they all attempted to graft Islam onto the logics of their ideological, state-centric projects. Alongside these political movements, a modernist literary movement emerged which, much like the political organizations, was either absorbed into the state apparatus or resisted it (Ahmadi 2008).

'Fundamentalist' Islam has its origins in student politics, when the Sazman-e Jawan-e Musulmin (Muslim Youth Organization) was founded to oppose leftist influence in Kabul University campus in 1969 (Edwards 2002: 203–4). Once the leadership were exiled, the student organization would evolve into the western-backed mujahidin, an insurgency that would eventually crystallize as the *ahzab haftgana* (the Seven Parties). Though decidedly not the only backlash to Sovietization and Soviet invasion, the two main factions of mujahidin in Jamiat-e Islami Afghanistan (led by Burhanuddin Rabbani) and Hizb-e Islami Afghanistan (led by Gulbuddin Hekmatyar) subscribed to 'fundamentalist' Islam. In the post-2001 Afghanistan, Al Qaeda and ISIS carry the mantle while the Taliban, though more ambivalent, demonstrate leanings towards similar ideological currents.

In Afghanistan, traditional Islam is signified by a millennium-old history of *tasawuf* (Sufism) and its dynamic coexistence with the dominant Hanafi *fiqh* (jurisprudence) and *sunat-hai mardumi* (popular customs), both tribal and regional, pre- and post-Islamic. The cultural and topographical landscape across Afghanistan signifies the salience of this 'Islam' and traditional knowledge perspectives, beyond disciplinary and institutional bounds. The typical Afghan setting is saturated with Sufi iconography, manuscripts, practices and rituals, and traditional social organization mechanisms have developed alongside these. These include 'heaven-sent stones, saintly footprints (*qadamgahs*), sites of visions (*nazargahs*), remnants of the Prophet Mohammad's mantle or cloak (*khirqa-yi sharif*), and the sacred hairs of his beard (*mu-yi mubarak*) – around which shrines have formed' (McChesney 2018: 191). Each site, in its localized ways, offers the 'downtrodden' a route to seek help 'beyond what could be negotiated personally', with the government, family or community (McChesney 2018: 232), just like the ascetic (*faqir* or *malang*) does for the Muslim faithful through dispensing of performed devotion (*dhikr*) or the holy person (*pir*) does by guiding their disciples in the path to spiritual intuition. In postcolonial Afghanistan, institutionally, traditional Islam and its teachings tend to be transmitted through the Deoband Darul Ulum, a transnational religious seminary founded around the same time as the rise of Wahhabists in Arabia and of the Islamic modernists in the Subcontinent. Their call for an 'inward turn of resistance' (Ingram 2018) was so detested that in 1928 Amanullah Khan barred all Deobandi *mullās* from entering the country (Stewart 1973: 379).

Unlike modernist and 'fundamentalist' Islam which, convinced of the validity of its argument, rejects alterity, traditional Islam, as knowledge, is not absolute; it intermingles historically and epistemically with Eurocentrism and the habitus of Muslims. In this, traditional Islam serves as 'border thinking', in form (as guided knowledge originating in love, ecstatic intuition and *mu'arifah*) and as subaltern knowledge perspectives that are at once distinct from and engulfed in coloniality of power. Border thinking can be viewed as a site of 'abstract universals', one that 'brings to the foreground the irreducible epistemological difference, between the perspective from the colonial difference, and the forms of knowledge that, being critical of modernity, coloniality, and capitalism, still remain "within" the territory, "in custody" of the "abstract universals"'

(Mignolo 2012: 88). In this sense, tradition is not immune from organized politics in the institutional and state-form. Whether it was manifest in the more experimental Kalakani uprising in 1929, in the actions of some of the mujahidin factions or the ambivalences of the Taliban to esoteric, village Islam, like any other social identity, traditional Islam can be entrapped into institutional forms of power. As discourse, however, these institutionalizing projects are a reification and cannot, by definition, capture traditional Islam in its entirety.

This tension is not lost on the broader Afghan society. There is a certain conception of time-space, from the Afghan perspective, that does not subscribe to the same linear accounts universalized by the modernist perspective. Nationalists, subscribing to socialist, Islamist or developmentalist teleology, have internalized a spatiotemporal perspective that is set on fixed timelines. This is countered by a different spatiotemporal perspective, a salient epistemological perspective and ontological experience that is rooted in traditional Islam, one that continues to live on in confrontation or parallel to the postcolonial nationalist struggles of Afghanistan. And despite the deployment of successive assimilationist projects, this articulation of traditional Islam was never eliminated. Towards a more productive understanding of the Taliban, therefore, I next seek to analyse the Taliban movement in the *longue durée* tradition within this historicity.

Insurgency: Ascent of the Taliban as a Traditional Force

The 1994 rise of the Taliban, a 'wild card in the Afghan turmoil' (Burns 1995), came as a shock to many observers and to their political opponents, the warring mujahidin factions whose 'Islamic fundamentalism' had, famously, led them to victory over the Soviet-backed Marxists but not to a 'winning of the war'. Conventional scholarly explanations tend to associate the rapid rise of Taliban with the Pakistani intelligence agency ISI (see Maley 2002; Nojumi 2002; Rashid 2010). They frame the Taliban claim to a village identity as a strategic move – Taliban fighters, after all, had only experienced life in the refugee camps and *not* in the villages. However, these 'conspiratorial' accounts, in the words of David B. Edwards (2002: 291), often fail to report the great conformity in cultural and political priorities that the ragtag and austere student group had with a large sect of the populace: the society at large sought a conduit to channel its disdain for the largely debased mujahidin. The Taliban faced little to no resistance as it emerged from obscurity after disarming a mujahidin militia group at the Chaman border and, then, proceeded to take control of the south, pushing westward and arriving at the doorsteps of Kabul by the fall of 1996. For the first time since the beginning of the conflict, a seemingly genuine traditional movement, bent on upending the dominant modernist-nationalist politics of the Islamist factions in favour of an indigenous approach to power that was diffuse, incoherent and fragmented, had entered the contest. This resonated as familiar, and comfortable, in those pockets of Afghan political life marked by anarchy.

The Taliban movement originated as a rural 'peasant' backlash against the excesses of 'fundamentalist' Islamist groups – though, as the name implies, the label of 'student' would be as fitting. Early on, the rank-and-file of the nascent movement seemed to share rural Afghan people's disenchantment with organized politics. Abdul Salam Zaeef deliberately conflates the Taliban with the people, explaining how the 'Taliban mostly eschewed politics, but the government tried to draw them in by pressuring them to be involved in the land reform, or by threatening them in other ways' (Zaeef and van Linschoten 2011: 5). Though the decade-long anti-Soviet struggle led to the recruitment of large numbers of Afghans into Islamist factions, in the immediate aftermath of the Soviet withdrawal, many chose quiet retirement back to their families and villages. According to Zaeef, while the mujahidin factions fought over control of Kabul and major cities:

> The Taliban didn't involve themselves in these disputes, and in any case most had returned home by now. Mullah Muhammad Omar turned our old mujahidin base in Sangisar into a madrasa. I briefly considered staying there as well, but without any work it would be difficult. I decided to return to my wife and children.
> (Zaeef and van Linschoten 2011: 52)

This recollection can be viewed as a throwback to the Sufist and Deobandi disavowals of organized politics in the state-form. In the encounter with western imperialism, colonial powers often projected a dichotomy on Sufis, describing them as either docile or rebellious (or as the French did, 'quietist' or 'activist'), without truly grasping the worldviews and cosmologies of traditional Islam. Though the 'vast majority of Sufis' were not involved in power struggles, or simply 'ignored the new conditions to the best of their ability' (Vikør 2014: 212), resistance to colonial powers never subsided; it simply manifested differently, through, for example, non-cooperation, non-violence, and *jihad akbar* or inner-purification of the Muslim subject. Nile Green notes how, after the failure of the 1857 Indian Mutiny, many leading Sufis 'adopted a strategy of avoidance rather than co-operation ... some [developing] theories disconnecting Sharia (and through it Muslim life more generally) from any links to the colonial state' (Green 2012: 194).

The Taliban's stated mission was to revive and reimagine a political discourse for Afghanistan in the image of the country's long-dismissed indigenous sensibilities, and it did this by discovering a self-identity vis-à-vis its Other in the form of the mujahidin. In the words of a Taliban spokesperson, 'Our culture has been greatly changed over the past 40 or 50 years, particularly in Kabul. In the villages the culture has not changed much ... We are trying to re-establish a purist Islamic culture and tradition' (Edwards 2002: 294). Hizb-e Islami and Jamiat-e Islami, in particular, had lost their foundations in society, the Taliban alleged. Taliban, in 'identifying purist culture and tradition with the Islam of the village', criticized the Islam of Hekmatyar and Rabbani, targeting their urban-educated middle-class sensibilities and their empiricist rationalism (Edwards 2002: 294). Mullah Omar, in a May 1995 speech, would allude to these 'tyrants', lamenting that the Taliban's calls on these 'corrupt leaders ... to stop the intimidation of their people and put an end to the crisis in the country' had fallen on deaf ears (van Linschoten and Kuehn 2018: 54). In the same speech, he also disavowed any collusion with outside powers, claiming the Taliban had no 'material wishes', that their fighters 'have done nothing against the nation during the crisis of the past few years [referring to the civil war]' (van Linschoten and Kuehn 2018: 55).

There is a metaphysical and epistemological context to Taliban politics and to the charismatic leadership of the Amir-ul Mominin (Mullah Omar). Mullah Omar's followers and commanders believed in his divine call to action. Rahimullah Yusufzai, a BBC journalist who regularly interviewed Mullah Omar, relays numerous accounts of the leader's strong belief in dreams (Edgar 2006). Shrine veneration, Sufism, *tariqah* (the spiritual path) and *irfan* (personal awareness, knowledge), all brought back the esoteric dimensions of Islam to the fore, as a backlash against the rationalism of 'fundamentalist' Islam. There is evidence of intense devotional practices in Taliban leadership, making such traditional and Sufi practices a fixture of the Emirate. Bette Dam's book *Looking for the Enemy* (2021) investigated the whereabouts of the Taliban leader Mullah Omar, discovering that he spent his final years as a hermetic recluse devoted to prayer. Whatever the veracity of this journalistic account, the impulse to spiritual retreat is worth noting.

The Taliban affinity for the intuitive 'beating heart of Islam' was reciprocated at least by some of the prominent Sufist mainstays, as can be seen in the Kenneth Lizzio's *Embattled Saints: My Year with the Sufis of Afghanistan* (2014). The author lived at a *khanaqah* (Naqshbandi order), in the mid-1990s. The lodge favoured the Taliban as an 'indigenous and constructive' force that desired to install a genuinely Islamic order. To them, that the Taliban had no associations with the largely discredited mujahidin or communists – even though both served in their ranks – and, for these observers, the group's largely peaceful ascent to power promised a period of stability and peace that the country had not experienced in almost two decades (Lizzio 2014). In the *khanaqah*, this enthusiastic support cut across ethnic and linguistic lines, Lizzio observed. The Pir (leader of a Sufi order who often claim noble religious lineage) had regular Taliban visitors who sought spiritual guidance.

The Taliban's cultural and literary heritage, captured in part by a closer examination of its poetry corpus, indicates local orientation and indigeneity, more so than transnational or even 'national' consciousness. Part of this canon is included in a collection edited by Van Linschoten and Kuehn (2012). According to Faisal Devji, Taliban literature, well known for its affinity for verse, is 'overwhelmingly Afghan in its emphasis, and dispenses with the desert scenes, tents, charging horses and other themes popular with such militants' (2012: 21). It is not exclusively fixated on the religious element; rather, even in deploying religious metaphor or practices, Taliban literature can be 'seen as being part of a broader cultural landscape and in any case to Afghanistan in particular' (Devji 2012: 21). The content of the collection reveals a delicate dance on the part of poet-warriors lower in the rungs of leadership, oscillating between propaganda and autonomous expression, seeking to find a voice perhaps beyond the reach of the leadership and its disciplining power. Much of this literature is concerned with human cost of the conflict, highlighting the Afghan tragedy, alongside defiance, resistance and discontent. These themes, for example, are reflected in a short poem by Muhammad Hanif Hairan, which includes the lines: 'O God! Change these people so that/Nobody will die anymore by another's hand' and 'O God, for anything to which you have given a soul /These things should never die by someone else's hand' (van Linschoten et al. 2012: 194).

Historically, as resistance, traditional practices have tended to be non-violent and *khudjush* (spontaneous), aspiring for individualized reassertion of threatened subjectivities in a range of creative, evasive or unpredictable ways. If we look at the Afghan struggle against Sovietization, especially early on, many among the Afghan populace would attempt to undermine the revolutionary PDPA government by relying on tactics of everyday resistance, as seen, for example, in the Kabul Hut Uprising. On the evening of 21 February 1980, Kabul, with its half a million population, would follow the example set by other major cities when the public engaged in similar tactics to disrupt the new regime. At about 7.00 pm, before most homes had served dinner, 'Allah Akbar' chants could be heard from rooftops of the city. Initially, they were isolated and spontaneous, but by 8.00 pm echoes of the *takbir* were increasing. By 9.00 pm the chant could be heard everywhere, on either side of Mount Asma'I in central Kabul, from Paghman to Khyer Khana, 'as if the voiced anger and frustrations of the masses against the invaders had reached the skies' (Sediq 1985: 24). Later, some areas of the city would start a chant, which would be carried over to other parts of the city, echoed by intermediary populations (Kakar 1997: 98). The commotion expanded into the streets the next day.

Much has been made of who organized the insurrection. Kakar, in providing his own eyewitness account, is adamant 'no group of protesters was organized', that all involved were common people (Kakar 1997: 101). I take this detour to make a point about the coexistence of competing discourses on everyday resistance, depending on who one reads, but also to demonstrate attempts by modernist forces to 'organize' the recalcitrant population along its own architecture of power. The mujahidin would come to, retroactively, claim involvement and absorb this backlash into its own activist movements: organized, militant insurgencies contesting for control of the state. Materially and discursively, attempts were made to absorb the traditional spaces (and sentiment) into political movements, so that what started as disorganized, spontaneous action and 'night letters' had, towards the end of the war, mushroomed into elaborate and tightly controlled insurgencies and information systems.

There is no reason to believe that these cultural perspectives would not persist. It is unlikely, however, that the Taliban were as pragmatic as the mujahidin. They originated in this milieu in mid-1990s, in opposition to Islamists and their excesses, and then in the post-2001 Afghanistan, as an insurgency, they would emerge from within or tap into the wider discontent with the 'war on terror' and the state building project. As a whole, the rise of the Taliban indicates a certain proximity to traditional Islam, where power is negotiated differently, with a commitment to community, socialization of power, traditional knowledge perspectives and coexistence.

Taliban Emirate: Custodianship of the State

While the rise of the movement promised authenticity and purity, assuming power made it clear that there were tensions inherent in the effort, by a traditional, fragmentary and unconsolidated force, to take ownership of the modern nation-state. The surety and confidence of the cultural perspective that legitimized Taliban in the eyes of Afghans, once running the state, also became its undoing. The tension emerges when this modernist, 'officializing', and hegemonic conception of *the* modern nation-state, in the words of Bernard S Cohn and Nicholas Dirk (1988), coexists, seemingly, with a 'traditional', relatively less hierarchical and non-hegemonic conception of *a* 'state'. The theatre of power in 'pre-modern state', to them, required 'varied forms of knowledge, historical, mythical, cosmological, ritual', a sort of ritual performance and dramatic display. The modern state, in stark contrast, would further add to this theatricality and performativity by also governing 'through the gradual extension of "officializing" procedures and routines, through the capacity to bound and mark space' (Cohn and Dirks 1988: 224).

For the Taliban, it was becoming apparent that an improvisational and incoherent, localized approach to power would need to be reworked in light of quick gains in territory, in encounters with western forces defined by asymmetry of power, and in discovering new governance and administrative responsibilities. Edwards, rather brilliantly, captures this tension: there is inherent value in incoherence when confronted with hostile imperial forces or heterogeneous local identities that flourish under the internal flexibility offered by 'the existence of separate realms of discourse and moral expectation' (Edwards 2002: 299). The Emirate's approach to power destabilized this equilibrium.

> In their zeal to overcome the abuses of the previous twenty years and to create a new foundation for the country, the Taliban have instituted an uncompromising moral severity and inflexibility that, abuses aside, does not mesh well with Afghan sensibilities, especially the valorization of individual autonomy that is shared across the ethnic and regional spectrum.
>
> (Edwards 2002: 300)

In the First Emirate (1996–2001) and since the post-2021 return, once in power, the Taliban has swiftly evolved from a 'Third Way' movement grounded in indigenous, traditional priorities into a totalizing regime that seeks to unify the state, Islam and 'tribe'. This has led to the adoption of repressive policies. For example, the Emirate has passed edicts and *layehas* (codes of conduct) that repress women and femininity, while instituting extreme social reforms and austerity measures. In the past and (increasingly) now, it violently polices such banal facets of private life as entertainment consumption and fashion. The movement has committed itself to what it considers a re-Islamification of society through its Ministry for Promotion of Virtue and Prevention of Vice. In the 1990s, the earlier Pashtun-based rule 'through consensus', which privileged 'agreement and cooperation' and invited others to advise the movement, would come to be replaced by a demand for obedience to the authority of the amir (van Linschoten and Kuehn 2018: 97).

It is reported that by 1998 Mullah Omar started handing out copies of Mufti Rasheed Ludhianvi's *Obedience to the Amir* to his visitors, instructing them to read it if they hoped to understand the Taliban. The Ludhianvi thesis maintains that 'foundations of religion are impossible without consensus and unity', and that any thought or action that leads to dissent is, in fact, in defiance of and 'against Islam' (quoted in van Linschoten and Kuehn 2018: 118). Since returning to power, the movement has reneged on many of its promises about inclusivity and 'progressive' governance (Zaland 2023: 41). The posture and politics in the lead up to the signing of the Doha Agreement and the armed takeover, about inclusion, respect for human rights and women's rights turned out to be, to the utter horror of millions of Afghans, empty rhetoric in the theatre of realpolitik. While during the insurgency the leadership subscribed to a sort of collective decision-making ethos in the *rahbari shura* (Quetta Shura), since the return to power, Mullah Haibatullah Akhundzada has amassed immense power in his position as the spiritual and political Commander of the Faithful. Alongside a dominant class of radicals, progressively pushing the group closer to its more overtly nativist orbits, the leadership demands absolute obedience.

Signs of dissension on key questions such as rights of women, rights of minorities and girls' education are apparent, but they seem to hold little sway. So far, internal challenges have been either violently repressed (Goldbaum 2022) or explained away under the pretence that pushing back might harm the unity of the movement and 'cause division' (Healy 2023). While alternative imaginaries continue to be echoed by some from within the movement, sometimes as voices of dissent, the Taliban proper have unmistakably turned to hardline politics. In its zealous call for assimilation, as a bid to institute conformity and uniformity, it finds itself in a poverty-stricken and devastated society that is inherently dynamic and incoherent – made up of a medley of ethnic and tribal groups. In both iterations, as a state, the Taliban move from consensus and cooperation to obedience and autocracy, embodied in the person of the emir.

But there is an extra-constitutionality to this inward turn towards autocracy, one marked by an ambivalence towards drafting and adopting a foundational document. Once in power, in mimicking statehood, several enduring legal contradictions become apparent, pointing to the dilemma at the heart of the Taliban as a governing force. The movement reasserts the nation-state as the sole organizer of power, but states rely on centralization, codification and discipline. The Taliban have remained ambivalent on the question of a constitution, either putting off the question or rejecting the premise entirely, instead privileging Sharia as the organizing framework. Comments from the Taliban authorities have been mixed and misleading. If the messaging in the first year of their rule in 1996 or the 2022 pseudo-official book written by the Taliban Chief Justice are anything to go by, the door on constitutional governance is closed due to the 'completeness' of Sharia (Zaland 2023: 41). On the other hand, an official announcement in September 2021 quoted the Taliban acting minister of justice as stating the interim government would use the 1964 constitution, so far as its content did not contradict 'Islamic Sharia and the principles of the Islamic Emirate' (Gul 2021). Since then, the constitution has not been cited, nor has it been invoked. Beyond that, as Haroun Rahimi has pointed out, the Taliban governance model departs dramatically from the principles enshrined in the Zahir Shah-era constitution which envisioned popular elections, formalized separation of power and considered Hanafi jurisprudence as supplementary to state legislation (Rahimi 2022).

There is also the looming shadow of an existing Taliban constitution, a phantom document that is part of the original Emirate's attempt to pass a constitution. In October 1996, seemingly at the request of Mullah Omar, the Jamiat-e Ulema-Islam of Pakistan, a Deobandi political party with close ideological ties to the Taliban (Muzhda 2003), drafted a constitution for the newly minted government (van Linschoten and Kuehn 2018: 209). The fate of this document is unknown, but a year later the Ministry of Justice reported that it had begun working on drafting a constitution. On 20 June 1998, Mullah Omar issued an official decree that tasked the Chief Justice Nur Mohamamd Saqib and the Supreme Court with drafting a constitution and reviewing all the other laws. By May 1999, the team was still working on drafting the document. While they never managed to submit their final draft for approval by the time of the regime's removal from power in 2001, the publicly available text of the constitution offers a contradictory account. It notes that the 'basic document' was 'arranged and approved and was named the constitution of the Islamic Emirate of Afghanistan', presumably only internally (quoted in Van Linschoten and Keuhn 2018: 210).

More importantly, the introduction to the draft claims that the document was 'once again' approved by the *rahbari shura* on 23 June 2005. Written in 10 chapters and 110 articles, there are many similarities with the Constitutions of 1964 and the post-1992 interim mujahidin government, and rather interestingly, in terms of the centralization of power, a strong Supreme Court, and council of ministers, it shares much in common with the 2004 constitution. Elsewhere, it enshrines the fundamental rights and duties of citizens, ensuring equality before the law (Article 18), powers and duties of the Amir-ul Mominin (Article 52), and proposes a selective Islamic council with councillors from each province. Some of its content was appropriated in the 2006 wartime *Jihadi Layeha*, a code of conduct for Taliban fighters. Neither that, nor the claim that it was formally adopted in exile, however, has made itself manifest in any material sense since the movement's return to power. The document languishes in obscurity.

One way to read the regime's hesitance about adopting a constitution lies in pragmatic decision-making. Criticism can be deflected if the regime leaves the door open on constitutionalism even as it invokes Sharia as the supreme – and only – law of the land, thereby empowering the amir and the Leadership Council. Another way to read this hesitance is the Taliban's veiled disdain for disciplinary power, putting on hold the officializing imprint of the state for as long as possible. There is a tendency for delayed decision-making in the Taliban that is quite unusual for revolutionary governments. After more than two years in power, the Taliban government calls itself *sarparast* or 'caretaker', with no clear timeline for a transition. Decisions on sensitive 'national questions', like the national flag, remain postponed to an unspecified time in the future, when the conditions are right (TOLOnews 2023). Decisions on girls' education and work rights have also been consistently delayed. This would point to the Taliban struggles to recalibrate its traditional sensibilities – ones that have tended to be local, familiar and de-hierarchical – with the demands of running a modern nation-state. Perhaps a fear exists that a decisive move against traditionalism would alienate the people.

During both iterations of the Emirate, the Taliban approach to governance has been defined by its proximity to a certain modernity in 'fundamentalist' Islam. Enacting national edicts based on provincial (or even village) sensibilities, calling for uniformity, excessive policing and counterproductive policy positions based on the whims of a few at the top of the leadership are made possible with the engine of the modern state at the disposal of the leadership. But there seems to be a sense of unease that persists in the Taliban about their relationship with this state. The movement is seemingly more comfortable viewing itself as a custodian of the state rather than its outright owner.

Conclusion

If one aims to produce a more locally intuitive, productive and non-violent discourse on Afghanistan, it is imperative to complicate accounts of power from multiple locations, transcending the epistemic violence levied so unabashedly by Eurocentric scholarship. In the context of ideological contestations, this means that the binary of modernist Islam and 'fundamentalist' Islam could be juxtaposed vis-à-vis another ontological reality, a traditional subjectivity that constitutes the lived experiences of a majority of Afghans. In this chapter, I have attempted to demonstrate how the Taliban, as a movement and a regime, can be analysed with reference to this historicity.

There is an ideological dilemma that lies at the heart of the Taliban movement: in a triumvirate of modernist Islam, Islamic 'fundamentalism' and traditional Islam, the Taliban disavows the former while embracing the latter two simultaneously. The genealogies of traditional and 'fundamentalist' perspectives could be traced to the origins of the Taliban and to its ascent into power. Bifurcating the Taliban into its insurgency form and its state custodianship form can be helpful in highlighting the salience of either political orientation, the rise defined by a closer proximity to traditionalism, while the ascent to and capture of power exposes a more fundamentalist undercurrent. Tensions, nonetheless, persist within the group. They result in a confluence of traditionalism and Islamic fundamentalism, each taking their cues from seemingly opposing master texts/cultural perspectives, which can then explain the coexistence of hardline, exclusionary policy positions alongside an aptitude for socialization of power.

Though the ambivalence persists, the Taliban in the last two years have turned inwards, embracing an exclusionary nativist impulse, and in doing so have increasingly dismissed other Afghans or their interests (see Adili, this volume). Compared to the 1990s, policies enacted immediately after their return to power – on media, gender, education and so on – tended to be somewhat less repressive. Over the last two years, however, these policies have been revisited for a more repressive reinterpretation (Zaland 2023: 43). Some have, quite appropriately, argued that the current iteration of the Emirate is equipped with a more complex approach to power, one less reliant on corporal punishment, for example in policing the observation of *hijab* (veiling), prayer or other aspects of religiosity, and more on information campaigns (Rubin 2022). This newfound appreciation for the more opaque tactics of power is at least in part an outcome of the devastating and transformative encounter with the West. The group struggles to overcome an enduring paradox: it replicates that which it seeks to dismantle. In repressing women and femininity, for example, the Taliban live up to the colonial fantasy that 'all Afghan women became powerless victims of their backward, misogynist, and villainous brethren' (Osman 2017: 355), mythologies that were originally (re)constructed to justify the 'war on terror' (see Zeerak, this volume). The Taliban is at a crossroads. It must re-evaluate its relationship with 'fundamentalist' Islam and its proximity to a traditional approach to power so that the attempt at delinking from hegemonic, Eurocentric ideology does not result in another articulation of hegemony.

In locating the Taliban in the 'inbetweens', and not necessarily conceding totality to their power, we then also open the plains for resistance. Taliban power, despite the wishes of some within its ranks, cannot be absolute because it is contaminated by traditional underpinnings. The local population have already taken to everyday resistance, to resurgence and acts of renewal, in the face of their oppressive, decree-based, unconstitutional governance. They push back in subtle and subterfuge forms, whether it is women protesting, activists using the internet and social media to highlight injustice and human rights violations, YouTubers and vloggers reporting on everyday life, or Kabul-based critics like Mehbouba Seraj who was recently seen in *Al Jazeera*'s *Witness* programme questioning, rather transgressively, the internalized logics of the Emirate (Healy 2023). So, we are to extend this logic to any understanding of power and resistance in Taliban-ruled Afghanistan: the Taliban can exercise power in a hegemonic manner, that is, leaving little room for negotiation of difference and disciplining alterity, but they can also be undermined and undone, and not necessarily by the only tactics that come easy to Eurocentric ideology (organized, violent resistance). Those who live in their midst struggle through diffused, everyday acts of resistance as agents who would not necessarily subscribe to western civilizational or cultural perspectives.

References

Ahmadi, W. (2008), Modern Persian Literature in Afghanistan: Anomalous Visions of History and Form. Oxford: Routledge.

Alatas, S. H. (1974), 'The Captive Mind and Creative Development'. *International Social Science Journal*, 26: 691–700.

Burns, J. F. (1995), 'Islamic Rebels Renew a Siege to Win Kabul'. *New York Times*, 16 October 1995.

Cohn, B. S. and Dirks, N. B. (1988), 'Beyond the Fringe: The Nation State, Colonialism, and the Technologies of Power'. *Journal of Historical Sociology*, 1: 224–9.

Dam, B. (2021), *Looking for the Enemy: Mullah Omar and the Unknown Taliban*. Delhi: HarperCollins India.

Devji, F. (2012), Preface, in Van Linshoten A. S., Kuehn, F., Rahmany, M., Stanikzai, H. and Devji, F. (eds.) *Poetry of the Taliban*. New York: Columbia University Press.

Edgar, I. R. (2006), 'The "True Dream" in Contemporary Islamic/Jihadist Dreamwork: A Case Study of the Dreams of Taliban Leader Mullah Omar'. *Contemporary South Asia*, 15: 263–72.

Edwards, D. B. (2002), *Before Taliban: Genealogies of the Afghan Jihad*. Berkeley: University of California Press.

Goldbaum, C. and Najim, R. (2022), 'From the Untamed North, Resisting the Taliban'. *New York Times*, 20 August 2022.

Green, N. (2012), *Sufism: A Global History*. Oxford: Wiley.
Gregorian, V. (1967), 'Mahmud Tarzi and Saraj-ol-Akhbar: Ideology of Nationalism and Modernization in Afghanistan'. *Middle East Journal*, 21: 345–68.
Gul, A. (2021), 'Taliban Say They Will Use Parts of Monarchy Constitution to Run Afghanistan for Now'. *Voice of America*.
Hanifi, S. M. (2016), 'The Pashtun Counter-Narrative'. *Middle East Critique*, 25: 385–400.
Healy, M. and Najibullah, Q. (2023), 'Taliban Palace: The Second Year of Taliban rule in Afghanistan'. 15 August 2023, *Al Jazeera*.
Ingram, B. D. (2018), *Revival from Below: The Deoband Movement and Global Islam*. Berkeley: University of California Press.
Kakar, M. (1997), *Afghanistan: The Soviet Invasion and the Afghan Response, 1979–1982*. Berkeley: University of California Press.
Lizzio, K. P. (2014), *Embattled Saints: My Year with the Sufis of Afghanistan*. Wheaton, IN: Quest Books.
Maley, W. (2002), *The Afghanistan Wars*. Basingstoke: Palgrave Macmillan.
McChesney, R. D. (2018), *Reliquary Sufism: Sacred Fiber in Afghanistan*. Leiden: Brill.
Mignolo, W. (2012), Local Histories/Global Designs: Coloniality, Subaltern Knowledges, and Border Thinking. Princeton: Princeton University Press.
Moaddel, M. and Talattof, K. (2002), *Modernist and Fundamentalist Debates in Islam: A Reader*. Basingstoke: Palgrave Macmillan.
Muzhda, W. (2003). Afghanistan wa panj sal-i salta'i taliban. Tehran: Nashre Ney.
Nasr, S. H. (1990), *Traditional Islam in the Modern World*. London and New York: K. Paul International Publishers.
Nasr, S. H. and Chittick, W. C. (2007), *The Essential Seyyed Hossein Nasr*. Bloomington, IN: World Wisdom.
Nawid, S. (1997), 'The State, the Clergy, and British Imperial Policy in Afghanistan during the 19th and Early 20th Centuries'. *International Journal of Middle East Studies*, 29: 581–605.
Nojumi, N. (2002), The Rise of the Taliban in Afghanistan: Mass Mobilization, Civil War, and the Future of the Region. Basingstoke: Palgrave Macmillan.
Osman, W. (2017), 'Jamming the Simulacrum: On Drones, Virtual Reality, and Real Wars', in Marilyn, D. and Moritz, F. (eds.), *Culture Jamming*. New York: New York University Press.
Quijano, A. (2007), 'Coloniality and Modernity/Rationality'. *Cultural Studies*, 21: 168–78.
Rahimi, H. (2022), 'Afghanistan's Laws and Legal Institutions under the Taliban'. *Melbourne Asia Review*, Edition 10, 6 June 2022. Available at: https://www.melbourneasiareview.edu.au/afghanistans-laws-and-legal-institutions-under-the-taliban/.
Rashid, A. (2010), *Taliban: The Power of Militant Islam in Afghanistan and Beyond*. London and New York: I.B.Tauris.
Sediq, M. Z. (1985). Juma-i khunin [Bloody Friday]. Kumita Farhangi, Itihad Islami Mujahidin: Peshawar.
Shariati, A. (1971), *Cheh bayad kard? [What Is To Be Done?]*. Tehran: Shariati Cultural Foundation.
Stewart, R. T. (1973), *Fire in Afghanistan, 1914–1929: Faith, Hope, and the British Empire*. New York: Doubleday.
TOLOnews (2023), 'De defah wuzarat la sarparast Muhammad Yaqoob Mujahid sarah zangali maraka [Exclusive Interview with the Interim Defence Minister Muhammad Yaqoob Mujahid]'. 17 June 2023. Available at: https://www.youtube.com/watch?v=Old0Qo-L944.

Van Linschoten, A. S. and Kuehn, F. (2018), *The Taliban Reader: War, Islam and Politics in Their Own Words*. Oxford: Oxford University Press.

Van Linschoten, A. S., Kuehn, F., Rahmany, M., Stanikzai, H. and Devji, F. (2012), *Poetry of the Taliban*. New York: Columbia University Press.

Vikør, K. S. (2014), 'Sufism and Colonialism', in Ridgeon, L. (ed.), *The Cambridge Companion to Sufism*. Cambridge: Cambridge University Press.

Zaeef, A. S. and Van Linschoten, A. S. (2011), *My Life with the Taliban*, C. London: Hurst (Publishers) Limited.

Zaland, F. M. (2023). 'The Conflicting Synthesis of the Taliban's Religious and Cultural Identity'. *The Review of Faith and International Affairs*, 21: 38–45.

Zeweri, H. (2022), 'Between Imperial Rule and Sovereignty: Rethinking Afghanistan Studies'. *Interventions*, 24: 1–11.

5

Neopatrimonial Perspectives on Political Structures in Afghanistan

Zinab Attai, Maryam Jami and Boshra Moheb

Throughout Afghanistan's protracted history as a target of foreign intervention, external powers have sought to influence or directly transform political order in the country. Whether in support of communist or democratic models of governance in the country, outside forces have pursued large-scale efforts to bolster or impose and sustain bureaucratic structures. At the same time, different leaders and the regimes they have created have nurtured various forms of patrimonial politics, thereby facilitating the persistence of informal norms and institutions in spite of ostensibly radical change. We contend that the lens of neopatrimonialism offers the best way to understand the intersection of these two phenomena – external influence and patrimonialism – and the institutional continuities that this intersection has brought about.

Neopatrimonial rule is the imposition of a set of bureaucratic institutions that reside on top of and intermingled with pre-existing practices and associations (Bratton and van de Walle 1994). We suggest that, in Afghanistan, these practices and associations date back at least to the Musahiban era (1929–78). An examination of how they have intersected with foreign attempts to support, bolster or impose bureaucratic governance allows for a better understanding of political outcomes and institutions in the Afghan case.

The use of neopatrimonialism as a lens invites scholars to understand foreign support and intervention as an imperialist phenomenon similar to colonialism, in which new systems of governance are imported into a host country. While never formally colonized, Afghanistan has experienced multiple layers of significant external intervention at different points in its modern history, most notably during the international intervention of 2001 to 2021. Political outcomes in the country can be usefully compared to those in countries that were directly colonized. Abundant historical institutionalist literature on African politics (Englebert 2000; Michalopoulos and Papaioannou 2013; Wilfahrt 2018) not only offers insight into what constitutes a neopatrimonial regime, but also provides key insight into its characteristics and outcomes that may allow scholars to better navigate political authority and its consequences in Afghanistan. A neopatrimonial frame also allows us to take into account other descriptions of political interactions in Afghanistan including those that focus on informal institutions (Murtazashvili 2016) and informal patronage networks (Hess 2010; Coburn 2013; Mukhopadhyay 2009 and 2014; Adel 2016; Maley 2018; Malejacq and Sandor 2020), and explain how these have interacted with the formal institutions that were introduced or bolstered by intervening forces. As many authors note, Afghanistan's informal and formal political institutions have long been intertwined: neopatrimonial analysis sets these overlapping institutions against the backdrop of external influence over governance structures. In this reflection, we offer a synthesized application of neopatrimonialism to Afghanistan and trace its historical progression through a selection of the country's recent political developments.

Neopatrimonialism: An Overview

Neopatrimonialism as a concept stems from Max Weber's work on patrimonialism, a term he used to describe political systems in which a ruler exerts authority on the basis of kinship ties, patron–client relationships and personal relationships wherein administrative staffing is organized around personal loyalty (Weber 1922). In the 1970s, academics expanded upon this concept, adding the prefix 'neo' to describe political cohesion and transition in postcolonial African states. Neopatrimonialism can be described as the 'usurpation of imported formal governance structures by indigenous informal societal forces' (Boege et al. 2009). Bratton and van de Walle explain that, in contemporary systems of neopatrimonial governance, 'relationships of loyalty and dependence pervade a formal political and administrative system' (Bratton and van de Walle 1994). In these systems, political leaders occupy bureaucratic offices less to perform public service and more to acquire personal wealth and status. Accordingly, public and private interests are indistinguishable, with public officials awarding personal favours both within the state and across society. In such governance systems, informal rules permeate the day-to-day operation of ostensibly rational legal institutions, and a hybrid form of governance emerges at the nexus of informal and formal institutions (Erdmann and Engel 2007).

Adopting this conception of neopatrimonialism, Bratton and van de Walle's seminal article on political transitions in Africa asserts that political outcomes in African countries have been distinct from political outcomes in other regions of the world (Bratton and van de Walle 1994). The authors attribute the distinct political outcomes of democratization in different countries in Africa to the political institutions of the preceding regimes in each country. Their reasoning contends that contemporary political outcomes are shaped by mechanisms of rule that were embedded in the pre-existing regime (Bratton and van de Walle 1994). Leaders in these types of neopatrimonial regimes remain in power for long periods of time (regardless of, and perhaps even as a result of, the holding of elections) and define rules about who can participate in the polity and the level of political competition permitted. Moreover, these rules shape the future outcomes of a regime and determine whether elites and masses can arrive at new parameters for political negotiation. Bratton and van de Walle explain that to be characterized as a neopatrimonial regime, personal relationships must constitute the foundation of that regime's political institutions. Many scholars have adopted a neopatrimonial lens to explain political outcomes including legitimacy crises in Ghana (Brobbey 2014), insecurity in the Central African Republic (Vlavonou 2016) and poverty in Latin America (Giraudy et al. 2020).

We contend that Bratton and van de Walle's conception of a neopatrimonial regime can be applied to Afghanistan. Informal, personal or patronage-based relationships have comprised a central component of the country's bureaucratic systems since the Musahiban era and earlier, resulting in a significant overlap between informal and formal institutions. Further, Afghanistan's political history resonates with the experiences of African colonial occupation in which western legal, rational bureaucratic design was imported and applied to (or at least inspired) a pre-existing, native political context by European colonists, albeit in varying ways. Several moments in Afghanistan's modern history – the British East India Company's ill-fated experience in the 1840s, the Soviet interventions in the 1980s and the US-led presence from 2001 to 2021 – demonstrate sustained attempts by foreign powers to influence, formalize and in some cases, transform existing structures of governance.

Neopatrimonialism in Afghanistan: A Brief Literature Review

The application of neopatrimonialism to Afghanistan can be seen as a streamlined consolidation of existing attempts by scholars to assess the various intersections of formal and informal politics in a context deeply influenced by colonial interventions. Direct application of the framework to Afghanistan has been relatively limited, but scholars using the term directly to apply to various periods in Afghan history include Geller and Moss (2007), Adel (2016), Mehran (2018) and Maley (2018).

This research has produced mixed findings. Some applications of the concept in Afghanistan suggest that neopatrimonial networks may have a stabilizing impact in facilitating political development (Hess 2010; Mehran 2018). For instance, Dipali Mukhopadhyay (2009; 2014) finds that the hybrid form of warlord-governor, under certain conditions, delivered services and maintained security subnationally in key provinces where the weak central government often had limited access. Mukhopadhyay (2009) viewed the performance of 'strongmen-governors' such as Atta Muhammad Noor and Gul Agha Sherzai as 'exceptional'. While not overtly using the 'patrimonialism' or 'neopatrimonialism' labels, research by Englehart and Grant found that Afghan provincial governors with patronage-based practices were more effective at deterring insurgent attacks (Englehart and Grant 2015).

Other scholars have found neopatrimonial practices to be obstacles to capacity building and long-term stability in Afghanistan (Giustozzi and Orsini 2009; Maley 2018; Bihzan 2018). William Maley describes how Afghanistan's 'neopatrimonial drift' occurred because President Karzai came to office using patronage and clientelism to navigate the incongruence of a new, highly centralized state with the reality of fragmented power on the ground. Maley argues that Afghan bureaucratic institutions became dominated by these practices at all levels of governance, which led to rampant corruption and counteracted the initial gains made in the state building process. Wilde and Mielke's work describes how patron–client relationships, eldership and other pre-existing characteristics of the underlying social order of Afghanistan influenced modern state building processes and led to the dominant influence of patronage networks and asymmetric power relations. These authors suggest that the western state building project failed in Afghanistan because these characteristics were insufficiently recognized and understood by foreign state builders (Wilde and Miekle 2013).

Given the varied nature of these findings, additional scholarship is necessary to determine how the dynamics of neopatrimonialism have affected political outcomes in Afghanistan. We assert that the value of this framework stems from its recognition of the quasi-colonial (Manchanda 2020) nature of foreign influence in Afghanistan and its simultaneous capacity to illuminate the interaction between native and foreign governance systems within the country's formal institutions. It is also important to explore the effects of merging informal, patrimonial practices with formal governance systems on political outcomes at various levels, from local to provincial and national. In the following historical overview, we begin to unpack some of these intersections as they have played out over the last century, focusing on select cross-sections of Afghanistan's history to draw out areas for future research.

The Development of Neopatrimonialism in Afghanistan's Modern History

1. The Musahibans (1929–78): Patrimonialism Meets 'Neutral' Foreign Policy

The historical roots of patrimonialism can be traced back to the Durrani Empire in which the *jagir* system of land grants preferentially distributed land to elite groups to incentivize loyalty to the monarchy (Qadir and Asghar 2016). But, for expedience and relevance, we begin our review in the twentieth century with the Musahiban dynasty, and specifically the forty-year reign of Zahir Shah. The governance systems of this regime were deeply rooted in patronage-based forms of rule and could be characterized as hybrid systems, emphasizing legal-rational institutions in urban areas and informal practices in rural regions. Learning from past failures, particularly the downfall of Amanullah Khan, the Musahiban rulers established relationships with local leaders to bridge the gap between the central government and rural communities (Shahrani 1986: 49; Barfield 2010: 185; Ibrahimi 2019: 50).

As others in this volume contend, the core policy of the Musahiban dynasty leaders was to prioritize the country's internal stability as a means of maintaining sovereignty. Amanullah Khan's policies had led to rebellion and dissatisfaction, prompting the Musahibans to focus on long-term stability by recalibrating government–society relations and avoiding the top-down imposition of social norms (Barfield 2019: 310). For instance, their approach to the unveiling of women was not as ambitious as Amanullah Khan's, presenting it as an optional choice for women rather than a wide-ranging imposed reform (Barfield 2019: 316). Additionally, the Musahibans aimed to alleviate economic pressures in rural regions to prevent potential uprisings. They gradually reduced taxes on rural products to address grievances that had fuelled rebellion against their predecessor (Barfield 2019: 307).

Accordingly, a kind of composite governance system emerged under the Musahiban rulers, incorporating both formal and informal governance structures. The formal municipal governance in Kabul adhered to established laws and regulations, while informal practices prevailed in rural areas based on customary laws (Barfield 2010: 222–3; Ibrahimi 2019: 49). This blended governance approach facilitated the formation of patron–client relationships between the central government and rural areas. Links with local leaders who acted as intermediaries strengthened patron–client networks that bridged the gap between Kabul and the countryside. However, this linkage came with drawbacks, such as inhibiting the state's reach to rural communities and hindering deeper institutional connections (Ibrahimi 2019: 49).

Critical to the Musahiban leaders' claims to national sovereignty and their ability to maintain internal cohesion was their 'neutral' stance towards foreign policy. They declared neutrality in the Second World War and, then, during the Cold War, received aid from both the United States and the Soviet Union. This meant that, while both countries had some influence over internal development programmes, for example, neither was in a position to impose new structures of governance.

In the 1960s, the rise of educated social groups led to the emergence of various political parties and movements, including the pro-Soviet People's Democratic Party of Afghanistan (PDPA), the Maoist Progressive Youth Organization and the Islamist-guided Muslim Youth Organization. These groups gained momentum and eventually the PDPA orchestrated a military coup against Muhammad Daoud Khan, the last representative of the Musahiban dynasty, in 1978. Despite the regime change, Afghanistan's hybrid political system persisted into the PDPA's rule, with patrimonial practices infiltrating the more formal structures of central and local government. This critical juncture in Afghanistan's history is a key window for understanding the path dependence of patrimonial politics in Afghanistan.

2. The PDPA (1978–92): Patrimonialism Meets a Single External Funding Source

The political project of the PDPA regime provoked a significant shift in the state's approach to governance. While the patrimonial systems of the Musahiban era remained largely intact, the balance of influence between two external powers had dissolved into an influence of one. The regime operated with the material and military support of the Soviet Union, aiming to establish socialism in Afghanistan (Nojumi 2002: 31; Hess 2010: 175). Comprising two factions, Khalq and Parcham, the PDPA shared an ideology heavily influenced by Soviet socialist thought (Barfield 2019: 354). Its objectives encompassed social reform, the introduction of attempts to change people's lives and mindsets as part of transforming Afghanistan into a socialist state.

The interaction between Soviet influence and existing strategies of Afghan governance materialized in two ways during the PDPA's tenure in Afghanistan. First, patrimonial practices were evident in strategies to mobilize support. Both leaders of Khalq (Noor Muhammad Taraki) and Parcham (Babrak Karmal) engaged in clientelism within their respective tribes, appointing supporters and co-ethnics to positions of power (Hess 2010: 175). Their loyalty and personal connections permeated formal institutions, solidifying their patrimonial governance approach.

Second, leaders attempted to replace local-level patrimonial practices and appointments with party committees functioning at all levels, favouring individuals *without* local affiliations over traditional powerbrokers. Formal initiatives such as land ownership, loans and marriage incentives were introduced by these party committees to legitimize the government's agenda.

This divergence between the PDPA's patrimonial strategies for party mobilization on the one hand and their top-down anti-patrimonial state building agenda on the other reflected the ways in which the government attempted to maintain support both from within Afghanistan and from its external patron simultaneously.

3. Dr Najibullah (1986–92): Patrimonialism Meets Waning External Influence and Funding

The rivalry between Khalqi and Parchami leaders, driven by modernization ambitions, marginalized various Afghan factions and led to the shift of the USSR's support to Dr Najibullah amid an increasingly costly war to quell Afghan resistance to the Soviet intervention (Halliday and Tanin 1998: 1366; Hess 2010: 177). Najibullah used patronage strategies to secure loyalty from local power holders and to stabilize his position. He aimed to connect formal government bodies with regional figures through decentralization (Hess 2010). While he introduced a new constitution during his time, it functioned as a tool for the president to establish a network of personal patronage within and beyond the PDPA. While Soviet funding was flowing freely, this bolstered his political influence and quelled internal party rivalries. His efforts included promises of land ownership, powerful bureaucratic roles and incentives like debt forgiveness and healthcare. He also pledged salaries to those joining the pro-state militia (Giustozzi 2000: 163–4; Hess 2010: 178).

Najibullah adeptly used formal structures to define participation criteria in the polity, relying on loyalty nurtured through patronage. Loyalty and support from his followers and rival factions stemmed not only from allegiance to him but also from the benefits his regime offered (Hess 2010: 179). This approach can be understood as a strategic attempt at papering over the ideological divide that had previously triggered a revolutionary war against the PDPA. His patrimonialism, while stabilizing in some respects, was heavily dependent on Soviet aid. As this external support declined, Najibullah found himself unable to continue rewarding loyalty, which led to the faltering of his regime. The government's reliance on a single source of aid, now significantly reduced, hampered his ability to provide essential services and maintain his patronage networks.

4. Hamid Karzai (2004–14): Patrimonialism Becomes Neopatrimonialism

For the purposes of our analysis of the development of neopatrimonialism it makes sense here to move forward to 2004, because this is the point in time when the form of institutionalized patrimonialism that had developed by the end of Najibullah's regime combined with the outright imposition of western models of governance. As Maley asserts, from 2004 onwards the government in Afghanistan experienced a 'neopatrimonial drift' (Maley 2018). President Karzai emerged from a background steeped in the political dynamics of the 1980s, where survival had hinged on patronage, clientelism and alliance management (Maley 2018). Upon assuming the presidency in 2004, Karzai brought this paradigm to Kabul and, within the parameters of externally imposed democratization, furthered his own personal influence and patronage network. In this way, Afghanistan's political landscape took on a distinct neopatrimonial character.

Networks of familial relationships thrived within the multi-layered patron–client system (Maley 2018), which, critically, now functioned in a new context – one in which the United States was not only funding state building efforts but also, in conjunction with the international community at large, dictating its parameters from the outside. The Karzai government remained reluctant to counter the pervasive corruption that gradually ensued from plentiful external resources in combination with patron–client politics, resulting in forms of governance that focused on short-term stability and the consolidation of power through patronage.

In the aftermath of the 11 September attacks in 2001, Afghanistan had experienced the Taliban overthrow by the United States and coalition forces. This transformation notably reshaped political dynamics with powerful mujahidin strongmen gaining additional legitimacy from the United States on the basis of their anti-Taliban stance. Many as a result played formal roles in national government (Giustozzi 2004; Mukhopadhyay 2009; Malejacq 2020). This was notably different to the roles that regional notables had played during the Musahiban era. After the international intervention in 2001, mujahidin strongmen consolidated their authority by maintaining armed groups access to international funds, some of which were channelled through the central government (Wide and Mielke 2013: 360–1; Ibrahimi 2019: 55). In this way, President Karzai facilitated the expansion of the influence of select local elites, and in turn relied on their local influence to reinforce his authority. For instance, General Raziq, while Kandahar's police chief, provided financial support to President Karzai's re-election campaign in 2009 and manipulated elections in his favour (Giustozzi and Mangal 2014: 3).

President Karzai's two terms as president witnessed the full transformation of patrimonial practices into neopatrimonial ones against the backdrop of internationally sponsored democratization. Karzai harnessed his position to allocate foreign aid, weaponry, finances and influential government roles as political rewards, not unlike many of his predecessors. Critically different, however, was the way in which this approach aligned both with the US military goals of cultivating relations through mujahidin strongmen in the regions and, on the surface at least, with the introduction of internationally sponsored and imposed state building parameters. This consolidation of a neopatrimonial state would continue, albeit with different characteristics, beyond Karzai's two terms as president and throughout the administration of Ashraf Ghani, who, while coming to office promising to establish a merit-based civil service – and initially filling government positions with young, qualified, English-speaking and computer literate staff to this end – oversaw an administration that increasingly emphasized ethnic divisions and personal loyalties.

5. The Taliban (2021 to the Present): A New Patrimonial Paradigm?

The Taliban, in its latest incarnation, has shed (at least performatively) externally imposed bureaucratic norms and lost substantial international financial support. In that sense, the new regime seems to be reverting to a more orthodox patrimonial system. As noted by Van Bijlert (2021), this evolving political landscape has revealed a distinctive form of patrimonialism that appears tightly knit and coherent at the centre. However, many questions remain unanswered: how do we make sense of the new regime's inclination to graft its radical project onto the republican architecture (bureaucratic and otherwise) that survived 2021? How will its seemingly cohesive core establish stable ties with segments of the citizenry that operate by very different understandings of state–society relations? How do we explain the Taliban's simultaneous insular ideological stubbornness alongside its persistent inclination to court foreign aid, investment and recognition? And, in that vein, can the Taliban regime sustain itself without the extensive external support that has historically shaped Afghanistan's political fabric?

References

Adel, E. (2016), 'Understanding and Explaining Corruption: A Case Study of Afghanistan' (Master's thesis). Södertörns University, Department of Social Science.

Barfield, T. (2010), *Afghanistan: A Cultural and Political History*. Princeton: Princeton University Press.

Bijlert, M. (2021), 'The Focus of the Taleban's New Government: Internal Cohesion, External Dominance'. Afghanistan Analysts Network.

Bizhan, Nematullah (2018), 'Aid and State Building, Part II: Afghanistan and Iraq'. *Third World Quarterly*, 39(1): 1–18.

Boege, V., Brown, A. and Clements, K. (2009), 'Hybrid Political Orders, Not Fragile States'. *Peace Review*, 21(1): 13–21.

Bratton, M. and Van de Walle, N. (1994), 'Neopatrimonial Regimes and Political Transitions in Africa'. *World Politics*, 46(4): 453–89.

Brobbey, C. A. (2014), 'Neopatrimonial Logic and National Programmatic Policies in Ghana: A Case of Rice Importation and Production Policies under the Administrations of J. A. Kufuor and J. E. A. Mills'. *African Journal of Political Science and International Relations*, 8(2): 43–53.

Coburn, N. (2013), 'Informal Justice and the International Community in Afghanistan'. U.S. Institute of Peace.

Erdmann, G. and Engel, U. (2007), 'Neopatrimonialism Reconsidered: Critical Review and Elaboration of an Elusive Concept'. *Commonwealth and Comparative Politics*, 45(1): 95–119.

Englebert, P. (2000), 'Pre-colonial Institutions, Postcolonial States, and Economic Development in Tropical Africa'. *Political Research Quarterly*, 53(1): 7–36.

Englehart, N. and Grant, P. (2015). 'Governors, Governance, and Insurgency in Karzai's Afghanistan: The Limits of Professionalism'. *Asian Survey*, 55(2): 299–324.

Geller, A. and Moss, S. (2007), 'The Afghan Nexus: Anomie, Neo-patrimonialism and the Emergence of Small-world Networks'. Available at: https://www.researchgate.net/publication/241754514_The_Afghan_nexus_Anomie_neo-patrimonialism_and_the_emergence_of_small-world_networks (Accessed: 1 May 2024).

Giraudy, A., Hartlyn, J., Dunn, C. and Carty, E. (2020), 'The Impact of Neopatrimonialism on Poverty in Contemporary Latin America'. *Latin American Politics and Society*, 62(1): 73–96.

Giustozzi, A. (2000), *War, Politics, and Society in Afghanistan, 1978–1992*. Washington, DC: Georgetown University Press.

Giustozzi, A. (2004), *'Good' State vs. 'Bad' Warlords? A Critique of State Building Strategies in Afghanistan*. London: London School of Economics Crisis States Program.

Giustozzi, A. and Mangal, S. (2014), '*Violence, the Taliban, and Afghanistan's 2014 Elections*. Washington, DC: U.S. Institute of Peace.

Giustozzi, A. and Orsini, D. (2009), 'Centre–Periphery Relations in Afghanistan: Badakhshan between Patrimonialism and Institution-building'. *Central Asian Survey*, 28(1): 1–16.

Halliday, F. and Tanin, Z. (1998), 'The Communist Regime in Afghanistan 1978–1992: Institutions and Conflicts'. *Europe–Asia Studies*, 50(8): 1357–80.

Hess, S. (2010), 'Coming to Terms with Neopatrimonialism: Soviet and American Nation-Building Projects in Afghanistan'. *Central Asian Survey*, 29(2): 171–87.

Ibrahimi, S. Y. (2019), 'Afghanistan's Political Development Dilemma: The Centralist State Versus a Centrifugal Society'. *Journal of South Asian Development*, 14(1): 40–61.

Lyall, J. and Wilson, I. (2009), 'Rage against the Machines: Explaining Outcomes in Counterinsurgency Wars'. *International Organization*, 63(1): 67–106.

Malejacq, R. and Sandor, A. (2020), 'Sahelistan? Military Intervention and Patronage Politics in Afghanistan and Mali'. *Civil Wars*, 22(4): 543–66.

Maley, W. (2018), 'Institutional Design, Neopatrimonialism and the Politics of Aid in Afghanistan'. *Asian Survey*, 58(6): 995–1015.

Manchanda, N. (2020), *Imagining Afghanistan: The History and Politics of Imperial Knowledge*. Cambridge: Cambridge University Press.

Mehran, W. (2018), 'Neopatrimonialism in Afghanistan'. *Journal of Peacebuilding & Development*, 13(2): 91–105.

Michalopoulos, S. and Papaioannou, E. (2013), 'Pre-colonial Ethnic Institutions and Contemporary African Development'. *Econometrica*, 81(1): 113–52.

Mukhopadhyay, D. (2009), *Warlords as Bureaucrats: The Afghan Experience*. Washington DC: Carnegie Endowment for International Peace.

Mukhopadhyay, D. (2014), *Warlords, Strongman Governors and the State in Afghanistan*. New York: Cambridge University Press.

Murtazashvili, J. B. (ed.) (2016), *Informal Order and the State in Afghanistan*. Cambridge: Cambridge University Press.

Nojumi, N. (2002). *The Rise of the Taliban in Afghanistan: Mass Mobilization, Civil War, and the Future of the Region*. New York: Palgrave Macmillan.

Qadir, A. and Asghar, F. (2016), 'Peshawar Valley under Durronos with Focus on Its Administration, 1747–1818'. *Journal of the Pakistan Historical Society*, 1(64): 57.

Shahrani, N. M. (1986), *State Building and Social Fragmentation in Afghanistan: A Historical Perspective*. Bloomington, IN: Indiana University Press.

Shahrani, N. (2013), 'Center–Periphery Relations in Afghanistan', in Schetter, C. (ed.), *Local Politics in Afghanistan: A Century of Intervention in Social Order*. London, UK: Hurst & Company.

Sharan, T. (2011), 'The Dynamics of Elite Networks and Patron-Client Relations in Afghanistan'. *Europe–Asia Studies*, 63(6): 1109–27.

Vlavonou, G. (2016), 'An Uncertain Transition: Security, Violence, and Neopatrimonialism in the Central African Republic'. *Revue Tiers Monde*, 228: 121–42.

Waldman, M. (2013), 'System Failure: The Underlying Causes of US Policy-Making Errors in Afghanistan'. *International Affairs*, 89(4): 825–43.

Weber, M. (1922), *Economy and Society*. Berkeley: University of California Press.

Wilde, A. and Mielke, K. (2013), 'Order, Stability, and Change in Afghanistan: From Top-Down to Bottom-Up State-Making'. *Central Asian Survey*, 32: 353–70.

Wilder, A. (2005), *A House Divided? Analyzing the 2005 Afghan Elections*. Kabul: Afghanistan: Research and Evaluation Unit.

Wilfahrt, M. (2018), 'Pre-colonial Legacies and the Contemporary Politics of Public Goods Provision in Decentralized West Africa'. *World Politics*, 70(2): 239–74.

6

Civil–Military Relations, Battlefield Performance and the Disintegration of Afghanistan's Security Forces

Abdul Basir Yosufi

For roughly two decades, Afghanistan's government and international partners invested ample resources in building Afghanistan's National Defense and Security Forces (ANDSF). Security expenditures constituted about 30 per cent of Afghanistan's GDP and nearly 50 per cent of the Afghan government budget (Haque 2019). The United States alone spent roughly $90 billion in developing, sustaining and equipping the ANDSF, while other international partners contributed financial and technical support as well (Sopko 2022a). Despite all of these investments, with the withdrawal of US and NATO troops, the ANDSF could not withstand the Taliban's pressure. While the Taliban made incremental gains in the previous year, it took them only ten days to capture thirty-three of the country's thirty-four provincial capitals, including Kabul; the Government of the Islamic Republic of Afghanistan (GIRoA) collapsed thereafter, on 15 August 2021 (Sopko 2022a).

Given the means by which the United States withdrew from Afghanistan, it could be argued that the collapse of the ANDSF was inevitable. The 2020 Doha US–Taliban Agreement and the subsequent troop withdrawal led to a sense of abandonment within the ANDSF and society in Afghanistan. At the same time, the Taliban viewed these events as a victory, providing them with a boost of morale and momentum. For almost two decades, the ANDSF had relied on the US and allied troops for air support and on contractors for maintaining equipment and logistics services. The precipitous withdrawal of both deprived ANDSF of these vital force multipliers and enablers (Sopko 2022a). The release of 5,000 Taliban prisoners of war based on the US–Taliban agreement further strengthened the Taliban.

While counterfactual arguments are inherently tricky, without the underlying structural problems discussed in this chapter, I would contend that the ANDSF would not have collapsed as quickly as it did. An effective military with solid leadership, clear political goals and an actionable strategy could have defended major population centres for years. Foreign dependence made the ANDSF unsustainable in the long run. However, Afghanistan's political leaders could have used the two-decade international support, including defence and security assistance, to develop self-reliant and capable military forces to protect the state against the Taliban and other insurgents, at least for a period of time. Moreover, although they withdrew their troops from Afghanistan, western governments remained committed to maintaining financial and political support for the Republic. The ANDSF were well-trained and equipped, had access to large quantities of modern weapons and ammunition, and significantly outnumbered the Taliban. With a total of 288,702 forces or 82 per cent of authorized *tashkil* (billets) as of July 2020, the ANDSF still enjoyed a roughly 1.5:1 numerical advantage, better equipment and technical capabilities (Schroden 2021a).

Despite the perception among some that Afghanistan's military did not fight, Afghan soldiers fought bravely in adverse conditions, sometimes without sufficient food supplies, ammunition or medical evacuation facilities due to poor planning and leadership. In the first ten days of August 2021 alone, more than 4,000 wounded soldiers were treated by the International Committee for the Red Cross and many more by Afghan military and civilian hospitals (Schroden 2021b). Over the years, more than 66,000 ANDSF were killed, and tens of thousands were injured (Sopko 2022b). Moreover, the ANDSF took over the responsibility for combat operations from US and NATO troops in 2014. For several years, they were able to defend major cities and population centres (with some exceptions) against the Taliban. They also provided security for four presidential and parliamentary general elections. It was little surprise, then, that most Afghan and international analysts, including US policy makers, thought the ANDSF would fight longer and more effectively than they did.

So, what explains the dramatic collapse of ANDSF? Some have argued that the Doha United States–Taliban agreement and the subsequent US departure from Afghanistan had a devastating psychological and operational impact on the ANDSF. The withdrawal of US air support and enablers undermined the operational capabilities of Afghanistan's military forces, as did corruption and lack of a national security strategy (Sopko 2022a). Structural problems such as a highly centralized political system (Murtazashvili 2022), politicization, poor discipline and leadership, and low morale have also been cited for the fall of the Islamic Republic of Afghanistan (IRoA) and its security forces (Andisha 2022).

While all these factors contributed to the collapse of the ANDSF, there has been insufficient systematic analysis and theorization as to *why* Afghanistan's political leadership squandered opportunities to build strong and cohesive forces that could stand the Taliban's onslaught. In particular, why did President Ghani resort to micromanagement, the appointments of incompetent loyalists and frequent leadership reshuffles? How did his behaviour undermine the effectiveness and battlefield performance of Afghanistan's military forces? This chapter tries to address this gap and answer these questions by drawing on theories of civil–military relations. This approach offers important insights into the outcome of international security assistance, conflict and state building in Afghanistan. It sheds light on how the design and management of defence and security forces to serve parochial interests and ensure political leaders' hold on power undermined institutional continuities that could have led to the development of professional and effective military forces.

I argue that the Republic's leaders, particularly President Ghani, undermined the effectiveness of the ANDSF through loyalty-based appointments, disregard for personal competence, ethnic manipulation and excessive centralization of command and control. The aim of these politics was to coup-proof the presidential palace and create a loyal and subordinate (if ineffective) security sector, even though the ethnic diversity of ANDSF and the presence of international troops made coups very unlikely. This politicization of military management led to poor leadership and battlefield performance, high casualties, low morale and lack of cohesion, all of which led to military collapse. The same problems were mirrored in civilian state institutions, resulting in a lack of accountability, corruption and the inability of the state to provide essential services or gain the legitimacy needed to maintain public support and motivation to fight for the state.

In this chapter, I first provide an overview of research literature on civil–military relations and military effectiveness, assessing coup-proofing's impact on military performance. Second, I discuss the development of the ANDSF. Third, I explain how political intervention and coup-proofing undermined the effectiveness and battlefield performance of ANDSF. Finally, I conclude with some implications for international security assistance and political leaders.

Civil–Military Relations and Military Effectiveness

Military effectiveness can be defined as 'the capacity to create military power from a state's basic resources in wealth, technology, population size, and human capital' (Brooks and Stanley 2007). Measuring military effectiveness and battlefield performance is complicated and challenging. First, it is an inherently dyadic concept in that it can only be evaluated in relation to an enemy's effectiveness and performance. A country's armed forces could be highly effective but still destroyed by a superior military or vice versa. Second, while the two concepts are related, military effectiveness differs from victory or defeat during the war. A country's military forces may perform well but still lose the war. Conversely, they may perform poorly in specific battles but win the war. Third, military effectiveness also depends on the effective utilization of technology, force size, and situational and environmental factors, all of which are difficult to measure (Pilster and Böhmelt 2011).

Existing literature suggests that the relationship between military and civilian political leadership shapes military effectiveness (Huntington 1957; Feaver 1999; Pilster and Böhmelt 2011; Bausch 2018). The central question of civil–military relations is how to balance the two vital but potentially conflicting goals of building military forces that are strong enough to defend and protect society against external (or internal) threats and, at the same time, obedient enough not to threaten or prey on the people they are supposed to protect. Given that the military's central skill is the management of violence and, by nature of duties, holds coercive power, it has the potential to impose its will on society and political leadership. A classic concern is the direct seizure of political power through coups, but there are other ways that the military can pose a threat, including resource draining, war provocation or simply disobedience vis-à-vis civilian leadership in the service of parochial interests (Feaver 1999).

So, how to achieve this delicate balance and, in doing so, achieve the dual goals of strong but obedient armed forces? Samuel Huntington, one of the most influential theorists of civil–military relations, argued it could be done through the professionalization and depoliticization of the armed forces. To ensure that the military is both obedient to its civilian masters and effective in defending the country against external threats, Huntington proposed his concept of 'objective civilian control' of the military: the military must be recognized as an autonomous, professional and politically neutral institution that is a tool of the state and obeys whoever secures political office through legitimate means. In return, civilians or, more broadly, political leaders must not intervene in the military profession or try to impose their personal control – in Huntington's vernacular, 'subjective control' – over the armed forces. Given the multitude of civilian groups in society, subjective civilian control of armed forces makes itself manifest as a function of competition between different groups, each of which seeks to subordinate the military to its own will, thereby undermining its political neutrality, professionalism and effectiveness (Huntington 1957: 80–5).

While most established western democracies – for many different but overlapping reasons – have achieved relatively harmonious civil–military relations and military effectiveness, autocratic leaders often resort to coup-proofing to control their armed forces and retain power. Coup-proofing can be defined as 'the strategies and tactics employed to prevent the military from seizing power' (Pilster and Böhmelt 2011: 331). The threat, real or perceived, of coups and seizure of power by the military means political leaders need to make a trade-off between building a strong and effective military on the one hand and holding on to power on the other. When leaders perceive a higher threat to their political power from the country's military than from external enemies, they often weaken their military to ensure regime survival (Bausch 2018). While political leaders could engage in coup-proofing irrespective of the regime type, autocratic leaders are more concerned with holding on to power and coup-proof more frequently (Bausch 2018). That is because coup-proofing is associated with higher costs and lower benefits for leaders in democratic states than their autocratic counterparts (Pilster and Böhmelt 2012).

Political leaders employ several strategies to coup-proof and ensure a loyal and subordinate military. First, they interfere in recruitment, promotion and assignment by exploiting family, ethnic and religious ties to ensure loyalty. A second strategy involves centralizing decision-making and a strict command system that limits operational and tactical autonomy, initiative and innovation (Talmadge 2011). A third strategy involves frequently rotating military leaders to prevent them from building strong relationships and following among their officers. Finally, political leaders try to create subordinate militaries by dividing the military into rival organizations to counterbalance each other (Pilster and Böhmelt 2011). Counterbalancing is used to create coordination problems among military organizations so that some rival armed forces can fight back and defend the regime against potential coups (De Bruin 2018).

Examples of coup-proofing abound. Togolese president Eyadema Gnassingbe filled the vast majority of officer positions with ethnic Kabye (making up about 20 per cent of the population), with almost all senior commanders coming from his own village (Decalo 1989). Zairian president Mobutu dissolved his military's entire general staff to centralize command and control of smaller military units under his own leadership (Emizet 2000). Saddam Hussein counterbalanced the regular Iraqi Army with the Republican Guard and the Special Republican Guard (Kiyani 2022). Coup-proofing is argued to have negatively affected the battlefield performance of Arab militaries, leading to the poor performance of Iraqi forces in the Gulf Wars and the dismal performance of the Syrian military against Israel on Golan Heights in 1973. Similarly, ethnic manipulation (Shiafication) by Prime Minister Noori al-Maliki led to the collapse and disintegration of the Iraqi armed forces even though they had a fifteen times numerical advantage against ISIS fighters as well as superior training and equipment (Bausch 2018).

To sum up, undue political intervention, coup-proofing efforts, ethnic manipulation, loyalty-based appointment and promotions, or what Talmadge (2011) calls 'worst practices' of interference, undermine military effectiveness, leadership qualities and tactical capabilities of armed forces.

Development of the ANDSF

Over the past 150 years, Afghanistan has had to rebuild its military several times. In the 1870s, Amir Sher Ali Khan re-established the country's army, which had disintegrated due to the Second Anglo-Afghan War. Abdur Rahman Khan redeveloped the army when he consolidated his rule over the country in the 1880s. Afghanistan's army was again reorganized under Amanullah Khan in 1919 and by Nader Shah in 1929. The 1960s saw the development of the Soviet-sponsored army (Jalali 2002). In 1992, when the communist regime collapsed, the Afghan National Army (ANA) and other military institutions disintegrated once again.

The ANDSF was founded in 2002 in the aftermath of US intervention and the defeat of the Taliban. From 2002 to 2021, the Afghan government and its international partners invested ample resources in developing the ANDSF. The US government spent upward of $145 billion on the overall reconstruction of Afghanistan (Sopko 2021), of which $90 billion was allocated to building and sustaining the ANDSF (Sopko 2022a). The security sector absorbed about half of the Afghan government budget and approximately 30 per cent of Afghanistan's GDP, almost ten times the 3 per cent average in other low-income countries. Total on-budget per capita public expenditure on security was around $50 per year compared to just $17 for education and $8 for health. In absolute terms, the ANDSF budget added up to about $5.5 billion, which is very high compared to per capita military expenditure in the region (Haque 2019).

Most resources came from international partners, specifically the United States and its allies. Based on its commitment at the 2012 NATO Chicago Summit, Afghanistan's government contributed $500 million towards ANDSF expenses, and the rest came from international partners (NATO 2012). From 2005 to 2019, the US Department of Defense (DOD) disbursed $69.22 billion ($47.43 billion to the ANA and $21.4 billion to the Afghan National Police [ANP]). Tens of thousands of American and NATO troops fought alongside or advised and mentored the ANDSF against the Taliban (Sopko 2019).

The over-reliance on the United States and full payment of ANDSF by international partners made the ANDSF financially unsustainable in the long run (Rubin 2006). However, without coup-proofing and with the right strategy, the investment of ample resources, technical support and training by the US and NATO troops during the two-decade engagement could have turned the ANDSF into one of the best-trained and equipped military forces capable of providing security for the Afghan government and people. Had the ANDSF managed to defend major cities and population centres in the short run, the outcome could have been less disastrous than a complete collapse of the Republic. In the medium and long term, the withdrawal of the US and NATO troops would have deprived the Taliban of the strategic cause that enabled them to recruit and motivate their foot soldiers in the name of jihad. It might have also changed the strategic calculations of key foreign and domestic players, perhaps leading to a re-alignment of the Taliban's foreign supporters and allowing for a more effective mobilization of anti-Taliban constituencies. These developments might have forced the Taliban to enter a negotiated settlement.

Ethnopolitics as Coup-proofing in the Afghan Security Sector

While the United States and most NATO allies have professional and politically neutral military institutions, they showed little interest in developing the same type of civil–military relations in Afghanistan and, in particular, in preventing the politicization and ethnicization of ANDSF. In fact, with their unconditional support for Ghani and his policies, the western powers contributed to the further politicization of the ANDSF. Political intervention, especially the 'worst practices', was the norm, not the exception. Political leaders intervened to ensure that appointments and promotions were based on political and ethnic loyalties; command structure and decision-making authority were highly centralized in the presidential palace, and the Office of the National Security Council (ONSC) interfered in military operations in disregard of the chain of command.

Given the ethnic diversity of the ANDSF, the presence of US and NATO troops, and the financial dependence of Afghanistan on international assistance in the past two decades, the possibility of a military coup was negligible. Nevertheless, political leaders attempted to maximize their subjective control and coup-proof the ANDSF to ensure their hold on power. According to Amrullah Saleh, the former chief of the National Directorate of Security (NDS) and later vice president, about 90 per cent of senior military officers were appointed based on relations and political loyalties (Giustozzi and Quentin 2014). In the absence of an effective performance evaluation system, competence and battlefield performance had little weight in assignments and promotions. In 2013, an evaluation committee of the Ministry of Defense (MoD) identified 30 poor performers among 500 senior commanders, but only 10 were reassigned. Of 46 officers promoted to general rank, only 10 were professional military officers. For example, a well-connected 26-year-old man with no military background was promoted to colonel rank after spending two weeks in the military academy. Both General Wardak, former minister of defence, and General Karimi, former defence chief of staff, complained that they were under pressure to appoint politically connected people (Giustozzi and Quentin 2014). While political intervention in ANDSF goes back to President Karzai's term, it increased significantly when President Ghani took power in 2014. Ghani bypassed formal institutions by personally appointing tactical-level ANDSF officials, a practice which not only hampered the institutional development of ANDSF but also undermined state authority and public confidence (Jalali 2016).

Ethnicity is a salient source of group identity, loyalty and mobilization in ethnically divided societies. Ethnic favouritism has contributed to underdevelopment across the world (Franck and Rainer 2012), while ethnonationalist leaders have used government policies to keep non-co-ethnics from availing themselves of the benefits of public goods (La Porta et al. 1999). The role of ethnicity in power relations in post-2001 Afghanistan was not new. Abdur Rahman Khan deployed his Pashtun army against Hazaras and other non-Pashtun groups in Hazarajat and parts of the north. Nader Khan mobilized Pashtun tribes in eastern Afghanistan based on ethnicity and deployed them in Kabul and the country's north, especially north of Kabul.

During the Soviet invasion of Afghanistan, most resistance groups fighting the occupation organized themselves along ethnic lines. Most Pashtuns joined the Hizb-e Islami of Gulbuddin Hekmatyar and some other smaller parties, while Tajiks formed the backbone of Jamiat-e Islami, led by former president Burhanuddin Rabbani. Hazaras came together around Abdul Ali Mazari and the Wahdat party. Uzbeks joined para-military groups led by Abdul Rashid Dostum and later founded the National Islamic Movement or Junbish-e Milli Islami. In the early 1990s, ethnic tensions among senior members of the communist party led to a weakening and contributed to the eventual collapse of Najibullah Ahmadzai's government. In the final days of the communist regime, senior military and security officers defected and joined their respective ethnically aligned mujahidin parties. For instance, senior military officers like General Watanjar, General Rafi, Manoki Mangal and Asadullah Payam tried to infiltrate Hekmatyar's forces into Kabul and hand over the government to Hekmatyar to ensure Pashtuns' supremacy. At the same time, the non-Pashtun, particularly Tajik members of the communist party of Afghanistan, helped Ahmad Shah Masood to seize political power in April 1992. President Najibullah was stopped from leaving the country by General Dostum's troops, had to take refuge at the UN political office in Kabul, and was eventually killed by the Taliban in 1996 (Azimi 1997, 565–92).

Given the ethnic relations and context discussed above, ethnicity played an important role in political leaders' perception of a military officer's loyalty and the subsequent fate of powerholders. This was particularly true for President Ghani, whom many saw as a Pashtun ethno-nationalist leader (Ayoobi 2018). Ghani's ethno-nationalism could explain the unprecedented level of ethnic manipulation as coup-proofing witnessed in the last few years of the Republic, a critical factor in the weakening and eventual collapse of the ANDSF. As quoted in a Special Inspector General for Afghanistan Reconstruction (SIGAR) report, former minister of the interior Masoud Andarabi and former Joint Special Operations commander, General Sami Sadat, believed President

Ghani feared the military would stage a coup against him. He sidelined experienced non-Pashtun military leaders, particularly Tajiks, whom he believed were connected to the former Northern Alliance. Moreover, Ghani perceived many effective US military-trained ANDSF officers (including Pashtuns) as more loyal to the Americans than the Afghan government. As the United States–Taliban negotiation continued, those fears intensified, and he tried to further push out the non-Pashtun officers who could potentially threaten his presidency (Sopko 2022a).

A 2018 presidential decree promoted twenty-three two-star and three-star army generals: nineteen were Pashtuns, two Tajiks, one Hazara and one Uzbek, creating serious resentment among non-Pashtun military officers (Sharan 2022). In 2017, an internal memo from the president's office was leaked to the media, providing detailed guidance on replacing non-Pashtun officers with fellow ethnic Pashtuns (Reuters 2017). Another internal memo from the head of the Afghan National Civil Order Police (ANCOP) cited President Ghani's instructions to avoid the recruitment of Tajiks officers and non-commissioned officers (NCOs) into the force (BBC 2017).

In 2017, President Ghani had already amended the Inherent Law of Officers and NCOs' Affairs (*Qanoon e Umoor Zati Afsaran, Bridmalan Wa Satanmanan*) through a presidential decree, reducing the retirement age by several years. This amendment led to the early retirement of several thousand military officers. The move was presented as a reform initiative to provide opportunities for a new cadre of trained officers. However, it was used to manipulate the composition of ANDSF and replace the existing officers with those perceived to be more loyal to the regime. It also led to the retirement of most senior officers with decades of professional experience without the opportunity for the younger officers to receive experience before undertaking higher positions.[1] Non-Pashtun politicians complained that this was an ethnically and politically motivated move to cleanse ethnic minorities from the ANDSF. Muhammad Mohaqqeq, the leader of Hizb-e Wahdat-e Mardum, published a list of twenty-three ethnic Hazara generals who were forced to retire while most of their positions were filled by Pashtun officers based on loyalty (MidEast Press 1398).

It is important to note here that when the ANDSF was initially developed, it was ethnically imbalanced in favour of non-Pashtuns, particularly Tajiks, who had fought against the Taliban as members of the Northern Alliance with Allied support. The Bonn Agreement gave the three security institutions, MoD, Ministry of Interior (MoI) and NDS, to the Northern Alliance, whose members had already taken over most security positions when they entered Kabul. The new government's international partners supported the introduction of ethnic quotas in 2002 to create balanced security forces. While Pashtuns' underrepresentation was addressed in the subsequent years, the quota system continued to be misused. It was applied selectively and became a convenient tool for justifying appointments and promotions of underqualified officers who were perceived as loyal to political leadership. It was, in turn, disregarded when its employment did not serve the political interests of those in power. Ethnic quotas did not lead to the appointment and promotion of Uzbeks and Hazara officers to leadership positions as per their proportion of the general population and ANDSF soldiers. From the founding of the ANDSF post-2001 until their collapse in 2021, no ethnic Hazara or Uzbek was appointed as the minister of defence, minister of interior, chief of the defence staff or senior deputy minister for security, the highest-ranking positions at MoD and MoI. In June 2021, out of the MoI's sixty-eight highest-ranking officials, including director generals, directors and senior advisors, only one was Hazara and one was Uzbek (Figure 6.1).

When the Taliban signed the Doha Agreement with the United States, Ghani grew more fearful of being overthrown or removed from power, intensifying his efforts to coup-proof by further Pashtunizing the ANDSF. While the Taliban were expanding their control by capturing districts, Ghani replaced Masoud Andarabi, a well-respected interior minister with extensive security and intelligence experience, with Hayatullah Hayat, a Pashtun from Nangarhar province with no policing or security experience. Even though his tenure lasted for only four months, he carried out one of the most drastic ethnic restructurings of the MoI, which came to be seen by many as the ministry's 'Pashtunization'. In this short period, he replaced thirty-five out of the sixty-eight most senior officials, including director generals, directors, department heads and advisors, with Ghani loyalists. Most sacked or demoted officials were Tajiks from Kabul, Panjshir and Parwan provinces. Hazaras and Uzbeks, who had already been excluded, were further marginalized in this new reshuffle (Sharan 2022). Such ethnic and political manipulations undermined competence-based promotions, cohesion and esprit de corps within the ANDSF.

In 2018, Ghani appointed Asadullah Khalid, an ethnic Pashtun accused of severe human rights abuses, as the minister of defence (Adams 2019). He was wounded in a Taliban suicide attack in 2012 and never fully recovered, spending much of his time under treatment abroad while the Taliban continued to make gains. Less than two months before the collapse of the government, Ghani replaced Khalid with General Bismillah Muhammadi as the ANDSF began to unravel (on 19 June 2021). Mr Muhammadi, an ethnic Tajik, was the commander of anti-Taliban forces north of Kabul in the 1990s and later served as the chief of staff of ANA and MoD (Clark and Ali). Even with this new appointment, the decision-making rested within Ghani's inner circle and the ethnic Pashtun army defence chief of staff, General Wali Muhammad Ahmadzai. Meanwhile, the Ministry was not given sufficient authority to do what was

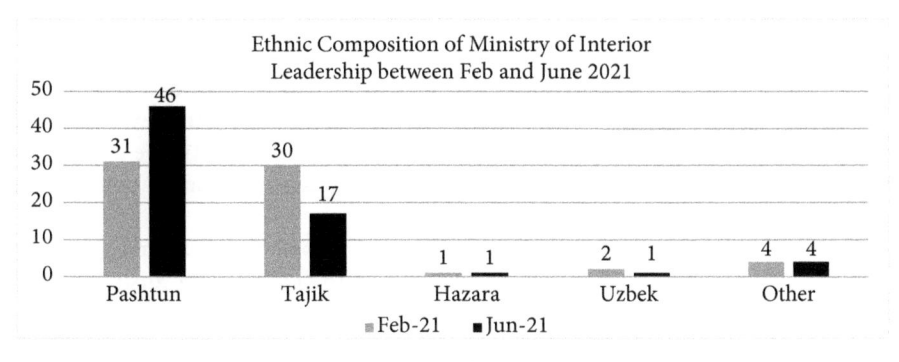

Figure 6.1 Ethnic composition of Ministry of Interior leadership between February and June 2021.

Source: Sharan (2022).

needed. After the collapse of the government, Muhammadi tweeted this indictment of Ghani and his team: 'They tied our hands behind our backs and sold the homeland' (Sier et al. 2021).

President Ghani and his close circle never acknowledged the urgency of the situation and the threat his government faced from the Taliban. Ghani was more concerned with removing the 'islands of power', a term that referred to anti-Taliban regional strongmen such as Atta Muhammad Noor and General Abdul Raziq, Balkh's governor and Kandahar's police chief, respectively, even as undermining them might well most benefit the Taliban. Even in the last months of the Republic, when the Taliban were taking Afghanistan's districts, Ghani did not provide resources to anti-Taliban figures such as Ismail Khan to fight. After the collapse of the government, Ghani and his national security advisor, Mohib, stated that they left the country to avoid a civil war, a statement many interpreted as a preference on Ghani's part for the Taliban over a victory by the country's non-Pashtun political contenders.

Excessive Centralization of Command and the Politics of Appointments

The 2004 constitution of Afghanistan created a highly centralized and powerful presidency. After President Ghani came to power in 2014, decision-making was progressively centralized further in the palace and the ONSC. Not only did the palace's inner circle choose who should be appointed or promoted, but it also intervened in the operations, command and control of forces. This bypassing of the chain of command and directly instructing field commanders dealt a devastating blow to the accountability, cohesion and effectiveness of the ANDSF (Jalali 2016).

Local commanders often complained that the ONSC intervened in their operational and tactical plans and activities. In 2021, Khan Aqa Rezayee, the chair of the Internal Security Commission of Afghanistan's parliament, said that the ANDSF ministries did not have sufficient authority and that the ONSC micromanaged their work. Some lawyers argued that ONSC was a policy development and advisory body and that its intervention in the appointment and removal of ANDSF officers was against the law (Amiri 2021). While deployed to combat missions, security forces had to wait in a defensive posture, making themselves static targets for the Taliban and suffering high casualties as a result (Sorosh 2019). Intervention by the ONSC and insufficient authority also inhibited commanders' initiative and ability to adapt plans and activities based on changing battlefield dynamics and enemy strategy.[2]

Many American military and ANDSF officials believed that frequent and unnecessary changes in leadership contributed to the collapse and disintegration of ANDSF. According to former acting defense minister Shahmahmood Miakhel, frequent leadership changes and rotations created a vacuum, undermined leadership quality and chain of command, diminished morale and reduced trust within the ANDSF while creating coordination problems across different security institutions. According to former US Secretary of Defense Lloyd Austin, 'We did not grasp the damaging effect of frequent and unexplained rotations by President Ghani of his commanders ... which degraded the confidence of the troops and their leadership' (Sopko 2022a).

The ANDSF were fighting an insurgency, a type of warfare where the support of the local people is an essential determinant in the success of either side. To use Mao Tse-tung's analogy, insurgents are like fish who can only survive in the sea of local people. At least in theory, the support of the local people for security forces makes the environment less habitable for insurgents. In Afghanistan, the frequent rotation of military leaders and commanders made it difficult to build connections and gain support within the local population. For instance, from December 2018 to August 2021, Afghanistan had four ministers of interior.[3] Meanwhile, from January 2020 to August 2021, four commanders were appointed to lead the ANA 209 Shahin Corp.[4]

To strengthen the national character of military forces and reduce the influence of regional strongmen, the ANA commanders and officers were usually appointed to other provinces and regions. In practice, this meant that in most cases, Pashtuns were appointed in non-Pashtun areas, while Tajiks, Uzbeks and Hazaras were usually appointed in Pashtun-majority provinces. Given the existence of ethnic tensions, it may have made it that much more difficult for them to earn the trust and support of the local people.[5]

In October 2020, Ghani replaced 100 existing district police chiefs with special forces commanders and intelligence officials. While these changes might have removed some corrupt or incompetent officials, they also contributed to the breakdown of command and ties to the local communities. The newly appointed police chiefs lacked experience, managerial skills and community support crucial to policing activities. Most of the police chiefs who were replaced had been closely linked to the local community for decades (Sharan 2022). The removal of these officials, who played a crucial role in defending their communities with the support of local people, created a vacuum that the Taliban exploited.

The removal of Faryab province's governor amid the Taliban offensive represented another prime example of problematic rotations. Faryab is an Uzbek-majority province, considered the gateway to the north of Afghanistan. The collapse of Faryab in 1998 allowed the Taliban to capture the country's north, including the key city of Mazar-e Sharif. In 2021, Faryab province witnessed some of the fiercest ANDSF battles against the Taliban. In June 2021, in Faryab's Dawlatabad district, the Taliban overran and executed twenty-four ANDSF commandos in what observers deemed the result of disastrous planning that led to nationwide mourning and despair for the forces meant to defend the country (Clark and Ali 2021).

A month earlier and amid some of the worst Taliban offensives, Ghani removed a dynamic ethnic Uzbek leader and governor of Faryab, Naqibullah Fayeq, who had strong local ties. The removal of Mr Fayeq, who was replaced by an ethnic Pashtun Daoud Laghmani, provoked a local backlash and led to weeks of public protests. Eventually, the new governor was inaugurated inside the ANA HQ in Faryab because protestors had blocked the governor's office and threatened to disrupt the event (Tolo News 2021).

Impacts of Coup-Proofing: Measuring the Effectiveness of ANDSF

Coup-proofing and political manipulation to create loyal subordinate security forces severely undermined the ANDSF's leadership cohesion, initiative and ability to coordinate among different units and logistics services. While political intervention, loyalty-based appointments and ethnic manipulation always existed in one form or another, these problems progressively increased when Ghani came to power. Ghani concentrated power and authority, including appointment and promotions in the Presidential Palace. During President Hamid Karzai's term, ANDSF ministers and commanding officers had much more authority in appointment and promotions. Ministries would propose a list of officers for positions, and the president usually agreed to those proposals. Sometimes vice presidents could sign the ministries' requests. While not all appointments and promotions were competency based, they provided more opportunities for performance assessment of officers and better accountability. For example, when Bismillah Muhammadi was appointed minister of interior, he reappointed all deputy ministers and many regional and provincial police chiefs who were underperforming. However, when Ghani took office and concentrated power in the Palace and ONSC, security ministers could not even appoint a provincial district police chief or head of Kabul city's police *houzas* (districts).[6]

With the progressive increase of coup-proofing, the ANDSF's effectiveness continued to decrease, and the Taliban were able to expand their area of control and influence continuously. According to the US SIGAR, while the Afghan government controlled 71 per cent of districts in 2016, it was reduced to only 56.3 per cent of districts in 2018. Meanwhile, the Taliban control of districts increased from 6 per cent in 2016 to 14.5 per cent in 2018. Moreover, the 'contested' area increased from 23 per cent to 29.2 per cent over the same period (Sopko 2018).

The ANDSF managed to defend major cities and population centres for many years, but they continued to lose ground to the Taliban. The Taliban had managed to nearly or briefly capture the provincial capitals of Kunduz, Ghazni, Farah, Uruzgan and Helmand in preceding years (Sabawoon 2019). In September 2015, the Taliban launched a major attack on Kunduz, the country's sixth-largest city and the capital of the northeastern provinces of Afghanistan. In less than twenty-four hours, a few hundred insurgents captured the city from roughly 7,000 ANDSF, who panicked and disintegrated in the face of the advancing enemy. While the Afghan army managed to regain control of Kunduz city with the US and NATO troops' support, the city's fall was a salient example of poor battlefield performance by the ANDSF (Wolf 2015).

In August 2018, the Taliban attacked Ghazni, another major city and provincial capital. While intelligence existed about an imminent Taliban attack and provincial members of parliament were warning about impending disaster, the ANDSF were caught unprepared. Most of the city was overrun by the Taliban, and the ANDSF suffered heavy casualties. More than 120 soldiers were killed and about 60 injured, while up to 250 civilians lost their lives. ANDSF elite commando troops with quick and heavy US air support pushed back the Taliban, but physical destruction and casualties were very high (Hennigan 2018). Beyond these gains, the Taliban had managed to overrun different districts across the country, killing ANDSF members and taking military equipment with them.

The ANDSF suffered mounting casualties from the Taliban, another indicator of relative ineffectiveness, due to poor leadership and planning, inability to support besieged posts, insufficient medical evacuation and simply not wearing protective gear. For instance, over 250 soldiers were killed in an attack on 209 Shahin Corps, where the Taliban entered the HQ posing as an ANA truck carrying an injured soldier (Ayaz Gul 2017). Over fifty were killed in an Army hospital in Kabul (Nordland and Sukhanyar, n.d.), and at least forty were killed in a single Taliban attack in Zabul in March 2020.

President Ghani reported that more than 45,000 ANDSF were killed between 2014 and 2018 (BBC News 2019). This is a staggering casualty figure, with thirty soldiers killed daily, and the actual numbers may have been even higher, up to fifty-seven a day in 2016 (Nordland 2018). In 2019, fatalities witnessed a further 5 per cent increase compared to 2018. According to Resolute Support (RS) Command, 60 per cent of casualties resulted from defensive operations as opposed to 40 per cent from offensive operations (Sopko 2019).

As US and NATO troops began their withdrawal, panic took hold within the ANDSF; the Taliban managed to capture thirty-three out of thirty-four provinces, including the capital, Kabul, between 6 August and 15 August 2021. On 15 August, President Ghani fled the country, and a few hours later, the Taliban captured the Presidential Palace. The last provincial capital, Panjshir, fell to the Taliban on 6 September 2021 (Sopko 2022a). This rapid unravelling reflected fundamental weakness in leadership, poor discipline, initiative, coordination and overall inefficacy resulting from years of political intervention, ethnic manipulation and subjective control by politicians.

Conclusion

The ANDSF were heavily reliant on the United States and its allies financially and technically, making the force unsustainable in the long run. The withdrawal of US and NATO troops from Afghanistan had acute negative operational and psychological impacts on them. However, the immediate collapse of ANDSF was not inevitable, and with effective leadership, command and control, and higher morale and cohesion, they would likely not have collapsed as quickly as they did.

In the medium term, the Afghan government and international partners could have worked together to gradually adjust the ANDSF budget to more sustainable levels. Meanwhile, the withdrawal of the US and NATO troops would have deprived the Taliban of the most important strategic cause to recruit and motivate their fighters. It would have also changed the strategic calculations in the region, perhaps leading to realignments in favour of the government. Given that ANDSF had overwhelming public support and foreign financial assistance, the Taliban may well have been forced to accept a negotiated settlement or remain in a less acute but protracted conflict, both distinct outcomes from a complete republican collapse.

Ultimately, Afghanistan's political leadership could have used the two-decade international security support to develop effective and capable military forces to protect the state against the Taliban and other insurgents. Instead, President Ghani resorted to coup-proofing, the appointment of loyalists, ethnic manipulation, excessive centralization of command, meddling in operational and tactical planning of military units, and frequent rotation of commanders to create loyal and subordinate military forces. Not surprisingly, this undermined the effectiveness and battlefield performance of ANDSF.

The US and NATO allies paid little attention to civil–military relations in their security assistance and reform in Afghanistan. They even inadvertently facilitated further politicization, coup-proofing and ethnic manipulation of ANDSF through their unconditional support for President Ghani and his close circle. The reasons for this neglect merit further research. But one lesson is clear: international partners that seek to enable security sector reform should include depoliticizing and harmonious civil–military relations among the primary objectives of their programming. They might undercut regime impulses for coup-proofing by linking security assistance to the depoliticization of armed forces while supporting democratic processes that engender accountability instead of picking leaders and supporting them against rival political forces. They might also provide more explicit guarantees to prevent coups.

As the collapse of the Islamic Republic of Afghanistan and Ghani's escape from the country showed, the threat to regimes from insurgencies or external enemies may well prove the truly existential threat, far more serious than concerns about a less-than-perfectly loyal army. Politicization and micromanagement of the security sector can spell the demise of these regimes, not their preservation. Political leaders can reduce the risk of a coup by limiting their intervention to oversight, policy and budget issues and delegating military affairs to professional officers. They can work towards professional and politically neutral military forces by reinforcing competency-based recruitment and promotion systems, decentralizing and strengthening the chain of command, and promoting accountability and ethnic diversity. These military forces are more likely to serve the interests of the country and even those of political leaders better than incompetent and corrupt loyalists.

Notes

1. Author's personal notes. From June 2010 to July 2018, the author served as Senior Policy Advisor to different ministers of interior and as Director General for International Cooperation with continuous involvement in policy issues and discussion with senior ANDSF officers. The author coordinated efforts to make sure retired officers were paid a promised lump sum retirement pay.
2. Author's personal notes.
3. During this period, Amrullah Saleh, Masood Andarabi, Hayatullah Hayat and Abdul Satttar Mirzakwal were appointed as ministers of interior.

4   These commanders included Major General Haibatuallah Alizai, Major General Mustafa Wardak, Major General Khanullah Shoja and Major General Zabiullah Mahmand.
5   Author's personal notes.
6   Author's personal notes.

References

Adams, B. (2019), 'New Afghan Defense Minister Should Face Investigation, Sanctions'. Human Rights Watch, 12 January 2019. Available at: https://www.hrw.org/news/2019/01/12/new-afghan-defense-minister-should-face-investigation-sanctions.

Amiri, S. (2021), 'Naqshe Shorai Amniat dar Umoor Nehand Hai Amniati'. *Tolo News Farsi*, 26 July 2021. Available at: https://tolonews.com/fa/afghanistan-173786.

Andisha, N. A. (2022), 'The Collapse of State in Afghanistan: A Repeat of History?' *Journal of Asian Security and International Affairs*, 9(3): 369–82.

Ayaz Gul. (2017), 'Attack on Afghan Army Base Reportedly Killed Over 250 Soldiers.' *VOA News*, 25 April. Available at: https://www.voanews.com/east-asia-pacific/attack-afghan-army-base-reportedly-killed-over-250-soldiers.

Ayoobi, E. K. (2018), 'Ashraf Ghani: "Philosopher King" or Ethnonationalist?' *Al Jazeera*, 5 February 2018. Available at: https://www.aljazeera.com/opinions/2018/2/5/ashraf-ghani-philosopher-king-or-ethnonationalist (Accessed: 18 May 2023).

Azimi, M. N. (1997), *Urdo wa Siyasat Dar Seh Daha e Akhir Afghanistan (Army and Politics in the Last Three Decades in Afghanistan)*. Saba Publishers. Available at: https://rahparcham1.org/wp-content/uploads/2019/11/اردو-و-سیاست-ـ-نبی-عظیمی.pdf.

Bausch, A. W. (2018), 'Coup-Proofing and Military Inefficiencies: An Experiment'. *International Interactions*, 44(1): 1–32. Available at: https://doi.org/10.1080/03050629.2017.1289938.

Brooks, R. A. and Stanley, E. A. (2007), *Creating Military Power: The Sources of Military Effectiveness*. Palo Alto, CA: Stanford University Press. Available at: http://ebookcentral.proquest.com/lib/oculcarleton-ebooks/detail.action?docID=3037552.

Clark, K. and Ali, O. (2021), 'A Quarter of Afghanistan's Districts Fall to the Taleban amid Calls for a 'Second Resistance'. Afghanistan Analysts Network, 2 July 2021. Available at: https://www.afghanistan-analysts.org/en/reports/war-and-peace/a-quarter-of-afghanistans-districts-fall-to-the-taleban-amid-calls-for-a-second-resistance/.

De Bruin, E. (2018), 'Preventing Coups d'état: How Counterbalancing Works'. *Journal of Conflict Resolution*, 62(7): 1433–58. Available at: https://doi.org/10.1177/0022002717692652.

Decalo, S. (1989), 'Modalities of Civil-Military Stability in Africa'. *The Journal of Modern African Studies*, 27(4): 547–78.

Emizet, K. N. (2000), 'Explaining the Rise and Fall of Military Regimes: Civil-Military Relations in the Congo'. *Armed Forces & Society*, 26(2): 203–27.

Feaver, P. D. (1999), 'Civil Military Relations'. *Annual Review of Political Science*, 2(1): 211–41. Available at: https://doi.org/10.1146/annurev.polisci.2.1.211.

Franck, R. and Rainer, I. (2012), 'Does the Leader's Ethnicity Matter? Ethnic Favoritism, Education, and Health in Sub-Saharan Africa'. *American Political Science Review*, 106(2): 294–325.

Giustozzi, A. with Quentin, P. (2014). 'The Afghan National Army: Sustainability Challenges beyond Financial Aspects'. Kabul: Afghanistan Research and Evaluation Unit (AREU).

Haque, T. A. (2019), *Afghanistan: Public Expenditure Update*. 139732. Washington, DC: World Bank Group. Available at: http://documents.worldbank.org/curated/en/696491564082281122/Afghanistan-Public-Expenditure-Update.

Hennigan, W. J. (2018), 'Exclusive: Inside the U.S. Fight to Save Ghazni from the Taliban.' *TIME*, 23 August. Available at: https://time.com/longform/ghazni-fight-taliban/.

Huntington, S. P. (1957), *The Soldier and the State: The Theory and Politics of Civil-Military Relations*. Cambridge: Harvard University Press.

Jalali, A. (2002), 'Rebuilding Afghanistan's National Army'. *Parameters: U.S. Army War College Quarterly* 32(3): 72–86.

Jalali, A. A. (2016), *Afghanistan National Defense and Security Forces*. Washington DC, UNITED STATES: United States Institute of Peace. Available at: https://www.usip.org/sites/default/files/PW115-Afghanistan-National-Defense-and-Security-Forces-Mission-Challenges-and-Sustainability.pdf.

Kiyani, G. (2022), 'Coup-Proofing and Political Violence: The Case of Iraq', *Middle Eastern Studies*, 58(1): 167–83. Available at: https://doi.org/10.1080/00263206.2021.1939690.

La Porta, R., F Lopez-de-Silanes, F., Shleifer, A. and Vishny, R. (1999), 'The Quality of Government'. *The Journal of Law, Economics, and Organization*, 15(1): 222–79.

Murtazashvili, J. B. (2022), 'The Collapse of Afghanistan'. *Journal of Democracy*, 33(1): 40–54.

NATO (2012), 'Chicago Summit Declaration on Afghanistan'. NATO. Available at: https://www.nato.int/cps/en/natolive/official_texts_87595.htm.

Nordland, R. (2018), 'The Death Toll for Afghan Forces Is Secret. Here's Why.' *The New York Times*, 21. Available at: https://www.nytimes.com/2018/09/21/world/asia/afghanistan-security-casualties-taliban.html#:~:text=Here's%20Why.,-Share%20full%20article&text=PUL%2DI%2DKUMRI%2C%20Afghanistan,keep%20battlefield%20death%20tolls%20secret.

Pilster, U. and Böhmelt, T. (2011), 'Coup-Proofing and Military Effectiveness in Interstate Wars, 1967–99'. *Conflict Management and Peace Science*, 28(4): 331–50. Available at: https://doi.org/10.1177/0738894211413062.

Pilster, U. and Böhmelt, T. (2012), 'Do Democracies Engage Less in Coup Proofing? On the Relationship between Regime Type and Civil–Military Relations 1'. *Foreign Policy Analysis*, 8(4): 355–72. Available at: https://doi.org/10.1111/j.1743-8594.2011.00160.x.

Reuters Staff (2017), 'Leaked Memo Fuels Accusations of Ethnic Bias in Afghan Government'. *Reuters*, 21 September 2017. Available at: https://www.reuters.com/article/afghanistan-politics-idINKCN1BW147.

Rubin, B. R. (2006), 'Peace Building and State Building in Afghanistan: Constructing Sovereignty for Whose Security?' *Third World Quarterly*, 27(1): 175–85.

Sabawoon, A. M. (2019), 'Government Rule Confined to District and Provincial Centres: Zabul's Capital under Threat.' *Afghanistan Analysts Network* [Preprint]. Available at: https://www.afghanistan-analysts.org/en/reports/war-and-peace/government-rule-confined-to-district-and-provincial-centres-zabuls-capital-under-threat/.

Schroden, J. (2021a), 'Afghanistan's Security Forces versus the Taliban: A Net Assessment'. *CTC Sentinel*, 14: 1.

Schroden, J. (2021b), 'Lessons from the Collapse of Afghanistan's Security Forces'. *CTC Sentinel*, 14(8): 1–61.

Sharan, T. (2022), 'What Went Wrong: The 2021 Collapse of Afghan National Security Forces'. Afghanistan Analysts Network, 15 December 2022. Available at: https://www.afghanistan-analysts.org/en/reports/war-and-peace/what-went-wrong-the-2021-collapse-of-afghan-national-security-forces/.

Sier, A. (2021), 'Taliban Sweep into Afghan Capital after Government Collapses'. *Associated Press*, 15 August 2021. Available at: https://apnews.com/article/afghanistan-taliban-kabul-bagram-e1ed33fe0c665ee67ba132c51b8e32a5.

Sopko, J. F. (2022a), 'Collapse of the Afghan National Defense and Security Forces: An Assessment of the Factors That Led to Its Demise'. Available at: https://www.sigar.mil/pdf/evaluations/SIGAR-22-22-IP.pdf.

Sopko, J. F. (2022b), 'Why the Afghan Government Collapsed'. Available at: https://www.sigar.mil/pdf/evaluations/SIGAR-23-05-IP.pdf.

Sopko, J. F. (2018), 'SIGAR Special Inspector General for Afghanistan Reconstruction, April 2018 Quarterly Report'. Special Inspector General for Afghanistan Reconstruction Arlington U.S. Available at: https://www.sigar.mil/pdf/quarterlyreports/2018-04-30qr.pdf.

Sopko, J. F. (2019), 'SIGAR Quarterly Report to the United States Congress'. SIGAR. Available at: https://www.sigar.mil/pdf/quarterlyreports/2019-10-30qr.pdf.

Sopko, J. F. (2021), 'What We Need to Learn: Lessons from Twenty Years of Afghanistan Reconstruction', 1 August 2021. SIGAR. Available at: https://www.sigar.mil/pdf/lessonslearned/SIGAR-21-46-LL.pdf.

Sorosh, E. (2019), 'Du Rewayat az Talafat Niro Hai Amniaty Afghan: Sigar Drust Migoyad Ya Wazarat Defa?' *Etila'at Roz*, 3 November 2019. Available at: https://www.etilaatroz.com/86890/two-narratives-of-afghan-security-forces-deaths-sigar-true-or-department-of-defense/.

Tolo News (2021), 'Daoud Laghmani Introduced as New Governor of Faryab at Army Base', *Tolo News*, 17 May 2021. Available at: https://tolonews.com/index.php/afghanistan-172214.

Wolf, S. (2015), 'The Battle Over Kunduz and Its Implications.' *South Asia Democratic Forum* [Preprint]. Available at: https://www.sadf.eu/the-battle-over-kunduz-and-its-implications/.

Part Two

Intervention and Its Legacies

7

Ghost Schools: Imperial Debris and the Erasure of Educated Women

Marya Hannun

A barren classroom, a shuttered window, a dusty and deserted tract of land – images of the so-called 'ghost schools' are one of the many forms of imperial debris that linger after the last US troops left Kabul in August 2021. 'Ghost schools' is a term used to describe the hundreds of schools that were supposed to have been constructed with American military and development funding during the twenty-year intervention in Afghanistan. In some cases, these schools were never built or never used; in others, they were misused or vastly underused. Despite their name, which hints at the absent or intangible, they are physical embodiments of an illusion underpinning the US occupation of and NATO intervention in Afghanistan. And they signify the discursive role played by the project of educating Afghan 'women and girls' in the construction of this illusion.

From the war's inception, postcolonial feminist critics pointed to the way women's rights were instrumentalized in support of the occupying forces. The most consequential of these critics is Lila Abu-Lughod, who in 2002 published her groundbreaking essay, 'Do Muslim Women Really Need Saving?' It would not be an exaggeration to say this essay informed how a generation of scholars contemplating gender in the Middle East engaged with Afghanistan (while an imperfect metric, I was surprised to find the essay is one of the most-cited articles mentioning Afghanistan on Google Scholar, far outperforming the work of political scientists, historians and anthropologists whose research explicitly focuses on the country).

Abu-Lughod was the first to point out how the rights denied to Afghan women and girls under the Taliban of the 1990s, including access to education, became a public justification for the shadowy and ill-conceived 'war on terror' (2002: 783). As Shenila Khoja-Moolji has observed, education formed one layer in the 'sedimented knowledges' that have coalesced around Muslim women in recent decades and as a result of this so-called war on terror (2018: 5). Both the barring of Muslim girls from schooling and the advocacy around teaching them have been at the centre of a reductionist logic applied to the geographies that make up the war on terror, including Afghanistan and Pakistan. This discourse positioned the lack of (primarily) girls' education as the cause for violence and the education of girls as a key antidote.

In so doing, it elided other material realities for women as well as the longer histories and context for violence (against them and others). Moreover, the term 'ghost school' most frequently appeared in reports on Afghanistan and Pakistan. A product of the significant funding poured into education in these areas by the US government and western aid organizations following 2001, it also reinforced the imaginary of 'Af-Pak' as a homogeneous region, forged by unique violence and requiring distinctive, targeted and gendered interventions (Hanifi 2022).

In *Imagining Afghanistan: The History and Politics of Imperial Knowledge*, Nivi Manchanda critiques the 'cruel optimism' behind the leveraging of pedagogy (and pity) to buttress American military involvement in Afghanistan. She notes the way it is productive of racialized difference: to position Afghan women as in need of saving by intervention also places Afghan society's problems on the shoulders of Afghan women (2020: 180). As Manchanda writes, 'In the discourse of "saving" Afghan women, we have a promise that is unlikely to be fulfilled, indeed that cannot be fulfilled – stemming from the fundamentally different nature of the Other' (2020: 181). If, as Manchanda argues, the intervention's goals around women's literacy were 'chimerical at best', the ghost schools capture the material ways in which this dream was perpetually deferred.

When it comes to western engagement with Afghanistan, on the other side of the ghost school fantasy were the thousands of girls who received some form of education in the country in the first two decades of the twenty-first century and did so within the context of war and intervention. If the ghost schools make visible certain absences and contradictions, the extreme politicization of women's education makes ghosts of the women for whom education in the context of intervention, occupation and war was a messy reality (Musawi Natanzi 2023). When US troops withdrew in August 2021, these women were held up by proponents of the war as the other side of the coin, a symbol that the US intervention was perhaps justified and a corresponding belief that, if the new Taliban would allow 'women and girls' to attend school, this group might somehow gain legitimacy.

Where do educated women, themselves, fit into this story? I think of the women activists who were forced by the framework of the withdrawal agreement to concede to the loss of certain rights as the price to be paid for the end of the 'forever war'. Is there room for their voices? I think of the open letter representing more than one thousand Afghan women, attempting to stave off just such a Faustian bargain. Published in *TOLOnews* in 2020 and available in English, it was avowedly anti-war and supportive of the ongoing peace talks insofar as they had the potential to put an end to ceaseless violence. It took up the Taliban's public dismissal of 'women's rights' and education as 'western', asserting instead that the 'rights that [Afghan women] espouse and work towards are fundamental human rights enshrined in the holy religion of Islam and other faiths practiced in Afghanistan' (*TOLOnews* 2020). Unlike the letters co-signed by North American feminists, Margaret Atwood and Gloria Steinem, this letter was not reprinted in major American or British news outlets (*The Guardian* 2019).

As a historian researching Afghanistan's first state school for girls, established precisely one century before the withdrawal, in 1921, I am haunted by such erasures. This ghosting reverberates deep into the historical record of Afghanistan, in which so little work has been done in the realm of Afghan women's history, despite the centrality of both gender and women to the processes of state formation (Kandiyoti 2005). Indeed, paralleling the first decades of the twenty-first century, the period of Amanullah Khan's rule in Afghanistan (1919–29) was marked by a top-down project of reforms, a number of which targeted women's social status and education. Afghanistan's first constitution, engineered by Amanullah Khan and a team of advisors and promulgated in 1923, established laws governing polygamy and requiring a minimum marriage age. The first hospital and newspapers for women were opened in this period, as was the Society for the Protection of Women. The constitution also had a provision for universal education, and the first schools for girls opened in Kabul in 1921.

At that time women's education was a source of tremendous contention between predominantly male elites. Amanullah Khan and the intelligentsia in Kabul with ties to the state found themselves in heated debates with those who stood in opposition to public schooling for women outside of the home. It is this contention that has largely occupied historians. For the state and its supporters, educating women was a way to assert national progress and, equally, a means of projecting political authority. For the opposition, questions of women's roles outside of the home represented both a threat to traditional authority and a convenient avenue by which to question the legitimacy of the state and its encroachment into social life. This form of contestation mapped onto other arenas, including land reforms, marriage reforms and taxation (Caron 2009: 38–9).

Amid these debates, women's voices and actions, the complexity around women's organizing and the diversity amongst women were all too often, if not entirely, collapsed or overlooked. The tendency to flatten a plurality of perspectives took hold in two directions, both of which were mirrored in accounts of Afghan women after 2001: the women of that time period were either dismissed as exceptional elites (and the project of schooling dismissed as ephemeral) or they were held up as representing all Afghan women (thereby enabling a reading of the Amanullah Khan years as a golden age for women's rights and education). In truth, that first generation of women educated in Kabul found themselves in messy and complex situations. As is often the case, they benefitted from their proximity to power to carve out space for their participation. From that proximity to power, both nationally and transregionally, they formed Afghanistan's first women's movement in the early twentieth century (Hannun 2020).

Deeper probing reveals that, while they were connected to the state, these women were not merely acting on its behalf. Thanks, in large part, to oral histories conducted in the 1960s and 1970s by historian May Schinasi, we have records of those who attended the Masturat School and what their experiences of learning were like. These were women from families connected to the state through service or kinship: daughters of trade agents, ministers and the royal family itself. While their education took place in a school paid for by the state's coffers and with textbooks printed by the Ministry of Education, they were gaining access to a set of skills that stretched far beyond the state building project of the Amanullah Khan years. Through these textbooks, for example, women were learning how to read, write and debate. They were gaining knowledge of their rights within the existing Islamic legal frameworks and learning about women's contributions to political and social history ('Abd al-Haqq 1923).

Moreover, for all of the ruptures that came with the overthrow of Amanullah Khan, a tracing of these women's lives after the 1920s reveals a number of continuities. Many of them employed their education to play important roles in women's education across Afghanistan in the subsequent decades. According to available oral histories, at least one of the teachers at Masturat continued to teach in secret after the school was shuttered. Another helped to establish a school for midwives in the subsequent decade. Yet another continued to pursue a career in education even after the girls' school closed. In the 1950s, she returned to her ancestral province of Faryab, where she founded the first school for girls in the province, *Maktab-i Niswan-i Sitar*. Yet another student at Masturat helped to found the Women's Welfare Association in 1946 and worked in the arena of adult women's literacy. Any dismissal of their participation as ephemeral or instrumental negates the ways in which women's education, much like Afsaneh Najmabadi's observation of the contemporaneous Iranian context, could be at once 'disciplinary and emancipatory' (1998: 107).

I have found myself thinking about these women a great deal since the US withdrawal from Afghanistan. Like the women educated in Afghanistan in the first decades of the twenty-first century, they are ghosts of a sort, haunting the historical record but just out of full view. They too benefitted from a central state, which, despite its nominal independence, was marked by a kind of crypto-coloniality. This term, borrowed from anthropologist Michael Herzfeld, describes how countries that bordered empire were compelled to buy their independence at the cost of dependence on foreign capital and the institution of suitable socio-political reforms (Hanifi and Hanifi 2021). Also like the women educated in Afghanistan in the first decades of the twenty-first century, my historical interlocutors did not represent all Afghan women. Their education worked to reproduce class distinctions and hierarchies between women in ways that have not been sufficiently explored in either time period. These women, too, were suddenly and violently denied access to public schooling with regime change.

Most of all, like the women educated in the first decades of the twenty-first century, their individual narratives and the broader movements they were part of do not fit neatly into the masculinist frames for apprehending this history. The complexity of their voices and experiences has been eclipsed by the wider constellations of politics and power that reflect patriarchal authority, whether it be of the crypto-colonial state, international coalition forces, or the Taliban government that has continued to weaponize and instrumentalize women's education since its return.

References

'Abd al-Haqq (1923), *Kitab-i Panjum-i Diniyat, Makhsus-i Makatab-i Niswan*. Kabul: Matba' Vizarat-i Jalilah-i Ma'arif.

Abu-Lughod, L. (2002), 'Do Muslim Women Really Need Saving? Anthropological Reflections on Cultural Relativism and Its Others'. *American Anthropologist*, 104(3): 783–90.

Caron, J. (2009), 'Cultural Histories of Pashtun Nationalism, Public Participation, and Social Inequality in Monarchic Afghanistan, 1905–1960'. Ph.D. thesis, University of Pennsylvania.

The Guardian (2019), 'Afghan Women's Voices Must Be Heard in US-Taliban Peace Talks', 26 February. Available at: https://www.theguardian.com/world/2019/feb/26/afghan-womens-voices-must-be-heard-in-us-taliban-peace-talks (Accessed: 1 June 2023).

Hanifi, S. M. (2022), 'Imperial Cartography and National Mapping in Afghanistan'. *International Journal of Middle Eastern Studies*, 54(2): 340–6.

Hanifi, J. and Hanifi, S. M. (2021), 'Crypto-Colonial Independence Rituals in Afghanistan'. *Afghanistan*, 4(1): 70–8.

Hannun, M. (2020), 'From Kabul to Cairo and Back Again: The Afghan Women's Movement and Early 20th Century Transregional Transformations'. *Genre et Histoire*, 25 (Spring 2020). https://journals.openedition.org/genrehistoire/5017#quotation.

Kandiyoti, D. (2005), *The Politics of Gender and Reconstruction in Afghanistan*. Geneva: UN Research Institute for Social Development.

Khoja-Moolji, S. (2018), *Forging the Ideal Educated Girl: The Production of Desirable Subjects in Muslim South Asia*. Oakland, CA: University of California Press.

Manchanda, N. (2020), *Imagining Afghanistan: The History and Politics of Imperial Knowledge*. Cambridge, UK: Cambridge University Press.

Musawi Natanzi, P. (2023), 'Gender Studies in Afghanistan or Jender Bazi: The Neoliberal University, Knowledge Production and Labour under Military Occupation'. TRAFO Blog For Transregional Research. Available at: https://trafo.hypotheses.org/47763 (Accessed: 1 August 2023).

Najmabadi, A. (1998), 'Crafting an Educated Housewife in Iran', in Abu-Lughod, L. (ed.), *Remaking Women: Feminism and Modernity in the Middle East*. Princeton, NJ: Princeton University Press.

Schinasi, M. (1995), 'Femmes Afghanes. Instruction et Activités Publiques Pendant Le Règne Amaniya (1919–1929)'. *Annali Dell'Istituto Universitario Orientale Di Napoli*, 55(4): 446–64.

TOLO News (2020), 'Open Letter by Afghan Women to the Taliban', 13 August. Available at: https://tolonews.com/opinion/open-letter-afghan-women-taliban-0 (Accessed: 1 August 2023).

8

Peace Building and State Building in Afghanistan: Constructing Sovereignty for Whose Security?

Barnett R. Rubin
Third World Quarterly, 27(1), 'From Nation-Building to State Building'
(2006), 175–85. Reprinted with permission.

In the aftermath of civil wars, international actors often worry about the incoherence, tribalism and division of war-torn nation-states like Afghanistan. However, the problems encountered in the Afghanistan recovery and reconstruction effort illustrate that the divisions, rivalries and fragmentation of authority of the 'international community' have constituted just as big an obstacle to what the UN now calls 'peace building'. Sustainable stability and peace, to say nothing of democracy, require international actors to delegate some sovereign functions to a multilateral entity that can reinforce rather than undermine the institutions responsible for the reconstruction of the nation-state. The history and contemporary situation in Afghanistan make clear that there is an important need for the peace building mechanisms proposed by the UN secretary-general's High-level Panel. This would involve a unified international decision-making body that would act as a counterpart to the recipient national government and potentially bring order to the anarchy that invariably flows from the multiple agendas, doctrines and aid budgets of the array of external actors involved in 'peace building' in Afghanistan and elsewhere.

Afghanistan provided the United Nations with its first chance to implement the recommendation of the Brahimi Report for 'integrated missions', which would exercise unified control over the political, assistance and peacekeeping functions of the UN.[1] This would take place under a mission headed by Lakhdar Brahimi himself, who returned to the UN as the Special Representative of the Secretary-General (SRSG) for Afghanistan. During and in the aftermath of civil wars, international actors often fret about the incoherence, tribalism and division of war-torn countries like Afghanistan. The Brahimi Report, however, recognizes that the divisions, rivalries and fragmentation of authority of the UN system and the rest of the 'international community' have constituted just as big an obstacle to what the UN calls 'peace building'.

The December 2004 report of the UN secretary-general's High-level Panel (HLP) on Threats, Challenges, and Change took the proposal for integrated missions even further by proposing the establishment of an inter-governmental Peace Building Commission to oversee UN operations to rebuild states after armed conflict. This Commission would exercise budgetary authority over a Peace Building Fund, which would be kept fully replenished in advance of operations and would contain unearmarked contributions. A Peace Building Support Office with the UN Secretariat would support the Commission.[2] The creation of a unified, multilateral decision-making body as a counterpart to the national government receiving the aid aims to bring order into the anarchy often created by multiple agendas, doctrines and aid budgets. Examining the attempts to rebuild a state in Afghanistan illustrates the deficiencies of the current international institutions that the HLP wished to address.

While political sensitivities prevented the HLP from using the term 'state building', such operations have the paradoxical mission of helping others build sovereign states. They constitute the contemporary version of a long-standing security task: the stabilization of the periphery by great powers, which must now be carried out in a globe governed by a regime of universal juridical sovereignty of the nation-state. Even the administration of US President George W. Bush, which has adopted a doctrine of preventive war on the basis of unilateral judgement that governments might threaten US security, has been constrained to act within the same regime. Its inability to motivate Iraqis or international partners to collaborate with an occupation regime forced the administration to call on the UN to assist in the initially unwanted transfer of sovereignty to Iraqis.

This recourse to the UN, despite political differences between proponents of multilateral peace building and prosecutors of unilateral preventive war, shows that these projects respond to a common security environment. The central fact of the environment in the past half-century has been the replacement of global juridical imperialism by global juridical national sovereignty. The UN incorporates this organizing principle into its Charter. Hence, when the collapse of public security in Afghanistan threatened its neighbours, Pakistan responded through covert actions to sustain the Taliban as a client regime, rather than by splitting the weakened country's territories with its neighbours. When the Taliban's grant of refuge to Al Qaeda proved to be a threat to the United States, Washington responded not simply by overthrowing the government but by calling on the UN to oversee a political transition and a programme of 'reconstruction'. Despite the intentions of the Bush administration, that programme moved beyond humanitarian action to a comprehensive, if at times distorted and poorly coordinated programme of state building, in which Washington, NATO and reluctant European states have all participated.

From Imperialism to Peace Building: Doctrines in Historical Context

The use by various states and organizations of sui generis terms such as 'peace building', 'post-conflict reconstruction', 'nation building' or 'stabilization' displaces these operations from their historical context. The United States' pursuit of security from both terrorism and challenges to its strategic dominance has different implications from the pursuit of human security through processes of global governance; the two converge to some extent over the intervention in Afghanistan and diverge over the invasion of Iraq. These doctrines, however, constitute different responses to a common problem: maintaining order and security, however and for whomever defined, in an increasingly integrated global system juridically and politically organized around universal state sovereignty.

For centuries stronger powers have intervened along their peripheries to establish politically acceptable forms of order. Before the arrival of European imperialism in Asia, the territory of today's Afghanistan constituted a shifting frontier among empires based in the neighbouring regions. The arrival of British and Russian Empires led to the demarcation of the country as a buffer state between these empires, and British aid enabled the Afghan Amir to 'stabilize' the country with a repressive state that lacked full external sovereignty. The 1905 Anglo-Russian treaty on Afghanistan, Persia and Tibet, which established the status of Afghanistan, illustrates the fact that, during this period, the European states that constituted the core of the imperial state system tried to regulate their competition through a stable division of colonial rule. Great powers cooperated to impose a common juridical framework over the entire globe, but one that institutionalized unequal political and legal status for different territories and peoples.

Afghanistan, which gained full independence in 1919, eventually joined the League of Nations. Other states followed it out from under imperial domination as the contemporary global framework for security developed with the foundation of the UN system after the Second World War. The UN oversaw the extension of decolonization, extending the international regime of national sovereignty enshrined in its Charter to the entire globe, a process that continued through the UN-supervised transition to independence of Timor Leste.

During the Cold War the struggle over building postcolonial states largely took the form of competing foreign aid projects among the alliance systems led by the United States and Soviet Russia. Afghanistan received aid from both camps. The end of United States–Soviet *de facto* cooperation tore the country apart. After the end of the Cold War regional competition continued the process of state destruction. The same global change freed the UN Security Council to undertake multilateral state building efforts, especially in the aftermath of conflict, but the failure to undertake any such effort in Afghanistan showed that, while the end of zero-sum strategic competition made cooperation possible, it also lowered the stakes for major powers, who were content to allow some problems to fester.

The attacks of 11 September 2001 showed that the United States could now be attacked from even the weakest state and hence reignited US nationalists' strategic interest in the periphery. The regime of universal sovereignty, however, requires more powerful states and international organizations to work through the institutions of nation-states. Post-war operations attempt to *transform* states, rather than *absorbing* them into other, more powerful, units.[3]

Peace Building and Stabilization as State Building

At the most schematic analysis, state formation consists of the interdependent mobilization by a sovereign of three types of resources: coercion, capital and legitimacy.[4] The sovereign wields coercion, in the form of what we hopefully call security institutions, to exercise a monopoly of (legitimate) force over a territory. He needs the accumulation of capital to produce income that can be extracted as revenues to fund state functions and services. Symbolic and cultural resources consecrate the use of force and public revenues as legitimate and link them into a meaningful whole to induce people to comply voluntarily as citizens. The state claims to exercise its power as the delegate of an imagined community – the nation.

These three types of resources have been mobilized in different combinations and contexts to build, destroy or undermine states. When the British transformed Afghanistan into a buffer state, they provided weapons and money to the ruler, Abdur Rahman Khan, but they did not impose any standards of legitimacy. They simply insisted, as provided in the Treaty of Gandamak (1879), that the Amir not extend his administration beyond the Durand Line. Thus the Amir received power resources, which he used to wage internal war, deport populations, massacre, execute and torture. Rudyard Kipling wrote verses about these practices, but as long as they served to maintain a stable border for the British Empire, no one attempted to reform them.

The Amir foreshadowed a familiar pattern of the postcolonial state. Epigrammatically, during the formation of national states in Europe, rulers struggled and negotiated with subjects who became citizens to extract resources to wage war against external threats. In the postcolonial world rulers struggled and negotiated with external powers to gain aid or capital to protect themselves from domestic threats. Citizens often became disenfranchised, as rulers looked to foreign patrons rather than citizens for power resources. External powers were motivated not by concern for apolitical 'stability', but by the strategic competition of the Cold War and now the global 'war on terror' as well as by economic interests.

This process of extroverted state formation underlies many changes in the international system, including the shift from interstate to intrastate warfare and the crises of legitimacy and capacity of postcolonial states, leading to the violent contestation and collapse of many. Afghanistan's rulers built a state with coordinated flows of foreign aid; the state exploded in civil war when the aid flows instead subsidized competing military forces; and the state collapsed when the aid flows ended. The post-2001 effort constitutes a new round of internationalized state building, with the UN formally recognized as the coordinator of international assistance.

Participants in peace building or stabilization operations attempt to use foreign resources of the same types to build acceptable states in areas that pose a perceived threat to powerful actors. Afghanistan became a point of consensus among international actors in part because it united characteristics of a 'rogue state', of concern to the United States, and a 'failed state', of concern to globalist humanitarians. The partial contradiction between the US military mission of hunting down the Taliban and Al Qaeda, even in collaboration with Afghan warlords, and the mission of the UN-authorized International Security Assistance Force (ISAF), to secure the nascent administration from warlord pressure, constitutes a concrete example of what Ghassan Salame calls the 'dual legitimacy' problem of global state formation.[5]

Internationalized State Building

The doctrines of the states and organizations engaged in this effort often contradict the goal of state building. Building a nation-state means creating a sovereign centre of political accountability, which is not necessarily the same as building an ally in the war on terror. Multilateral operations often consist of juxtaposing existing capacities – humanitarian aid, war fighting, peacekeeping, economic guidance and assistance, civil society support, democracy assistance – without a coherent strategy. A strategic decision-maker would require command and budgetary authority over the entire operation, which was the rationale for the Brahimi Report's proposal for 'integrated missions', but the Afghan operation, for instance, despite an attempt at such integration and being founded by Brahimi himself, continued to suffer from lack of coherence. In 2002 the UN issued a Consolidated Appeal for Afghanistan with no reference to the reconstruction strategy or the national budget. At the same time, the United States' own reconstruction plans were being formulated in Washington without international consultation.

Such operations make use of the same types of resources as other processes of state building: coercion, capital and legitimacy. The core tasks of security provision are peacekeeping or other forms of international transitional security provision. In Afghanistan these include operations with different, though now converging, goals by the Coalition and ISAF; dismantling irregular militias that compete with the state's monopoly of coercion (demobilization, disarmament and reintegration, or DDR); and building new security forces, called Security Sector Reform (SSR), which includes building the Afghan National Army (ANA) and Afghan National Police (ANP).

As in all such operations economic resources for public services in Afghanistan have almost entirely come from international assistance, rather than from domestic capital accumulation and resource mobilization. Donors have largely delivered assistance through their own implementing agencies and national NGOs. According to the minister of finance of Afghanistan, in 2004–5, out of a total of $4.9 billion of public expenditure, only $1.4 billion was channelled through the government budget.[6] Aid outside the budgetary control of the national government may block growth of state fiscal capacity, capital accumulation and economic management, undermining the state's accountability to citizens.

The legitimacy of the operation derived initially from a combination of international legislation (Security Council resolutions supporting the coalition military action) and the political agreement reached under UN chairmanship at Bonn. The Bonn Agreement outlines a process to increase the legitimacy of the interim administration to that of a fully elected constitutional government through internationally supported political processes. The UN, troop providers and donors, however, have tried to constrain these processes so as not to contradict international standards of human rights and key foreign interests.

Coercion and Security

In the period before the rise of the Taliban the Afghan army disintegrated, and Afghanistan had the pattern of fragmented control of armed forces characteristic of 'failed states'. The Taliban largely recentralized control over coercion, but the US intervention destroyed their forces, while rearming the same commanders and warlords who had previously dominated the country. The US-led coalition and ISAF, however, enjoyed an overwhelming preponderance of military force, which made a state building project possible.

The Bonn Agreement partly signified that Afghanistan would undergo 'warlord democratization', in which armed groups would demobilize in order to resolve a security dilemma, deciding to arbitrate their differences via elections rather than violence. Such a process requires confidence building measures and transparency enforced by peacekeepers.[7] This constituted only part of the mission of the coalition and ISAF, however. While the Northern Alliance factions consented to the power sharing in the Bonn Agreement, its precise terms were obtained under pressure and required subsequent enforcement by the coalition and ISAF, generally through coercive diplomacy rather than direct exercise of force. The deposed groups (Al Qaeda and Taliban) were not parties to the Bonn Agreement, and successful state building required eliminating or co-opting them, the main job of the coalition.

State building operations following internal armed conflict must include measures for DDR of combatants and for the changes in government security agencies – SSR – but the Bonn Agreement, concluded in great haste under pressure from the US military campaign, referred to these in only the most general terms. The subsequent negotiations over these programmes were key to the nature of the new political order. The mujahidin groups demanded that the new security forces should consist primarily of their own militias with new weapons and training. Accepting this model would have deprived political reforms of their meaning by assuring that the armed forces remained under the personal control of faction leaders. Only the leverage provided by the coalition and ISAF enabled the UN to negotiate a different outcome. The unwillingness of either the United States or Europeans to exert much military pressure against the warlords and faction leaders, however, meant that their agreement to the building of depoliticized armed forces had to be obtained largely through incentives, mainly through the offer of political incorporation. Hence co-optation rather than marginalization had to be the main strategy towards the former warlords.

Training and reforming security agencies are equally political. The intense, quasi-religious esprit de corps of military organizations derives from the human need to believe intensely in something for which one risks one's life. Forming effective armies and police requires formation of a national authority that can command such loyalty, not just technical training. The formation of an officer corps particularly depends on forming its coherence and spirit in service to a mission. High salaries bring recruits but do not inspire them to sacrifice. Neither the ANA nor the ANP was able to provide most of the security necessary for the two *Loya Jirgas* (Grand Councils) or the October 2004 presidential elections. It is no wonder that in Afghanistan as elsewhere the first post-war elections required international security forces.

A longer-term problem is that the Afghan state may not be able to sustain its security forces. Given current salary levels and future staffing plans, maintaining the ANA will eventually impose a recurrent cost estimated at about $1 billion per year on the Afghan government. In order for Afghanistan to cover the cost of the ANA with 4 per cent of legal GDP, near the upper limit of the global range of defence spending, it would have to more than quintuple its legal economy. Nor can any state long survive the funding of its army and police by foreign powers. An 'Afghan National Army' fully paid for by the United States and deployed with embedded US trainers, can be only a transitional measure. States must eventually develop an economic and fiscal capacity to pay for their security forces. Economic development, capital accumulation, the collection of revenue and the suppression of illegal, untaxable parallel economies (such as trafficking in drugs and other forms of smuggling) all require effective security forces. Thus, among the tasks of transitional international security providers should be strengthening the government's fiscal capacity and providing security for property rights. Despite initial resistance, the coalition and ISAF now seem to have realized that they will have to help the Afghan government secure its borders against evasion of customs revenue, not just terrorists or narco-traffickers.

Public Finance, Assistance, Capital Accumulation

Afghanistan was among those post-war countries where the local economy and the capacity of the state to deliver services were most damaged in decades of violence. Many people needed humanitarian assistance to return to their homes and survive. Basic assets such as roads, schools, power supplies and financial institutions had to be rebuilt or built from scratch. With its human development indicators tied for last place in the world, Afghanistan needed massive building of human capital through education, training and health care. Much of the economy was and is informal or illegal, producing incomes for mafias or patronage networks engaged in drug trafficking and for other businesses which have captured parts of the state but do not contribute to it.

The dominant modes of assistance delivery, however, ignore and indeed often undermine the fundamental strategic goal of economic assistance to state building: strengthening sustainable state capacity to mobilize resources to deliver services, which requires the growth of licit economic activity, which in turn requires public services such as security, rule of law, fiscal and monetary management, and education.

The central state institution that coordinates mobilization of resources, provision of services and legitimation of state power is the budget. And it is the process of mobilizing these resources domestically, and particularly the struggle over the budget, which is at the centre of the process of state formation and legitimation.

International donors contributed to a UNDP trust fund for government salaries during the first six months of Afghanistan's interim government, but only a few have been willing to continue budgetary support or make it into their main means of contribution. Rather than disbursing money from a common account under the control of a political authority that can be held accountable to the nation receiving the aid, most donor countries or agencies, notably the United States, have maintained separate spending mechanisms and procedures that are accountable to its own political authority. In the 2005 budget presented by the Afghan authorities, for instance, less than 30 per cent of all expenditures were channelled through the Afghan government's budget.[8] What former Afghan finance minister Ashraf Ghani has called the 'dual public sector' operates according to its own rules. Its salary scales suck capacity out of the national government by drawing most qualified nationals into the service of international organizations. Its inflationary effect on price levels depresses the value of state salaries.

Accountability also suffers. As far as donor states are concerned, aid money is 'spent' when it is disbursed to an agency, not when the agency implements a programme. Hence the Afghan Donor Assistance Database (DAD), which is the most advanced system of donor accountability yet devised, keeps no accounts of expenditure by the numerous implementing agencies.[9] Instead it tracks 'disbursements', that is, the deposits by donors of funds into the accounts of implementing agencies, much of which is still sitting in these accounts. Since Afghans, who hear reports of huge figures unmatched by perceived results, have no way to demand accountability for the funds, the frequent result is populist politics. In Afghanistan this has taken the form of a campaign against NGOs, whom the government and press accuse of massive corruption. The campaign reached such a level that the Afghan government passed a decree forbidding the use of government funds for NGOs only a week before the annual Afghanistan Development Forum in April 2005, sparking a conflict with donors.

This method of giving aid fails to build the legitimacy and capacity of the recipient government. The government cannot make decisions about what services are to be provided, track expenditures or gain experience in providing public goods. Multilateral operations risk creating elected governments fragmented among clienteles of different aid agencies, with no political authority having the power to pursue a coherent strategy for building sovereignty. Elected governments without budgetary authority or control over security provision hardly merit the term 'democracies'.

Of course, the governments of countries such as Afghanistan are often incapable of exercising such responsibilities. International organizations have created a number of mechanisms to enable the Afghan government to increase its responsibility and build capacity. The Afghanistan Reconstruction Trust Fund (ARTF), administered by the World Bank, provides support for the government's recurrent and development expenditures. The Law and Order Trust Fund for Afghanistan (LOTFA) provides support for SSR. A new trust fund provides support for counter-narcotics programmes. Donors deposit unearmarked contributions into these funds in return for a voice in the management of the fund. The Afghan government must provide full documentation of expenditure for approval by the fund's governors. The joint governance of the fund provides both aid donors and the recipient government with a voice in accounting for expenditure, while empowering the government to make policy decisions.

The problem of dual legitimacy can also occur in the area of economic policy. In many post-war countries governments that rely on state patronage for support may clash with international financial institutions trying to implement liberal market policies. In Afghanistan the clash focuses more on the approach to counter narcotics. After ignoring the problem for several years, the United States now apparently wants to solve it quickly, ignoring the fact that this 'criminal' activity accounts for 40 per cent of the total Afghan economy, by UN estimates. The decrease in planting in 2005, partly motivated by a drop in prices caused by a glut of supply, is not likely to be sustainable as promised aid fails to materialize. Armed clashes with eradication teams have already occurred in some areas, and conflict over opium eradication may give new life to a declining insurgency.

Legitimacy, Transitional Governance and Democracy

Almost by definition international state building operations begin under conditions where states lack not only capacities to provide security and services but also legitimacy. The legitimacy of the state in Afghanistan had fallen to historic lows in the course of the previous decades' conflicts.

Legitimacy begins with that of the international operation. The intervention in Afghanistan enjoyed international legitimacy (no state opposed it) and considerable support in Afghanistan, where Afghans saw it less as destroying sovereignty than as potentially restoring it after years of interference by neighbouring countries. Involvement by the UN provided a more credible interlocutor for political groups than direct action by the occupying power, as the Bush administration found to its apparent surprise in Iraq. The next stage was the establishment of a transitional administration. The Bonn Agreement established a process of political transition marked by an emergency *Loya Jirga*, adoption of a constitution at another *Loya Jirga* and election of a 'fully representative' government.

Although the UN, unlike some regional organizations, has no clear standards for the type of government legitimate for its members, its operational doctrine requires that the transition lead to adoption of a constitution providing for at least an appearance of liberal democracy, with elections constituting the principal benchmark. The United States has, even more explicitly, made 'democracy' (defined as a government elected by universal adult suffrage) as the goal of such operations. International actors also require that any constitution or basic law profess adherence to international standards of human rights. This led to an agreement that appeared to require Afghanistan to become a consolidated and 'gender-sensitive' democracy within two and a half years.

This goal was clearly not attainable. Like many such agreements, the Bonn Agreement had timetables and benchmarks for political changes, but no mechanism to coordinate these political measures with timetables and benchmarks for the creation of security institutions and fiscal capacity. Electing officials to preside over a non-functional pseudo-state that can provide neither security nor services does not constitute democracy. The struggle over how militias were to be disarmed and new security institutions built was at least as essential to any democratic character of the regime as holding elections.

Elected governments presiding over a society that visibly supports them, however, will be better able to mount campaigns for empowerment by international actors than interim governments of dubious legitimacy. Thus the first election of a legitimate government, while a key step in the state building process, is far from its termination point and may mark its true beginning. After his election, Afghan President Hamid Karzai openly opposed US plans for aerial eradication of the opium poppy, showing greater independence than previously.

Conclusion: Constructing Sovereignty for Whose Security?

Studies of state building operations often try to identify 'best practices' without asking for whom they are best. While actors can learn how better to achieve their goals, every step of the process of internationally sponsored state building generates political conflict. Nonetheless, in a strategic environment where the goals of actors are interdependent, negotiation may lead to convergence among actors with different motivations. The Bush administration entered Afghanistan committed not to engage in 'nation building'. Eventually, however, it needed an 'exit strategy' which would be sustainable only if the United States and other international actors helped Afghans build institutions that would serve the common interests of Afghanistan and the international community.

Hence the nationalist concept of 'exit strategy' and the globalist concept of 'sustainability' may converge on the mission of building a legitimate and capable state. Doing so effectively requires transitional governance institutions that incorporate the need for both national and international legitimacy. The problems encountered in the operation in Afghanistan illustrate how the institutions proposed by the HLP endorsed by the UN secretary-general would provide an institutional framework to make this possible.[10] These institutions would create a single counterpart for the national sovereign of the recipient countries that would provide a forum for donors and troop contributors, as well as a fund through which they could coordinate their decisions.

This organizing principle of the contemporary global system requires that state building, and particularly multilateral state building, be placed at the centre of the global security agenda. To do so will require negotiated delegation of some sovereign functions, not only of the reconstructed country, but also of the donor countries. They will better serve their own needs by giving aid in ways that are more accountable to the reconstructed country's citizens, not just to their own.

Notes

1 Report of the Panel on United Nations Peace Operations (A/55/305–S/2000/809).
2 'A more secure world: our shared responsibility', *Report of the Secretary-General's High-level Panel on Threats, Challenges and Change* (A/59/565 2004); and the

secretary-general's report on the implementation of the recommendations of the High-level Panel, 'In larger freedom: towards development, security and human rights for all', *Report of the Secretary-General* (A/59/2005).
3   Jackson and Rosberg (1982). For a more recent interpretation, see Barnett (1995).
4   Tilly (1992).
5   Salamé (1996).
6   Dr Anwar-ul-Haq Ahady, Minister of Finance, 'The budget as a tool for accelerating economic development and poverty reduction', presentation to the Afghanistan Development Forum 2005, Kabul, 4 April 2005, p 6.
7   Walter and Snyder (1999). See also Wantchekon (2004).
8   Ahady, 'The Budget as a Tool'.
9   For a link to the DAD, see http://www.af/dad/index.html.
10 'A More Secure World'; and 'In Larger Freedom'.

References

Barnett, M. (1995), 'The New United Nations Politics of Peace: From Juridical Sovereignty to Empirical Sovereignty.' *Global Governance*, 1(1): 79–97.

Jackson, R. and Rosberg, Carl G. (1982), 'Why Africa's Weak States Persist: The Empirical and the Juridical in Statehood.' *World Politics*, 35(1): 1–24.

Salamé, G. (1996), *Appels d'Empire: ingérences et résistances à l'âge de la mondialisation*. Paris: Fayard.

Tilly, Charles. (1992), *Coercion, Capital, and European States, AD 990–1992*. Oxford: Blackwell.

Wantchekon, L. (2004), 'The Paradox of "Warlord" Democracy: A Theoretical Investigation.' *American Political Science Review*, 98(1): 17–33.

Walter, Barbara F. and Snyder, J. (eds.) (1999), *Civil Wars, Insecurity, and Intervention*. New York: Columbia University Press.

9

Afghan Subjectivities and US Foreign Policy: Postcolonial Perspectives

Nasema Zeerak

Isn't this difficulty of finding adequate forms of struggle a result of the fact that we continue to ignore the problem of power? After all, we had to wait until the nineteenth century before we began to understand the nature of exploitation, and to this day, we have yet to fully comprehend the nature of power ... The question of power remains a total enigma. Who exercises power? And in what sphere?

(Michel Foucault 1972, cited in Lemke 2019: 51)

On 15 August 2021, the Islamic Republic of Afghanistan fell to the hands of the Taliban, and the Islamic Emirate of Afghanistan was restored once again, twenty years after its initial collapse. The fall of the Republic came after unilateral peace talks between the Afghan government and the Taliban stalled and the Biden administration followed through with total troop withdrawal, agreed upon in a separate unilateral peace deal between the Taliban and the US government under the Trump administration in 2020. The withdrawal of troops was followed by deadly, frenzied evacuations as thousands of those who had supported the US mission and opposed the Taliban – including human rights defenders, women in government, political activists and others at risk – tried to flee the country. Devastating scenes of panic and desperation at Kabul Airport ensued.

Against the backdrop of withdrawal and chaotic evacuations, the discourse of tribalism, as a reifying mechanism of 'us' versus 'them' found renewed resonance among international observers. American foreign policy officials, and President Biden himself, deployed this discourse to describe Afghans seeking a means of escape. On August 26, President Biden declared Afghanistan 'a country that has never once in its entire history been a united country ... made up of different tribes who have never ever gotten along with one another' (President Biden, August 2021). In saying this he effectively naturalized the troop withdrawal as an inevitable and desirable policy choice vis-à-vis a tribal non-nation. Why was this discourse – and the relationships of power it taps into – readily available to President Biden and other American officials at this particular moment in time and place? And how did its use make possible the political effects witnessed after its invocation? More specifically, what social and political processes have underpinned the production of Afghanistan as a tribal country, and, as a result, a country with limited capacity to be united? How has the framing of Afghanistan as a country without the capacity to be united shaped and justified specific policy objectives? And how was the American policy of unconditional withdrawal made (to seem) inevitable by this discourse?

The discourse of tribalism is co-constituted by and with that of saving 'the Afghan woman'. Allegedly, it is the tribesman and the tribal codes of conduct that repress and violate 'the Afghan woman', as exemplified in the justification of the American liberation project in 2001. But even as they affirm each other, these two discourses also alienate each other: the dream of a 'free' and 'modern' 'Afghan woman' is, after all, in direct contradiction with the image of Afghans as unchanging tribesmen who lack the capacity to embrace modernity. As such, Afghanistan and its inhabitants are imagined as embodying two entangled and contradictory discourses – at once static (tribesmen) and dynamic (free and fit for modernity) – leaving us with a fundamental question: how can we understand *why and for what purposes* Afghanistan is represented through contradictory yet mutually constitutive discourses? What can the timing of discourse-usage tell us about their intended political effects?

Far from undermining the coherence or epistemological authority of each other, these dissensions and internal contradictions are sites of productive power (Foucault 1980) as they render particular policy agendas inevitable and 'right' at particular geopolitical moments. In other words, the continual paradoxical production of Afghan subjectivities works as a mechanism of governmentality (Foucault 1980) – a mode of power concerned with rendering Afghans 'legible' (Scott 1999) as governable and manageable.[1] Although it is tempting to look for resolutions of these apparent dichotomies, the persistence of these oppositions in the twenty years of American intervention (and previous imperial interventions) in Afghanistan does not permit this. Rather, in placing these two discourses in relation to the role of the United States as an imperial power, I argue that the two discourses – saving 'the Afghan woman', as deployed in 2001 and tribalism as deployed two decades later – are simultaneously constituted by and co-constitutive of imperial power relations and governmentality.[2]

A concomitant reading of the two discourses – as exemplified in presidential (and other political) speeches, talks and policy documents (broadly defined) – exposes the power of language in *producing* Afghan identities and subjectivities through systems of meaning. As such, the discourse of saving 'the Afghan woman' has coincided with the desire of the US foreign policy apparatus to highlight the capacity of Afghans to evolve beyond repressive tribal codes of conduct and avail themselves of modern forms of governance and sovereignty. Paradoxically, Afghanistan is (re)produced as a tribal nation to activate the representation of Afghanistan as unchanging and timeless, defined by its otherness vis-à-vis modern forms of citizenship and capacity for unity, as a way in which to justify and/or explain away military defeat. It is the ambivalence and contradictions at the heart of these interlocking discourses that render Afghans 'legible' or manageable for American governmentality by naturalizing American foreign and military policies – as exemplified in the naturalization of intervention and withdrawal of troops in 2001 and 2021, respectively.

To understand the force and political effects of discourses at particular moments, I employ Foucauldian discourse analysis (Foucault 1980) to explore the long-term

Orientalist and colonial architecture (Mills 1997) that provides the context in which these discourses emerge. The postcolonial theoretical perspective helps capture and contextualize the continuities, overlapping and emerging configurations of power-knowledge in consolidating imperialism and colonialism in both colonial and postcolonial eras across the globe. Discourse theory and postcolonial theory combined help consider contemporary American discourse as part of a long history of colonialism and imperialism in Afghanistan. This enables us to move beyond oft-cited narratives claiming that the country has never been colonized, which obfuscates and/or renders invisible coloniality (Gani 2022).

The significance and contribution of this critical analysis – in line with the overarching theme of this edited volume – are to reveal the complex workings of diffuse forms of power operating in American discourse on Afghanistan and to investigate its political effects at particular geopolitical moments. It is undeniable that the United States and its foreign policy apparatus wield material capabilities in the international arena. However, their power cannot be reduced to material capabilities and its effects cannot be conceptualized only in realist theoretical perspectives that privilege coercive force (Dahl 1957: 202–3). American power in the international system often operates in diffuse micro-level social processes, through the construction of social identities, capabilities and relations.[3] Particular 'realities' are discursively constituted, creating spaces in which specific policy choices come to be seen as natural, even desirable. More broadly, this analysis illuminates how the twenty-year war in Afghanistan was, in part, a discursive war fought through morphing discourses on a discursive field.[4]

Seen from this perspective, the importance of discourses at the 'beginning' and the 'end' of American military intervention in enabling American power and governmentality in Afghanistan makes itself clear. Put differently, discursive constructions, alongside military operations, have worked as a mechanism of governmentality, a way of rendering Afghans and Afghanistan 'legible' for a variety of American political and military policies. As will become clear by the end of this chapter, the war, discursively naturalized as 'over' with the invocation of tribalism, has only ended *until* the next iteration of imperial interventionism is made (to seem) natural and desirable with the invocation of a different discourse in line with the geopolitics of a global superpower. Or as Nivi Manchanda (2022) poignantly reminds us, 'historical intervention in Afghanistan, suggests that periods of heightened Western engagement have almost always been followed by disengagement and indifference'. As such, the end of the occupation and the 'end' of the war is not in contradiction, but rather in line with an imperialist agenda that has only stabilized and maximized the effects of the occupation.

This chapter first lays out the context for the use of postcolonial theory as a framework. I then present and discuss Foucault's productive power to frame the analysis of the discursive constitution of Afghanistan through the discourses of saving 'the Afghan woman' and tribalism. Next, I examine the constitution of Afghan subjectivities (and Afghanistan), focusing on two geopolitical moments – 2001, the invasion, and 2021, the withdrawal – and their shared political effect, namely the consolidation of US political and military power. The chapter concludes by reflecting on the role knowledge and policy making play in producing Afghanistan (and Afghans) as an object(s) of (non)intervention.

Afghanistan and the Postcolonial

Post coloniality represents a response to a genuine need, the need to overcome a crisis of understanding produced by the inability of old categories to account for the world.
(Arif Dirlik quoted in Hall 2021: 311)

The war in Afghanistan, now in its fifth decade, is multifaceted and cannot be understood solely in terms of colonial and postcolonial encounters or discourse theory.[5] Nonetheless, establishing the important role colonial legacies and power-knowledge configurations have played is important to understanding the contemporary war and its aftermath. As such, herein, I read Afghanistan as a postcolonial polity with a history of encounters with various colonial and imperial powers.

Following Stuart Hall, I use the definition of colonialism as referencing 'something more than direct rule over certain areas of the world by the imperial powers' and, instead, 'signifying the whole process of expansion, exploration, conquest, colonization and imperial defeminization which constituted the "outer face", the constitutive outside, of European and then western capitalist modernity after 1492' (Hall 2021: 302). Postcolonial is what follows, as the 'aftereffects' of this pervasive type of indirect colonial hegemony (Hall 2021: 307). As the 'after' connotes the moment that follows the colonial moment, in which the colonial relation was dominant, colonialism and postcolonialism can be seen as two distinct forms of inequality and domination, each with features specific to the context and time (Hall 2021). Crucially, larger-scale discursive frameworks have played a central role in the consolidation of colonial and imperial power.[6] As such, postcolonial discourse theory is the 'critical study of non-literary writings which were produced within the period and context of British imperialism, and the effect of colonialism and colonial texts on current societies' (Mills 1997: 105).[7]

Proceeding from the perspective that colonialism is more than direct rule and that the power-knowledge configuration has conditioned the consolidation of domination, Afghanistan can be understood as a postcolonial state with histories of imperial encounters underpinned by imperial discursive frameworks. Manchanda (2020) traces the origins of Afghanistan (although never directly colonized) as an imperial formation – an entity that has been constituted by imperial practices – hinged on the familiar 'logics of mystification, hierarchy, and fetishism' (6).[8] And, as Manchanda notes, the difference between direct colonization and the imperial formation of Afghanistan is the establishment of Afghanistan as a quasi-colonial state, a state 'sporadically subject to invasive imperial intervention', but never fully folded into the British Empire (2020: 226). This is significant as Afghanistan becomes the object of interest (and intervention) at particular geopolitical moments, and it is at these moments that imperial logics of Orientalism work to produce subjectivities and naturalize geopolitical strategies.[9]

Importantly, much as in other colonial formations, subject categories were created by imperialists and became linked to indigenous identities in Afghanistan. More recently scholars have turned to the interrogation of historical knowledge production practices on Afghanistan and its exigencies to colonialism and imperialism. Citing Jon

Anderson, Manchanda argues that 'nearly all the colonial ethnography that emerged on the North-West Frontier of British India, and Afghanistan more generally, was gathered, sifted and culled for political intelligence' (2020: 141). Similarly, Robert Crews, writing on the importance of knowledge production 'for ruling places as cheaply as possible', notes this as the reason that the 'British in the nineteenth and early twentieth centuries and the Soviets in the late twentieth centuries and the Americans in the twenty first century would invest so much in devising highly racialized typologies of tribes and ethnic types' (2015: 4).[10]

In these ways, Afghanistan post-independence in 1919 *could* be understood as a postcolonial state. In 1919 Amanullah Khan gained autonomy over Afghanistan's foreign policy from the British, putatively ending British influence. Yet, Afghanistan was to experience a number of quasi-colonial interventions thereafter, a fact in line with the notion of postcoloniality, a label that does not signify the end of colonial rule, but rather captures its continuities and aftereffects. Colonial logics continue to live, in particular, in the discourses deployed to constitute Afghan subjectivities in relation to intervening powers. The end of colonialism does not necessarily imply the suspension of domination, and 'it certainly does not mean that we have passed from a regime of power-knowledge into some powerless and conflict-free time zone' (Hall 2021: 307). More importantly, as Hall notes, postcolonialism 'stake[s] its claim in terms of the fact that some other, related but yet "emergent" new configurations of power-knowledge relations are beginning to exert their distinctive and specific effects' (Hall 2021: 307). As such, postcolonial analysis is vital for analysing and interpreting contemporary discursive practices in light of the power relations and regimes of truth (Foucault 1980) that have contributed to their definition and evolution. To frame the exigency of productive Afghan subjectivities at two geopolitical moments – 2001 and 2021 – I now turn to Foucault's conception of discourse and productive power.

Discourse Theory and Productive Power

We must cease once and for all to describe the effect of power in negative terms: it 'excludes', it 'represses', it 'censors', it 'abstracts', it 'masks', it 'conceals'. In fact, power produces; it produces reality; it produces domains of objects and rituals of truth.
(Foucault 1995: 194)[11]

Discourse is 'groupings of utterances or sentences, statements which are enacted within a social context, which are determined by that social context' and which 'systematically form the objects of which they speak' (Foucault quoted in Mills 1997: 11). As such, 'discursive practices – through which texts are produced (created) and consumed (received and interpreted) – are viewed as an important form of social practice which contributes to the constitution of the social world including social identities and social relations' (Jørgensen and Phillips 2002: 61). For instance, the use of binaries, such as 'civilized' and 'uncivilized', can be understood as statements enacted within the context of imperialism, determined by unequal imperial power relations, and *deployed to reproduce* those unequal power relations.

Importantly, discourses, even as they produce regimes of truth (Foucault 1980), are sites of constant contestation through the production of meaning, and, as such, there is no unified, homogeneous or permanent discourse.[12] In other words, a discourse is not 'an ideal, continuous smooth text that runs beneath a multiplicity of contradictions and resolves them in the calm unity of coherent thought … It is rather a space of multiple dissensions; a set of different oppositions whose levels and roles must be described' (Foucault quoted in Carlson 2005: 135).[13] Far from permanent, discourses represent 'fluid constellations', constantly challenged and modified by other discourses (Mills 1977). It is this morphing nature – the ambivalence, impermanency and contradictions of the American discourse – that work to create paradoxical subjectivities that can justify geopolitical strategy at two different moments in time.[14] Such an understanding of power does not imply a disregard for Afghan sovereignty and agency. As I illustrate in the coming pages, Afghans – themselves struggling to overcome structures of coloniality through anti-colonial discursive (and other) moves – may actively engage with, (re)produce and perpetuate colonial discourses as well.

In this sense, power, always entangled and co-constituted with discourse, produces an effect (or many) (Mills 1997: 17).[15] And as the social and political life is discursively constituted; discursive practices both construct representations of the world, social subjects and social relations, including power relations, and play a role in furthering the interests of particular social groups (Jørgensen and Phillips 2002: 63). Using this understanding of productive power and discourse as an analytical model, I turn to an analysis of American discourse on Afghanistan to delineate the making of Afghan subjectivities and US political and military strategy in 2001 and 2021, respectively.

'A Nation of Muzzled Women'[16]

When I write these stories, I realize that they may be co-opted by those who want to wage wars through the bodies of Muslim women. I understand the global power dynamics that seize these stories as fodder for programs of imperialism.
(Ahsan-Tirmizi 2021: 198)

The discursive formation of 'the Afghan woman'[17] in need of saving (Abu-Lughod 2013) by imperial power relations has coincided with the constitution of particular subjects and modes of subjectivity so as to make possible the US interventionist policy in Afghanistan in 2001. The discourse was relied on to produce an effect (Mills 1997) by attributing differential qualities (capacities) to social subjects and positioning them in relation to one another. The entanglement between the discourse of emancipating women and imperialist interventions is not new, and much critical scholarship has been dedicated to the interrogation of 'colonial feminism',[18] both historically and in contemporary discourses (Cronin-Furman, Gowrinathan, and Zakaria 2017). Understanding Afghan women's production as an object of imperial intervention (Zeweri 2017: 11) requires investigating how 'the Afghan woman' was discursively produced as silent, captive and 'hidden beneath burkhas' (Fernandes 2017: 647) in 2001. In particular, what this discourse made possible at this specific moment in time and space, despite (1) the evidence of women's subjugation for at least two decades before 2001 and (2) the many ways in which women had resisted and fought against this subjugation. How did it come to be that an international military intervention could be regarded as the only (and the desirable) course of action vis-à-vis the victimized 'Afghan woman'?

First, a brief annotation: In tracing the geopolitical genealogies of 'the Afghan woman', I am interested in making visible the operation of power and its effects in consolidating American political and military power. As discourses are constituted in relation to (and constantly modified by) other discourses, necessarily Afghans themselves (including Afghan women) engage and interact with such discourses. As such, the pernicious effects of these discourses are traceable to Afghan women themselves in their embodying, performing and benefitting from reproducing the discourses. A whole cadre of 'expert' and 'activist' Afghan women have built their career and reputation, validating and supporting American discourse on Afghan women, serving as on-the-ground 'informants' (Azarbaijani-Moghaddam 2022). A detailed analysis of this is not possible here, but suffice to say, while I trace the exigencies of this discourse to American power in Afghanistan, Afghans themselves (especially Afghan women's rights activists) are implicated in reproducing and appropriating them for their own self-interest.

The making of 'the Afghan woman' – as a productive subjectivity and not as a specific person or real people – in 2001 necessarily relied on the discourse of liberation. By 2001, Afghan women had lived through the decade of Soviet occupation of Afghanistan (1979–89) (Ahmad and Avoine 2018), a civil war (1989–96) (Osman 2020) and the subsequent Taliban regime (1996–2001). Yet, published weeks after the US intervention, a State Department report (2001) entitled 'The Taliban's War Against Women' described that 'prior to the Taliban, women in Afghanistan were protected under the law and increasingly afforded rights in the Afghan society'. In effect, this characterization overshadowed Afghan women's victimization prior to (and beyond) the Taliban reign. This explicit linking of 'the Afghan woman's' oppression to the Taliban was to produce an effect – the legitimization and consolidation of the US-led intervention as a liberation mission. An excerpt from the report cited above is useful to illustrate the reliance on the discourse of liberation:

> Today, with Kabul and other Afghan cities liberated from the Taliban, women are returning to their rightful place in Afghan society – the place they and their families choose to have. Schools are preparing to reopen, and women are praying again in mosques.
>
> (Department of State 2001)

The report not only frames the Taliban regime as at war with the *women* of Afghanistan, as indicated in the title and text of report, but it also works to absolve any American role in the oppression of Afghan women in the 1980s by arming and funding the warring factions (Samar 2019).[19] Instead, it reproduces the United States as the liberator. Positioning the Taliban (as oppressor) and the United States (as liberator) in a binary opposition, Afghan women are rendered as free and rightful *after* the military intervention.[20] Significantly, Laura Bush's weekly radio address on 17 November 2001 explicitly framed the US-led international intervention in terms of liberating Afghan women:

> *Because of our recent military gains*, in much of Afghanistan women are no longer imprisoned in their homes. They can listen to music and teach their daughters without fear of punishment. Yet, the terrorists who helped rule that country now plot and plan in many countries, and they must be stopped. The fight against terrorism is also a fight for the rights and dignity of women.
> (Bush 2001, emphasis added)[21]

Here, Laura Bush draws the discursive boundaries of what is imaginable for Afghan women according to a western discourse of freedom. She produces Afghan women as a category with the capacity to be free, illustrated in their ability to listen to music without fear of punishment.[22] The effect of the discursive formation is the idea that Afghan women *can*, in fact, be saved (have the ability to be free and exercise their agency), and that the saving was done with US support and specifically, military intervention against Afghan women's oppressors – the Taliban.[23]

The creation of the Afghan Women's Writing Project (AWWP), a series of online creative writing workshops conducted by US-based mentors with Afghan women in 2009, is another important entry point for understanding the making of Afghan subjectivities in the service of consolidating American power. The creation of the AWWP is an exemplar of the neoliberal (mis)appropriation of the epistemic authority of Afghan women (and women of colour more generally) while hollowing out its potential to create knowledge and do politics. As the epigraph by Ahsan-Tirmizi reminds us, the knowledge produced by women of colour (from the Global South) is deployed just as readily within dominant discourses, obscuring and misappropriating the critical space that is carved for alternative ways of knowing and politics.[24] The writing project was created 'with the belief that to tell one's story is a human right', and with 'the aim of teaching women in Afghanistan how to write essays, poems, short stories and other literary genres in English'.[25]

In the words of Lori Noak, the American founder of AWWP, 'in telling their [Afghan women] own stories, we've seen these women gather strength, courage, and self-confidence. They become empowered to make change within their homes, their communities, and eventually their country' (AWWP website). In this sense, Zeweri (2017) strikes a chord when she asks, 'what does it mean to empower women across a vast geographic divide, through a digital interface and during a time of protracted conflict, insecurity and uncertainty?' While Zeweri poses the question in a rhetorical fashion and deems it unresolved, albeit a productive exercise for critical analysis, Melamed (2011) reminds us that writings 'by or about women in the South gets recruited not only for discourses of legitimation but also, importantly … cast as transparent and easily accessible "evidence," function in place of or alongside scholarship' (92). In this sense, 'the Afghan woman's' writings are recruited as 'evidence' of the Taliban's brutalities and Afghan women's desire to be part of this western liberation project (Zeweri 2017).

As Fernandes (2017) points out, what is critical to note about the project is its timing. AWWP was created after the CIA called directly for the use of Afghan women's stories as a weapon:

> Afghan women could serve as ideal messengers in humanizing the ISAF [International Security Assistance Force] role in combating the Taliban because of women's ability *to speak personally and credibly about their experiences under the Taliban, their aspirations for the future, and their fears of a Taliban victory.* Outreach initiatives that create media opportunities for Afghan women to share their stories with French, German, and other European women could help to overcome pervasive skepticism among women in Western Europe toward the ISAF mission.
>
> (CIA Red Cell Special Memorandum, 11 March 2010, emphasis added)

As Fernandes also notes, the memo points to the exigencies of storytelling in pursuit of geopolitical strategy (2017: 643). Indeed, AWWP was created to highlight the capacities of Afghan women for change, constituting them as subjects with agency and freedom *only* in the presence of American (or western) political and military operatives.[26] And, more importantly, Afghan women's epistemological authority was instrumentalized as evidence (Melamed 2011) of their oppression, highlighting their liberation in the absence of the Taliban. Of course, in the face of threats of a Taliban victory, US (and international) military intervention was made to seem indispensable to the protection of their freedom and in the service of the larger imperial project of 'freedom'.

In addition to the ways the discourse of a victimized 'Afghan woman' has been productive of/for imperial projects, it has also worked to repress the agency and resistance of Afghan women. In 2001, the discourse of saving the passive and victim 'Afghan woman' was produced by erasing Afghan women's resistance before, during and after the Taliban regime – to enable the twin notions of the United States as liberator and Taliban as oppressor (Fernandes 2017: 647). To be sure, the discourse also worked to preclude the possibility that Afghan women might have actively supported the Taliban. Distinguishing western feminism from its conceptual 'other' – patriarchy under the Taliban – the discourse positioned the intervention as the only possible means for Afghan women to access rights or liberation. As a result, Afghan women's suffering through other intersecting national-global forces – such as militarism and neoliberalism – was rendered irrelevant.[27] Similarly, since 2001, the discourse of saving 'Afghan women' has necessarily relied on erasing the Afghan women's resistance to US-led international military and imperialism (Fernandes 2017) (Zeweri and Osman 2022).

Crucially, the making of 'Afghan women' in need of saving has relied on producing Afghanistan as a society marked by a male-dominated tribal culture (Manchanda 2020). As Ahsan-Tirmizi contends, the apparent American mission of gender relations reform and women's liberation has emerged in opposition to a notion of Pashtun tribalism (2021: 30) and as such, tribalism has always necessarily been implicated in and entangled with the image of women held captive. As Homi Bhabha (1997) contends, for the imperial discourse to be effective, 'it must continually produce its slippage, its excess, its difference' (153). The slippage here is that the Afghan women cannot be saved if Afghans are timelessly and hopelessly tribal, set in their tribal ways – there is, in other words, an inherent ambivalence in these two interlocking discourses. The discourses necessarily alienate each other, even as they co-constitute each other. As such, the logic of tribalism is ever present in the background, and as Manchanda reminds us, 'already offering a way out'. If the United States fails to defeat the Taliban and save Afghan women, 'it is because they are too different, too retrogressive and too obdurate to be saved' (2020: 168). It is this constructed impermeable otherness – that continuously alienates the authority of liberation discourse – to which I now turn.

Enter the 'Armed and Uncontrolled Tribesmen'[28]

To understand the interplay of the discourse of tribalism with the exigencies of imperialism, it is worth contextualizing the constitution of Afghanistan and Afghans through the concept of tribalism at historically and politically contingent junctures. This kind of historical analysis reveals the work that power does for these discourses and the work these discourses do, in turn, for power.[29] Similar to any imperial discourse, a full understanding of the force and persistence of the discourse of tribalism is not possible without accounting for Afghans' reproduction and perpetuation of it. Afghans, as imperial subjects, are hardly passive victims vis-à-vis American discourse, and instead, exercise their agency in actively engaging with, resisting and benefitting from the discourse. In this sense, the turn to everything tribal and an uncritical celebration of local customary forms of governance have benefitted traditional elite Afghans themselves.

For instance, *jirgas* (tribal councils), as one of the privileged and putatively ideal types of informal justice, are regarded as 'a key tenet of Pashtunwali and can be understood as an exercise of affirming identity and community, whether positioned against adversaries, the state, or other localities, ethnicities, or tribes' (Wimplemann 2013: 408). In other words, far from 'a kind of enlightened tradition, devoid of power relations and hierarchies and cleansed of their excesses by the training and monitoring programmes carried out by NGOs' (Wimplemann 2021: 131), *jirgas* are located within the ongoing contestation and negotiation of power and political hierarchies. In including references to the informal customary justice in Afghanistan's National Justice Sector Strategy in 2008, much power was ceded by international policy makers and their Afghan counterparts to *jirgas* (much to the dismay of Afghan human rights activists), whose representatives are drawn from a small and relatively fixed roster of senior Pashtun men. In this sense, the turn to incorporating informal justice mechanisms, mediated through western expert knowledge (Wimplemann 2013, 2021), into the formal Afghan judicial system was picked up and reproduced by traditional Pashtun elites who benefitted from being rendered as 'more Afghan', or 'real Afghans' (Wimplemann 2013).

Tracing a genealogy (Schaffer 2015) of tribalism as a politicized concept to the initial colonial encounters with the country, Manchanda contends that the discursive production of Afghanistan through the concept of tribe is typical of imperial modes of thought, 'not unlike those of "race", "caste" and "ethnicity" found elsewhere in the colonies' (2020: 140) that have been mined and instrumentalized in the service of empire. It is typical of imperial knowledge to read Afghanistan through the lens of repressive tribal norms, which served to cast Afghans as 'others' against which the nation-state is posited by representing Afghanistan at times 'as a security problem, a political threat and as something that needs "engaging with"' (2020: 109). More importantly, the term was politically deployed for the purpose of '"pacification" and control of the frontier and its population' (2020: 131). Relating the images of autonomous and sovereign tribes – governed through traditional authority – to the British strategic objectives in the 'frontier' region, Wimplemann asserts that the objective of questioning Afghan statehood and sovereignty was nothing other than to wrest the area away from the Afghan king (Abdur Rahman Khan) at the end of the nineteenth century (2013: 412). In effect, Afghans were made (to seem) a threat that needed to be pacified, controlled and positioned in relation to the European 'self', legible as the figure of a specific modern form of citizenship and national sovereignty.

The image of Afghanistan as a country of 'free' tribesmen was resurrected again in the 1980s, motivated by Cold War geopolitics. Afghans were insidiously constituted (and celebrated) as 'freedom fighters' (Stanski 2009) and 'brave mountain people', to fuel resistance not only against the Soviet army, but also against an inherently alien central state (Wimplemann 2013: 120).[30] The discourse of tribalism *both* constructed the capacities of Afghans as 'freedom fighters' *and* facilitated the advancement of the American interest in fighting the Soviet army in Afghanistan.[31] The work of discourse in consolidating American national identity (in relation to Afghans and the Soviets) is exemplified in the then-US President Reagan's remarks: 'to watch the courageous Afghan freedom fighters battle modern arsenals with simple hand-held weapons is an inspiration to those who love freedom' (Manchanda 2020: 131). Here, positioned in relation to both the Americans and the Soviets, Afghans are endowed as courageous, freedom-loving and an inspiration even as they are also positioned at the bottom of the hierarchy for their use of 'simple hand-held' weapons against the modern Soviet arsenal. Constructed around an ambivalence, as Bhabha notes, the discourse purports that they are almost like us, but not quite (1997: 153). The Afghans, no matter how brave and freedom-loving, are not capable of asserting national sovereignty and consolidating national identity in quite the same way the United States does – as came to be claimed in the coming decades.

The discursively constructed tribal character of Afghanistan, in turn, facilitated the eventual return of the emirate as the failing international state building project and its *sine qua non* – good governance – proved increasingly elusive. Earlier calls for recognition of and support for informal justice processes (the US Institute of Peace was an early advocate and at the forefront of these calls) culminated in the establishment of a working group in 2009 to create a national policy to form a hybrid (formal and informal) justice sector (Wimplemann 2013). Wimplemann contends that the fascination with everything tribal and its entanglement with the military strategies and rationales at this juncture 'did not differ from other historical processes in which rulers have set up or co-opted courts and justice bodies with the view to consolidating power' (2013: 419).

In the face of a failing international state building project, the discourse of tribalism was deployed only after the military had expressed interest in 'winning hearts and minds' by emphasizing the possibilities for informal justice systems to enable stability (Wimplemann 2013).[32] The conception of Afghans as static – in this case, hopelessly and timelessly tribal – undergirded the inclination to engage with the tribes on their own *tribal* terms, this time to defeat the Taliban. The turn to 'understanding' and 'engaging' with the tribes worked not only to absolve the United States for its failure to bring good governance, but also to discursively render desirable its latest military doctrine – counterinsurgency – 'premised on hearth and home, kin and kith' in the words of Kinsella (2020: 120). Also worth noting is that the counterinsurgency doctrine was in direct contradiction to the discourse of saving 'the Afghan woman' for it underwrote the very same practices that precipitated the victimization of Afghan women. As Wimplemann (2013) notes, Afghan feminist activists were increasingly alienated at this time when they objected to the turn to delivering justice through informal tribal codes of conduct.

With repetition and over time, these morphing discourses worked to draw boundaries around what was worthy of attention, thinkable and desirable. This is perhaps most evident in the aftermath of the collapse of the Islamic Republic, on 16 August 2021, in President Biden's speech. Recounting President Trump's unilateral deal with the Taliban, Biden stated: '[T]here was only the cold reality of either following through on the agreement to withdraw our forces or escalating the conflict and sending thousands more American troops back into combat in Afghanistan, lurching into the third decade of conflict' (President Biden August 2021). Further, he stated, 'Afghanistan['s] political leaders gave up and fled the country. The Afghan military collapsed, sometimes without trying to fight' (President Biden August 2021) In repeatedly, chronicling the Afghan leaders' corruption, lack of political and military will, and the inability to unite politically, Biden discursively constructed the Afghans as tribesmen, inherently and permanently incapable of fighting for their country, and unfit for modern forms of governance and sovereignty. This constructed otherness and the corresponding unsuitability of Afghans for unity and sovereignty always already work as a kind of imperial disavowal.

The naturalization of the withdrawal and even the Taliban's return was produced through rhetoric in the weeks leading up to the fall of the Republic. Ultimately, Afghans' inability to evolve beyond tribalism and their negotiations of a series of surrender agreements (Lubold and Trofimov 2021) were framed as the 'way out', 'a sort of "get out of jail free card"' (Manchanda 2020: 168). Thus, it was the tribalism and the American failure to *understand* the tribes, not its *twenty-year misdeeds* that was to be blamed. Michael Zacchea, a retired US Marine who led an American-trained Iraqi Army battalion during the Iraq War, put it this way:

> We did not understand the tribal dynamics ... we think everybody wants what we have. It's cultural obtuseness, obliviousness to their reality and their lived

experience …. we assumed they wanted what we had – liberal democracy, Judeo-Christian values … and [thought] they'd just automatically convert. And that is not the case.

(Turak et al. 2021)

Biden reinforced this conclusion: 'American troops cannot and should not be fighting in a war and dying in a war that Afghan forces are not willing to fight for themselves' (August 2021). Attributing the fall of the country to the fact that tribal alliances and loyalties supersede national ones (Turak et al. 2021), the impermeable and entirely constructed otherness of Afghans came to be naturalized as the 'truth'.[33]

The turn to a discourse of tribalism was motivated by a new (if temporary) alignment between Afghans' constructed otherness and American geopolitical interest – the withdrawal of troops. The turn to Afghans' tribalism was not a recognition of a legitimate political organization; rather, its mobilization constituted 'an erasure of Afghanistan from the dominant political narrative' (Manchanda 2022), in order to consolidate consensus for the American policy of troops withdrawal. Because Afghan women's liberation was always imagined in and through a western discourse of freedom, Afghan tribalism – this unsuitability for political modernity – always stood in contradistinction. This is not an erosion of the epistemological authority of the discourse. On the contrary, the continual contradictions, tensions and slippages are instrumental in the perpetuation and production of Afghans as (only) governable and manageable through contradictory discourses.

Discourse as/in Governmentality

In scholarly and policy discussions, 'power' is imagined to mean coercive and material power, obscuring diffuse and complex forms of power operating in micro-level social processes. As such the role of power-knowledge configurations in mediating and perpetuating governmentality – a mode of power concerned with rendering subjects legible and controlled – is overlooked. In exposing the politics of discourse and its linkages to power, mechanisms of governmentality and historical processes, I have highlighted the ways in which US discourses on Afghanistan are constituted by and constitutive of imperial relations. I have argued that the constructed otherness of Afghans, and their differentiation from the American 'self', is sustained through scholarly and policy practices that obfuscate and distort American power in mobilizing, sustaining and reifying this otherness.[34]

Empirically, in the concomitant reading of two seemingly unrelated and disparate discourses – saving 'the Afghan woman' and the tribalism of Afghans – I have illustrated the intricate and intimate ways they are attached to and co–constitute each other, even (or, perhaps, especially) as they simultaneously contradict each other. Afghan tribalism is always implicated in the violation of Afghan women, while the possibilities and potential for a liberated Afghan woman are always in contradistinction to the tribalism of Afghan men. Even when imagined suitable for liberation and freedom, those Afghans constructed as fundamentally *different* are not imagined as capable of asserting national sovereignty and consolidating national identity in quite the same way as citizens of modern states do. Similarly, in invoking Afghans' customary and tribal forms of governance, far from a kind of legitimate pluralism, imperial narratives construct Afghanistan as defined by its non-stateness.

Rather than undermining the epistemological authority and force of each other, the internal tensions between these two discourses *in fact authorize* American power in Afghanistan and constitute a politics of imperial disavowal (Mantena 2010). Individually and conjoined, both discourses work to constitute paradoxical subjectivities for Afghans in relation to American empire at different geopolitical moments. Making visible the connections (to coloniality) and contradictions of the discourses – and their precariousness – I have illustrated that their mobilization as a mechanism of governmentality has been instrumental in both waging and ending the American imperial war in Afghanistan.

Finally, in revealing the genealogies of contemporary policy making and the academic scholarship they are anchored in, the preceding discussions enclose a critique of liberal (American) empire's interventionism. Exposing the continuities and innovations that connect structures of coloniality to their liberal 'alibi' (Mantena 2010), I illustrate the ways in which contemporary American policy making is imbued and imbricated with colonial logics of engagement. The fall of the Afghan Republic, and the eventual return of the Taliban, can be understood not as incidental and/or an exception, but rather constitutive of liberal interventionist politics.[35] Constituting an imperial mechanism of governmentality to create and maintain a racialized hierarchy between American 'self' and Afghan 'other', the discourses and the inevitable (non)interventionism under the pretext of liberation and sovereignty are a profound subversion and erasure of Afghanistan's sovereignty and Afghans' political consciousness.

In Closing

Invoking the discourse of liberation for Afghans and Afghanistan, as a senator in 2002, President Biden was a staunch advocate for continued engagement in Afghanistan. He asserted, 'history is going to judge us very harshly, I believe, if we allow the hope of a liberated Afghanistan to evaporate because we are fearful of the phrase, nation building, or we do not stay the course' (2002). Paradoxically in 2021, in the aftermath of the fall of the country, as president (2021), he declared that 'Afghanistan is made up of different tribes who have never ever gotten along with one another', and that the mission in Afghanistan was never 'supposed to have been nation building. It was never supposed to be creating a unified, centralized democracy' (August 2021). The ambivalence and the inconsistency with which the discourses of liberation and tribalism have been invoked point to the inherent power of language in negotiating unequal power relations.

Significantly, beyond reductive conceptions of power, productive power helps us map out the crucial role micro-level social processes play in the legitimization of violence and war. In this chapter, I have illustrated the ways in which (post)colonial discursive frameworks have worked to constitute and position Afghans and Afghanistan vis-à-vis American political and military power at two different geopolitical moments – 2001, the invasion and 2021, the withdrawal. The project of liberating 'Afghan women' worked to signify capacity and to position Afghans as free agents and fit for modern forms of governance and sovereignty in relation to the US military intervention. In so doing, it defined the terms of an engagement in which Afghan women were the permanent victim in need of American rescue. Meanwhile, the casting of Afghans as tribesmen served to signify Afghans (and Afghanistan) as static and unchanging in time, solidified in their collective incapacity to transcend tribal codes of conduct and their place in a global matrix of imperial power as 'other'.

As for the United States, once situated against a tribal country unable to change and unite, the policy decision to withdraw troops became inevitable, desirable and natural in response to an immutable enemy. The ways in which the interlocking discourses of liberation and tribalism co-constitute (and alienate) each other worked to 'warrant a sort of imperialism in perpetuity' (Manchanda 2020: 173). In the words of Zeweri, 'the portrayal of Afghan women as always already oppressed by their societies creates a kind of infinite timeline to imperialism itself' (2021: 8). Thus, the hope of a liberated Afghan woman lives on (in the future) until the next iteration of imperial intervention is made (to seem) natural and desirable vis-à-vis an immutable enemy – the tribesmen of Afghanistan.

Notes

1   Anna Larson (2019) makes a similar application of Scott's notion of 'legibility' to the Afghan context in her critique of the 'fragile state' label and the parameters of the international intervention more broadly.
2   While colonialism generally refers to situations where representatives of one country invade and settle in another country, imperialism is the more general term, signifying other and indirect exploitative relations, but no large-scale settlement by civilians. Or in the words of Chen (2010), 'colonialism is a deepening of imperialism. Whereas colonialism is necessarily a form of imperialism, imperialism is not necessarily a form of colonialism' (6). As there is a variety of differences in colonial and imperial relations over time and in different contexts, and postcolonial theory does not generally make a distinction between the two, following Mills, I use the terms interchangeably to refer to the texts that were produced within colonial and imperial contexts. For more, see Mills (1997).
3   For an excellent recent example of discourse analysis of (shifting) US foreign policy vis-à-vis Afghanistan (and the Taliban), see Ibrahimi and Farasoo (2023). Their analysis reveals that, rooted in colonial thought, the discursive oscillation between various aspects of the Taliban movement (an insurgency, a terrorist group and a proxy of Pakistan's foreign policy), was more a reflection of shifting US policy priorities rather than a shift in Taliban behaviour or self-identification as a group.
4   For a useful discussion of war beyond conventional understandings, see Roennfeldt (2011: 41). Roenfeldt defines productive war 'as a discursive conflict about socio-

political hegemony, which is produced by expedient discursive effects, created by networks of heterogeneous actors operating from local centers of power-knowledge to influence the discursive battlefield with the strategic objective of winning the will of the people'. This conception is an important shift towards accounting for micro socio-political dynamics that legitimate geopolitical strategies and intervention policies.

5   For twenty years, Afghans were told that the US intervention was a liberal war – for Afghans' protection against the evil and oppressor Taliban. Failing to deliver the promised liberation and in returning Afghanistan to the Taliban, the framing of the war as 'over' can be understood in and of itself a technology of war, an obfuscation of the reality of/for Afghans. Dispossessing Afghans of their meaning making ability, the (epistemic) violence is deployed as an ontological destruction: 'aimed to remove their connection to their (past) selves to gain strategic supremacy over their future' (Caron 2022: 349). Thus, while western (and specifically American) epistemologies subjugated to the will of geopolitics speak of the 'end' of the war, to be sure, Afghans are haunted by an ongoing deadly war. For instance, see Human Rights Watch (2022).

6   Also, it is worth noting that discourses simultaneously constitute the imperial power as it constitutes the colonized. For example, the fact that the colonized and colonizer are mutually implicated through power-knowledge configuration is a central theme in Manchanda's book, *Imagining Afghanistan* (2020).

7   For instance, Hall makes connections between colonialism and the use of binary opposites, such as 'civilized' and 'uncivilized' in the context of colonialism and their utility for domination of the non-western world (2021). Similarly, Edward Said (1977) introduced the concepts of Orientalism and 'Othering' – understood to be a complex set of relationships between knowledge, power and representation – to examine the ways in which western agents expressed their understanding of non-western worlds and their role in consolidating colonial and imperial rule. For Said, 'knowledge of subject races or Orientals is what makes their management easy and profitable; knowledge gives power, more power requires more knowledge, and so on in an increasingly profitable dialectic of information and control' (Said 1979: 36).

8   Manchanda contrasts this use of the concept from the way Stoler uses the concept to refer to the colonizing power itself. See also Crews (2015) for another in-depth discussion of the emergence of the Afghan state, at multiple levels, as part of a series of global processes, particularly the role of empire.

9   In short 'subject to a form of the euphemistic indirect rule that turned out to be every bit as invasive as direct rule' (Manchanda 2020: 6), Afghanistan is 'a territorial ambiguity that's constituted by an imperial macro-polity that's Britain, Russia, to an extent, and later the USA' (2020: 69).

10 See also Hanifi (2018) and his discussion of how stereotypical and oriental representation of Afghanistan has become a form of knowledge about the country.

11 As Lemke (2019) notes Foucault was struck by the shortcomings of the analytical focus on negative forms of power such as exclusion, constraint, repression and prohibition in his engagement with the prison movement in May of 1968. Focusing on clarifying the micro-political dynamics that direct societies by shaping perceptions, Foucault focused on discursive formations, rendering social, political and economic contexts as non-discursive factors (24).

12 As Foucault reminds us, 'Truth, therefore, is something which societies have to work to produce, rather than something which appears in a transcendental way' (quoted in Mills 1997: 18).
13 Particularly, as Mills notes, 'writing about another culture is heterogenous, marked by gaps, contradictions, inconsistencies, and even characterizing the indigenous subject in positive ways' (1997: 117).
14 See *supra* note 3.
15 See also Barnett and Duval (2004: 55) for another good discussion of productive power in IR. Barnett and Duval note that structural power and productive power concern both how the capacities of actors are socially produced and how these processes shape actors' self-understandings and perceived interests. However, productive power and structural power also differ in a critical respect: whereas the former works through direct structural relations, the latter entails more generalized and diffuse social processes.
16 As articulated by Lori Noack, the Associate Director at the Afghan Women's Writing Project: https://delphiquarterly.com/recent-issues/current-issue-2-2/interview-with-the-afghan-womens-writing-workshop/.
17 It's important to note here that I am interested in illustrating the productive nature of discourse in producing something else – an effect – and not 'arguing with the real', in the words of Butler (1993). As I will discuss in the coming pages, Afghan women *were* victimized by the Taliban (and other forces) *and* that the discourse was intentionally invoked to signify capacity and position Afghan women in relation to the US military intervention, defining the terms of engagement in which Afghan women were the permanent victim in need of American rescue.
18 Leila Ahmed defines colonial feminism 'as the use of feminist ideas and the notion of men oppressing women in the rhetoric of colonialism to "render morally justifiable its project of undermining or eradicating the cultures of colonized peoples"' (cited in Fernandes 2017: 644).
19 Amongst the groups supported by the Reagan administration, Gulbuddin Hekmatyar, who received the largest sum of CIA funding, has the notorious reputation as the misogynistic extremist who threw acid on schoolgirls and college women's faces (Osman 2020). See also *infra* note 33.
20 Not to mention that the announcement of Afghan women praying in mosques is illustrative of a kind of ignorance that guides analysis on Afghanistan. Here, Afghan women's experiences are extrapolated from the experiences of 'veiled Muslim women' as women don't pray in mosques in Afghanistan.
21 While already substantially analysed and rather 'old', the speech is important to tracing the genealogy of this discourse as it is the first instance in which Afghan women were produced as a category victimized by the Taliban – and therefore also as a concept that *could* be invoked to mobilize public support of US intervention – and provides a temporal marker from which to measure the effect of the discourse. See also Abu-Lughod (2013) for an excellent analysis of Laura Bush's radio address.
22 She goes on to define (and pre-emptively justify) the role of the United States in all those places where terrorists might be present to limit the possibility of freedom for women, effectively entangling terrorism with rights and dignity of women – to much political effect.

23 Osman (2020) reminds us that within the US socio-political context in the early 2001, intervention without the pretext of saving 'Afghan women' would have been even less popular than it was.
24 For an in-depth discussion of misappropriation of women of colour's writings in the service of imperialism, see Melamed (2011) in Hong and Ferguson (2011).
25 AWWP website accessible here: https://awwproject.org/discover-awwp/history-mission/.
26 Another strand of analysis on AWWP focuses on the 'positional superiority' that's granted to western women by deflecting attention away from entrenched gender inequalities in western countries. As noted earlier, the discourse simultaneously constitutes subjectivities for both western and non-western women. See, for example, Fernandes (2017). Also, worth noting, the memo's framing of Afghan women's stories against Western women's scepticism is relevant to understanding the role that making the Afghan woman into the productive subjectivity must also position the European woman as the figure of liberated womanhood attached to the imperial power.
27 For an excellent discussion, see Enloe (2010).
28 Crews (2015: 183).
29 See *supra* note 20, it is again worth clarifying that while it may be true that tribes do exist in Afghanistan and Afghans do subscribe to tribal codes of conduct, my focus here is on the ways in which the discourse of tribalism has been deployed at the service of empire to discursively constitute social identities and social relations through distancing and the reification of differences. Nonetheless, one view on the salience of tribalism, as argued by Crews, is that what might appear on the surface as tribal, or highly localized, were in fact much more complex affairs that drew together the local and the global (2015: 57). He writes, 'what many observers in the late 20th and 21st centuries took to be timeless, traditional, and all-encompassing modes of political and social organizations were in these early modern imperial settings instruments that rulers used to govern their peripheries' (2015: 39).
30 Absent here is the criticism of Afghan feminist organizations such as Revolutionary Association of the Women of Afghanistan (RAWA) who warned that the mujahidin parties – the freedom fighters – were guilty of atrocities against other Afghans and that their vision for the future was an unattractive one for many Afghans (Crews 2015: 261–2). See also Manchanda (2020) and Crews (2015).
31 Of course, as has been extensively documented, during the Soviet occupation of Afghanistan in the 1980s, the CIA gave billions of dollars in aid money to mujahidin fighters commanded by regional Afghan warlords to induce a proxy war (Fernandes 2017: 653). See also Osman (2020) and Crews (2015).
32 It is precisely the emphasis on the informal practices of justice that attach the discourse of tribalism to the discourse of saving 'Afghan women'. Because the focus of these tribal processes is restoration and compensation for the aggrieved party, women seldom take part in the proceedings and can find themselves used as objects to mediate disputes – for instance, Wimpleman (2013) notes a practice called *baad*, where women are given away in marriage as compensation to the offended party.
33 Exposing the absurdity of representing Afghanistan as characteristically unchanging through time as tribal and dismissing its complex historical context, Osman contends that fixating on the tribal nature of Afghanistan, and its inability to change, is: 'Akin to stating that in the U.S. White Anglo-Saxon Christian men have ruled for more than two centuries over an ethnically heterogeneous society – and on that basis to

discredit all Americans within and outside the government who led social justice and civil rights movements for and by women and minorities like African Americans, Native Americans, and immigrants' (2020: 41).

34   For an excellent contemporary example of the relationship between Orientalism and (its mediation in) policy making, see Gani (2022).
35   See *supra* note 3; As Ibrahimi and Farasoo (2023) argue the policy shift to negotiate a political settlement with the Taliban was a reflection of US policy priorities, not peace or stability for Afghanistan.

References

Abu-Lughod, L. (2013), *Do Muslim Women Need Saving?* Cambridge, MA: Harvard University Press.
'Afghanistan: Taliban's Catastrophic Year of Rule' (2022), Human Rights Watch, 11 August. Available at: https://www.hrw.org/news/2022/08/11/afghanistan-talibans-catastrophic-year-rule (Accessed: 1 September 2022).
Ahmad, L. and Avoine, P. (2018), 'Misogyny in "Post-war" Afghanistan: The Changing Frames of Sexual and Gender-Based Violence'. *Journal of Gender Studies*, 27(1): 86–101. Available at: https://doi.org/10.1080/09589236.2016.1210002.
Ahsan-Tirmizi, S. (2021), *Pious Peripheries: Runaway Women in Post-Taliban Afghanistan*. Stanford: Stanford University Press.
Azerbaijani-Moghaddam, S. (2022), 'Afghan Women in the Wonderland of the International Community's (Mis)Adventures in Afghanistan'. United Against Inhumanity, July 2022.
Barnett, M. and Duvall, R. (2004), 'Power in Global Governance', in Barnett, M. and Duvall, R. (2004) (eds.), *Power in Global Governance*. Cambridge: Cambridge University Press.
Bhabha, H. K. (1997), 'Of Mimicry and Man: The Ambivalence of Colonial Discourse', in *Tensions of Empire Colonial Cultures in a Bourgeois World*. Berkeley: University of California Press.
Biden Addresses Nation after Attacks at Kabul Airport – 8/26 (2021). Available at: https://www.youtube.com/watch?v=9tBR5cMoiOA (Accessed: 11 December 2021).
Butler, J. (1993), *Bodies That Matter: On the Discursive Limits of 'Sex'*. London: Psychology Press.
Carlson, L. (2005), 'Docile Bodies, Docile Minds: Foucauldian Reflections on Mental Retardation', in S. Tremain, S. (ed.), *Foucault and the Government of Disability*. Michigan: University of Michigan Press, 133–52.
Caron, J. (2022), 'Why Decenter the "War on Terror" in Histories of the "War on Terror"?' *International Journal of Middle East Studies*, 54(2) (May 2022): 347–51. https://doi.org/10.1017/S0020743822000411.
Chen, K. -H. (2010), *Asia as Method: Toward Deimperialization*. Durham, NC: Duke University Press. Available at: https://doi.org/10.1215/9780822391692.
Crews, R. D. (2015), *Afghan Modern: The History of a Global Nation*. Cambridge, MA: Harvard University Press.
Cronin-Furman, K., Gowrinathan, N. and Zakaria, R. (2017), *Emissaries of Empowerment*. New York: City College of New York. Available online: https://www.ccny.cuny.edu/colinpowellschool/emissaries-empowerment

Dahl, R. A. (1957), 'The Concept of Power'. *Behavioral Science*, 2(3): 201–15. Available at: https://doi.org/10.1002/bs.3830020303.

Department of State (2001), 'Report on the Taliban's War against Women'. Department of State. The Office of Electronic Information, Bureau of Public Affairs. Available online: https://2001-2009.state.gov/g/drl/rls/6185.htm (Accessed: 10 January 2022).

Enloe, C. (2010), *Nimo's War, Emma's War: Making Feminist Sense of the Iraq War*. Berkeley: University of California Press.

Fernandes, S. (2017) 'Stories and Statecraft: Afghan Women's Narratives and the Construction of Western Freedoms'. *Signs: Journal of Women in Culture and Society*, 42(3): 643–67. Available online: https://doi.org/10.1086/689631.

Foucault, M. (1972), *Intellectuals and Power. Language, Countermemory, Practice: Selected Essays and Interviews by Michel Foucault*. Ithaca: Cornell University Press.

Foucault, M. (1980), *Power/Knowledge: Selected Interviews and Other Writings, 1972–1977*. New York: Pantheon Books.

Foucault, M. (1990), *The History of Sexuality. Volume 1, An Introduction*. Vintage Books Edition. Translated by R. J. Hurley. New York: Vintage.

Foucault, M. (1995), *Discipline and Punish: The Birth of the Prison*. New York: Knopf Doubleday Publishing Group.

Gani, J. K. (2022) 'From Discourse to Practice: Orientalism, Western Policy and the Arab Uprisings'. *International Affairs*, 98(1): 45–65.

Hall, S. (2021), 'When Was "the Postcolonial"?: Thinking at the Limit', in G. McLennan (ed.), *Selected Writings on Marxism*. Durham, NC: Duke University Press, 293–315. Available online: https://doi.org/10.2307/j.ctv1j9mjwm.18.

Hanifi, S. M. (2018), 'A Genealogy of Orientalism in Afghanistan: The Colonial Image Lineage', in *Middle East Studies after September 11*. Leiden and Boston: Brill, 50–80. Available online: https://brill.com/view/book/edcoll/9789004359901/BP000003.xml (Accessed: 12 December 2021).

Ibrahimi, N. and Farasoo, A. (2023), 'Understanding Shifts in US Policies towards the Taliban: A Critical Analysis'. *Millennium*, 50(3): 810–38. Available online: https://doi.org/10.1177/03058298221130114.

Jørgensen, M. and Phillips, L. (2002), *Discourse Analysis as Theory and Method*. London: SAGE Publications Ltd. Available online: https://doi.org/10.4135/9781849208871.

Kinsella, H. M. (2020), 'Sleeping Soldiers: On Sleep and War'. *Security Dialogue*, 51(2–3): 119–36. Available online: https://doi.org/10.1177/0967010619897243.

Larson, A. (2019), 'More Legitimate, Less Fragile, Less Liberal? The Adoption and Adaptation of Elections in Afghanistan', in Lahai, J., Von Strokirch, K., Brasted, H. and Ware, H. (eds.), *Governance and Political Adaptation in Fragile States*. London: Palgrave Macmillan.

Lemke, T. (2019), *Foucault's Analysis of Modern Governmentality: A Critique of Political Reason*. Translated by E. Butler. New York: Verso Books.

Lubold, G. and Trofimov, Y. (2021) 'Afghan Government Could Collapse Six Months after U.S. Withdrawal, New Intelligence Assessment Says – WSJ'. Available online: https://www.wsj.com/articles/afghan-government-could-collapse-six-months-after-u-s-withdrawal-new-intelligence-assessment-says-11624466743 (Accessed: 31 August 2022).

Manchanda, N. (2020), *Imagining Afghanistan: The History and Politics of Imperial Knowledge*. Cambridge: Cambridge University Press.

Manchanda, N. (2022), 'Colonial Amnesia and Imperialism in Afghanistan'. *Jamhoor*, (7), 10 August 2022. Available at: https://www.jamhoor.org/read/colonial-amnesia-and-imperialism-in-afghanistan.

Mantena, K. (2010), *Alibis of Empire: Henry Maine and the Ends of Liberal Imperialism*. Princeton: Princeton University Press.

Melamed, J. (2011), 'Reading Tehran in Lolita: Making Racialized and Gendered Difference Work for Neoliberal Multiculturalism', in Kyungwon Hong, G. and Ferguson, R. A. *Strange Affinities: The Gender and Sexual Politics of Comparative Racialization*. Durham, NC: Duke University Press.

Mills, S. (1997), *Discourse*. London, UK: Routledge.

Mrs. Laura Bush Delivers the President's Weekly Radio Address – November 17, 2001 – YouTube (2001). Available at: https://www.youtube.com/watch?v=gr6liwDJMoU (Accessed: 11 December 2021).

Nguyen, M. T. (2012), *The Gift of Freedom: War, Debt, and Other Refugee Passages*. Durham, NC: Duke University Press. Available at: https://doi.org/10.1215/9780822391845.

Osman, W. (2020), *Television and the Afghan Culture Wars: Brought to You by Foreigners, Warlords, and Activists*. Champaign, IL: University of Illinois Press.

President Biden Delivers Remarks on Afghanistan – 8/26 (2021), Available at: https://www.youtube.com/watch?v=kIxyYU227mM (Accessed: 31 August 2022).

Remarks by President Biden on Afghanistan (2021), Available at: https://www.youtube.com/watch?v=kIxyYU227mM (Accessed: 25 August 2022).

Roennfeldt, C. F. (2011), 'Productive War: A Re-conceptualisation of War', in *Journal of Strategic Studies*, 34(1): 39–62.

Said, E. W. (1979), *Orientalism*. Delhi: Penguin Books India.

Samar, S. (2019), 'Feminism, Peace, and Afghanistan'. *Journal of International Affairs*, 72(2): 145–58.

Schaffer, F. C. (2015), *Eluciditating Social Science Concepts: An Interpretivist Guide*. New York: Routledge. Available online: https://doi.org/10.4324/9780203814932.

Scott, J. C. (1999), *Seeing Like a State: How Certain Schemes to Improve the Human Condition Have Failed*. New Haven: Yale University Press.

Stanski, K. (2009), '"So These Folks Are Aggressive": An Orientalist Reading of "Afghan Warlords"'. *Security Dialogue*, 40(1): 73–94.

Trofimov, G. L. and Y. (2021), 'WSJ News Exclusive | Afghan Government Could Collapse Six Months after U.S. Withdrawal, New Intelligence Assessment Says'. *WSJ*. Available online: https://www.wsj.com/articles/afghan-government-could-collapse-six-months-after-u-s-withdrawal-new-intelligence-assessment-says-11624466743 (Accessed: 31 August 2022).

Turak, N., Macias, A. and Ng, A. (2021), '"Intelligence Failure of the Highest Order" – How Afghanistan Fell to the Taliban so Quickly', *CNBC*. Available online: https://www.cnbc.com/2021/08/16/how-afghanistan-fell-to-the-taliban-so-quickly.html (Accessed: 25 August 2022).

U.S. Foreign Policy (2002), Available at: https://www.c-span.org/video/?168516-1/us-foreign-policy (Accessed: 1 September 2022).

Wimpelmann, T. (2013), 'Nexuses of Knowledge and Power in Afghanistan: The Rises and Fall of the Informal Justice Assemblage'. *Central Asian Survey*, 32(3): 406–22. Available online: https://doi.org/10.1080/02634937.2013.835200.

Wimpelmann, T. (2021) 'Gender, Violence, and Competing Sovereign Claims in Afghanistan', in The *Everyday Lives of Sovereignty: Political Imagination beyond the State*. Ithaca: Cornell University Press, 114–34.

Zeweri, H. (2017), 'The Specter of Failure: Rendering Afghan Women as Sites of Precarity in Empowerment Regimes'. *International Feminist Journal of Politics*, 19(4): 441–55. Available online: https://doi.org/10.1080/14616742.2017.1303335.

Zeweri, H. (2021), 'Between Imperial Rule and Sovereignty: Rethinking Afghanistan Studies'. *International Journal of Postcolonial Studies*, 24(1): 1–11. Available online: https://doi.org/10.1080/1369801X.2021.1885465.

Zeweri, H. and Osman, W. (2022), 'Afghan Women: Always Resisting Empire'. *Against the Current: A Socialist Journal*. Available online: https://internationalviewpoint.org/spip.php?article7550 (Accessed: 31 August 2022).

10

Leased Power and Vague Authority: The Political Culture and Economy of Rule in Afghanistan

M. Nazif Shahrani

In this short essay I will argue that the powers of Afghanistan's rulers, since its creation as a buffer state by the British Raj in the 1880s, can be best characterized as 'leased/borrowed', bestowed upon them by their various foreign patrons. This condition, and the political culture it engenders, has affected both the long-term political economy of the state and impeded the rulers' need for and inclination to seek popular political legitimacy. These unusual colonial circumstances, which involved the empowerment of Afghanistan's first rulers as a modern nation-state by British India, have shaped the problematic dynamics of state–society relations in Afghanistan for nearly one and a half centuries. And they have culminated in the 2021 restoration of Taliban militant rule. It is the dynamics of this political culture of dependency – on leased power by the rulers and its tragic consequences for the subjugated peoples of Afghanistan, the *ru'aya* (sing. *ra'yat*) and *ittiba'* (sing. *taba'a*), both meaning *subjects* – which I explore briefly here.

For the sake of clarity, I will briefly describe the difference between power (*qudrat*) and authority (*qudrati mashru'*) and clarify what is meant by political culture (*farhangi siyasi*). Both power and authority are forms of influence over others' conduct but with the critical difference being as to how or by what methods that impact is achieved. Power emanates from a person due to his or her force of personality, skills, experience or access to economic and military assets to impose his or her will on others, without the necessity of consent. Authority on the other hand is *legitimated power* and the sources of legitimacy according to Max Weber are three: 'tradition' (justified by the 'eternal yesterday' such as ancestry or other claims), 'personal charisma' (marked by extraordinary personality and communication skills with messages attracting mass following)and 'rational-legal' (conferred or delegated via elections or appointments within a formalized hierarchical institutional structure) (Weber 1919). Political culture refers to the operating principles, major beliefs, attitudes, values, ideals and sentiments that shape the exercise of power and authority within a society. That is, political culture provides a *model of* and *model for* a political process. This model then gets produced and maintained through the collective history of members of a society and gets demonstrated through the life experiences of its ruling elites and those of ordinary folks. It also gets reflected in the quality of their public and private lives (for detailed discussion, see Shahrani 2012).

The signal events shaping the contemporary political culture of modern Afghanistan were the late-nineteenth-century 'Great Games' of European colonial empires in Central Asia, which resulted in the creation of Afghanistan as a buffer state between Tsarist Russia and British India. The principal architect and stage manager of this imperialist project was Britain. The British Raj defined the country's boundaries, selected its first ruler, Abdur Rahman Khan, from among the warring Durrani princes for succession and crowned him as the Amir of Afghanistan (1880 to 1901). Amir Abdur Rahman was offered substantial annual cash subsidies as well as considerable modern weapons with the task of 'taming' his people and ruling over the many diverse tribal and ethnolinguistic-sectarian communities while relinquishing the country's foreign policy to his patron, the British Raj. He used the weapons he was given mercilessly against the people gaining the title of the 'Iron Amir' and tamed them into becoming his subjects, *taba'a wa ra'yat* (subjects) – the labels still used by the Taliban and inscribed in the constitutions of Afghanistan until now. The amir also attempted to sacralize the state by claiming that God chose him to be the leader of the country, a claim that instrumentalized Islam as part of the national political culture thereafter.

The British practice of leasing power (political and economic) to the Muhammadzai rulers continued with Abdur Rahman Khan's son, Amir Habibullah (1901 to 1919), but was interrupted by his grandson, Amanullah Khan (1919 to 1929) when he declared Afghanistan's national independence at the expense of losing the British subsidies and their frustration to boot. The declaration of independence earned Amanullah Khan popularity. Additionally, his notable oratory skills calling for reforms gained him popular support but did not last long. His ambitious imitative reform projects – like that of Ataturk in Turkey, but with less religious sensitivity in a more conservative Afghanistan – required funds, power and authority that he lacked. He raised taxes from his subjects, which also led to illegal extractions by his officials; multiple domestic revolts forced him to abdicate his throne in less than a decade. His successor, a rebel Habibullah Kalakani, could not obtain external recognition or foreign subsidies to extend his rule. His reign lasted only nine months. Similarities and differences of that historic event to the Taliban today are instructive about the Taliban's prospects to continue their misrule.

Britain then leased power to General Nader Khan and his brothers, lateral members of Amanullah's clan of Barakzai. Nader Khan, with British weapons and cash subsidies was quickly installed as Nader *Shah*, the new ruler of Afghanistan. His brutal reign of four years led to his assassination followed by fifty years of monarchic rule by his brothers and nephews. The Musahiban period (1929 to 1979) also saw some investment in education and communication infrastructure peppered with considerable doses of Pashtun (Afghan) nationalism. In retrospect, some consider that half century as the golden age of relative stability if void of real peace with justice in the country. Afghanistan's rulers continued to remain under the tutelage of Great Britain through the Second World War.

After the Second World War and the rise of anti-colonial wars of independence against the UK, its dominion around the globe gave way to a new form of ideologically defined imperial structures, which can be referred to as 'Empires of Trust' or 'Empire by Invitation' (Lundestad 1999; Madden 2008). The new global forces of domination came to be the American 'empire of trust' leading the capitalist West against the Soviet Union's 'empire by invitation' heading the socialist/communist Eastern bloc. Their so-called Cold War launched a new competition for leased power through educational-technical, military and economic assistance, to the rulers of postcolonial nation-states in Asia, Africa and Latin America (see Shahrani 2016).

The Cold War offered the rulers of Afghanistan – strategically proximate to the USSR and Pakistan and Iran, strategic allies of the United States – new opportunities for leased power and resources in the forms of military, technical, economic and educational assistance from both superpowers. Both sides, especially the Soviets, offered considerable military weapons in the 1950s, military training to the officers corp and some development assistance (the Salang Tunnel and road construction, irrigation and hydropower on the Kabul River, for example) thereafter. The United States also offered financial and development assistance for education, road construction and the Helmand River hydropower and irrigation projects. Some assistance was also drawn from Germany, especially for the Sarubi hydropower and the Jabalus Saraj textiles factory and more. During the decades of the 1960s and 1970s, more than 70 per cent of the country's annual operating budget was supported by foreign assistance (Fry 1974; Dupree 1980).

Soviet investments in Afghanistan, especially training to military officers and support for the Khalq and Parcham communist parties, paid off. But the successful military coup d'état of 1978 met with factional infighting and stiff popular jihad resistance, leading the Parcham faction to invite the Soviets in December of 1979 to intervene militarily, which they did (from 1979 to 1989). The Soviets became the new leaseholders for the power of the communist regimes in Afghanistan until their defeat and removal from power by the foreign armed and financially supported Afghan mujahidin in 1992.

The mujahidin groups were also quickly turned into leaseholders for power by their various outside military and financial supporters especially Saudi Arabia, Pakistan, Iran and covertly the US CIA (1980–92). Their internecine fighting during the early 1990s and later with the Taliban were financed by the many regional proxies (Pakistan, Saudi Arabia and the United Arab Emirates [UAE] versus Iran, Russia and India) that fought for influence and control of Afghanistan. This environment enabled a globalized jihadism, including the formation of the Al Qaeda network by Osama Bin Laden within the Taliban-controlled Afghanistan (1996–2001). From Afghanistan they allegedly planned and carried out the 11 September tragedy in the United States.

Over twenty years, the United States and its allies intervened in Afghanistan to wage global war 'on terrorism', costing the United States alone over two trillion dollars plus an estimated eighty-billion-dollar investment in Afghanistan's governance and reconstruction projects.[1] The powers of the rulers of Afghanistan from 2001 to 2021 were also leased by the United States to an unprecedented extent. Not surprisingly, the Taliban were also aided and abetted by Pakistan and their other allies in their fights against the US-NATO forces. In their presumed victory in 2021 they earned *ghanimat* (war booty) of more than seventy billion dollars-worth of modern weapons left behind by the United States. Even now, the Taliban collects a widely reported $40 million in cash per week from the United States which helps keep them in power (Wissing 2012; SIGAR 2023)

The consequences of these historic rulers' dependencies on leased power for the politics and political economy of the state have been clear – such dependencies have produced an *extractive economy* with *exclusionary politics* (see Sharan 2023, also Acemoglu and Robinson 2012). Because of the outside subsidies and foreign aid given to Afghanistan's rulers, they became the wealthiest segment of the population in the country. Simultaneously, they and their officials extracted even more money and resources from their subjects legally in the form of taxes (directly or indirectly) and illegally in bribes and extortion. All large productive enterprises (manufacturing industries, factories, banks, mines, energy production, etc.) became government monopolies or were owned by select members of the ruling elites. Opportunities for wealth production outside of traditional means (agriculture, small trade and crafts production) by ordinary people were rare until the US intervention (2001–21). Even then, these opportunities became available only for the well-connected, those able to get contracts from the US or other foreign military and logistics entities (Coburn 2018). As a result, the Afghan masses remain in extreme poverty with the situation under the Taliban rule even more dire.

The reality of an extensive and expansive political economy of rulers' dependency – economic, military, security, technology and education among other things – on outside powers has become part and parcel of the extant dysfunctional political culture of Afghanistan. This unfortunate historical reality has created and promoted person-centred political structures. Politics centred on individuals, families, tribes and ethnicities remain pervasive at the expense of values-centred, ideas-centred and programmes-focused political institutional structures. The results of this political culture have been a politics of exclusion that denies the peoples of Afghanistan the rights to participate in their own governance and political decision-making. They have not been able to shed their roles as subjects (*taba'a* and *ra'yat*), or to transform themselves into truly empowered citizens (*shahrwand*). The rulers have shown no real interest in seeking popular legitimacy (i.e. authority) since they have enjoyed access to leased powers that enable them to control a tamed nation of subjects. When necessary, they have shared power with a few token, hand-picked, non-representative ethnic entrepreneurs and claimed inclusiveness as a deceptive measure, a dubious claim now made by the Taliban as well.

The politics of exclusion was and is justified by demands for special privileges on behalf of rulers, their family, clan and select members of their ethnolinguistic cohorts. As such, the discrimination against and exclusion of many Afghans from all ethnolinguistic communities, including most members of the ruling elites' own communities, have become the norm. In the over-centralized system of governance, power and resources are monopolized by the select few. Those in power have used their privileges of appointing virtually all government officials from Kabul, promoting nepotism, cronyism, bias and corruption, further enriching themselves and creating vast chains of dependency across society. Appointed officials to the provinces and districts have long been viewed by local inhabitants as outsiders interested in economic extraction and weakening or destroying the fabric of their local communities of trust.

Because of the avaricious practice of government-appointed officials, local communities have formed their own authoritative parallel local leadership structures to protect themselves against the menace of the corrupt officials sent by the central government (see Shahrani 1986). Instead of building, reforming and strengthening such horizontal democratic structures at the local levels to build the vertical structures of the central government, Kabul's rapacious officials have consistently relied on their leased powers from outsiders to weaken or destroy these local communities of trust (Shahrani 2013). Indeed, securitized regimes in Kabul – reliant on leased military and financial powers from hostile, mostly colonial Islamophobic outsiders – have felt no real need to seek popular legitimacy from the peoples of Afghanistan. Elections held in the name of adherence to globalized democratic practices have been for the most part fraudulent and a sham, whether during the monarchies, the communist rule of the 1980s or the two decades of the US-NATO intervention (2001–21).

Rulers have generally pandered to their foreign patrons to secure their rule, and not always successfully, instead of seeking popular support. Since the late 1960s, governments have not relied on direct taxation from the increasingly poverty-stricken bulging rural population. Since the 1970s, many educated or skilled youth have left the country (or at least tried) to seek work in Iran. Meanwhile, large numbers of rural youth, especially from the very poor families from the northern provinces – much like the Pashtuns in the south – have been attracted by the prospects of free madrasa education in Pakistan since the 1980s. This latter phenomenon, together with dysfunctional political culture, sadly have made it possible for the Pakistani ISI and other hostile Islamophobic international intelligence agencies to instrumentalize and successfully weaponize Islam. These tragic outcomes are the products of a distorted trajectory fueled by a political culture of dependency produced and maintained in collaboration with the leased leaders of rented regimes in Afghanistan for almost a century and a half. The near-term prospects for radical shift to transformation of *ru'aya* and *ittiba'* into an empowered *shahrwandan* seem rather dim for the long-suffering people of Afghanistan.

Note

1   The initial intent of the United States may have been a 'war on terror', but this war – instead of reducing terrorism – increased the emergence of more terrorist groups globally. For this reason the term 'war FOR terrorism' might be more appropriate.

References

Acemoglu, D. and Robinson, J. A. (2012), *Why Nations Fail: The Origins of Power, Prosperity, and Poverty*. New York: Crown.

Coburn, N. (2018), 'Merchant-Warlords: Changing Forms of Leadership in Afghanistan's Unstable Political Economy', in Shahrani, M. N. (ed.), *Modern Afghanistan: The Impact of 40 Years of War*. Bloomington, IN: Indiana University Press.

Dupree, L. (1980), *Afghanistan*. Princeton: Princeton University Press.

Fry, M. (1974/1997), *The Afghan Economy: Money, Finance and the Critical Constraints to Economic Development* (Social, Economic and Political Studies of the Middle East and Asia, No. 15). Leiden: Brill.

Lundestad, G. (1999), '"Empire by Invitation" in the American Century'. Diplomatic History, 23(2): 189–217.

Madden, T. F. (2008), Empires of Trust: How Rome Built-and America Is Building-a New World. New York: Dutton.

Shahrani, M. N. (1986). 'The Kirghiz Khans: Styles and Substance of Traditional Local Leadership in Central Asia'. *Central Asian Survey*, 5(3/4): 255–71.

Shahrani, M. N. (2012). 'Approaching Study of Political Culture in Afghanistan with Institutional Analysis and Development (IAD) and Social-Ecological Systems (SES) Frameworks', in Brooks, B. E., Brooks Babin, L., Ramsden Zbylut, M and Roan, L. (eds.), *Sociocultural Systems: The Next Step in Army Cultural Capability* (ARI research Product 2012-XX). Arlington, VA: U.S. Army Research Institute for the Behavioral and Social Sciences, 169–92.

Shahrani, M. N. (2013), 'Center-Periphery Relations in Afghanistan', in Schetter, C. (ed.), *Local Politics in Afghanistan*. London: Hurst Publishers, 23–38.

Shahrani, M. N. (2016), 'Why Muslim Sectarian Politics of Rage in the Age of "Empire of Trust"?' *Journal of Islamic and Muslim Studies*, 1(1): 28–46.

Sharan, T. (2023), *Inside Afghanistan: Political Networks, Informal Order, and State Disruption*. London and New York: Routledge.

SIGAR (2023), 'Quarterly Report to the U.S. Congress'. Available at: https://www.sigar.mil/pdf/quarterlyreports/2023-04-30qr.pdf (Accessed: 5 September 2023).

Weber, M. (1919 [1970]), 'Politics as a Vocation', in H. H. Gerth and C. W. Mills (eds). *From Max Weber: Essays in Sociology*. London: Routledge, 77–128.

Wissing, D. (2012), *Funding the Enemy: How US Taxpayers Bankroll the Taliban*. Amherst, NY: Prometheus Books.

11

Legitimacy by Design

Astri Suhrke

About forty years ago I travelled to Pakistan to interview the mujahidin fighters who had established themselves in Peshawar, making it the headquarters for their campaign to oust the Soviet armed forces from Afghanistan and defeat the Najibullah government. The so-called moderate factions were installed in a large, barrack-looking building with offices well equipped to receive visitors who came to collect information or offer support. Gulbuddin Hekmatyar lodged separately in a comfortable, large compound where he held court among his numerous supporters and ceremoniously welcomed even a stray researcher like myself. Much smaller factions, such as that led by mujahidin commander Amin Wardak, were also fully cognizant of the power of performative politics. Wardak's office was located in an affluent-looking house with a bright new sign that announced 'The Peshawar office of the Wardak Command'. The commander himself graciously welcomed his European visitor with an elegant speech in French. When it was time for a photo-op, his followers quickly arranged themselves in a perfect formation – the man at the back hopping up on a table to complete the triangle. The sun streaming through the window caught his light-coloured turban and made it look like a flaming torch.

The hopes for the future suggested by that torch were soon extinguished by a new civil war (1992–96) and then the suppressive rule of the Taliban's first Islamic Emirate (1996–2001). The international coalition that led Afghanistan for the subsequent two decades (2001–21) had little appreciation of the way symbolic politics, including types of performativity, can generate and nourish legitimacy. Instead, the legitimacy of the new order was constructed around a utilitarian programme where actual performance, rather than the symbolic presentation of such, mattered the most. To justify the grand state building venture launched in 2001, its international architects drew up plans for an effective and benevolent state. Yet, this ideological platform was beset with contradictions that undermined its legitimating functions, as I wrote in my book on the international project in 2011 (Suhrke 2011).

The main justification for the new order, I argued, was to establish at least a minimally effective state out of the chaos left by revolution, invasion and civil war. This was implicit in the popular aspirations for peace and security that were captured in surveys, public opinion polls and much anecdotal information. The broader rationale was laid out in the preamble to the Bonn Agreement, which embodied the goals of 'national reconciliation, lasting peace, stability and respect for human rights', as well as 'the principles of Islam, democracy, pluralism and social justice'.

A state that provided a measure of security, justice, basic social services and good governance would seem to carry its own source of legitimacy. That belief was repeatedly expressed in the public discourse among the coalition partners, in the aid community and among Afghan reformers. The problem with this essentially utilitarian source of legitimacy, however, is that it exerts no normative force merely by virtue of its ideational existence. The state has to actually deliver in order to cash in on its legitimacy potential. The same applies to elections. In order to legitimate a political contest, elections have to be seen as reasonably free and fair.

Ultimately, the Afghan state mostly did not deliver on this potential. There were the oft-cited advances in education and health, and on women's rights in the urban areas. Yet the new order failed to provide the basic elements of human security in almost all parts of the country; to halt the growing abuse, corruption and incompetence in public administration; to stem the mounting insurgency and the perception that the international forces were responsible for excessive or unjustly inflicted violence; and – perhaps most important – to provide a political exit from the war. Whatever legitimacy was bestowed by the first presidential and parliamentary elections seemed lost in the violence and fraud that marred the subsequent rounds.

The daily realities of violence, inequality and corruption overshadowed the liberal democratic vision initially promoted by international and Afghan reformers and supported through numerous governance projects. Increasingly, the vision faded even in the declaratory policy of donors, as their goal slid from 'good' to 'good enough'.

I made this assessment in 2011. It involved a discussion of two major, alternate sources of legitimacy – religion and nationalism. For obvious reasons, neither was readily available to the internationally constructed new order. With respect to religion, the Taliban had laid claim to an ostensibly purer form of Islam to justify their struggle against the western forces; meanwhile, internationally, the leaders of the coalition remained locked in a globalized armed struggle against forces of militant Islam. Nationalism was clearly out as well. A political order that was heavily dependent on international capital, consultants and foreign military forces to survive could not credibly invoke nationalism as a legitimizing ideology.

Reviewing this analysis today, almost two years after the fall of that order, I think I would sharpen it in two respects. Most obviously, I would underscore the failure of performance: the effective, benevolent state did not materialize. But there was also a problem with symbolic politics. The declaratory role of Afghans as creating a distinctly Afghan version of the new order was rarely promoted by appropriate symbolic actions. Hamid Karzai, readers may recall, made a rare effort to the contrary by creating, and frequently wearing, a dress that symbolized the multicultural traditions of the Afghan nation. The practice lasted throughout his presidential tenure. His successor, Ashraf Ghani – perhaps realizing the potential power of performativity – donned a turban. Yet that proved inadequate to conceal his dominant western-modern image and background.

More generally, the pervasive presence of foreigners – civilian and military – at public ceremonies as well as daily life in both urban and many rural areas sent signals that conveyed the importance of foreign, not Afghan leadership. The point was captured in the stale joke over the donor slogan that 'the Afghans are in the driver's seat'. 'But', ran the bottom line, 'who owns the car and pays for the fuel?'

The substantive as well as symbolic power of elections – a key institution in a democratic political system – was likewise negated not only by violence and fraud, but perhaps more devastatingly by the aftermath of the 2014 presidential elections. After two rounds, both Ashraf Ghani and Abdullah Abdullah claimed victory and accused each other of fraud. It took forceful mediation by Secretary of State John Kerry to end the stand-off. The photo showing Kerry standing behind the two Afghans, physically towering over both, told it all. The elections really meant nothing much; it was American power that again determined the outcome.

By expressing the dominance of foreign leadership, symbolic politics conveyed a material reality that made it impossible for nationalism to serve as a source of legitimacy for the new order. The two decades of international state building consequently lacked the type of ideational foundation that historically has been a critical element in the formation of states and nations, as well as the historically exceptional cases of successful state building. Writing today, in 2024, this is the second point I would like to sharpen.

Externally directed state building as it took form in Afghanistan from 2001 to 2021 now seems to me more clearly to have been a form of neo-colonialism. The label is complicated; it probably has become more so after the recent revival of critical analysis of the colonial period and material actions against its remaining structures and symbols. Here I want only to emphasize that the structures of foreign dominance in Afghanistan in the international coalition period were quite clear. The economic dominance was expressed in striking figures provided by the World Bank in 2019: a stunning 75 per cent of Afghan public expenditure was financed by foreign aid in the form of grants (World Bank 2019). Aid flows in 2020 represented 42.9 per cent of the country's GDP.

Coalition forces, particularly US air power and logistics, remained central to the operation of the Afghan armed forces against the insurgents even after the change in the NATO mission from armed combat to 'advise and assist' at the end of 2014. The new mission – ambitiously named Resolute Support – did not change the underlying structure of dependence. As dramatically demonstrated in the months leading up to the fall of the government on 15 August 2020, the Afghan armed forces were built to remain operationally dependent on US and allied support and collectively collapsed when that support ended.

The two-decade-long international project in Afghanistan had many benevolent and laudable goals. It improved the lives of some segments of the population, particularly urban women, and enabled a local professional class. Yet the economic and military dependence that the project entailed, and indeed fostered, sharply limited the power of the recipient government and the Afghan people more broadly. This political condition, I would now argue, offended a deep sense of national dignity and nationalist identity that transcend the ethnic and social diversity of Afghanistan. This made the international project vulnerable and brittle from the start, with the tensions increasingly evident until the project finally came apart in 2021.

References

Suhrke, A. (2011), *When More Is Less. The International Project in Afghanistan*. London: Hurst.

World Bank (2019), 'Afghanistan: Public Expenditure Update'. https://www.worldbank.org/en/country/afghanistan/publication/afghanistan-public-expenditure-update.

12

Brokerage, Business and the Continuities in Power

Noah Coburn and Arsalan Noori

The Collapse

In the chaotic days leading up to the collapse of the Islamic Republic of Afghanistan on 15 August 2021, political actors scrambled to position themselves for a potential change of regime. They crossed borders, both international and those between Taliban territory and government-controlled territory, attempting to position themselves for what was to come next.

One week earlier, Abdul Rashid Dostum, the Uzbek warlord and former vice president, and Atta Muhammad Noor, the former governor of Balkh, flew north to the strategic city of Mazar-e Sharif, which was increasingly under siege by advancing Taliban troops. They announced that they were rallying Afghan National Army and other irregular forces to prevent the takeover of the city by the Taliban. The two men had dominated the north of the country politically since the 1980s war against the Soviet Union, oftentimes as rivals to one another – and had both enriched themselves and further solidified their own authority through a series of political appointments under the internationally sponsored republican government (Giustozzi 2009; Mukhopadhyay 2014; Malejacq 2020). In short, these men were consummate survivors in Afghan politics.

Yet on 14 August, the two leaders abruptly abandoned the city, fleeing north overland to Uzbekistan and essentially handing their region to the Taliban. Atta sent a tweet to his followers that stated: 'My dear countrymen! Despite our firm resistance, sadly, all the government and the #ANDSF equipments were handed over to the #Taliban as a result of a big organized and cowardly plot. They had orchestrated the plot to trap Marshal Dostum and myself too, but they didn't succeed' (14 August 2021 Tweet).

Around the same time, a small convoy of construction vehicles, belonging to a businessman named Mirwais and his brother, drove north from Kabul towards the province of Baghlan.[1] Mirwais' plan was to provide the heavy equipment to resistance groups to further solidify the military defences around the province to fortify it in

Arsalan Noori is a pseudonym.

preparation for a potential Taliban attack. Meanwhile, Ashraf Ghani's vice president, Amrullah Saleh, had driven north to the Panjshir valley, his birthplace, to help lead the resistance from there. These pockets of resistance hoped to unite and push back the Taliban given their belief that the insurgents had overreached in their seizure of these territories.

However, in the two weeks following the Taliban takeover of Kabul, it became clear no significant resistance would be mounted against Taliban forces, at least in the near term. Within weeks Saleh and other leaders moved to Istanbul, leaving behind small groups of fighters inside Afghanistan and in Tajikistan.

Around the same time, the convoy of construction vehicles owned by Mirwais rolled back through Taliban checkpoints and into Kabul. Not long after, Mirwais was back working in his office, having agreed to work on several construction projects for the new Taliban authorities. The same excavators that had been digging positions for resistance fighters were working on public work projects for the Taliban within a week.

In this chapter, we ask: how, in the face of such rapid government collapse, did the Taliban authorities, out of power for twenty years and with limited administrative experience, stabilize the country with limited local resistance? The answer, we believe, lies in part with a group of hybrid businessmen and brokers who successfully navigated relationships on both sides of the war and maintained these relationships even the regime in Kabul changed. This assertion does not overlook the Taliban's violent acts, retributive killings and perpetrated disappearances as human rights groups have recorded them. However, the lack of a coherent resistance two years into their rule, particularly considering the deplorable economic conditions their return has brought, suggests that the Taliban's power has found buttressing from within.

Based on interviews with Mirwais, as well as interviews both with close associates and those in his orbit, this chapter argues that his ability to maintain a flexible network of allies and business contacts – and the success that has produced – is based, at least in part, on a continuity of power structures from one era to another. In particular, we would argue, the continuity of power relations just below that of the national elite has proved salient. This is both a recent phenomenon and one that follows a historical pattern: as Thomas Barfield described it, leadership in Afghanistan has come and gone, but much of the government bureaucracy and the bureaucratic officials have remained in place through those transitions (Barfield 2012). In this case, the government bureaucracy has been supplemented by the myriad deals and networks that Mirwais and others have cultivated. These alliances are in part built upon some long-commented-upon aspects of Afghan political life, such as reputation, but also through an ability to work with international contractors and military, drug dealers, smugglers and criminal networks, and to serve as brokers between these multiple groups. As we will argue, these brokers have a long history in Afghanistan, but the nature of the last twenty years of war, followed by the collapse of the Ghani government, have given them new prominence as uniquely suited navigators within this early period of renewed Taliban rule.

Studying Power in Afghanistan

A robust field of political studies has emerged over the past twenty years from Afghanistan. As Robert Crews argues, far from being peripheral, Afghanistan has been at the centre of how many of the world's empires have defined themselves. And, in turn the global forces emanating from Afghanistan have deeply shaped these empires (Crews 2015). In more recent years, Afghanistan has been at the forefront of projects that aim to redesign political society. Western organizations and governments turned Afghanistan into a laboratory for democratization projects, such as the $717 million World Bank-funded Citizens Charter Program that aimed to grow grassroots democracy through local development councils (World Bank 2021). In decades past, these projects were shaped by socialist visions of the 1980s as well as al Qaeda's employment of the territory in the 1990s as a place from which to imagine a global caliphate. And, for some within the Taliban, inspiration came from images of an Afghan nation built on Pashtun culture alongside more localized readings of the Quran (Strick van Linschoten and Kuehn 2012). As such, Afghanistan has been continually used by both intervening forces and Afghan elites as a site for the construction and performance of strategic political narratives. Those Afghans outside the most elite circles have lived through these experiments but rarely bought into the extreme versions of political ideology espoused by their leaders. If we look at how they attempt to navigate these changing regimes, we can learn much about the lived experience of political power (Barfield 2012).

While the academic study of politics in Afghanistan has expanded significantly in the past twenty years, scholarly studies as well as media accounts of politics in Afghanistan tend to focus either on the ultra-local or ultra-elite level of politics with less focus on those actors that actually bridge the gaps between the two. This is partially a result of western disciplinary approaches to Afghanistan, where anthropologists have tended to focus on the local, while political scientists and scholars of international relations have focused on the national, but it is also something of a consequence of the ways in which much of Afghan political life is organized. Most Afghans, particularly in rural areas, rely on elders and religious leaders to resolve disputes and organize small-scale public works projects (Coburn 2013). At the same time, national-level figures often control key resources, such as government revenue and international aid flows that shape broader development and economic trends across the country.[2]

As Jennifer Brick Murtazashvili lays out in her study of subnational politics: 'The most important public goods in rural Afghanistan are things like basic law and order, dispute resolution, and small-scale infrastructure. Despite chaos in Kabul, these goods are often provided through customary channels at the village levels.' Communities, often on their own, cooperate to ensure that these resources are preserved, whether it means the allocation of water or collective forms of justice (Murtazashvili 2018).

Much of the rural order in the country was shaped by the violence and instability brought on by the influx of international funds of the 2000s and 2010s, but it was less impacted by the actual state institutions themselves, particularly since district- and village-level elections were never held as mandated by the Afghan constitution of 2004. In fact, as Dipali Mukhopadhyay points out, the state often relied on 'strongman governors' and other officials with connections to more grassroots forms of authority to help strengthen state institutions in post-2001 Afghanistan (Mukhopadhyay 2021).

While state institutions may have had a more minimal impact on local structures, this is not to imply that these more local structures were static, nor that they were devoid of connections to state institutions. In fact, ethnographic accounts of politics in Afghanistan have long pointed out the ways in which so-called traditional forms of leadership are highly dynamic and adapt to shifting economic and political conditions, particularly during periods of upheaval. Classic examples of this include the move by Khirgiz *khans* to extract resources from the state to build their legitimacy, as studied by M. Nazif Shahrani, but also the delegitimization of Uzbek *khans* as the state-coopted traditional roles, as in the case of the shifting significance of the game of *buzkashi* in the late twentieth century as studied by Whitney Azoy (Shahrani 1986; Azoy 2012).

This adaptability was particularly important during the twenty years of the US-led war in Afghanistan. This era saw a weakening of tribal structures, as well as some of the mechanisms that kept commanders and Islamist political parties in place during the 1980s and 1990s.[3] Similarly, warlords and commanders who had been influential in past periods, were no longer important just because they controlled territory (Malejacq 2020). Instead, as Romain Malejacq has pointed out, their authority was based on the ability to exert influence or *nafuz* in different ways. Some of these figures maintained influence by participating in the shadow economy, including smuggling or the drug trade (Goodhand 2005). Many others, however, allied themselves more closely with the state, particularly with the influx of international resources in the form of developmental funds and military spending (Coburn 2011b).

Amidst this massive influx of aid (US funds for reconstruction went from $1 billion in 2002 to $3.5 billion in 2006 and $16 billion in 2010), government institutions in Afghanistan continued to struggle to gain authority or influence as institutions in and of themselves. Instead, the system evolved into a kind of 'fragile limited access order', which Douglass North, John Wallis and Barry Wiengast define as one where weak rule of law and economic oversight produce a political economy dominated at the national level by a small group of powerful actors (North et al. 2013). Within this group, William Byrd points out 'economic and political spheres overlap', making political organizations, followers of ethnic leaders and even companies 'vehicles for armed political groups to access rents' (Byrd 2015). Little incentive to reform, or even upend, the system exists as long as rents continue to flow. As national-level actors and their local allies negotiated for resources in this system, other local structures remained more robust, though, by definition, more limited in scale.

Between these two groups, however, a connective tissue of political and economic actors like Mirwais existed, which managed to knit together the state- and local-level structures to great personal effect. These figures are understudied in part because disciplinary approaches to politics tend to favour the national or local level, but also because these figures gained their strength by operating quietly in and across multiple realms. Their hybridity made them difficult to define, but, particularly as the Taliban advanced in the late 2010s, and control of the country became more splintered, they operated very much like brokers, navigating a series of geographic, political and social boundaries across the country.

Brokers

There is a symbiotic relationship between borders and brokers. The political and social disjunctions that borders create open up opportunities for brokers to take advantage. Jonathan Goodhand, Jan Koehler and Jasmine Bhatia suggest that paying attention 'to the edges tells us important things about the whole; the lives of seemingly marginal borderland brokers provide a privileged vantage point for understanding the wider political economy of (licit and illicit) trading systems, how they change over time and their distributional effects within and across borders' (Goodhand, Koehler, and Bhatia 2021). Taking this argument one step further, it is useful to think of how internal borders, both formal and informal, create opportunities for multiple forms of brokerage within a country.

This is certainly true of Afghanistan during the 2010s, when, depending upon the year, the Taliban controlled between a third and a half of all of the country's territory. These borders were, at times, very real and there were physical checkpoints set up by the Taliban to control who passed through certain territory. At other times, these internal boundaries were more subtle, but still made themselves manifest in daily life, from control over violence in a certain area to the practices of (not) sending daughters to school to decisions about dress and comportment. Those brokers who thrived in the 2010s had to contend with a set of incentives and realities created by the international intervention, particularly that of the US government, the Taliban and the Afghan government. The ability to cross from Taliban to government-controlled territory thus became an increasingly valuable skill and provided brokers with the opportunity to take advantage of the scarcity of certain resources on different sides of the border.

There is an established history of thinking about Afghanistan as a space with different territories and internal borders. Both Thomas Barfield in his political history of the country and Ashley Jackson in her more recent study of civilian–Taliban relations have pointed to the ways in which maps of political control in Afghanistan resemble Swiss cheese, with distinguishable 'holes' or gaps in government control (Barfield 2012; Jackson 2021). At the same time, however, the ideological differences between the political and economic order of the internationally backed government's realm and the realm held by the Taliban created almost completely different rhetorics and forms of social and political capital.

While these internal borders demarcated different political 'countries' with different orders, this difference did not preclude their being (frequently) crossed. In fact, ordinary Afghans often had to cross these boundaries daily. The borders themselves could also shift rapidly, with some territory being government-held by day and Taliban-controlled by night. As Jackson writes:

> The lines between combatants and civilians are slippery in real life: ... an aid worker could at one point have been a Taliban fighter; a government worker, likely to be seen by the Taliban as a combatant, would be a civilian in my view ... Some civilians were seen as Taliban 'in their hearts' even if they did not take an active role in the conflict.
>
> (Jackson 2021)

In government-controlled territory there were resources to be had for those that could speak the language of USAID and military contracts, as well as those projects encouraging democratization and other forms of liberal reform. In Taliban-controlled territory, ties between fighters and their kin networks, connections to specific *madrasas* (religious schools) or militia leaders created very different forms of capital. And ultimately, those brokers that could navigate between both of these worlds were best positioned not just to survive, but actually to thrive during periods of transition from one form of government to the next.

By the time the Ghani government collapsed in 2021, many members of the political elite, like Dostum and Atta, had grown overly reliant on the Islamic Republic, and, more importantly, the donors funding it, without maintaining sufficient connections on the other side of those internal boundaries. That meant, at least at first, they had few choices, but to move into exile. At the same time, for figures like Mirwais, who could cross those boundaries successfully, the new *de facto* authorities allowed them to remain. Moreover, the new government created opportunities for these brokers, given their experience and expertise in service delivery and the bureaucratic workings of the state, both of which members of the Taliban sorely lacked.

Mirwais

In their 2021 study, Goodhand, Koehler and Bhatia argue for a scholarly focus on both the positionality of brokers ('their personal backgrounds, their ability to straddle lifeworlds, the "deal spaces" they occupy, the resources and commodities they move, and the key pathways, corridors and choke points that channel and direct trade flows'), as well the dynamics of brokering ('including the ways that brokers find solutions or "fixes" to problems but rarely resolve them, and how brokers adapt to [or fail to adapt to] moments of rupture in fluid trading environments') (Goodhand, Koehler, and Bhatia 2021: 118). Our case study of Mirwais – an analysis of both his positionality and the dynamics of his brokerage, the ways in which he developed his own power and authority – demonstrates the international reshaping of Afghanistan's political economy in terms that allowed figures like him to thrive.

Mirwais came from a poor family in Baghlan province, which during earlier generations would have been badly positioned to rise in social or political class. Indeed, because of their poverty, his brother migrated to Iran to find work as a labourer, joining over two million Afghan refugees there (UN High Commissioner for Refugees 2001; Monsutti 2005). Mirwais remained in Afghanistan and, as he described it, his first real opportunity came during the 1990s when he was hired by a relief agency as a driver, earning $70 a month. As the civil war went on, he moved between agencies, slowly advancing in each while building a regionally and ethnically diverse network that also captured internationals working in the humanitarian industry.

Shortly after the US-led invasion, his brother returned to Afghanistan, bringing home his construction experience as well as new social connections with Afghan migrants he had met in Iran. Together with some friends, they set up a construction and logistics firm, which focused on small-scale construction projects in response to the building boom in Kabul. During the early 2000s, western organizations set up offices and financed projects, while Afghans who had previously lived abroad returned to rebuild family homes. Mirwais and his partners worked on many of these small building projects. His big break, he said, came when he won a contract to paint some of the new government offices funded by a US contract.

It was not a large amount of work, he said, but was spread out across several sites around the city. When he went to pick up payment for the project, he described how the finance officer overseeing the project handed him 25 million *afghanis* (or approximately $250,000) instead of the 2.5 million *afghanis* ($25,000) that he had thought that he was owed. He tried to give the money back, but the officer insisted it was the correct amount and that he take it. When he returned to his office, he rechecked the contract, and saw that in the estimate there was a typographical error. The firm had meant to bid 2.5 million on the project, but had instead put down 25 million. Whether Mirwais' tale was apocryphal or not, this was a story that Mirwais both told about himself and that others told about him. It spoke to local assumptions about the poor oversight of international funds and the limited interest internationals appeared to have in spending efficiently.

Most importantly, Mirwais said, his successful completion of this project gave him access to other US military-sponsored construction and logistics projects. Over the next few years, as his business expanded, he began turning down any project that was less than $500,000. During this phase of expansion, Mirwais worked closely with Hanif Atmar, who at the time (2008–10) was minister of the interior, along with several powerful parliamentarians from the Parwan district which housed Bagram Airbase.[4] While the workers they hired were often from Baghlan, they also made it a point to hire groups from other areas, which would help ensure connections to other parts of the country where new contracts might be released. This multi-ethnic, geographically widespread network of allies built on some of Mirwais' ties to his home area of Baghlan, but often crossed typical regional and ethnic-based networks.

As his business grew, the brothers worked to diversify their opportunities while building on the connections they had in both the US and Afghan militaries. They bought real estate around Kabul and elsewhere. In particular, they turned two large compounds into private military bases with guard towers, multiple layers of security and private security forces. They then rented these compounds to UN offices, US military contractors and other large NGOs who housed their employees and, in some cases, offices, there. In these instances, Mirwais benefitted from the rent they collected, and also the further connections they made with these international organizations. Mirwais explained that the attitude of the internationals controlling the contracts generally was 'If you've found an Afghan businessman you trust, why not continue working with him, considering how incompetent and corrupt the alternatives could be?' This ultimately contributed to the concentration of international funds within a select class of brokers like Mirwais.

Afghan politicians were particularly eager to work with Mirwais because of his connections to and understandings of the US military contracts on the base. During this period, when the US government was especially concerned with what it perceived as Afghan corruption, politicians like Atmar struggled to profit directly from the construction and logistics contracts available on US military bases. They could profit, however, by partnering with intermediaries, like Mirwais, who would hold the main contract and then subcontract out to companies associated with these politicians or their families. The networks that Mirwais relied on were often based on kin and ethnicity, with many of his closest associates being from Baghlan. But this did not prevent him from making alliances with politicians and businessmen from various ethnic groups and representing various political interests. And, so, his business grew even as the Afghan government lost ground to the Taliban.

Throughout the 2010s, as the Taliban footprint expanded, more territory across the country became contested. In June 2021, *The Long War Journal* estimated that only 80 of 407 districts were under government control, while the Taliban controlled 160 districts, leaving 167 districts 'disputed' (Roggio 2017). In many of these disputed districts (and in some of the 'government-controlled' ones as well), there was an ostensible government presence, particularly during the day and in the district centre, but, often, the Taliban had control of the roads at night. Insurgents could freely set up checkpoints, collect taxes or, more typically, monitor the various projects ongoing in the districts (Giustozzi 2019; Jackson 2021; Amiri and Jackson 2022).

This gave the Taliban *de facto* veto control over projects and, depending upon the political situation in a specific area, Talibs could demand a tax to allow projects to continue. In Wardak, for instance, projects sponsored by the Afghan government, World Bank and other international organizations continued, since the government ostensibly maintained control of the province for much of the 2010s; but in fact, for those organizations working in the province, it was necessary to pay a tax to local Taliban officials to keep projects going (Amiri and Jackson 2022). Afghan construction companies almost always implemented these projects, hiding the fees in their accounting (sometimes by inflating material costs, but also by pushing local labourers, who often wanted to see these projects completed, to accept lower wages).

At first, Mirwais said he tried to avoid working in these contested territories. Instead, if he had a road building contract, for instance, he would first make sure that he had the approval of local elders to begin the work. As time went on, however, in a growing number of areas, the Taliban began to threaten projects associated with either the international community or the national government. In many of these instances, Mirwais realized that he could not rely on the government to protect his work or equipment.

To function in this environment, companies and individuals required the ability to navigate across the boundary between the Islamic Republic and the Taliban. International contractors were more hesitant to take contracts in these areas because of the threats to their employees and the complexity of managing relations with Taliban officials. In contrast, Mirwais and his associates were ideally placed to run projects of this kind. They had connections with various local elders who could put them in contact with local Taliban officials, and, when absolutely necessary, they had access to armed security contractors to protect their projects and equipment.

Mirwais' firm proved able to cross these kinds of invisible boundaries in the paradigmatic province of Wardak. Wardak is a province located very close to Kabul, but still difficult to access due to its mountainous terrain; it is known for its resistance to the British presence in Kabul in the nineteenth century (Dupree 1997). Since then, its inhabitants have maintained a proud narrative of independence: Wardakis resisted the communist government of the 1980s, but also produced very few members of the initial Taliban movement of the 1990s. The province witnessed some of the fiercest fighting between local Wardakis loyal to Gulbuddin Hekmaytar and the Taliban (Elias 2009). Yet, the province was one of the first in the centre of the country where the Taliban gained a firm foothold as early as 2006. By 2008, the province had a complex Taliban shadow government with representation at the district and sub-district levels (Elias 2009).

Despite the Taliban's *de facto* control, international organizations and the Afghan government continued to run substantial projects in the province. They did so by contracting work to a variety of NGOs and Afghan firms; Mirwais' company had some of these contracts. To work in Wardak, it was necessary to have Taliban permission. At the start of a project, Mirwais would reach out to elders he knew in the community with contacts in the Taliban shadow government. Often it was unnecessary to meet directly with the Taliban members themselves, as these elders would serve as intermediaries between the two sides. Mirwais would share project documents with the Taliban as well as a budget. The two sides would agree on a tax, usually paid in cash; the arrangement might also involve the promise to hire allies of the Taliban from the area. The brothers' success in completing projects even in contested areas led to more contracts for them.

Meanwhile, they continued to pursue contracts that required close government ties. After around fifteen years of growth, the brothers realized that a direct connection to the government would potentially open up even more contracts to them. Since so much of their business relied on direct contracts with international groups, they saw an opportunity to expand by situating themselves *within* the Afghan government in Kabul (Coburn 2011a). In 2018, Mirwais' brother ran for parliament and Mirwais served as his campaign manager. The campaign was well-organized and they managed to mobilize voters both through their family connections in Baghlan, but also through their business partners and those politicians with whom they had worked over the past decade. Mirwais' brother won a seat easily.

By the time Mirwais' brother joined the parliament in 2018, the parliament was largely at odds with President Ghani. Growing accusations of parliamentary corruption (Bjelica and Sorush 2018) and the absence of substantive political parties meant that the legislature's activities had little bearing on the lives of ordinary Afghans. Indeed, as Jennifer Brick Murtazashvili put it, the parliament 'never managed to play a constructive role in Afghan society' (Murtazashvili 2022). At the same time, however, a seat in the parliament did provide access to certain resources, both international and Afghan government based, from which the brothers could benefit (Coburn 2010). And, so, even as the Taliban advanced in the final years of the Afghan Republic, the brothers continued to win contracts and work on a variety of construction projects.

The New Taliban Era: Why Brokers Survived

Given the influx of weapons and funds to Afghanistan over the past forty years, it is remarkable just how many groups and leaders proved *unable* to hold on to power after 2021. National-level elite figures like Dostum and Atta, even when at odds with the government in Kabul, grew deeply connected to and implicated in the Afghan Republic and the international community that supported it. As a result, when the government started to crumble, they were not able to regroup their followers and resist the Taliban on terms independent from government structures as they had in previous decades. Mirwais and other brokers who worked with both the government and the Taliban were far more likely and able to remain in the country after the Taliban's return and continue their business with new patrons. The ability of these mid-level brokers to navigate internal boundaries and to maintain power and authority independent from the Afghan state ultimately protected them during the most turbulent times of transition back to Taliban rule.

Over the Islamic Republic's twenty years, sources of external funding for brokers like Mirwais evolved significantly. Starting with a light military and development spending footprint in the early 2000s, the United States later ramped up troops' levels and flooded the country with funds during Obama's 2009–13 surge. American money, troops and influence would decline slowly in the years that followed. Likewise, Mirwais' influence and business expanded as international funds came in, but as funding started to decline, he looked elsewhere for opportunities. Ultimately, the vagaries of funding and troop levels did little to change the way authority worked on the ground level versus the preferences and politics of those local figures with whom Mirwais engaged as he set up projects.

As Murtazashvili has remarked, despite the range of forms of local governance, 'fieldwork in rural Afghanistan revealed surprising similarity in the organization of village governance across a diverse ethnic, religious, and tribal landscape'. In general, rural areas have maintained 'polycentric governance … centers of decision-making are independent, yet overlapping … in most communities, there is not one individual or organization who rules authoritatively over others' (Murtazashvili 2018: 3–4). Those who wished to work across these communities required political and social networks encompassing an array of actors. They could establish these networks by hiring close kin, holding formal and informal meetings, and participating in local rituals, such as visiting on holidays. Such small acts allowed actors like Mirwais to traverse the blurry boundaries between government- and Taliban-held territories. Ultimately, for those that could consistently cross those boundaries and maintain relationships on both sides, there were significant gains to be made.

Much remains unknown about what form the state will take under the new Taliban regime. Certainly, the centralized tendencies of the group are at odds both with the political diversity of the country and its ability to enforce decisions locally. However, the fact that the Taliban have, in recent years, organized themselves more and more horizontally has certainly contributed to the ability of individuals like Mirwais to remain politically and economically active (Watkins 2022). The unsettled nature of the governance structures after the collapse of the Republic also suggests that there is space for brokers, even those with some affiliation to the former government, to continue operating.

In June 2022, Farooq Wardak, former minister of education in the Republic government returned to Kabul, the highest official to return in the year following the fall of the Republic. He made this return after several of his representatives, themselves brokers not unlike Mirwais, had long been in contact with Taliban officials. These brokers looked to recuperate properties that had been confiscated from Farooq Wardak and determine what steps the Taliban officials would take upon his return.

At the same time, Mirwais and other brokers continued to have ties to the international community that paid dividends. As countries including the United States proved reluctant to formally recognize the Taliban government, nearly all of the more formal diplomatic channels had been cut off. As such, international groups continuing to deliver hundreds of millions of dollars in humanitarian aid to the country, were more and more reliant on non-state actors in Afghanistan. Those individuals and organizations that could facilitate aid distribution stood to benefit significantly.

All of this suggests that brokers have not just been *responding* to the shifting conditions of the Afghan political economy, but they have, in fact, helped to remake it. As Goodhand, Koehler and Bhatia argue, brokers 'are not merely mediators; they play a role in transforming and reconfiguring connections and relationships within political and market systems' (Goodhand, Koehler and Bhatia 2021). Brokers will continue to help define the extent to which international aid does or does not flow into the country, and, more broadly, how relationships are negotiated across the country's deep political divides.

But the case of Mirwais also demonstrates the ways in which, as Robert Crews argues, those inside Afghanistan have impacted the various forms of imperialism that have intervened upon their country. Brokers like Mirwais helped to define the very nature of American intervention in Afghanistan and the narrative the US government presented to the outside world. They shaped and implemented various projects, ranging from development initiatives to programmes meant to nurture grassroots democracy. These programmes were designed in Washington, Brussels and elsewhere, but, ultimately they were implemented by these actors, in consultation with local groups, including the Taliban.

The American imperial era in Afghanistan was not, in fact, as hegemonic as the intervention's narrative suggested: on the contrary, the US government rarely controlled the ways in which Mirwais and others implemented their visions of democracy or development. Instead, the American approach relied largely on the outsourcing of construction and logistics to various Afghan firms and the outsourcing of violence to the internationally supported Afghan National Army and private security firms. This system emerged not by accident but, rather, by design: American presidents from both political parties worked to limit the presence of US troops in Afghanistan even as they continued to expand development, governance promotion, security sector assistance and other forms of aid and intervention.

After 2021, as the new Taliban authorities rolled back nearly every policy and law which they perceived as promoting western values, the violence of American imperialism had outlasted the presence of American troops. After all, brokers like

Mirwais helped to build Taliban security installations and supply Taliban security forces using none other than facilities and equipment funded (and then left behind) by the Americans.

The Future of Brokers

The failure of American-led state building and counterinsurgency has led to disengagement with Afghanistan. It is likely that legacies of the war will contribute to a broader reluctance to commit massive numbers of troops or spending in the near term. At the same time, however, the real question for the future of American interventionism may be more about a reliance on contractors and other brokers than it is about more ambitious efforts at governance promotion through military might. These contractors and brokers used many of the mechanisms that have historically given Afghan political actors power – the reliance on kinship networks and various forms of reciprocity. At the same time these brokers excelled because they proved able to develop a network of international contacts and connections that extended far beyond Afghanistan's borders, adopting the language and ways of their new foreign patrons as appropriate and, ultimately, embedding themselves deeply in the global economy. Their presence and persistence became defining features of the Afghan political economy in the later years of the 2010s, feature that were created by international, and particularly US policies even as they ultimately eroded American military and diplomatic influence on the ground.

US policies in Afghanistan empowered brokers and other contractors to implement much of the international programming on the ground, draining funds and leading to outcomes far different than those originally envisioned. As this chapter has argued, the ways in which power was structured in Afghanistan over the past twenty years uniquely empowered those actors who positioned themselves to work across the boundaries between the Afghan government, the international community and the Taliban. These 'borders' were physical, as well as cultural and linguistic, and required an agility that figures like Mirwais possessed and many Afghan national-level elites gave up when they committed themselves to the Republic. So long as similar actors play a major role in international intervention, they will continue to affect unintended outcomes of the kinds seen in Afghanistan.

Meanwhile, Mirwais has continued to pave roads and run construction projects. The sources of his income have changed significantly, but his practices of working with elders, navigating local political boundaries and taking advantage of state resources have altered little. The borders have moved, but the brokers have moved with them.

Notes

1 Names and some distinguishing details of non-national-level figures have been changed to preserve their identity.

2   This was caused by forces on both sides of the conflict. See, for instance, the weakening of the Alikozai tribal structures by the Karzai government, but also the targeting of traditional leaders by Taliban suicide bombers (Malkasian 2021).
3   He served later as national security advisor and minister of foreign affairs at the time of the collapse of the Republic.
4   Anna Larson and I particularly explore this intersection of local and elite politics in Coburn and Larson (2014).

References

Amiri, R. and Jackson, A. (2022), 'Taliban Taxation in Afghanistan: (2006–2021)'. Working Paper 138, February 2022. International Centre for Tax and Development. Available at: https://www.ictd.ac/publication/taliban-taxation-afghanistan/ (Accessed: 25 August 2022).

Azoy, G. W. (2012), *Buzkashi: Game and Power in Afghanistan*. 3rd ed. Long Grove, IL: Waveland Press.

Barfield, T. J. (2012), *Afghanistan: A Cultural and Political History*. Princeton: Princeton University Press (Princeton studies in Muslim politics).

Bjelica, J. and Sorush, R. (2018), 'Lost in Procedure: How a Corruption Case in the Afghan Parliament Was (Not) Dealt With'. Kabul: Afghan Analysts Network. Available at: https://www.afghanistan-analysts.org/en/reports/political-landscape/lost-in-procedure-how-a-corruption-case-in-the-afghan-parliament-was-not-dealt-with/ (Accessed: 20 September 2022).

Byrd, W. (2015), *Understanding Afghanistan's 2014 Presidential Election*. Washington, DC: USIP. Available at: https://www.usip.org/publications/2015/04/understanding-afghanistans-2014-presidential-election (Accessed: 24 June 2021).

Coburn, N. (2010), *Connecting with Kabul: The Importance of the Wolesi Jirga Election and Local Political Networks in Afghanistan*. Kabul: Afghanistan Research and Evaluation Unit.

Coburn, N. (2011a), *Political Economy in the Wolesi Jirga: Sources of Finance and Their Impact on Representation in Afghanistan's Parliament*. Kabul: Afghanistan Research and Evaluation Unit.

Coburn, N. (2011b) 'The International Community and the Shura Strategy', in Kyed, H. M., Albrecht, P., Isser, D. and Harper, E. (eds.), *Perspectives on Involving Non-state and Customary Actors in Justice and Security Reform*. Rome, Italy: IDLO.

Coburn, N. (2013), 'The Politics of Dispute Resolution and Continued Instability in Afghanistan', in Smith, S., Yusuf, M. and Cookman, C. (eds.), *Getting It Right in Afghanistan*. Washington, DC: USIP.

Coburn, N. and Larson, A. (2014), *Derailing Democracy in Afghanistan: Elections in an Unstable Political Landscape*. New York: Columbia University Press.

Crews, R. D. (2015), *Afghan Modern: The History of a Global Nation*. Cambridge, MA: The Belknap Press of Harvard University Press.

Dupree, L. (1997), *Afghanistan*. Oxford and New York: Oxford University Press (Oxford Pakistan paperbacks).

Elias, M. O. T. (2009), 'The Resurgence of the Taliban in Kabul, Logar and Wardak', in *Decoding the Taliban: Insights from the Afghan Field*. New York: Columbia University Press.

Giustozzi, A. (2009), *Empires of Mud: War and Warlords in Afghanistan*. New York: Columbia University Press.

Giustozzi, A. (2019), *The Taliban at War: 2001–2018*. Oxford and New York: Oxford University Press.

Goodhand, J. (2005), 'Frontiers and Wars: the Opium Economy in Afghanistan'. *Journal of Agrarian Change*, 5(2): 191–216.

Goodhand, J. Koehler, J. and Bhatia, J. (2021), 'Trading Spaces Afghan Borderland Brokers and the Transformation of the Margins', in *The Routledge Handbook of Smuggling*. 1st edn. London: Routledge.

Jackson, A. (2021), *Negotiating Survival: Civilian-Insurgent Relations in Afghanistan*. Oxford: Oxford University Press.

Lutz, C. and Desai, S. (2015), *US Reconstruction Aid for Afghanistan: The Dollars and Sense*, Costs of War Project, Providence, RI: Watson Institute, Brown University.

Malejacq, R. (2020), *Warlord Survival: The Delusion of State Building in Afghanistan*. Ithaca, NY: Cornell University Press.

Malkasian, C. (2021) *The American War in Afghanistan*. New York, NY: Oxford University Press.

Monsutti, A. (2005), *War and Migration: Social Networks and Economic Strategies of the Hazaras of Afghanistan*. 1st ed. New York: Routledge (Middle East studies: history, politics, and law).

Mukhopadhyay, D. (2014), *Warlords, Strongman Governors, and the State in Afghanistan*. Cambridge: Cambridge University Press.

Mukhopadhyay, D. (2021), 'What's Next for Afghanistan? – The Washington Post'. *The Washington Post*, 8 July 2021. Available at: https://www.washingtonpost.com/politics/2021/07/08/taliban-isnt-only-challenge-afghanistan-government/ (Accessed: 17 July 2021).

Murtazashvili, J. B. (2018), *Informal Order and the State in Afghanistan*. First paperback edition. Cambridge and New York: Cambridge University Press.

Murtazashvili, J. B. (2022), 'The Collapse of Afghanistan'. *Journal of Democracy*, 33(1): 40–54.

North, D. C. et al. (eds.) (2013), *In the Shadow of Violence: Politics, Economics, and the Problem of Development*. Cambridge: Cambridge University Press.

Roggio, B. (2017), 'Mapping Taliban Contested and Controlled Districts in Afghanistan | FDD's Long War Journal'. *Long War Journal*. Available at: https://www.longwarjournal.org/mapping-taliban-control-in-afghanistan (Accessed: 17 June 2021).

Shahrani, M. N. (1986), 'The Kirghiz Khans: Styles and Substance of Traditional Local Leadership in Central Asia'. *Central Asian Survey*, 5(3–4): 255–71.

Strick van Linschoten, A. and Kuehn, F. (2012), *An Enemy We Created: The Myth of the Taliban-Al Qaeda Merger in Afghanistan*. Oxford and New York: Oxford University Press.

UN High Commissioner for Refugees (2001), 'UNHCR Afghan Refugee Statistics'. Situation Report. Available at: https://www.unhcr.org/en-us/afghanistan.html.

Watkins, A. (2022), 'The Taliban One Year On'. 15:8. Combating Terrorism Center at West Point. Available at: https://ctc.westpoint.edu/the-taliban-one-year-on/ (Accessed: 30 August 2022).

World Bank (2021), 'Development Projects: Citizens' Charter Afghanistan Project – P160567, World Bank'. Available at: https://projects.worldbank.org/en/projects-operations/project-detail/P160567 (Accessed: 8 October 2021).

13

Power, Ideas and the 'Taliban 2.0' Myth

William Maley

In *The General Theory of Employment, Interest and Money*, the economist Maynard Keynes famously wrote that 'the power of vested interests is vastly exaggerated compared with the gradual encroachment of ideas' (Keynes 1973: 383). The power of ideas in shaping political outcomes is easily overlooked, partly because of the difficulty of constructing simple causal chains that link a particular idea or set of ideas with a specific outcome. But to discount the significance of ideas on that basis is to risk producing explanations from which important explanatory variables are missing. Where this has surfaced with respect to post-republican Afghanistan is in the notion, circulated on social media in December 2022, that 'whitewashing' of the Afghan Taliban by western analysts played no role in the decision by US President Donald Trump to move to withdraw from Afghanistan, a decision that culminated in the Taliban takeover in August 2021. The following reflections seek to unpack some of the complexities that surround this notion. Was the myth of a 'Taliban 2.0' really of no significance?

The notion that the Taliban had changed, and for the better, had quite a long history. As Ibrahimi and Farasoo (2022) have shown, US discourse about the Taliban's character had shifted over time as the inclination to engage with them became more widespread. The idea that a 'Taliban 2.0' had reshaped or replaced the force that people remembered from 1996 to 2001 found a number of supporters (see Asey 2018). A certain tendency to 'normalize' the Taliban had been on display from the time of Richard Holbrooke's appointment as the US special representative for Afghanistan and Pakistan on 22 January 2009, although these efforts aborted spectacularly in 2013 when an attempt to engage with the Taliban unravelled (Coll 2018: 640). But, with the appointment of Zalmay Khalilzad as US special representative for Afghanistan Reconciliation on 5 September 2018, the tendency towards 'normalization' shot up. Khalilzad had a long history of optimism about the Taliban, going back to their first period of control (Khalilzad 1996); his spouse published an article trying to soften the Taliban's image (Benard 2021).

On the eve of 29 February 2020 United States–Taliban agreement, Barnett R. Rubin, wrote that that the Taliban had 'made an impressive offer of significant and lasting reductions in violence nationwide that cover both Afghan and U.S.-coalition forces'

(Rubin 2020). Most striking of all, however, was an op-ed article purportedly authored by Sirajuddin Haqqani, a senior Taliban figure but also a 'specially designated global terrorist', on the 'most wanted' list issued by the FBI. Published in the *New York Times*, the article claimed, 'We are committed to working with other parties in a consultative manner of genuine respect to agree on a new, inclusive political system in which the voice of every Afghan is reflected and where no Afghan feels excluded' (Haqqani 2020). The language of the article was far more that of a western official or think tanker than an Islamic militant, as any reading of authentic Taliban texts (see Johnson 2017) would show, and suggested a sophisticated whitewashing operation by supporters of engagement with the Taliban to which the *Times* had fallen victim.

Did any of this matter? The argument that it did not is based on President Trump's well-documented support for a withdrawal from Afghanistan, which he relentlessly asserted in meetings with senior US officials; and on his ultimate capacity as commander-in-chief to bring it about. Irrespective of any whitewashing of the Taliban, so the argument runs, a complete US withdrawal was bound to occur. But there is rather more to the story than this. During his 2016–20 term, Donald Trump was above all else an erratic president with a very limited attention-span (Drezner 2020; Baker and Glasser 2022; Freedman 2022: 474), and such figures can often be distracted from courses of action that might prove otherwise destructive. This was indeed the case where Afghanistan was concerned. Trump's approach was anything but linear. On 21 August 2017, he had argued that a 'hasty withdrawal would create a vacuum that terrorists, including ISIS and Al Qaeda, would instantly fill, just as happened before September 11th', and that '[c]onditions on the ground – not arbitrary timetables – will guide our strategy from now on. America's enemies must never know our plans or believe they can wait us out' (quoted in Maley 2018: 216). Of course, he pivoted away from this position when his administration tasked Khalilzad with negotiating with the Taliban, a process that came close to producing a meeting between Trump and the Taliban at Camp David in September 2019.

But it was also Trump who scuttled that meeting after an American was killed in a Taliban bombing in Kabul: as Trump tweeted at the time, 'I immediately cancelled the meeting and called off peace negotiations. What kind of people would kill so many in order to seemingly strengthen their bargaining position?' (quoted in Bolton 2020: 442). According to the military historian Carter Malkasian, Trump 'clarified to reporters at the White House that peace talks were "dead" and would not resume' (Malkasian 2021: 442). Talks with the Taliban soon resumed, but in their respective memoirs, neither Secretary of State Mike Pompeo nor Secretary of Defense Mark T. Esper claimed that it was *Trump* who ordered the resumption of discussions (Esper 2022; Pompeo 2023); Malkasian (2021: 443) rather implied that it was Khalilzad's initiative. And notwithstanding the signing of the United States–Taliban agreement, US troops were still in Afghanistan when Trump exited the Oval Office in January 2021, again suggesting that there were limits to how far Trump would go before a certain caution set in. The notion that an inexorable and irreversible push to withdraw made any whitewashing irrelevant does not stand up to detailed scrutiny (see also Barr 2022: 426).

If a whitewashing of the Taliban did have some effect on policy settings, the question still remains as to how. Here, there are two particular points that require discussion. One relates to the broad questions of the power of ideas, and of the framing of policy debate. The other relates to the ways in which whitewashing might have shifted the balance between different potential exit mechanisms, or to put it another way, between different policy options. The following paragraphs discuss these in turn.

The proposition that ideas form part of the landscape within which social life and policy activities occur is not an especially novel one, and it has been approached from varying directions by scholars. The crudest approach derives from classical Marxism, where the idea of 'false consciousness' was developed by Friedrich Engels (Lewy 1982); a more sophisticated version, grounded in a concept of 'hegemony', was associated with the prison writings of the Italian Marxist Antonio Gramsci (Kolakowski 1978: 240–4). In a famous study of political power, Steven Lukes looked beyond 'decisions', and even 'non-decisions', to focus on control over the political agenda through a kind of 'ideological power', a 'power to secure willing consent by shaping and influencing desires and beliefs' (Lukes 2021: 3). This, like 'constructivist' theory in international relations scholarship (Reus-Smit 2018: 119–54), is arguably too abstract to provide any direct illumination of very specific policy decisions, but it does capture the need to reflect on how ideas that have come to be accepted wisdom can influence policy outcomes.

Where this has obtained more concrete form is in the idea of *framing*. 'Framing', Chong and Druckman argue, 'refers to the process by which people develop a particular conceptualization of an issue or reorient their thinking about an issue' (2000: 107). Framing effects 'occur when (often small) changes in the presentation of an issue or an event produce (sometimes large) changes of opinion' (2000: 104). Where Afghanistan was concerned, whitewashing did not begin with twenty-first-century administrations. The Reagan administration used the blanket label 'freedom fighters' to frame the Afghan mujahidin, even though some resistance parties, such as Gulbuddin Hekmatyar's Hizb-e Islami, were better described as 'Islamo-Leninist' (Roy 1992: 113). This exercise in framing not only allowed Washington to avoid some very awkward questions over how and why US aid was finding its way to such a group; it served to transfer some reflected glory from the mujahidin's struggle to much more suspect groups backed by the United States at the time, notably the Nicaraguan Contras whom President Reagan also described as 'freedom fighters'.

It is in the context of framing that one begins to see ways in which whitewashing of the Taliban might have affected the course of policy decisions. To provide just one example, in a rigorous analytical discussion, Anthony Richards argues that 'terrorism is a method that entails the use of violence or force or the threat of violence or force with the primary purpose of generating a psychological impact beyond the immediate victims or object of attack for a political motive' (Richards 2015: 146). There are quite strong bases on which one could argue that the behaviour of the Taliban, in the period between the withdrawal of the bulk of western forces at the end of 2014 and the signing of the Doha Agreement, satisfied all of these criteria (Maley 2021a), which in normal circumstances could have activated a range of norms against negotiating with terrorists

(Pruitt 2006: 381). *If*, however, the Taliban were reframed as a 'reformed Taliban 2.0', and *not* to be seen as terrorists, this problem could be avoided. The genesis of such framing arguably went back as far as the establishment of Holbrooke's office, although it became public only at a later date. By 2018 it was prominently on display.

Whitewashing also potentially affected the choice between different *mechanisms* of withdrawal. On 26 April 2023, Khalilzad tweeted: 'The experience of the last two years is better than many expected – with no US loss of life since the withdrawal and with the saving of some $40 billion that we spent on the war there annually'. If this was intended as a retrospective defence of the agreement which he had signed with the Taliban in February 2020, it begged the question of whether there were alternative approaches that could have been taken to withdraw US troops if the Taliban had not been framed as acceptable negotiating partners. The answer is plainly yes.

One approach would have been to use diplomatic pressure on Islamabad to address much more seriously the problem of Taliban sanctuaries in Pakistan as a precursor to withdrawal from Afghanistan. The option of pressuring Pakistan, once advocated by Khalilzad himself (2010), was in effect foreclosed by the decision to seek to negotiate with the Taliban. In turn, this decision led the United States to engage in a subsidiary act of framing which depicted Pakistan, the Taliban's critical source of military support, as part of the solution rather than as part of the problem. In September 2021, the chairman of the US Joint Chiefs of Staff, General Mark A. Milley, identified never 'effectively dealing with Pakistan' as a critical error (Demirjian and Horton 2021).

A second approach would have been for the United States simply to withdraw its military in a staged transition process planned with the Afghan government itself. This was essentially the approach (*inteqal*) that was taken during the extraction of the bulk of foreign forces from Afghanistan in five tranches between 2010 and 2014, under the auspices of a 'Joint Afghan-NATO Inteqal Board' (Maley 2021b: 266). This transition did not trigger a crisis of morale for the Afghan National Defence and Security Forces (ANDSF) in the way that the US engagement with a whitewashed Taliban, and the United States–Taliban agreement, undoubtedly did (Jamal and Maley 2023: 160).

The whitewashing of the Taliban arguably had the effect of disguising the extreme dangers associated with negotiating with such a force (see Maley 2021c: 236–51) and tipping the balance away from the alternative of a withdrawal explicitly executed in cooperation with the Afghan Republic. It led instead to an agreement between the United States and the Taliban that had disastrous consequences (Maley and Jamal 2022). Thomas Hobbes famously remarked that the 'Reputation of power, is Power' (Hobbes 1996: 62) and the 2020 agreement, struck by the Taliban and the Americans behind the back of the Afghan Republic, gravely undermined the Afghan government's reputation of power and enhanced that of the Taliban (Miller 2020). The collapse of the Republic led to one other – distinctly unsavoury – exercise in framing, namely the attempt by President Biden and other US politicians to pin the blame for the collapse on the Afghans (Murtazashvili 2022) and blacken the names of Afghanistan's leaders, especially Ghani (Pompeo 2023). Here, however, it is likely that Biden's objective was to shape the judgement of history to his own advantage rather than to shape events on the ground.

Of course, nothing in the preceding discussion leads to the conclusion that whitewashing alone explains the US withdrawal in 2020 and 2021. Other factors indisputably came into play (Jamal and Maley 2023: 196–201). The key point is rather that whitewashing cannot be discounted as a relevant contributing factor. Politics and diplomacy are awash with fringe players, whose ideas typically count for little in the wider sway of things. In September 1939, the Under-Secretary of State at the British Foreign Office Sir Alexander Cadogan dismissed one such player as 'like a wasp at a picnic – one can't beat him off' (Dilks 1971: 220). But the methodical whitewashing of radical groups presents a more serious challenge. The problem here is not one of odd individuals hanging around the corridors of power, but of ill-judged ideas insidiously seeping into popular and elite consciousness through the kind of gradual encroachment that Keynes highlighted. If there is a lesson from the Afghanistan case, it is the importance of being watchful about this danger in the future.

References

Asey, T. (2018), *Taliban 2.0. – Have the Taliban Really Changed and Learnt Their Lesson?* Washington, DC: The Atlantic Council, 5 January 2018.
Baker, P. and Glasser, S. (2022), *The Divider: Trump in the White House, 2017–2021.* New York: Doubleday.
Barr, W. P. (2022), *One Damn Thing after Another: Memoirs of an Attorney General.* New York: William Morrow.
Benard, C. (2021). 'Afghanistan: Will Biden Cave to the Forever War Party?' *The National Interest*, 24 February 2021.
Bolton, J. (2020), *The Room Where It Happened: A White House Memoir.* New York: Simon and Schuster.
Chong, D. and Druckman, J. N. (2007), 'Framing Theory'. *Annual Review of Political Science*, 10: 103–26.
Coll, S. (2018), *Directorate S: The C.I.A. and America's Secret Wars in Afghanistan and Pakistan.* New York: Penguin Press.
Demirjian, K. and Horton, A. (2021), 'U.S. Lost War in Afghanistan through Miscalculations Spanning Multiple Administrations, Milley Tells Lawmakers'. *The Washington Post*, 29 September 2021.
Dilks, D. (ed.) (1971), *The Diaries of Sir Alexander Cadogan, O.M., 1938–1945.* London. Cassell.
Drezner, D. W. (2020), *The Toddler in Chief: What Donald Trump Teaches Us about the Modern Presidency.* Chicago: The University of Chicago Press.
Esper, M. T. (2022), *A Sacred Oath: Memoirs of a Secretary of Defense during Extraordinary Times.* New York: William Morrow.
Freedman, L. (2022), *Command: The Politics of Military Operations from Korea to Ukraine.* London: Allen Lane.
Haqqani, S. (2020). 'What We, the Taliban, Want'. *New York Times*, 20 February 2020.
Hobbes, T. [1651] (1996), *Leviathan.* Cambridge: Cambridge University Press.
Ibrahimi, N. and Farasoo, A. (2022), 'Understanding Shifts in US Policies towards the Taliban: A Critical Analysis'. *Millennium*, 50(3): 810–38.

Jamal, A. S. and Maley, W. (2023), *The Decline and Fall of Republican Afghanistan*. New York: Oxford University Press.
Johnson, T. H. (2017), *Taliban Narratives: The Use and Power of Stories in the Afghanistan Conflict*. London: Hurst & Co.
Keynes, J. M. [1936] (1973), *The General Theory of Employment, Interest and Money*. London: Macmillan.
Khalilzad, Z. (1996), 'Afghanistan: Time to Reengage'. *The Washington Post*, 7 October 1996.
Khalilzad, Z. (2010), 'Get Tough on Pakistan'. *New York Times*, 19 October 2010.
Kolakowski, L. (1978), *Main Currents of Marxism: The Breakdown*. Oxford: Oxford University Press.
Lewy, G. (1982), *False Consciousness: An Essay on Mystification*. New Brunswick: Transaction Books.
Lukes, S. (2021), *Power: A Radical View*. London: Bloomsbury.
Maley, W. (2018), *Transition in Afghanistan: Hope, Despair and the Limits of Statebuilding*. New York: Routledge.
Maley, W. (2021a), 'Terrorism and Insurgency in Afghanistan', in Izarali, M.R. and Ahlawat, D. (eds.), *Terrorism, Security and Development in South Asia: National, Regional and Global Implications*. London: Routledge.
Maley, W. (2021b), *The Afghanistan Wars*. London: Macmillan/Red Globe Press.
Maley, W. (2021c), *Diplomacy, Communication, and Peace: Selected Essays*. New York: Routledge.
Maley, W. and Jamal, A. S. (2022), 'Diplomacy of Disaster: The Afghanistan "Peace Process" and the Taliban Occupation of Kabul'. *The Hague Journal of Diplomacy*, 17(1): 32–63.
Malkasian, C. (2021), *The American War in Afghanistan: A History*. New York: Oxford University Press.
Miller, L. (2020), 'Will the U.S.–Taliban Deal End the War?' *New York Times*, 18 February 2020.
Murtazashvili, J. B. (2022), 'Biden Continues to Bungle Afghanistan'. *The National Interest*, 14 February 2022.
Pompeo, M. (2023), *Never Give an Inch: Fighting for the America I Love*. New York: Broadside Books.
Pruitt, D. G. (2006), 'Negotiation with Terrorists'. *International Negotiation*, 11(2): 371–94.
Reus-Smit, C. (2018), *On Cultural Diversity: International Theory in a World of Difference*. Cambridge: Cambridge University Press.
Richards, A. (2015), *Conceptualizing Terrorism*. Oxford: Oxford University Press.
Roy, O. (1992), *The Failure of Political Islam*. London: I.B. Tauris.
Rubin, B. R. (2020), 'In Long-Suffering Afghanistan, This Is a Peace Deal Worth Trying'. *The Washington Post*, 16 February 2020.

Part Three

The Politics of Recognition and Resistance

14

The State, the Clergy and British Imperial Policy in Afghanistan during the Nineteenth and Early Twentieth Centuries*

Senzil Nawid
International Journal of Middle East Studies, 29 (1997) 581–605. 2009 ©
Cambridge University Press. Reprinted with permission.

The great drawback to progress in Afghanistan has been those men who, under the pretense of religion, have taught things which were entirely contrary to the teachings of Mohammad, and that, being the false leaders of the religion, the sooner they are got rid of, the better.

– Amir ʿAbd al-Rahman[1]

The fiery cross, which was sped from end to end of the Scottish Highlands, in the old days, when the call to the arms was made, was no more powerful than is the Koran now carried from village to village by the moolah of Afghanistan.

– Howard Hensman[2]

The political and dynastic history of Afghanistan during the nineteenth and the early twentieth centuries is well known. So is British imperial policy towards Afghanistan.[3] However, very little attention has been paid to the role of the clergy, the guardians of the Islamic order and the representatives of the civil society in Afghanistan. They played a major role in domestic politics and in Afghanistan's challenges with foreign powers. This chapter attempts to fill the gap in information about the *ulama* by detailing their role in defending Afghanistan's territorial integrity and by examining the conflict over jihad between the ulama and Afghanistan's rulers, a conflict that adversely affected the legitimacy of successive regimes.

Due to the tribal nature of Afghan society, the central government has traditionally been weak in Afghanistan. Weak central governments were characteristic during the first three quarters of the nineteenth century as a result of dynastic conflicts, wars of succession and invasions by the British. These conflicts virtually demolished the infrastructure of the country. In the absence of a strong central government, peripheral authority became increasingly autonomous,[4] and the power of the ulama, the spiritual leaders of the masses, increased significantly. Except during the twenty-one-year reign of Amir ʿAbd al-Rahman, the Afghan clergy enjoyed enormous power as *de facto* leaders of civil society. Through the period of the Anglo-Afghan Wars (1839 and 1879), the influence of the clergy expanded as Afghanistan's rulers acquiesced to demands of foreign powers. At the instigation of the clergy, jihad became the pre-eminent political issue, and the ruler's role in jihad became the measure of his legitimacy. By the turn of the century, the forces of the power of the clergy and the forces of nationalism and pan-Islamism challenged the authority of the central government, particularly in the tribal zone along the border with British India.

The Division of Power and the Concept of Leadership

In October 1747, an intertribal assembly (*Loya Jirga*) of important Ghilzai, Abdali, Tajik, Uzbik, Hazara and Baluch chieftains met in Kandahar and elected Ahmad Khan Sadduzai (later called Ahmad Shah Baba or Ahmad Shah Durrani) as their sovereign. The tribal chiefs gave him their oath of allegiance, establishing the Sadduzai dynasty (1747–1842) in Afghanistan, ushering in two-and-a-half centuries of Pashtun rule. Under Ahmad Shah Durrani (1747–73), the region gradually coalesced to form modern Afghanistan.

Pashtun tribes, diverted by the shah from fighting one another, provided the military base for a central political authority. In 1747, Ahmad Khan was merely a leader among tribal chieftains, an intertribal patriarch (*bā bā*). His government resembled a federal republic rather than an absolute monarchy.[5] He was selected by the tribal leaders, and his decisions and actions were to comply with precepts of the Sharia and the tribal code of honour (*pashtūn wāli*), which prescribed relations between individuals and among tribes. His military expeditions, which built an empire, established him as a leader of jihad. For example, the Battle of Panipat (1761), the high point of his military feats in the Indian subcontinent, was deemed a jihad against the Maharata Hindus.

Afghan historians characterize Ahmad Shah as a genuinely religious man. According to ʿAbd al-Hai Habibi, he was a staunch Hanafi Sunni, well versed in the Sharia. As he consolidated power, he established the Hanafi doctrine as the official rite of Afghanistan.[6] Timur Shah (1773–93), Ahmad Shah's son and successor, was also a devoted adherent of Hanafism. During the latter's reign, all courts in Afghanistan were required to abide by tenets of the Hanafi school in every detail.[7] Timur Shah was also the founder of the Tasbih-Khana, a centre for religious scholarly activities in Kabul. Political instability persisted, however, and the influence of religious leaders increased steadily during the first three quarters of the nineteenth century. At Timur Shah's death in 1793, the Durrani kingdom was engulfed in fratricidal strife among his twenty-six sons. Between 1800 and 1834, there were four changes of rulers, from Zaman Shah to Mahmud, from Mahmud to Shah Shujaʿ, from Shah Shujaʿ back to Mahmud and then – a shift of dynasty – from Sadduzais to Barakzais (another branch of Durrani Pashtuns). Wars of succession among Sadduzai princes and power struggles between Sadduzai and Muhammadzai (Barakzai) sardars offered religious leaders and tribal chiefs opportunities to assume new power and influence. With decentralization of the Sadduzai kingdom, the elaborate state-sponsored clerical hierarchy began to disintegrate, and independent clergy and shaykhs of the *tarīqas* gained increasing power.

Religious leaders were increasingly called on to legitimize political authority. During succession disputes, claimants to the throne frequently sought out influential religious leaders to support their claims and undermine their opponents. For example, the shift of power from the Sadduzai to the Muhammadzai dynasty was endorsed by Mir Hajji, the son of the famous Mir Waʿiz (Mir Ahmad), when the former crowned Dost Muhammad Khan in 1834 at the ʿIdqah Mosque in Kabul.[8] During the Second Anglo-Afghan War (1879–80), Amir Shir Ali's widow solicited support from Mullah Mushk-i-ʿAlam to place her exiled son, Yaʿqub Khan, or grandson, Musa Jan, on the throne.[9] Various other claimants sought the support of high-ranking clergy until Amir ʿAbd al-Rahman gained the upper hand in 1880.

The coronation ceremony (*dastār-bandī*) was emblematic of the legitimating function of the clergy; it was usually performed by one or two religious leaders immediately following the accession of a new ruler, in order to legitimize the new regime. It involved wrapping a white muslin turban around the head of the new ruler and reciting verses from the Qurʾan, after which the conducting clergyman would give the amir a copy of the Qurʾan, signifying the new amir's pledge to rule in accordance with the teachings of the holy book. New rulers sought the most influential religious leader in the country to perform the ceremony, as the reputation of the clergyman to perform the *dastār-bandī* revealed to some degree the existing level of political support for the new ruler. Zaman Shah, one of Timur Shah's sons and his first successor, postponed his *dastār-bandī* rather than have it performed by lesser clergymen of the court, who were eager to do it. Instead, Zaman Shah went at night to the residence of Shah Saffi-Allah Mujaddidi, the most exalted spiritual leader in the country, to receive the ceremony.[10]

Thus, from the emergence of modern Afghanistan, the clergy influenced political life as well as religious life. Let us look more closely at the structure of the clergy.

Divisions among the Clergy

Within the Afghan ulama, there were three distinguishable groups: (1) the state-employed, high-ranking ulama; (2) the lower-ranking ulama, mostly local mosque functionaries; and (3) the ulama affiliated with Sufi orders, who were independent of state control.

The status of an individual member of the ulama varied according to his rank, knowledge, piety, position and relationship to other important ulama. An *ʿālim* benefitted from being the son, student or close associate of a prominent scholar. Those ulama who served the state held high religious positions and were directly answerable to the central civil authority. The lower-ranking rural ulama had much greater autonomy. Although they did not exert the same influence over matters of state as their urban counterparts, they exercised great influence over the lives of the local population.

The ulama usually carried titles indicating the level of their scholarly achievement and the school where they studied. 'Shaykh' referred to outstanding scholars who had completed their education in one of the leading madrasas in Hijaz or in Egypt and to the leaders of Sufi orders. According to the *Hidāyat al-ᶜUrfān*, a nineteenth-century Naqshbandi text, 'shaykh' referred to a person who is skilled in the Sharia, is a firm believer (*mutaddayyin*), and is a spiritual leader who has received permission from the leader of a Sufi order to preach (*muqtadā zi ijāzat al-irshād bāshad*).[11] The title 'Mawlawi' (my master), denoting a specialist in Islamic law, was originally borne by a graduate of a religious school in India; later, high-ranking state-employed ulama often adopted this title. 'Dahmulla' (*dah* meaning ten and *mullā* meaning learned man or scholar who can guide ten *mullās*) was used in northern Afghanistan for religious scholars who had received their training in Bukhara. 'Mullā' (learned man) was used for a graduate of a local madrasa. Until the beginning of the twentieth century, all religious scholars were called *mullās*, but the term was later restricted to mosque functionaries.

The high-ranking clergy were government-employed jurists, teachers in government-sponsored madrasas, courtiers who interpreted the law and advised the king, imams of the congregational prayer, and preachers at major mosques in the capital and other large cities. As the most highly educated citizens, they filled important administrative positions in the government. Several small, important families dominated the upper echelons of the ulama hierarchy. A prominent Barakzai family from Kandahar produced several generations of great *qāżīs* (Arabic, *qāḍḍī*). From the time of Ahmad Shah until the War of Independence in 1919, the office of *khān-i-ᶜulūm* was occupied exclusively by the Barakzai family. Another important clerical family descended from Qazi Faiz-Allah, the chief *qadi* under Timur Shah, who enjoyed great power and prestige and possessed a large estate. The office of *mīr wāᶜiz* was held for several generations by a clerical family for Chahardehi, near Kabul. The first prominent member of this family was Mir Ismaᶜil, an important Naqshbandi shaykh and *mīr wāᶜiz* under Timur Shah. His son, Mir Ahmad, was an eminent *ᶜālim* who held the same position under Timur Shah's successors, enjoyed enormous prestige, and had thousands of followers in the region.[12] The latter's son, Mir Muhammad Maᶜsum, also known as Hafizji or Mir Hajji, and his grandson, Mir ᶜAtiq-Allah, were among the most influential ulama of Afghanistan in the second half of the nineteenth century.

The increase in the ulama's political influence was accompanied by increased economic power. The higher ulama obtained a share of land revenues and even acquired large parcels of land in the capital. By 1879, about a third of the revenue of each province was dedicated to the upkeep of the religious establishment.[13] A district (*Guzar-i-Qāżī*), a park (*Bāgh-i-Qāżī*) and a fortress (*Qalaᶜa-i-Qāżī*) in Kabul were among the extensive property holdings of the descendants of Qazi Faiz-Allah. The extended estate of Sayyid Ahmad Mir Waᶜiz comprised almost one-third of the city of Kabul.[14]

The lower-ranking clergy, the *mullās*, served in the mosques of small towns and villages and in the more remote and smaller districts of large cities. They led daily prayers, conducted marriages and funerals, and taught in the mosque schools. In the absence of a *qadi*, they sometimes registered documents as notaries and issued judicial opinions on matters related to marriage and inheritance. Through involvement in their daily lives, the *mullās* greatly influenced the people. Unlike the high ulama, who depended on royal appointments, the local *mullās* were supported by their communities and were largely free of government control. The source of their income was fees from marriages and funerals, *zakāt*, and grants of land from tribal leaders and villagers.

Spiritual Leaders (The Rūḥānīyyūn)

The leaders of Sufi orders and their devout adherents and pious men, who claimed noble religious lineage, exercised 'leadership in piety'. Generally referred to as the *rūḥānīyyūn*, they commanded great respect among the people, who regarded them as friends of God (*awlīyāʾ*) who had reached the highest level of spirituality (*bajā rasīda*). They usually bore such appellations as *sayyid*, *hażrat*, *pādshāh*, *shāh*, *shāhzāda*, *naqīb*, *mīr*, *mīan*, *īshān*, *khwāja*, *ākhūndzāda* or *sāhibzāda*, denoting their noble ancestry. The leaders of the Sufi orders (*ahl-i-ṭarīqa*) were the most powerful group within the religious establishment. Most Sufi orders had numerous branches, each led by an appointee or deputy (*khalīfa*) or the leader (*pīr*). The function of the *khalīfa* was to provide spiritual guidance to the followers (*murīds*) and to initiate new members into the order; new members made an oath of allegiance known as holding the hand of the *pīr* (*dast-i-pīrī giriftan*). Miraculous deeds (*karāmāt*) were attributed to the *pīrs* and sometimes to their disciples, as well.

The leaders of *ṭarīqas* had many followers among the masses and enjoyed enormous prestige as religious scholars and as pious men who possessed mystical knowledge (*maʿrifa*). Their influence was pervasive in the population, even among the ulama. Without specific offices in the religious establishment, Sufi leaders derived their power from the number of *murīds* they attracted. The absolute loyalty of a *murīd* to the *ṭarīqa* gave Sufi shaykhs extraordinary power with which to motivate their followers. The influence of the *ṭarīqas* was so widespread in Afghan society that many people, including high government officials, members of the royal family and even the king, paid homage to Sufi leaders and were often the *murīds* of a *pīr*. In *An Account of the Kingdom of Caubul*, Mountstuart Elphinstone wrote about his visit in 1808 with a celebrated shaykh who 'was often visited by the King [Shah Shujaʿ al-Mulk] and his prime minister, neither of whom ever would be seated in his presence, till repeatedly commanded'.[15]

The most important *ṭarīqas* in Afghanistan were the Qadiriyya, the Naqshbandiyya, the Chestiyya and the Suhrawardiyya; the last two were the largest *tariqas* in Afghanistan during the nineteenth and twentieth centuries.

Leaders of the Qadiriyya Order

The Qadiriyya order was established in northern Afghanistan during the thirteenth century. Adherents of the Qadiriyya order were concentrated in eastern and southern Afghanistan, Turkistan, and Herat and among the Durranis. In the early nineteenth century, Shaykh Saʿd-Allah Gailani, a descendant of the order's founder ᶜAbd al-Qadir Gailani (d. 1166), established a Sufi headquarters (*khāniqāh*) in Siyawashan, south of Herat. Shaykh Saᶜd-Allah belonged to the Jundiyya Baghdadiyya branch of the Qadiriyya order and was the first member of the Gailani family to arrive in Afghanistan. Sayyid Hasan Affandi Gailani, known as the Naqib Sahib of Charbagh, also a descendant of the ᶜAbd al-Qadir Gailani, came to Afghanistan from Baghdad in the early 1900s. 'He and his brothers, who had their seat in Baghdad, had many followers in Muslim countries.'

Qadiriyya shaykhs and their disciples in southern and eastern parts of Afghanistan played significant roles as powerbrokers, instigators of jihad and mobilizers of the masses. Their influence was based on their noble ancestry, their reputation for scholarship and piety, and their large following. Many were also connected by family ties to powerful tribal leaders, who relied on them for advice. They exerted power through a network that linked them on the one hand to the *ṭarīqa*, and on the other to an important madrasa or shrine. Through subordinate *mullās*, usually their disciples, these Qadiriyya shaykhs wielded extensive power, especially with the people of their region. As independent scholars with madrasas, they trained a great number of local *mullās*. Some of them were also custodians (*mutawāllīs*) of important shrines and closely tied by tribal origin to the people.

Leaders of the Naqshbandiyya Order

The Naqshbandiyya order (named for its founder, Sayyid Bahaʾ al-Din Naqshband, 1317–81) was established in Afghanistan during the early period of the order's growth in Central Asia. Leaders of the Mujaddidi branch of the Naqshbandiyya order played especially significant cultural and political roles in Afghanistan. They were known as *hażrat* (majesty or highness), an appellation they carried with their names.

The most reliable source on the history of the Mujaddidi Naqshbandis, Muhammad Fazl-Allah, author of *ᶜUmdat al-Maqāmāt*, traces their origin to Shihab al-Din Farrukhshah. A descendant of ᶜUmar, the second caliph, Shihab al-Din Farrukhshah settled in Khurasan in the time of the Ghaznavids and was buried in the valley of Farrukhshah in Panjshir, north of Kabul. Imam Rafiᶜ al-Din, a lineal descendant of Shihab al-Din Farrukhshah, went from Kabul to Sirhind in India.[16] One of his offspring, Shaykh Ahmad Mujaddid Alf al-Sani, the son of Mawlana ᶜAbd al-Ahad, was born in Sirhind. Guided in the Naqshbandiyya order by Khwaja Muhammad Baqi Kabuli (d. 1602), Shaykh Ahmad Mujaddid Alf al-Sani became known as a great scholar and spiritual leader in India and Afghanistan.

On a visit to Sirhind, Ahmad Shah invited Shah ᶜIzzat-Allah Mujaddidi (known as Hazratji Sahib) and his brothers, Shah Ghulam Muhammad and Qayyum Jan, to Afghanistan. The three brothers accepted the invitation and settled in Kandahar. Later, with the transfer of the capital from Kandahar to Kabul, the three eminent men were invited to move with the state assemblage. Timur Shah, Ahmad Shah's son and successor, also treated Hazratji with great respect, granting him land, a residence in the Shurbazar district of Kabul, and an annual pension.[17]

Clerical Resistance to Foreign Occupation

During the nineteenth century, Afghanistan became a major playing field in the 'Great Game of Asia'. Great Britain had established control over India in the eighteenth century. In 1779, its sovereignty over the Indian subcontinent was recognized by the Treaty of Paris. During the first quarter of the nineteenth century, while the British consolidated their power in India, czarist Russia expanded the territory under its control to the south by subjugating and annexing Central Asian kingdoms and northern parts of Persia (the Caspian provinces and the towns of Darband and Baku). Russia's steady advances created anxiety in Great Britain for the safety of its Indian empire. Afghanistan's strategic location as the 'gateway to India' made it a focal point of British diplomatic and military strategy for decades. British invasions of Afghan territory resulted in the First and Second Anglo-Afghan Wars.

Every segment of Afghan society and every ethnic group was involved in Afghanistan's armed resistance against the British invaders. It is important to recognize the significance of the clergy in the First and Second Anglo-Afghan Wars, not just as participants and mobilizers of the masses but also as leaders of the war effort. While resentment towards the foreign occupiers had united diverse Afghan forces against the British, religious leaders stood at the forefront of the opposition as defenders of Islam and advocates of jihad. The call to jihad became the most effective catalyst to the defence of Afghanistan's territorial integrity and traditional culture. As instigators and leaders of jihad, the clergy became a commanding political force.

The First Anglo-Afghan War, 1838–42

The origin of British involvement in Afghanistan can be traced to Russian expansion into northwestern Persia during the 1820s. Ahmad Shah, the Qajar ruler of Persia, was encouraged by the Russians to compensate for losses in the northwest by seizing Herat, which at the time was ruled by Kamran, a grandson of Timur Shah Sadduzai. In 1837, the Russian-backed Persian army attacked and besieged Herat. The siege of the city aroused a general uprising against the Persians. Religious leaders raised the banner of jihad against the Persians. Mawlawi ʿAbd al-Haqq, a leading clergyman in Herat, declared that fighting the Shiʿi invaders was the 'great jihad' (*jihād-i-akbar*) and a religious duty of all citizens. The declaration was distributed in pamphlet form throughout the city and generated an immediate response. Thousands of citizens, wearing white shrouds and carrying banners, joined forces to defend the city against the invaders.[18]

While the Persians were engaged in the siege of Herat, a Russian mission led by Captain Vicovitch arrived in Kabul to establish commercial relations with the Afghan ruler, Amir Dost Muhammad Khan, who had seized power from the Sadduzais in 1834.[19] Great Britain perceived the attack on Herat by the Persians and the dispatch of a mission to Kabul as preludes to a Russian invasion of India through Afghanistan. The British responded by occupying Kharak, the Iranian island in the Persian Gulf, forcing the Persians to relinquish claims over Herat. The British further tried to extend their control northward in order to pre-empt further Russian manoeuvres. The best way to prevent Russian influence in Afghanistan was to install a ruler in Kabul who was well disposed to British interests. In 1838, Lord Auckland, the British governor-general of India, entered into negotiations with Shah Shuja^c, the deposed Sadduzai ruler of Afghanistan (1804–9) then in exile in India, and with Maharajah Ranjit Singh, the Sikh ruler of Panjab, who had steadily advanced into Sadduzai territory in northern India to enlist their cooperation in a joint military venture against Amir Dost Muhammad Khan. A treaty signed in 1838 by the three parties promised Shah Shuja^c the throne of Afghanistan on the condition that he accept permanent stationing of British troops in Kabul. Parts of Afghanistan, including areas that later came to be known as the North-West Frontier Province (of British India), were promised to Ranjit Singh. In 1839, the combined forces known as the Army of the Indus advanced towards Kabul, and on 7 August, they reinstalled Shah Shuja^c on the throne of Afghanistan with little resistance, forcing Amir Dost Muhammad Khan to flee to Bukhara.

Initially, the British invasion did not generate strong opposition, perhaps because Britain's coming was simply viewed as aid to the deposed Sadduzai king in a dynastic power struggle. The situation remained calm until 1841, when William MacNaughten, the British representative in Kabul, took charge of government affairs, and it became apparent that the king was only a puppet. Beguiled by the apparent tranquillity, MacNaughten issued administrative directives that adversely affected Afghans.[20] Significant among the adverse directives was a reduction of the tariff on imported merchandise intended to promote British trade. Shah Shuja^c, who had begun to realize the unfortunate consequences of his alliance, was offended by the British action and secretly authorized ^cAbd al-Shakkur, the prime minister, to raise import duties. A heated argument between MacNaughten and ^cAbd al-Shakkur ensued.[21] Sensing the prime minister's hostile attitude towards them, the British pressured Shah Shuja^c to replace him with Muhammad ^cUsman the Nizam al-Dawla, a man of their choosing. According to Ferrier, the British had also begun missionary activity in Afghanistan by distributing a Persian translation of the Bible.[22]

Opposition to British occupation began in Kabul and spread quickly to the provinces, with mosques serving as communications centres. The ulama refused to read the *khuṭba* in the mosques in the name of Shah Shuja^c, alleging they could do so only for an independent sovereign, and that Shah Shuja^c was not independent.[23] In the city of Ghazni, Sayyid Qasim, a local religious leader, led a challenge to British control that resulted in the death of Colonel Herring. Then, Mir Masjidi raised the banner of jihad against the foreign occupiers in Kuhistan, north of Kabul. Recognizing the gravity of the situation, MacNaughten imprisoned several leading clergy. Finally, on 2 November 1841, during the early morning prayer, Mir Wa^ciz Hajji Ma^csum, also known as Hafizji, proclaimed jihad in the Pul-i-Khishi Mosque in Kabul. Jihad was immediately proclaimed in other mosques.

The role of religious leaders was prominent throughout the war. Not only did they preach jihad; they also carried banners and fought alongside the military forces. Further, they travelled to villages to persuade the people not to sell food to the British. Key religious figures were Mir Hajji Ma^csum and Mir Darwish (both sons of Sayyid Ahmad, Mir Wa^ciz of Kabul), Mir Masjidi, Mir Mahbub Kabuli, Mir Junaid and Mullah Ahmad.

The uprising gained momentum with the return of Sardar Akbar Khan, the exiled son of Amir Dost Muhammad, from Bukhara, and ultimately resulted in the defeat of the British and the death of Shah Shujaᶜ, who had become the target of public hatred for his alliance with the British. MacNaughten and his assistant, Major Alexander Burns, were killed. British garrisons at Kabul, Ghazni and Kandahar were besieged, and communication with India was virtually cut off. Major Pottinger, the remaining British officer, precipitously concluded an agreement to evacuate the country. In January 1842, 4,500 British troops left Kabul for Jalalabad. Only Dr William Bryden, a medical officer, survived the continuous attacks en route through the passes. So ended in total disaster the first British invasion of Afghanistan. In 1869, Talboys Wheeler, the assistant secretary in the British Foreign Department in India, wrote that British occupation of Afghanistan was an incident that excites 'more painful feelings than any other episode in the history of British India, excepting perhaps the mutiny of 1857'.[24]

Although the British retaliated by attacking and burning the grand bazaar of Kabul in September of the same year, they made no attempt to remain in Afghanistan and withdrew immediately to India. The negotiations that followed resulted in a peace settlement. British policy makers saw it in their interest to adopt a policy of non-interference, or 'Masterly Inactivity'.

As the result of the conclusion of a peace settlement with the British, Dost Muhammad Khan of the Barakzai tribe, who had initially gained power in 1834, returned to the Afghan throne. His re-accession to power (1842–67) was made possible, in large measure, by the leading role that his son, Sardar Akbar Khan, had played in the jihad. Dost Muhammad Khan founded the Muhammadzai dynasty, which retained power in Afghanistan until the establishment of a republican government in 1973. Instead of the title 'shah', Dost Muhammad Khan adopted 'amir', a term with religious connotations given to him earlier by Mir Maᶜsum, the then Mir Waᶜiz of Kabul. The title signified his role as the commander of the faithful (*amīr al-muʾminīn*) and the leader of jihad (against Ranjit Singh at the time of Singh's initial encroachments on Afghan territory). Conceived as a religious duty, commitment to jihad was now a prerequisite for political legitimacy.

Amir Dost Muhammad's greatest achievement was the creation of a unified country. To retain power, he had to balance his relations carefully with politically ambitious brothers and with Great Britain. He had several clashes with religious leaders over his cautious dealings with the British. The ulama openly criticized him for agreements with the British in 1855 and 1857 that resulted in the loss of Peshawar and other southern territories to British India.[25] He resisted their pressure to wage jihad against the British to recover Peshawar and to defend Indian Muslims during the Sepoy Mutiny (May 1857).[26] Nevertheless, he managed to retain legitimacy, partly because in domestic matters he followed the rules of the Sharia and exhibited great piety.

The Second Anglo-Afghan War, 1878–80

The second British invasion of Afghanistan was provoked by a steady advance of czarist Russia into Central Asia in the 1860s and 1870s. When Benjamin Disraeli came to power in Great Britain, British policy towards Afghanistan was redefined. The policy of 'Masterly Inactivity' was abandoned in favour of what came to be known as the 'Forward Policy': move forward into Afghan territory, gain control and create a buffer state to protect India. By this time, the British had occupied Sind (in 1842) and Punjab (in 1849) and had positioned themselves more closely to the Afghan border.

In 1878, a Russian diplomatic mission headed by General Stelietov arrived uninvited at the court of Amir Shir ᶜAli Khan (1867–79), Dost Muhammad Khan's son and successor. Enraged at the Russian presence in Kabul, Lord Lytton, the viceroy of India, demanded that the amir promptly receive a comparable British legation in Kabul. Amir Shir ᶜAli Khan's refusal to accede immediately to the demand afforded the British an excuse to invade Afghanistan. In November 1878, British troops attacked Kandahar, Kurram and Kabul. As they approached the capital, Shir ᶜAli Khan, who was mourning the sudden death of the crown prince, fled north in hopes of receiving help from Russia, leaving a weak and ailing son, Yaᶜqub Khan, in charge. Lacking the will and ability to resist, Yaᶜqub Khan signed the Treaty of Gandamak in May 1879, which imposed on the new amir a permanent British mission in Kabul and ceded the Kurram Valley and Khayber Pass to British India.

On 3 September 1879, a mutiny over pay in the Herati regiment in Kabul gave rise to a violent revolt in the capital which resulted in the death of Sir Louis Cavagnari and several other British officers stationed in the city. This incident precipitated another British expedition into Afghanistan under the command of General Frederick Roberts, whose troops entered Kabul on 18 October. Amir Muhammad Yaᶜqub abdicated and agreed to go into exile in India.

In the absence of a strong political leadership, the clergy once again became the major force in mobilizing the Afghan population against the British. In the early stages of the war, the influential Mullah Khwaja Nazir rallied followers in Charasia, near Kabul, in a fierce battle that included female villagers among the combatants. Ulama in Ghazni began giving defiant sermons in the mosques, and the practice was quickly taken up in Kuhistan and Kabul.

The most important leader of the Second Anglo-Afghan War was Mullah Din Muhammad, known as Mushk-i-ᶜAlam (1790–1886), referred to by Archibald Forbes as 'Peter Hermit of Afghanistan'.[27] Mushk-i-ᶜAlam adhered to the Qadiriyya order and enjoyed great reverence for his highly acclaimed madrasas in Ander and Shilgahr (in Ghazni), which attracted many students from Lugar, Ghazni, Wardak, Qalat-i-Ghilzai, Hutaki and districts of Jalalabad. On 2 December, Mullah Mushk-i-ᶜAlam declared jihad in Ghazni and then proceeded towards Kabul with General Muhammad Jan Lugari, Mullah ᶜAbd al-Ghaffur Langari, Mir Bacha Kuhistani and Akhundzada Mir ᶜUsman Tagawi. Despite exceeding old age, Mushk-i-ᶜAlam launched a vigorous campaign against the British.

In the name of Musa Jan, the crown prince, Mushk-i-ᶜAlam took command of Afghan forces in Kabul. At midnight on 23 December, the night before the holy day of ᶜāshūrā, Mushk-i-ᶜAlam ascended the Asmai heights and lit a beacon, signalling various forces to attack Shirpur. While the onslaught forced the British to retreat within the walls of their Shirpur cantonment,[28] General Roberts regained control of Kabul. Howard Hensman, who accompanied the British army as a special correspondent for *The Pioneer* (published in Allahabad, India) and *The Daily News* (published in London), wrote in his diary:

> [N]early every fighting man in North-Eastern Afghanistan flocked to the banners consecrated by Mushk-i-ᶜAlam; and if the success of the jihad had been a little longer-lived – say by the interception of our reinforcements – there would have been streams of men setting in for Cabul [Kabul] from Turkistan, Badakhshan, and the Shutargardan district.[29]

In February 1880, the jihad led by Mullah Mushk-i-ᶜAlam regained momentum and prevented General Donald Stewart from advancing into Kabul. 'By July, Lord Lytton's views about occupying Afghanistan had undergone a complete *volteface*. Now he could not withdraw from Afghanistan quickly enough.'[30] Russia's change of attitude regarding Afghanistan provided a good reason for withdrawal. On 14 February 1869, Lord Clarendon, the British foreign secretary, had received a positive assurance from the Russian foreign minister, Prince Gortschakoff, that the Russian emperor considered Afghanistan outside the Russian sphere of influence and that Russian officers would no longer be allowed to visit Afghanistan.[31]

While anxious to leave, the British stayed on waiting for a sovereign to emerge who would be acceptable to the Afghans and with whom they could negotiate terms of a settlement. The arrival at this juncture of Sardar ᶜAbd al-Rahman, a nephew of Amir Shir ᶜAli Khan from Bukhara, seemed to satisfy everyone.

Diminution of Clergy Power during the Time of Peace: Centralization of Power under Amir ᶜAbd al-Rahman, 1880–1901

Following the Second Anglo-Afghan War, the influence of the ulama declined considerably when Amir ᶜAbd al-Rahman, the 'Iron Amir', succeeded in establishing a strong central government by military force. When ᶜAbd al-Rahman came upon the scene during the Second Anglo-Afghan War, support for jihad was at its peak among the masses. He used the mass sentiment for jihad for his personal political ends by sending messages to the leading chiefs of Turkistan, Kuhistan and Kabul, declaring his intent to expel the British. At this time, negotiations over succession to the Afghan throne had broken down. Neither of the most eligible candidates, Amir Muhammad Yaᶜqub and Sardar Muhammad Ayyub, the two sons of Amir Shir ᶜAli, was acceptable to all groups. The people of Herat, Kandahar and Farah favoured Sardar Muhammad Ayyub. *Ajirga* of 189 members, including Mullah Mushk-i-ᶜAlam, was held in Ghazni to support the deposed Amir Muhammad Yaᶜqub, but the people of Kabul, Kuhdaman and Lugar disapproved of both candidates. By July, Mushk-i-ᶜAlam, who supported succession in Amir Shir ᶜAli's line, had softened his position, and although his feelings towards the British did not change, he agreed to accept their choice as ruler of Afghanistan from among the claimants. In his war diary, Howard Hensman wrote: 'The old Moolla, Mushk-i-Alam, had, it is true, written to say he would accept the ruler whom we favored, but it was not expected that secessions from the Jacobin party would follow so rapidly.'[32]

The arrival of Sardar ʿAbd al-Rahman generated favourable reactions in Kuhdaman and Kabul, and on 20 July 1880, he was proclaimed king in Charikar, north of Kabul. He immediately entered into negotiation with the British, who were anxious to evacuate.

The popular religious fervour that ʿAbd al-Rahman had used to personal advantage was soon turned against him. Although negotiations with Britain's Lepel Griffin resulted in the complete withdrawal of British troops, the price extracted by the British was control over Afghanistan's foreign policy.[33] In July 1880, Griffin, then the foreign secretary to the government of India, sent a letter to the amir declaring that 'since the British government admits no right of interference by foreign powers in Afghanistan … it is plain that Your Highness can have no political relations with any foreign power except with the British government'.[34] Although ʿAbd al-Rahman never formally accepted the terms of the agreement,[35] he acquiesced to the British demands because of his delicate situation between two aggressive imperial powers and uncertainty about his own position. His willingness to forfeit Afghanistan's autonomy caused religious leaders to question his commitment to independence. They accused him of acceding to British demands in order to save the throne for himself, sacrificing Afghanistan's independence for personal gain.[36] By contrast, Sardar Muhammad Ayyub's continuing resistance to the British in Herat and Kandahar, combined with his decisive victory on the Maiwand front (near Kandahar) in 1880, increased his popularity with religious leaders, particularly with the influential Mujaddidis of Herat and Kandahar and Mullah Mushk-i-ʿAlam.

Many influential religious figures, such as Mushk-i-ʿAlam and some Kuhistani and Kandahari religious leaders, such as the *mullās* Amir Muhammad, ʿAbd al-Rahim and ʿAbd al-Ahad, began to oppose Amir ʿAbd al-Rahman. In 1883, Mushk-i-ʿAlam led a disturbance against the amir in Zurmat and Katawaz, urging the Waziris to resist his rule. In fact, Mullah Mushk-i-ʿAlam fought against ʿAbd al-Rahman until his death in 1886. His son, Mullah ʿAbd al-Karim, encouraged anti-government activity among the Ghilzais. In addition, Akhundzada ʿAbd al-Ghaffur, who was related to Mullah Mushk-i-ʿAlam by marriage, rose up against the government in Charasia, near Kabul.

Sahibzada ʿAta Muhammad, the spiritual leader of the Ghilzai and Durrani tribes, was also a staunch opponent of Amir ʿAbd al-Rahman. In Shinwar, the mullah of Hadda aroused the Shinwaris against the amir by accusing him of friendly relations with the British and of bringing Europeans into Afghanistan.[37] Mullah ʿAbd al-Karim, who had played a prominent role in the Ghilzai Rebellion of 1886–7, proclaimed the amir 'the worshipper of himself and the friend of an alien Government'.[38]

Despite considerable opposition among the ulama, Amir ʿAbd al-Rahman succeeded in consolidating his rule in Afghanistan. He crushed separatist movements and destroyed or banished suspect Barakzai *sardārs*, tribal *khāns* and potential claimants to the throne. To counter opposition from religious groups, he developed a threefold policy: (1) the use of force; (2) ostentatious piety; and (3) control of religious endowments (*awqāf*), making the clergy financially dependent on the state. Once Amir ʿAbd al-Rahman had defeated his rival cousins, Sardar Ayyub Khan in Kandahar and

Herat and Sardar Ishaq Khan in Balkh, he set about tightening control over the clergy. In 1882, he executed Muhammad ʿUmar Mujaddidi and his son, ʿAbd al-Baqi, who had supported Ayyub Khan, and he forced Mujaddidi's other sons into exile. Akhund ʿAbd al-Rahim Kakar, another influential leader who had proclaimed the amir an infidel, was executed along with several other *mullās* who had taken sanctuary (*bast*) in the Khirqa-i-Sharif, the shrine in Kandahar that contains a robe of the Prophet. Mullah Abubakr of Ghazni and his family were imprisoned in Kabul, and the allowances of Mushk-i-ʿAlam and his son were discontinued as early as 1881. In addition, the amir levied a tax of Rs. 15,000 on Mushk-i-ʿAlam's land and 'demanded seven years arrears at the above rate from his son [ʿAbd al-Karim]'.[39]

Leaders of the Sufi orders, particularly the Naqshbandiyya shaykhs, who had supported Ishaq Khan and Ayyub Khan against ʿAbd al-Rahman, also came under attack. While praising Shaykh Bahaʾ al-Din Naqshband, the founder of the order, as a sacred man and a hardworking potter, ʿAbd al-Rahman claimed that his followers were false. Their principal reason for seeking disciples, he wrote, 'was to extort money from them, that they themselves might lead a lazy life. They forget that it is entirely against the teachings, as well as against the practice of our Holy Prophet, who used to work hard himself'.[40]

To confound religious pretexts for opposing his rule, Amir ʿAbd al-Rahman practised strict orthodoxy. He placed himself imperiously at the head of a theocratic government and outmanoeuvred the ulama by claiming that 'kings stand to their countries as vice-regents of God .... [T]hey exercise the right of fortune or misfortune – of life and death – over those who are placed under his (*sic*) rule'.[41] Indeed, ʿAbd al-Rahman was the first ruler in Afghanistan to promote the divine right of the king as the *ẓill-Allāh*, the shadow of God on Earth. He even assumed the title *żiyāʾ al-Millat wa-l-Dīn* (Light of the Nation and the Faith) and claimed that as God's vice-regent on Earth, it was his duty to implement divine law. Under his direction, a number of pamphlets were printed, enjoining the faithful to the proper observation of the rules of the Qurʾan and the teachings of the Prophet. The implicit purpose of the pamphlets, however, was to provide religious justification for his policies. The tracts emphasized 'obedience to kings, paying of taxes, and steadiness in battle'.[42]

To strengthen his image as an orthodox religious man, ʿAbd al-Rahman hired subservient clergymen to implement the Sharia in a manner that conformed to his policies. He increased the power of the qadis, who enforced law and order and publicly sanctioned his policies. He increased the number of qadis and offered them positions as administrators of the Sharia and as overseers of the state's machinery in the capital and in certain provinces. Although the *qadi* retained the right to make discretionary decisions, they were required to act in compliance with codified procedures in the *Guidelines for Qadis* (*Asās al-Qużāt*). Along with other religious functionaries, the qadis were appointed by the amir and supervised by him.[43]

ʿAbd al-Rahman curbed the power of religious groups further by depriving them of their traditional sources of income. He brought the administration of religious endowments (*awqāf*) under direct governmental control. He imposed the first property tax on religious holdings and discontinued allowances to the heads of Sufi orders for the maintenance of Sufi headquarters (*khāniqāhs*). By making the ulama dependent on the government for their livelihood, he was able to subjugate most of them to the authority of the state.

In 1893, the amir was forced to sign what came to be known as the Durand agreement, under which parts of the Pashtun tribal area were divided into the British and Afghan spheres of influence. The demarcation of the Durand line reinforced hostility towards the British and strengthened the political position of the clergy in eastern Afghanistan. Earlier, Mullah ʿAbd al-Ghafur, the Akhundzada of Swat (b. 1794), a Qadiriyya shaykh, who was known for his piety and spiritual attainment and had great influence in the vicinity of Khaybar Pass, had issued a dictum to the effect that jihad against the British was a religious duty incumbent on all citizens.[44] The geographical location of Swat on the frontier between Afghanistan and British India facilitated the transformation of the Sufi order into a basis of holy war. Mullah ʿAbd al-Ghafur's influential *khalīfas*, such as Mullah Najm al-Din, known as the Mullah of Hadda; Mullah Hajji Akbar; Mullah Faiz-Allah; Mullah ʿAbd al-Wahhab Manki; and Mullah Hamz-Allah, were active in spreading the gospel of jihad throughout the region. Another leading figure involved in anti-British agitation was Mullah Saʿd-Allah, known as Mullah Mastan.

Amir ʿAbd al-Rahman tried to repress the activities of the tribal clergy by transferring the authority to declare jihad to the state. To justify the usurpation, he ordered books written asserting that no one but the caliph, amir or sultan was authorized to declare jihad.[45] At the same time, the amir enhanced his image as a pious amir, or sultan, possessing religious and secular powers – the imamate and the amirate. Heresy, even contact with 'infidels', was severely punished. Attempts were also made to enforce Hanafi doctrine on the Shiʿi population. In the name of Hanafi orthodoxy, the amir prosecuted leading clergymen whose influence posed a threat to the central authority. Mullah Najm al-Din of Hadda, the celebrated disciple of the Akhundzada of Swat, was arrested and 'was to be arraigned before a tribunal of *mullās* on a charge of disseminating Wahhabism',[46] a movement led by Sayyid Ahmad of Bareilly in India.

Amir ʿAbd al-Rahman enhanced his image as a Muslim ruler mostly as a result of his successful campaign in Kafiristan (1895–6) and the mass conversion of its people to Islam.[47] He skilfully turned the web of jihad towards the conquest of this isolated region in the northeast, whose inhabitants had retained their local creed for centuries. Leading tribal clergymen, including the Mullah of Hadda, the amir's staunch adversary, felt obliged to join the campaign. Upon the conversion of the Kafiri people to Islam, Kafiristan was given the name Nuristan (The Land of Light).

While ʿAbd al-Rahman significantly reduced the political influence of the ulama in Afghanistan by the end of the nineteenth century, he did not greatly reduce their influence as social and religious leaders. Clergy-backed skirmishes and sporadic warfare against the British continued along the frontier. Holy war became the dominant feature of tribal polity in eastern and southeastern Afghanistan. The clergy began to reassert its influence in the tribal regions along the borderline.

After the death of Mullah ʿAbd al-Ghafur of Swat, Hadda, seven miles south of Jalalabad, became the centre of anti-British activities. Hadda rose to prominence as a religious centre mostly because of the famous madrasa, Sufi headquarters and almshouse (*langer*) founded by the celebrated Mullah Najm al-Din of Hadda. According to British archival sources, the mullah of Hadda had more than 100,000 followers and was the most powerful mullah in Afghanistan at the end of the nineteenth century. As the most capable student of the famous Akhundzada of Swat, Mullah Najm al-Din commanded great reverence among the Pashtun tribes on both sides of the border. The disciples of the mullah of Hadda made up the most powerful group of ulama during the first quarter of the nineteenth century in Afghanistan. In the heart of the tribal region, Hadda became a convenient place for disciples to gather periodically to discuss important religious issues.

Although the clergy had begun to revitalize its power in the tribal region, they did not pose a challenge to ʿAbd al-Rahman's absolute power. The amir continued to rule with an iron hand until his death in 1901. By then he had created a united Afghanistan and a strong central government with effective administration. Lord Curzon, who visited ʿAbd al-Raman in 1894 in Kabul, described him as being

> at once a patriot and a monster, a great man and almost a fiend, [who] laboured hard and unceasingly for the good of his country .... He welded the Afghan tribes into a unity which they had never previously enjoyed, and he paved the way for [Afghanistan's] complete independence.[48]

A New Politicization of the Ulama under Amir Habib-Allah

During the reign of Siraj al-Millat wa al-Din Amir Habib-Allah (1901–19), son and successor of ʿAbd al-Rahman, the ulama gradually reasserted themselves as a political force, particularly along the frontier, which was populated by militant Pashtun tribes. Factors that permitted their resurgence were (1) royal patronage, (2) a relaxation of control by the central governmental and (3) the rise of nationalism and Pan-Islamism.

Habib-Allah, unlike his father, revered the ulama and the *pīrs*. He granted them land and allowances as high as Rs. 12,000 per annum, and he frequented the shrines. Even more important, he relaxed the state's control over religious institutions and practices, and the ulama gradually regained their influence. Although still appointed by the government, they reacquired full jurisdiction as judges, imams, instructors and custodians of shrines (*mutawāllīs*). The leaders of the *ṭarīqas* regained prominence. Members of the royal family, including the king himself, became aspirants of one or several *pīrs*.

Habib-Allah also granted amnesty to families forced into exile by ʿAbd al-Rahman, including important ulama families such as the Mujaddidis of Herat, exiled for twenty years in Persia. It was also during Habib-Allah's reign that the Sayyid Hasan Affandi Gailani (brother of the Naqib of Baghdad, head of the Qadiriyyah order) came to Afghanistan. Habib-Allah granted him a princely pension, land and a residence in Charbagh, near Jalalabad, and treated him with utmost respect.[49] The Mujaddidis of Kabul, also known as the Hazrats of Shurbazar, regained their former position as highly revered spiritual leaders and went on to play an important political role in the twentieth century in Afghanistan.

The revival of the ulama's influence was closely tied to renewed interest in jihad in Afghanistan during the first two decades of the twentieth century. Developments in and outside the country provoked strong anti-British sentiment and widespread support for jihad, which Habib-Allah encouraged in order to strengthen his hand in negotiations against the British. When Turkey entered the Great War against the Allies, which included the Afghan ulama's archenemy, Great Britain, the support for jihad was pervasive in Afghanistan. Given the traditional role of the ulama in jihad, as sentiment for jihad grew, so did the ulama's influence and involvement in politics. By the end of the First World War, the whole Afghan nation was ready to wage holy war against the British. As early advocates of war, the ulama were again at the forefront of Afghan politics.

Ironically, Habib-Allah first suggested the possibility of jihad against the Russians, not the British, in negotiations with the latter in 1904. The British were pressing him to accept an Anglo-Afghan military alliance, ostensibly to protect Afghanistan from possible attack by Russia. Habib-Allah insisted that, like Japan, Afghanistan could withstand Russian encroachment. All he needed from the British was financial assistance. He argued that he would, if necessary, enlist the Persians and Central Asian Muslims in a Pan-Islamic jihad against Russia.[50]

Three years later, in 1907, a diplomatic conference was held in St. Petersburg to define spheres of British and Russian influence in Afghanistan, Iran and Central Asia. After several months of negotiation, an agreement reached on 31 August 1907 stipulated equal commercial rights for both powers and demarcated a sphere of political influence for each. Afghanistan was declared outside Russia's sphere of interest, and Britain assumed political influence there in exchange for an agreement not to annex or occupy any part of Afghanistan and not to engage in any military action there that might threaten Russia. Russia was to engage only in commercial and non-political relations with Afghanistan.[51]

Repercussions in the Afghan court of the Anglo-Russian convention were far-reaching. The amir and members of the State Council (Majlis-i-Shura-i-Khas) expressed their displeasure publicly.[52] Habib-Allah called a national assembly (jirga), which included prominent religious leaders. After consulting the tribal leaders and the ulama, the amir and the State Council concluded that jihad against the British was inevitable.

Reluctant to see fighting begin, Habib-Allah hoped that by threatening holy war in the tribal zone, he could force the government of India to withdraw its acceptance of the convention. He established contact with Mullah Pawinda (a disciple of the mullah of Hadda), who exerted great influence among the Muhmand and Waziri tribes on the British side of the Durand line, offering ammunition, men and money. As efforts were made to enlist men for the jihad, several leading ulama, headed by the Padshah-i-Islampur, preached jihad in the Eastern Province. Enthusiasm for jihad swept across the country, and volunteer tribal warriors flocked into Kabul from every direction. The Padshah of Islampur raised a large tribal army in Kunar, near Jalalabad, to be led to the frontier by Shaghasi ʿAbd al-Quddus Khan Iʿtimad al-Dawla. Mullah Pawindah, Mullah Hamz-Allah, Lala Pir and several others engaged in stirring up tribes across the frontier. The anti-British sentiments aroused by the call for jihad were so intense that Habib-Allah and Nasr-Allah Khan Naʾib al-Saltana feared the situation would get out of hand. To avoid an outbreak of fighting, they blocked Sardar ʿAbd al-Quddus, the Iʿtimad al-Dawla, from joining the troops in Kunar, a decision that offended both the Padshah of Islampur and the Iʿtimad al-Dawla. Infuriated by this order, the fervid anti-British prime minister resigned his post and wrote to the amir and his brother that in the future he would 'never have anything to do with them or the business of the state'.[53]

Anti-British sentiment continued to escalate. It appeared as though the entire Islamic world was in danger of being partitioned by the Europeans. 'These fears received daily confirmation in the rumors of proposed railway construction across Persia, and the discussions about respective spheres of influence that [were] carried on in a cool proprietary tone in the newspapers.' [54] In 1908 and 1909, the ulama of the Eastern Province joined in calling for jihad against the British. The leading clergy involved in anti-British agitation included the Padshah of Islampur; the Sufi of Baikitut, Sayyid Laʿl Shah (Mullah Lalapir); the Hazrat Sahib of Charbagh; and the Akhundzada of Tagaw, all disciples of Mullah Najm al-Din of Hadda. In 1909, Mullah Najm al-Din issued a religious decree (*fatwā*) urging the people to join in a holy war against the British. His call for jihad aroused excitement in Kabul, Lugar, Kuhistan and the southern provinces. Another fatwa by Akhundzada Mussahi, the *pīr* of Amir Habib-Allah and Prince Nasr-Allah, had a similar effect.

The primary instigator of anti-British agitation was Nasr-Allah Naʾib al-Saltana, the amir's younger brother. A profoundly pious Muslim who was the commander of the Afghan army, he advocated Islamic perspectives in domestic and foreign policy, a predilection that made him popular among the ulama. Assisted by Mawlawi ʿAbd al-Raziq, the rector (*mullā-bāshi*) of the Madrasa-i-Shahi, the influential chaplain of the royal household (*mullā-i-huẓūr*), and 'the central wire-puller of all transborder priestly fanaticism',[55] the prince had established connections with virtually all of the religious leaders in Afghanistan and across the border in the North-West Frontier Province of British India. Through a network of loyal *mullās*, the Naʾib al-Saltana promoted a nationalism based on Islam. British authorities viewed him as the main force behind anti-British riots in the North-West Frontier and as the man who had united the various factions of clergy under the banner of Islamic patriotism.[56] According to Arnold Keppel, the Naʾib al-Saltana was also involved in smuggling some 30,000 rifles from the Persian Gulf through India in 1907. These rifles, brought to Kandahar via a network of *mullās*, were to be used to stir up the frontier tribes against the British.[57] In 1906, the Naʾib al-Saltana appointed Mullah Sayyid Laʿl Shah his agent to work in Khust among the Mangals, Waziris and Mashuds. On 14 July, Lord Hardinge, the British viceroy of India, complained to the amir:

> I regret to have to inform you that during the past three months a series of numerous raids have been committed into British territory, which I am informed are the results of efforts on the part of Mollah Pawindah to stir not only the Khust outlaws but the tribesmen of Waziristan to commit outrages against the Government. Mollah Pawindah is said to have paid recent visits to Kabul and to be using YM's name in his appeals to the tribesmen to commit mischief.[58]

The viceroy added that letters bearing the seals of Mullah Pawindah and Nasr-Allah Khan were found in the possession of those captured.

Despite being offended by the resolutions of the Anglo-Russian Convention, the amir, now inclined to avoid hostility with the British, gave in to the viceroy's pressure. He took repressive measures to stop the skirmishes instigated by the clergy near the frontier. He dismissed and reprimanded Mawlawi ʿAbd al-Raziq, Nasr-Allah Khan's protégé, and Nazir Safar, the chief steward and seal holder, who had collaborated with Mawlawi ʿAbd al-Raziq. Several leaders of the disturbance in the frontier area were arrested and brought to Kabul for trial.

The amir's change of attitude towards the British turned the ulama and the anti-British elements in the court against him. Habib-Allah Khan's relations with the ulama had, in fact, started to deteriorate earlier in 1906, when, despite strong opposition by the Naʾib al-Saltana and several high-profile religious leaders, such as the sultan of Islampur, he had accepted the viceroy's invitation to visit India. Clerical opposition to the amir's visit surfaced in the Eastern Province in response to rumours that he had become a Freemason.[59] The amir responded to the charged vigorously. Upon his return, he executed four *mullās*.[60]

The Ulama and Liberal Nationalism

At the outset of his reign, Amir Habib-Allah gave the impression of being a progressive, energetic ruler. He granted amnesty to exiled families, increased the power of the State Council, abolished torture in prisons and promoted modern education by establishing new schools, a printing house (*Matbaʿa-i-ʿInāyat*) and the Bureau of Translation (*Dār al-Tarjuma*). As time passed, however, he became more authoritarian and, like his father, began to claim 'divine rights'. According to Ghubar, he often stated publicly that the ruler was God's vice-regent (*nāʾib*) on earth and that his command was in fact the command of God.[61] Books were written, heavy with quotations from the Quʾan, the Hadith and medieval Muslim works, stressing that a Muslim state could not survive without the sultan, or *pādshāh*, who as the shadow of God (*ẓill-Allāh*) and a shepherd (*rāʿī*), was the nourisher, guide and protector of his subjects (*raʿīyya*). Submission to authority (*iṭāʿat-i-ūlū al-ʾamr*, which, based on the Qurʾanic verse [iv: 62], was interpreted to mean the ruler) was the religious duty of every Muslim. The ruler was responsible for maintaining order and providing safety and justice, according to the Sharia. In fulfilling those duties, the ruler was answerable only to God.[62]

Against this autocracy, a group of students and teachers, including some liberal ulama, formed the Secret National Party (*Ḥizb-i-Sirr-i-Millī*), also known as the Constitutionalists (*Mashrūṭa Khwāhān*). Their aim, as the name implied, was to bring to an end the autocratic regime of Habib-Allah and to establish a constitutional government. The head of the Mashruta Khwahan was Mawlawi Muhammad Sarwar Wasif, an eminent religious scholar from Kandahar.[63] Mawlawi Wasif and his close collaborator, Mir Muhammad Qasim, espoused progressive ideas and advocated legislative reform. Among other liberal ulama who advocated change were Mawlawi ʿAbd al-Raʾuf Kandahari (the son of Mawlawi ʿAbd al-Rahim Alikuzai, executed by ʿAbd al-Rahman) and his two sons, Mawlawis ʿAbd al-Wasiʿ and ʿAbd al-Rabb. Mawlawi ʿAbd al-Raʾuf was at the time the head of the Madrasa-i-Shahi and the chief alim in the royal court. A document in the Afghan National Archives reveals that a group of ulama of the Madrasa-i-Chubfrushi in Kabul and others, including Mawlawi ʿAbd al-Raʾuf, wrote a letter to Amir Habib-Allah requesting establishment of a biweekly paper in Kabul.⁶⁴ Iʿtimad al-Dawla submitted the request to the amir and received his approval. The first issue of the paper appeared on 11 January 1906, under the editorship of Mawlawi ʿAbd al-Raʾuf. A poem in that first issue called the amir's attention to progress made by other nations.⁶⁵

In the winter of 1909, the amir became aware of a plot by the Hizb-i-Sirr-i-Milli against the regime and ordered police action. Members of the Hizb were arrested. Some were sentenced to death and others to various terms of imprisonment. Among those arrested were several liberal ulama: Mawlawi Wasif, Mullah Muhammad Sarwar Alikuzai, Qazi ʿAbd al-Ahad Sulaimankhail, Mullah Mohammad Akbar Akhundzada, Mawlawi Ghulam Muhyi al-Din, Sahibzada ʿAbd-Allah Mujaddidi, Mullah Minhaj al-Din and Mawlawi ʿAbd-al-Wasiʿ Kandahari, son of Mawlawi ʿAbd al-Raʾuf.⁶⁶ That year, Mawlawi Wasif was executed with several other suspects on a charge of conspiring against the monarch. Moments before his execution, he slipped to a friend a piece of paper on which he had written a verse affirming that sacrifice was necessary in order to achieve liberal goals.⁶⁷

The events of 1909 turned Amir Habib-Allah against the liberal groups. Since the *mashrūṭa* movement had begun in the newly established Habibiyya College, the amir's interest in expanding the opportunity for education waned quickly. He refocused his energy on modernizing the court and spent the rest of his time on new hobbies – hunting and photography.

The First World War and Pan-Islamism

The reign of Amir Habib-Allah coincided with the epoch of Islamic nationalism and Pan-Islamism. The Turko–Italian War in 1911 and the Balkan Wars during the next two years generated a sense of solidarity in the Islamic world. Sultan ʿAbd al-Hamid II's revival of the prestige of the office of caliphate in Turkey and the Young Turks' campaign in the name of caliphate to promote Pan-Islam in India and Central Asia had already generated strong popular support for that office throughout the region, including in Afghanistan.

A group of Afghan nationalists, headed by Mahmud Tarzi, editor of the Afghan newspaper *Sirāj al-Akhbār*, set about reconciling tenets of Islam and nationalism. Publication of *Sirāj al-Akhbār* marked a watershed in the development of political consciousness in Afghanistan. The paper took the lead in promoting support for Ottoman Turkey and Pan-Islamism. The Ottoman sultan declared Turkey's entry into the Great War and called for an Islamic jihad against the Allies in defense of the caliphate (*khilāfat*).

The Afghan ulama and Afghan nationalists responded enthusiastically to the Ottoman sultan's call for jihad, not only because Turkey was the seat of the caliphate and all Sunni Muslims felt responsible for its defence, but also because an alliance with other Islamic forces against the Allies could strengthen Afghanistan's demand for complete independence from Great Britain. News of the jihad was spread quickly among the people by pilgrims returning from Mecca with leaflets seeking support for Turkey and by secret Turkish envoys in the tribal areas on both the Afghan and British sides of the Durand line. The influential tribal mullah, the hajji of Turanqzai, on the British side of the North-West Province's border, awaited the amir's lead to begin activities there.[68] *Sirāj al-Akhbār* expressed deep sympathy for Ottoman Turkey and called India the abode of war (*dār al-ḥarb*). Copies of this issue were distributed on the subcontinent and were read avidly. The Indian newspapers *Al-Hilāl* and *Comrade*, edited by Mawlanas Muhammad ʿAli and ʿAbd al-Kalam Azad, also printed stirring articles in favour of Turkey. Their common sympathy for Turkey reinforced ties between Indian Muslims and the Afghan ulama and nationalists.

In 1915, a joint Turkish-German mission headed by Oscar Niedermayer arrived in Kabul with a message from the German emperor and chancellor, encouraging the amir to join the jihad in favour of Turkey and asking him to allow troops of the Central Powers to pass through Afghanistan to India. The mission included several Turks and two Indian revolutionaries, Barakat-Allah and Mahandra Pratap, who later formed a provisional government in Kabul. At about the same time, Mawlana Muhammad Husain, a professor at Deoband College and one of the principal instigators of the Khilafat Movement in India, sent a disciple, Mawlana ʿUbaid-Allah Sindhi, to promote jihad in Afghanistan.[69] The news of the arrival of the Turkish-German mission electrified the entire frontier region.

While some influential members of the Afghan court, such as the Naʾib al-Saltana and the Iʿtimad al-Dawla, favoured an alliance with Turkey, Habib-Allah remained firm in his belief that it was not in Afghanistan's best interest to enter the war. The amir hoped that by remaining neutral he could later bargain effectively with the British for Afghanistan's unconditional independence. He believed that an escalation of hostility between Afghanistan and Great Britain would lead to a confrontation that would have negative results for Afghanistan, so he rejected the overtures of the Turkish-German Mission.[70]

Habib-Allah's resistance to entering the war and his unwavering policy of 'Cautious Alliance' intensified the resentment of religious groups. Simultaneously, he offended the nationalists who wanted complete independence from Britain and direct diplomatic and cultural relations with the rest of the world.

Religious leaders in the frontier zone, mostly disciples of the mullah of Hadda, encouraged raids on British territory. On 18 April 1915, the mullah of Chaknawur brought a significant tribal force to the vicinity of Peshawar, the border city between Afghanistan and British India, and crossed into British territory. In May, Lord Hardinge, viceroy and governor-general of India, informed the amir of the hostile ferment among the Muhmand tribes at the instigation of the Chaknawur mullah in the vicinity of Peshawar, and asked him to punish persons who had incited hostilities.[71] But by late summer, the mullah of Chaknawur again tried to gain the cooperation of the Sufi of Baikitut and Nazian mullah, also disciples of the mullah of Hadda, to promote jihad among the Afridi tribe.[72] Meanwhile, the mullah of Turanqzai, Sandakai mullah and Babri mullah were engaged in agitating jihad among the Muhmand tribesmen.[73] Plans for a combined attack on the British border were thwarted by an outbreak of cholera in August,[74] but anti-British activities started again in September.

The viceroy wrote to Habib-Allah that 'Mīr Sāhib Jan Padshah, *mullā* of Islāmpūr, in Your Majesty's territories, has moved into Mohmand country with a considerable following, for the purpose of creating trouble on that border'.[75] The amir tried to dissuade the independent frontier tribes from supporting the *khilāfat* cause. He sought the cooperation of a noted Nangarhari religious leader, Mullah ʿAbd al-Hamid, to control anti-British ferment on the frontier.

Ultimately, Habib-Allah convened a *jirga* consisting of 540 representatives in Kabul to discuss the request of the Turkish-German Mission. According to Ghubar, his real purpose was to keep all potential sources of anti-British agitation under his surveillance in Kabul.[76] Among those invited were leading supporters of jihad, including the Padshah of Islampur, Mullah Muhammad Mussahi, the Akhundzada of Tagaw, the Mian of Buru, the Mian of Hissarak, the Ustad of Hadda, the Mullah of Chaknawur and members of the Mujaddidi family.[77]

At about this time, Habib-Allah had a leaflet printed extolling the medieval doctrine of obedience to authority (*iṭāʿat-i-ūlū al-ʾamr*). Copies were distributed in the mosques and at military headquarters throughout the country, warning that according to the Sharia, jihad could not be waged without the order of the ruler.[78] In the meantime, he gave the British authorities his promise of continued neutrality 'so long as the internal interests of Afghanistan are not exposed to danger'.[79]

The Turkish-German Mission left in May 1916, after Habib-Allah's public announcement of Afghanistan's neutrality in January of that year. The amir's denial of the request of the Ottoman sultan disconcerted the nationalists and the ulama. Shortly after the departure of the mission, the British agent in Kabul reported that leaflets had been circulated in the major mosques in Kabul denouncing Amir Habib-Allah as the friend and servant of the British government and inciting the people to rebel against the orders of the amir.[80] Later in June, the padshah of Islampur announced at his daughter's funeral that the 'amir would never break his faith with the British unless coerced by overwhelming force'.[81]

Even as the amir attempted to keep Afghanistan out of the war, open as well as secret preparations for mobilization continued. *Pro-khilāfat* and anti-British sentiment was fuelled further by a British-inspired Arab revolt in Hijaz against the Turks. Mahmud Tarzi once again published a stirring article in *Sirāj al-Akhbār* on 16 July 1916, labelling the sharif of Mecca a traitor.[82] In Kandahar, a large group of *mullās* held a conference with the governor and asserted that the siege of the holy cities by the British had made jihad unavoidable. Despite his strong sympathy for the Turks, Sardar Nasr-Allah Khan did not act openly against his brother but was involved covertly in anti-British agitation among the tribes. Near the end of 1917, the amir came to suspect his brother's involvement in anti-British tribal revolts on the British side of the border; he then prevented his brother from conducting further frontier tribal affairs.[83]

Outside the capital, public opinion was unanimously pro-war. Some religious leaders were independently in contact with pro-*khilāfat* elements in India. In 1918, the Padshah Sahib of Islampur received a party of Indian Khilafatists in Islampur.[84]

In February 1919, when frustration over the amir's 'cautious policy' was at a critical level, Habib-Allah was shot and killed in his camp on a hunting trip in the Eastern

Province. A note prepared by the Political Department of the India Office on 17 May 1919 reads in part:

> The fidelity of the late ruler to the British connection is well known, and has formed the subject of eulogy in both Houses of Parliament. He had a difficult hand to play in the war, and he played it with consummate skill and success. He had to resist the pressure, not only of the German and Turkish agents who found their way to his capital, but of a large 'KDD' element among his own people (his brother Nasrullah Khan being the leading spirit) who constantly urged him to assume the role of a 'King of Islam' and declare war on the enemies of Khalif [sic] .... How far the unpopularity of his war policy may have been among the causes of his assassination, it is difficult to say.[85]

After Amir Habib-Allah's assassination, relations between the government and the ulama suddenly changed. Habib-Allah's son and successor, Aman-Allah (1919–29), who championed the nationalist cause, effectively pre-empted Sardar Nasr-Allah's claim to the throne through a swift course of action. First, he accused Nasr-Allah of involvement in the assassination. Then he unilaterally declared Afghanistan's independence and joined the clergy in calling for jihad against the British. In response, the religious forces rallied immediately to his support. During the initial years of his reign, Aman-Allah was able to maintain a coalition with the clergy on the issues of independence and Pan-Islamism. However, the alliance between the state and the ulama did not last long. Aman-Allah's reform policies soon created serious tension between the state and the clergy, resulting in clergy-backed revolts in the countryside and the eventual collapse of the central government in the winter of 1928. However, an analysis of the ulama's relations with Aman-Allah is outside the scope of this chapter.

Conclusion

The first three quarters of the nineteenth century formed a period of intense political turbulence in Afghanistan. Competition between two imperial powers – czarist Russia in the north and British India in the south – made Afghanistan the battle ground for what came to be known as the 'Great Game of Asia'. Foreign invasions and power struggles among Sadduzai princes, and struggles between the princes and the Barakzai leaders, led to the decline of the central government and the demise of the elaborate judicial administrative system set up by Ahmad Shah Durrani. In the absence of a strong centralized state and centralized economic structure, self-sufficient rural communities at the periphery assumed greater autonomy, opening the way for the religious establishment to expand its influence on social and legal matters and assert leadership in the political arena. Although the influence of high-ranking ulama, whose function was connected with the central administration, began to dwindle, the influence of the religious leadership in the countryside became expansive. As the result of the British invasions in 1839 and 1878, jihad became the dominant force in Afghan politics, with its clergy its most ardent advocates. Opposed to conciliation of any kind, the clergy forged a formidable force against the British. They exercised considerable political influence through most of the nineteenth century as powerbrokers, mass mobilizers and arbiters of political legitimacy.

Under the reign of Amir ʿAbd al-Rahman in the last quarter of the nineteenth century, the influence of the clergy in Afghan politics was temporarily curtailed. Amir ʿAbd al-Rahman established the authority of the central government throughout Afghanistan. He brought the religious establishment back under state control, reaffirmed traditional Islamic symbols of the monarchy and established himself as the leader of religious, as well as social, order. At the beginning of the twentieth century, however, the political influence of the clergy expanded anew with the rise of nationalism, liberalism and Pan-Islamism. The common goal to liberate Afghanistan from British control resulted in a coalition of the ulama and the liberal nationalists. In fact, a small group of ulama in the capital allied with liberals to curb Amir Habib-Allah's absolute monarchical power.

It was events primarily outside Afghanistan that brought the ulama back to the fore of Afghan politics. The tense climate surrounding the entry of Ottoman Turkey into the Great War once again politicized and mobilized Islamic forces in Afghanistan. By establishing links with anti-British and Pan-Islamic activists outside Afghanistan, the ulama and the nationalists became involved in regional and even international politics. The influential role of rural ulama as popular leaders of organized forces opposing foreign domination was re-established. Amir ʿAbd al-Rahman's son and successor, Amir Habib-Allah, was unable to control the political activity of the clergy. Habib-Allah's pro-British leanings and resistance to the popular demand for jihad were important factors in uniting the clergy with the liberal groups for the cause of Afghan independence.

The revival of clergy as a political force during the reign of Amir Habib-Allah opened a new phase in the state–ulama interactions. A number of government-appointed high-ranking ulama, affected by Muslim revivalist ideas of the late-nineteenth- and early-twentieth-century Muslim thinkers, expressed progressive views and allied themselves with the liberals. However, the majority of the high ulama who served in the government-controlled judicial department and filled some important posts in the administration remained to become a rubber stamp for the implementation of government policies. The leaders of the Naqshbandi and the Qadiri orders, who exerted great influence among the urban and rural population, assumed a greater role in Afghan politics.

By the time of Habib-Allah's assassination in 1919, the clergy had established for itself a compelling historical role as the defender of Islam against foreign invasion and as a bulwark of the rural civil society, a role it has traditionally asserted in times of political upheaval. Because of their affiliation with the militant Pashtun tribes along the border with British India, and their connection with the Qadiri and Naqshbandi orders, religious leaders in the Eastern and Southern provinces emerged as a compelling political force, posing a challenge not only to the British in India but also to the central government at home.

Notes

* Spelling and grammar (both English and Persian) have been kept as originally published in this chapter.

Author's note: This chapter is based on primary and relevant secondary sources in English and Persian. In addition to materials gathered from the India Office Records in London and the National Archives of India (NAI), I have used eyewitness reports by nineteenth-century western writers such as Mountstuart Elphinstone, who visited Kabul in 1808 during the reign of Shah Shujāᶜ, Joseph Ferrier, a French general who visited Afghanistan in the mid-1800s; Howard Hensman, special correspondence of the *Pioneer* (Allahabad) and the *Daily News* (London), who accompanied British troops in Afghanistan during the Second Anglo-Afghan War. I have also consulted the work of Mohan Lai, an Indian secretary who served under General MacNaughten and Major Burns in Kabul in the mid-nineteenth century; and the autobiography of Amir ᶜAbd al-Rahman, translated into English by his secretary, Sultan Mahomed (Muhammad) Mir Munshi. The most important sources in Persian are nineteenth-century and early-twentieth-century government publications; Naqshbandi texts written by Mujaddidi shaykhs, ᶜ*Umdat al-Muqāmāt* (written in the early 1800s by Muḥammad Fazl-Allah) and *Hidayāt al-ᶜUrfān* (written in the mid-nineteenth century by Muhammad ᶜUmar Jān); *Tāj al-Tawārīkh*, Amir ᶜAbd al-Rahman's autobiography; *Ṭuhfat al-Amīr fi Bayān-i-Sulūk wa al-Tadbīr* written by Muhammad Tāj al-Dīn Afghānī at Amir Habib-Allah's order; and *Sirāj al-Tawārīkh* written by Faiẓ Muhammad Kātib, court historian in the time of King Habib-Allah.

I am grateful to Ludwig Adamec for sharing materials from the NAI. The NAI files used in this work are from his library.

1. Mahomed Mir Munshi (1901).
2. Hensman (1881).
3. Ludwig Adamec's works on diplomatic history in Afghanistan covers in detail Afghanistan's relations with Great Britain during the late nineteenth and early twentieth centuries.
4. This theme is explored by David Gibbs to explain the tenacious resistance in the countryside to the Soviet invasion of Afghanistan and to the domestic Marxist regime in Afghanistan during the 1980s; Gibbs (1986).
5. Ferrier (1858).
6. Habībī (1970).
7. Fufalzai (1967).
8. Lai (1978); Ferrier, *History of the Afghans*, 203.
9. Lal, *Life of the Amir* 2:277.
10. ᶜAzīz al-Dīn W. Fufalzai, *Durrat al-Zamān fī Tārīkh-i-Shāh Zamān*, 22–3.
11. ᶜUmar Jan (1940).
12. ᶜAṭā Muḥammad Shikārpūri, *Nawā-I-Maᶜārik*, quoted by Fulfalzai, *Durrat al-Zamān*, 274.
13. Ghani (1978).
14. The part of Kabul that once belonged to the descendants of Mīr Ahmad was referred to as the *awqāf* of Mīr Wāᶜiẓ in the official listings of the revenue office.
15. Elphinstone (1972).
16. Faẓ 1-Allah (1355/1925).
17. Fufalzai, *Tīmūr Shāh Durrāni*, 2:309.
18. Kātib (1912); Muhammad Ghubār (1967); Fufalzai, *Durrat al-Zamān*, 116.

19 By 1838, as the result of intense internal strife among Durrani princes, large portions of Durrāni or Sadduzai territory such as Panjab, Kashmir and Moltan had been lost to the Sikhs, and local leaders in northern Afghanistan were proclaiming independence.
20 Ferrier, *History of the Afghans*, 331.
21 Ibid., 332.
22 Ibid., 334.
23 Ibid., 332.
24 Wheeler (1869).
25 Gregorian (1969).
26 Ibid.
27 Forbes (1906).
28 Ibid., 358.
29 Hensman, *The Afghan War*, 264.
30 Barthorp (1982).
31 India Office Records, L/P&S/10/125, 3082, A.165, confidential document, 1907. These preliminary negotiations formed the basis of the so-called Clarendon–Gortschakoff Agreement of 1872–3.
32 Hensman, *The Afghan War*, 435.
33 Adamec (1967).
34 India Office Records, L/P&S/10/125, 3082, A 165, 1907.
35 A report compiled by the political department of India office affirms that 'there is no record of any formal acceptance by Amir ʿAbd al-Rahman of the terms set forth in Mr. Griffin's letter of July 1880'; ibid. The amir did, however, assure the British that 'if I have the friendship of a great government like yours, how can I communicate with another power without advice from and consultation with you'; ibid.
36 Ghubār, *Afghānistān dar Masīr-i-Tārīkh*, 641. In his autobiography, ʿAbd al-Rahman felt compelled to respond to the allegations of apostasy levelled against him by the clergy because of his alleged friendly ties with the British. Mir Munshi, *The Life of Abdur Rahman*, 1:225.
37 Kakar (1979).
38 *Biographical Accounts of Chiefs, Sardars and Others of Afghanistan (Strictly Confidential)*, Foreign Office of India (Calcutta: Office of Superintendent of Government Printing, 1869), 112, cited by Adamec, *Historical and Political Who's Who of Afghanistan*, 98.
39 *Biographical Accounts*, 6.
40 Mir Munshi, *The Life of Abdur Rahman*, 1:265.
41 Ibid., 15.
42 Ghani, 'Islam and State-Building', 279.
43 Kātib, *Sirāj al-Tawārīkh*, 3:941. From this time until the end of King Zahir Shah's reign (1933–73) the qadis were appointed directly by the king.
44 Qureshi, 162. The Akhundzada of Swāt claimed spiritual leadership through a chain of predecessors (*silsila*), mainly Shaykh Junaid of Peshawar and Shaykh Ahmad of Delhi, to Sayyid Abdal-Qadir Gailani; interview with Padshah Sāhib Sayyid ʿAbd al-Qayyūm, the last shaykh in the line of the successors of Akhundzada of Swāt through the mullah of Hadda, Peshawar, 23 September 1994.
45 Kakar, *Government and Society*, 125.
46 *Biographical Accounts*, 147.

47 Kāfiristān, land of the infidels (*kāfirs*), is currently known as Nuristan.
48 Curzon (1923).
49 Adamec, *Historical and Political Who's Who*, 230; May Schinazi, *Afghanistan at the Beginning of the Twentieth Century: Nationalism and Journalism in Afghanistan – A Study of Siraj al-Akhbar, 1911–1918* (Naples: Instituto Universitario Orientale Seminaro di Studi Asiatici, 79), 117.
50 National Archives of India, January 1905, tel. 73k, 23 December 1904.
51 Adamec, *Afghanistan, 1900–1923*, 70.
52 National Archives of India, Foreign Department Notes, Secret File, July 1908, Nos. 276–8.
53 Ibid., nos. 276–8, 46.
54 Kepple (1977).
55 Government of India (1914).
56 Keppel, *Gun-Running*, 72–3.
57 Ibid., 52.
58 India Office Records, L/P&S/14/6, Kharita no. 11 p.o., Simla, 14 July 1913, from His Excellency the Viceroy to His Majesty Amir of Afghanistan.
59 National Archives of India, Foreign Secret File, nos. 23–32, February 1907.
60 Adamec, *Afghanistan, 1900–1923*, 67.
61 Ghubār, *Afghānistān dar Masī*, 711.
62 See, for example, Tāj al-Dīn Afghānī (n.d.), chaps. 1–5.
63 Ḥabībī (1986).
64 Kāẓim Ahang (1970).
65 Habībī, *Junbish-i-Mashrūṭiyyat dar Afghānistān*, 8.
66 Ghubār, *Afghānistān dar Masī*, 718–19.
67 Habībī, *Junbish-i-Mashrūṭiyyat dar Afghānistān*, 16; Ghubār, *Afghānistān dar Masir-i-Sarikh*, 718.
68 Husain Qureshi (1974).
69 Ibid., 246–7.
70 On 3 March 1915, the viceroy wrote to Habib-Allah: 'I am delighted to have proof that in spite of such influences as may be at work in your territories Your Majesty is steadily pursuing the policy of neutrality which throughout you have declared to the King Emperor's Government. I have had evidence of your Majesty's wise influence in the temperate preaching of mollahs on the frontier and in the improved tone of the "Siraj-ul-Akhbar [*sic*] newspaper."' India Office Library, L/P&S/14/6, Kharita no. 6, POA, 3 March 1915, from HE Viceroy and Gov. G. to HM A of Afghanistan.
71 India Office Records, London, L/P&S/14/6, Kharita no. 10, PO-A, Simla, 10 May 1915, from Viceroy to Amir Habib-Allah.
72 India Office Records, L/P&S/10/544, P 3352, 15 September 1915.
73 Ibid., P3845, 1915; P3258, 1915.
74 Ibid., P3553, 29 August 1915.
75 Ibid., L/P&S/14/6, tel. no. S.994, 28 September 1915.
76 Ibid.
77 Ibid.
78 Ibid.; *Sirāj al-Akhbār*, Kabul, vi, no. 15, 14 April 1916.
79 Adamec, *Afghanistan, 1900–1923*, 92.
80 India Office Records, L/P&S/10/202, P2805, 1916.
81 Ibid.; letter from George Roos-Keppel to the secretary of state for India, n. 4BN, 17 June 1916.

82 *Sirāj al-Akhbār*, vi., no. 22, 16 July 1916.
83 Adamec, *Afghanistan, 1900-1923*, 92.
84 Government of India, 'Who Is Who of Afghanistan', confidential unpublished file, British Government in India, 1920, 151.
85 'The Afghan Situation', National Archives of India, Political Department, India Office, A 177, 17 May 1919.

References

Adamec, L. 1967. *Afghanistan, 1900-1923: A Diplomatic History*. Berkeley: University of California Press, 14–15.
Afghānī, M. Tāj al-Dīn. (n.d.), *Ṭuhfat al-Amīr fi Bayān-i-Sulūk wa al-Tadbīr*. Kabul: Government Printing House.
Barthorp, M. (1982), *The North-West Frontier: A Pictorial History, 1859-1947*. Bristol: Blandford Press, 85.
Curzon, George N. (Marquess of Kedleston) (1923), *Tales of Travel*. New York: George H. Doran Company, 67.
Elphinstone, M. (1972), *An Account of the Kingdom of Caubul*, 4th ed., 2 vols. Karachi: Oxford University Press, 2:83.
Fażl-Allah, Muhammad. (1355/1925), ᶜ*Umdat al-Mūqāmāt*. Kabul: Nuᶜmānī Publishers, 99–102.
Ferrier, J. P. (1858), *History of the Afghans*. London: John Murray, 95.
Forbes, A. (1906), *The Afghan Wars, 1839-42 and 1878-80*, 4th ed. London: Seeley and Co., Ltd., 224.
Fufalzai, ᶜAzīz al-Dīn W. (1967), *Timūr Shāh Durrānī*, 2 vols. Kabul: Historical Society, 1:41.
Ghani, A. (1978), 'Islam and State-Building in a Tribal Society: Afghanistan 1880-1901.' *Modern Asian Society*, 12(2): 271.
Gibbs, D. (1986), 'The Peasant as Counter Revolutionary: The Rural Origins of the Afghan Insurgency.' *Studies in Comparative International Development*, 21 (Spring): 36–59.
Government of India. (1914), secret serial no. 88, *Who's Who in Afghanistan*. Simla: Government Monotype Press, 11.
Gregorian, V. (1969), *The Emergence of Modern Afghanistan: Politics of Reform and Modernization, 1880-1946*. Stanford, CA: Stanford University Press, 83.
Habībī, ᶜAbd al-Hayy. (1970), *Tārīkh-i-Mukhtaṣar-i-Afghānistān*, 2 vols. Kabul: The Book Publishing Institute, 2:99.
Ḥabībī, ᶜAbd al-Hayy. (1986), *Junbish-i-Mashrūṭiyyat dar Afghānistān*. Washington, DC: Private Press, 13.
Hensman, H. (1881), *The Afghan War of 1879-80*. London: H. Allen and Co., 336.
Husain Qureshi, I. (1974), *Vlema in Politics: A Study Relating to the Political Activities of the Ulema in the South-Asian Subcontinent from 1556-1947*, 2nd ed. Karachi: Maᶜaref Limited, 224.
Kakar, H. (1979), *Government and Society in Afghanistan: The Reign of Amir Abd al-Rahman Khan*. Austin: University of Texas Press, 164–5.
Kātib, Faiż Muhammad. (1912), *Sirāj al-Tawārīkh*. Kabul: Government Press, 1:135.
Kāẓim Ahang, M. (1970), *Sayr-i-Zhurnalizm dar Afghānistān*. Kabul: Historical and Literary Society, 72–3.

Kepple, A. (1977), *Gun-Running and the Indian North-West Frontier*, 2nd ed. Quetta, Pakistan: Gushae-Adab, 78.

Lai, Mohan. (1978), *The Life of the Amir Dost Muhammad Khan of Kabul*, Pakistan ed., 2 vols. Karachi: Oxford University Press, 1:168–9.

Muhammad Ghubār, M. G. 1967, *Afghānistān dar Masīr-i-Tārīkh*. Kabul: Publishing Institute, 406.

Munshi, Sultan Mahomed Mir. (ed. and trans.) (1901), *The Life of Amir Abdur Rahman: Amir of Afghanistan*, 2 vols. London: John Murray, 2: 251.

ᶜUmar Jan, Muhammad. (1940), *Hidāyat al-ᶜUrfān: Dar Baiyān-i-Azkār-i-Tarīqa-i ᶜĀliya-i-Naqshbandiyya*. Kabul: Nuᶜmāni Publishers, 59.

Wheeler, J. Talboys. (1869), *Memorandum on Afghanistan Affair from A.D. 1700*. Calcutta: Office of Super-intendent of Government Printing, 112.

15

The Pushback against the Hazara Rise in Afghanistan

Ali Yarwar Adili

This reflection examines the power and influence of the Hazaras of Afghanistan as one of the country's major ethno-religious groups during the Republic (2001 to 2021) and their current status under the Taliban regime. It argues that the Hazaras' overwhelming embrace of the post-2001 political order was seen by other ethnic polities as a resurgence that posed a political threat to the country's ethnic balance, resulting in a strong pushback against the community, including persistent targeted attacks. Additionally, the country's constitutional design encouraged a politics of patronage that left the Hazaras without institutional means to effectively resist marginalization and maintain and build on the relatively improved standing they achieved in the years following the Bonn Conference. Presently, the Hazaras are facing a further reversal of their political and civil rights under the current Taliban regime. The forthcoming reflection is based on the author's research about the Hazaras over the past several years. It begins with an analysis of the Hazaras' response to the post-2001 political landscape, including the backlashes against their perceived rise and the drivers behind them. It then considers the institutional constraints that stymied their ability to hold onto the progress made. Finally, it looks at their current status under the Taliban.

The Hazaras under the Republic

The US-led intervention in Afghanistan following the 9/11 attacks resulted in the establishment of a new political order in the country. The Hazaras, as one of the four largest ethnic groups – in addition to Pashtuns, Tajiks and Uzbeks – eagerly engaged with the political process of reconstruction, which in turn opened up new opportunities for the community to enhance their social, political and economic status. Their response was particularly noticeable in the education sector and in electoral politics. The Hazaras had faced systematic discrimination in educational institutions until late 1978 (Ibrahimi 2017: 101).[1] Motivated by this historical deprivation, they actively enrolled in schools and universities en masse after 2001.[2] Moreover, members of the community who had been in exile returned to the country with degrees and skills that they used to contribute to the emerging private university industry amongst others.³ These educated returnees also secured jobs with international organizations.⁴

Politically, in those early years, Hazara eagerness was sharpened by the participation of one of the community's leaders, Muhammad Mohaqeq, who ran for office in the country's first presidential election in 2004. His candidacy mobilized co-ethnics to vote. In that and consequent presidential, parliamentary and provincial council elections, Hazara citizens turned out to vote with great enthusiasm and motivation. Even in the 2019 presidential election in which the overall turnout was extremely low, the turnout in Hazara majority provinces was relatively high (Adili 2018).

Western journalists and experts began to refer to this socio-political phenomenon as the 'Hazara resurgence', or the 'rise of the Hazaras', with some also observing that this resurgence was causing its own problems.⁵ A number of political figures perceived this improved standing and its sensationalized media coverage as a threat to what they considered an 'ethnic balance' and thus reacted to it with virulent statements. For instance, former Taliban ambassador to Pakistan, Mullah Abdul Salam Zaeef, accused the Hazaras of overstepping and disturbing the balance with the support of foreigners, suggesting that this would be rectified once the foreigners left Afghanistan.⁶ Similarly, in an Eid message in August 2013, the then-fugitive leader of Hizb-e Islami, Gulbuddin Hekmatyar, criticized the Presidential Palace for upgrading the former Hazara-majority district of Daikundi in Urozgan province to a new province and appointing 'Hazaras and Shias' to various military and civilian positions. He also lashed out at the Hazara pushback against the movement of Kuchis (Pashtun nomads) into Hazara-majority areas of Maidan Wardak province and issued a warning of future reprisals against the community.⁷ While Zaeef's reaction stemmed from his concerns about ethnic balance, Hekmatyar worried about Hazara pushback against historical persecution and the movement of nomads across the central highlands. Additionally, according to analyst Michael Semple, the Hazaras' enthusiastic response to educational opportunities had given rise to concerns in certain circles, including the Taliban, that they were using education as a tool for their own progress. This in turn prompted the Taliban's 2011 decision to scale back their attacks on schools (Giustozzi and Franco 2011: 11–12; Semple 2011: 8), a campaign that had largely affected the Pashtun-majority areas under Taliban control. Andrea Chiovenda and Melissa Kerr Chiovenda conclude that the increase in Hazara engagement in public life produced significant concern among non-Hazara Afghans, who perceived this activity as 'subversive and perturbing' (Chiovenda and Chiovenda 2018: 169). On the basis of fieldwork conducted in southeastern Pashtun communities over several years, these authors contend that the knowledge of a sustained history of Hazara persecution from the late nineteenth century onwards aroused fears in the 'Pashtuns' collective imagery' in anticipation of 'equally murderous violence' as vengeance in the future (Chiovenda and Chiovenda 2018: 169).⁸

The Hazaras' full endorsement of the political order appeared to be one of the reasons why the Taliban began to target members of this community. For example, on 25 June 2010, eleven Hazara men were beheaded in Urozgan Khas district of Uruzgan province. This seemed to mark the beginning of the Taliban's attacks on Hazaras on highways and roads. A police official, Muhammad Gulab Wardak, as reported by *Reuters*, said that the Taliban had carried out the killing because they were Hazaras and Shias (Reuters 2010). The emergence of the Islamic State – Khorasan Province (ISKP) in Afghanistan in late 2014 as an affiliate of the Islamic State in Iraq and Syria (ISIS) dealt another severe blow to Hazara progress and their struggle to maintain or improve their political representation. ISKP holds a Salafist ideology and its fighters were primarily recruited from Salafist communities whose members had been fighting in the ranks of the Taliban (Osman 2016). However, they also included university students and remnants of other Islamic militant groups from the region (Osman 2020). Since 2015, following the ISKP emergence, the majority of attacks against Hazaras and Shias have been attributed to this group. For example, out of the twelve deadliest attacks against the community in Kabul between July 2016 and May 2021, ten were claimed by the ISKP (Adili 2022).

Institutional Constraints on Hazara Influence

In 2004, Afghanistan adopted a new constitution that established a highly centralized presidential system, granting the president more powers than the former king, including the authority to appoint government officials down to district levels (Shahrani 2018). Then-president Hamid Karzai also chose to implement a single non-transferable voting (SNTV) system for elections. This led to what analyst Thomas Ruttig (2018) described as a 'paradoxical political party system', in which the parties were legally inside the political system (because they could field party candidates for elections), but, in practice, outside it (because candidates were not required to declare party affiliation on the ballot and thus most ran as 'independent'). As a result, the country had a weak parliament with no strong political parties and no effective parliamentary form of loyal opposition (Coburn and Larson 2014: 36–8; Adili and Linke 2016). An inevitable corollary of this institutional design was person-centred politics at the expense of political party consolidation. Partly due to this person-centred politics and the absence of a parliamentary form of opposition, the Hazara leaders formed alliances with political leaders and parties from other ethnic groups outside the parliament. However, such informal coalitions only oiled the wheels of prevalent patronage politics because the Hazara leaders (like their counterparts from other ethnic groups) used the coalitions as vehicles to further their personal interests. In fact, Hazara politicians would often join these coalitions when they were unable to secure government positions or sought to increase their influence, hoping to be co-opted by the government (Adili and Linke 2016). By 2009, the Hazara-dominated Hizb-e Wahdat-e Islami Afghanistan (The Islamic Unity Party of Afghanistan) – which was established in 1989 and became a major political and military player in Afghanistan – had fragmented into a least four competing factions (Ibrahimi 2009: 1).

The only time Hazara leaders and factions had the chance to exert influence as powerbrokers within the formal system was during election seasons. While many of these leaders effectively articulated and conveyed the demands of their communities during electoral campaigns, after the elections, the ruling president frequently reneged on these agreements once in office. In order to maintain positive relations with the president and secure their inclusion in future election cycles, Hazara leaders within the ruling teams abandoned their previous demands despite popular support for them. Those who did not wish to go along with the status quo had no institutional means of opposition to challenge the ruling president.[9] They were, as a result, unable to hold the president accountable for his promises even if they had substantial community support behind them. Consequently, these demands became mere tools used by Hazara leaders to garner votes for their respective teams; they had no lasting impact on the subsequent well-being of the communities from which they came.

Despite their cooperation with the powers-that-were, the Hazaras encountered 'systematic and institutional discrimination' (Bose, Bizhan and Ibrahimi 2019). A Hazara was never appointed a chief security official – such as the minister of defence or interior or the head of the National Directorate of Security (NDS) (Adili 2022). US and NATO commanders reportedly contributed to this discriminatory practice as they often favoured candidates who had prior links to western intelligence services, including the CIA. These key ministries remained political battlegrounds dominated by Pashtuns and Tajiks. And, at the highest levels of power, the considerations of international actors, particularly the United States, also played a decisive role. The outcomes of presidential elections, in particular, were shaped by American influence, which included tacit approval of a Pashtun candidate for president.[10]

In addition to the targeted attacks that began in 2010 and intensified from 2015 onwards, and the persistent institutional discrimination, Hazaras' relatively proportional representation in the government declined significantly over the years. A January 2020 survey conducted by activists affiliated with then-Second Vice-President Sarwar Danesh showed that there was no Hazara minister in the cabinet at that time,[11] while there had been at least four Hazara and Shia ministers during the early years of the post-2001 political order (Sharan 2011: 1118).

A pervasive sense of marginalization took hold within the community, which gave rise to two noteworthy and unprecedented protest movements initiated by the Hazaras: the Junbish-e Tabasum, which was mobilized in protest to the beheading of seven Hazara travellers, including a nine-year-old girl named Tabasum who became the movement's main symbol, in Zabul province in late 2015 and Junbish-e Roshnayi (Enlightenment Movement), which was formed to protest the government's decision to reroute an important power line from Turkmenistan, bypassing the Hazara regions (Adili and Linke 2016). Hazara leaders in the government aligned themselves with these protest movements but only as a means to revive or safeguard their political influence. In keeping with the prevalent model of patronage politics, they were bought off by the Presidential Palace and ultimately stood in defence of the government's position.

All in all, the constitutional design that concentrated power in the hands of the president and fostered a politics of patronage altered the incentives of Hazara political leaders to shape government decisions and to challenge its discriminatory policies and practices. At the same time, the Presidential Palace engaged in a practice of co-option through patronage politics that also rendered Hazara political forces prone to fragmentation. As a result, even if they coalesced around a particular demand, they struggled to maintain unity as they put their personal gains from political patronage above their community's demands for protection, inclusion and development projects.

The Hazaras under Taliban Rule (Once Again)

During the Taliban insurgency under the Republic, the Hazaras managed to largely resist the Taliban infiltration into and control over their regions. Taliban insurgents launched massive attacks on the district of Khas Urozgan in Urozgan province and the Malestan and Jaghori districts of Ghazni in late 2018 after the local Hazara communities refused to comply with the Taliban's orders that they pay *ushr* (a 10 per cent Islamic tax on harvest). In response, the Hazara community displayed swift and determined reactions. They took to the streets in spontaneous demonstrations, launched social media campaigns and exerted pressure on the government to take decisive action against the Taliban's push into their regions. Moreover, locals also mobilized public uprising forces to defend their areas. Volunteers from other Hazara areas even travelled to Jaghori and Malestan to provide additional support to the local resistance and boost morale (Adili and Van Bijlert 2018a).

But the Hazaras' social progress suffered a monumental setback with the Taliban's sweeping return to power. Not only did the Taliban completely exclude the Hazaras (in fact, they offered minimal representation to all non-Pashtun ethnic groups) from their so-called interim cabinet, but they also made a series of policy decisions that instilled fear among the Hazaras. For example, Taliban officials, shortly after retaking power, indicated that they might revert to Zahir Shah's 1964 constitution (Adili 2023). Such a move would have effectively reversed the 2004 constitution's unprecedented formal recognition of the Shia Islamic sect and its preferred jurisprudential framework, the Jafari school.

In spring 2022, Taliban Chief Justice Abdul Hakim Haqqani published a book entitled *The Islamic Emirate and Its System*, which many consider the regime's manifesto. In this book, he declared that justice and judgements should be exclusively based on the Hanafi Sunni school of jurisprudence and rejected other religious denominations, as they would supposedly undermine their 'Islamic system'. He even asserted that the Afghan people did not wish to adhere to other religious schools of thought, an assertion that blatantly disregarded the country's Hazara and other Shia populations as well as other religious groups. This disdainful statement was not surprising, as the Taliban had held the same positions on jurisprudence during the intra-Afghan talks that preceded their return to power in August 2021. Although some of their members had suggested that Shia jurisprudence would be recognized at the time of constitution drafting, the chief justice's writing suggested otherwise (Adili 2021).

In January 2022, the Taliban dismissed all Hazara judges, arguing that the Hazaras were ineligible to serve in the judiciary (Adili 2023). The Taliban's emphasis on Hanafi jurisprudence is rooted in their conception of political authority as based on a literalist interpretation of Islamic Sharia under Hanafi jurisprudence. Moreover, as Niamatullah Ibrahimi (2023) explains, the Taliban combine religious fundamentalism with 'a particular form of exclusionary Pashtun ethnonationalism'. This combination makes the Taliban's exclusion of the Hazaras particularly noticeable, as their religious and ethnic differences reinforce each other as bases for discrimination. The Taliban's current exclusionary policy towards other religious denominations also demonstrates that they have reneged on their promises to minorities during the pre-takeover peace talks. Moreover, despite the Taliban's claims of establishing security nationwide, targeted attacks against the Hazara community persist. These attacks resumed just over a month after the takeover (Adili 2022).

In response to the new regime, Hazara leaders and representatives have adopted a strategy focused on survival. This approach has been characterized by denunciation of armed resistance and, instead, attempts at pragmatic engagement and collaboration with the Taliban aimed at minimizing harm to the community. In fact, the community's resistance against the Taliban ceased when the Republic's fall became inevitable. While the Taliban have been conveying conciliatory messages to the Hazara community publicly, the reality on the ground has produced a near-complete reversal of their political and civil rights. It is unlikely that the community's political leaders and forces can challenge the Taliban.

Conclusion

The Hazaras' enthusiastic response to a new political order following the ouster of the Taliban regime in late 2001 enabled them to enhance their social and political status. However, their progress was soon perceived by some as a resurgence that posed a threat to non-Hazara communities, especially Pashtuns. This anxiety stemmed from concerns about the country's ethnic power balance, the Hazaras' emerging pushback against the historical trends and injustices, and their imagined potential for violent reprisal. Hazara progress and political participation faced setbacks soon enough. A new wave of targeted attacks ensued, restricting their movement and limiting their participation in public life. Consequently, the Hazaras faced not only rising security threats but also increasing political exclusion, as they had no institutional mechanisms to influence policy decisions.

The Hazaras' concurrent success and struggle for progress and political participation under the Republic cannot be fully analysed without understanding the nature of political power and authority in Afghanistan. Ethnic affiliation and international support served as prevailing sources of power. For example, while Afghanistan held four presidential elections, the outcome of each election was largely determined by the considerations of international actors, particularly the United States, including their tacit approval of a Pashtun candidate for president. Since the ruling president was vested constitutionally with more power than a king, presidents had the latitude to engage in patronage politics in order to co-opt ethnic and factional leaders by leveraging their control over state resources. Their unchecked power also afforded opportunities to manipulate the electoral process.

Since the return of the Taliban, Hazara representation and rights have seen a near-complete reversal. This is not an unexpected outcome given the Taliban's conception of political authority, which is based on a combination of their literalist interpretation of Islamic Sharia under the Hanafi jurisprudence and their ethnonationalism. Absent any cross-cutting ethnic or religious cleavages between the Taliban and the Hazaras, the latter will continue to bear the brunt of political exclusions under the current regime, which also employs violence and coercion to suppress any dissent.

Notes

1. Zalmay Khalilzad also reports: 'The Hazaras were always given the hard, lowly jobs. In the national army, Hazara conscripts would be assigned as servants in the homes of state officials. There were Hazaras in my school, and I saw that there were limits to how high they could rise' (Khalilzad 2016: 24).
2. For example, Wadir Safi, a professor of political science at Kabul University, is cited in an *LA Times* article in 2010 as saying that the presence of the Hazaras at the university was expanding every year. 'They are the ones in power now. They are a minority, but they are very united' (Daragahi 2010).
3. These Hazara-run private universities include Kateb University, Avicenna University, Gowharshad University and Gharjistan University in Kabul.
4. This is noted by two Afghanistan experts quoted in an *LA Times* article in 2010: Candace Rondeaux, who worked for the International Crisis Group in Afghanistan at the time, said, 'Many Hazaras have become middle class. For the first time they have decent jobs, housing, a little money in their pockets and the ability to insulate themselves from political pressures.' In the same article, Martine van Bijlert, an analyst at the Afghanistan Analysts Network, is cited as follows: 'When you get job interviews, the best candidates will often be Hazaras' (Daragahi 2010).
5. For example, *The Economist* noted the post-Taliban Republic had 'made things a bit better for Afghanistan's underclass'. However, 'Hazara successes [were] breeding their own problems', see *The Economist* (2007).
6. Zaeef called it 'the conspiracy of the occupation' and claimed that '[t]he foreigners are supporting the minority against the majority'. He said that a 'balance' would return after the Americans leave. See Daragahi (2010).
7. Hekmatyar said in his message, 'The day will come when the oppressed people of Afghanistan will rise to claim their usurped rights and then they [Hazaras] will not find refuge in any part of the country. Some of them will flee to Iran and Iran will treat them brutally and without mercy,' see BBC Farsi (2013).
8. For example, Andrea Chiovenda and Melissa Chiovenda related that, in 2010, Andrea Chiovenda travelled from Jalalabad to Bamyan with a group of Pashtun friends who were NGO employees. Over lunch one day, Chiovenda appreciated the security in Bamyan. In the ensuing conversation, Asad, the team leader, a Pashtun from Jalalabad, said: 'If they [the Hazaras] become too powerful they will come after us … they say we have oppressed them, they always talk about all the times they have been killed by us … it's not going to be good for Pashtuns.' Chiovenda and Chiovenda (2018: 178).
9. One notable example is Muhammad Mohaqeq, the leader of Hizb-e Wahdat-e Mardom Afghanistan. He supported Hamid Karzai in the 2009 presidential election. The following year, he withdrew his support in protest against the government's inaction for stopping Kuchis from moving into the Hazara areas in Maidan Wardak and Ghazni. He later formed the National Front of Afghanistan with Uzbek leader Abdul Rashid Dostum and a Jamiat leader and former vice-president Ahmad Zia Massoud.
10. In the paper, Van Bijlert argues that 'the perception widely held among Afghans that the outcome of the elections is shaped by four main factors: (1) decisions by international actors, in particular the United States; (2) behind-the-scenes negotiations and deals among local leaders; (3) manipulation of the electoral process;

and – only in the fourth place, if at all; (4) the vote of the people', see Van Bijlert (2009: 1).
11 This survey was conducted by Hazara activists in 2020 and the results were shown to the author but were not made public.

References

Adili, A. Y. (2018), 'Afghanistan's 2019 Election (18): How the People of Bamyan, Daikundi and Lal wa Sarjangal Voted'. Afghanistan Analysts Network, 16 October 2018. Available at: https://www.afghanistan-analysts.org/en/reports/political-landscape/afghanistans-2019-election-18-how-the-hazaras-of-bamyan-daikundi-and-lal-wa-sarjangal-voted/.

Adili, A. Y. (2021), 'Intra-Afghan Talks (1): Rules of Procedure Agreed, but Still No Agenda as Talks Resume'. Afghanistan Analysts Network, 3 January 2021. Available at: https://www.afghanistan-analysts.org/en/reports/war-and-peace/intra-afghan-talks-1-rules-of-procedure-agreed-but-still-no-agenda-as-talks-resume/.

Adili, A. Y. (2022), 'A Community under Attack: How Successive Governments Failed West Kabul and the Hazaras Who Live There'. Afghanistan Analysts Network, 17 January 2022. Available at: https://www.afghanistan-analysts.org/en/reports/war-and-peace/a-community-under-attack-how-successive-governments-failed-west-kabul-and-the-hazaras-who-live-there/.

Adili, A. Y. (2023), 'The Politics of Survival in the Face of Exclusion: Hazara and Shia Actors under the Taleban'. Afghanistan Analysts Network, February. Available at: https://www.afghanistan-analysts.org/en/reports/political-landscape/the-politics-of-survival-in-the-face-of-exclusion-hazara-and-shia-actors-under-the-taleban/.

Adili, A. Y. and Linke, L. (2016), 'The Politics of Opposition: A Challenge to the National Unity Government?' Afghanistan Analysts Network, 27 October 2016. Available at: https://www.afghanistan-analysts.org/en/reports/political-landscape/the-politics-of-opposition-a-challenge-to-the-national-unity-government/.

Adili, Ali Y. and Van Bijlert, M. (2018a), 'Taleban Attacks on Khas Uruzgan, Jaghori and Malestan (I): A New and Violent Push into Hazara Areas'. Afghanistan Analysts Network, 28 November 2018. Available at: https://www.afghanistan-analysts.org/en/reports/war-and-peace/taleban-attacks-on-khas-uruzgan-jaghori-and-malestan-i-a-new-and-violent-push-into-hazara-areas/.

Adili, Ali Y. and Van Bijlert, M. (2018b), 'Taleban Attacks on Khas Uruzgan, Jaghori and Malestan (II): A New and Violent Push into Hazara Areas'. Afghanistan Analysts Network, 29 November 2018. Available at: https://www.afghanistan-analysts.org/en/reports/war-and-peace/taleban-attacks-on-khas-uruzgan-jaghori-and-malestan-ii-a-new-and-violent-push-into-hazara-areas/.

BBC Farsi (2013), 'Hekmatyar: Khariji-ha ba hemayat az aqaliyat-ha Afghanistan ra tajzia mekonand' (Foreigners Partition Afghanistan by Supporting Minorities), 7 August 2013. Available at: https://www.bbc.com/persian/afghanistan/2013/08/130807_zs_gulbuddin_hekmatyar_eid_message.

Bose, S., Bizhan, N. and Ibrahimi, N. (2019), 'Youth Protest Movements in Afghanistan: Seeking Voice and Agency'. U.S. Institute of Peace (USIP), Report No. 145, February 2019. Available at: https://www.usip.org/sites/default/files/2019-02/pw145-youth-protest-movements-in-afghanistan-seeking-voice-and-agency.pdf.

Chiovenda, A. and Chiovenda, M. (2018), 'The Specter of the "Arrivant": Hauntology of an Interethnic Conflict in Afghanistan'. *Asian Anthropology*, 17(3): 165–84. Available at: https://www.tandfonline.com/doi/epdf/10.1080/1683478X.2018.1480917?needAccess=true.

Coburn, N. and Larson, A. (2014), *Derailing Democracy in Afghanistan: Elections in an Unstable Political Landscape*. New York: Columbia University Press.

Daragahi, B. (2010), 'A Formerly Persecuted Minority Gains Clout in Afghanistan'. *Los Angeles Times*, 16 December 2010. Available at: https://www.latimes.com/archives/la-xpm-2010-dec-16-la-fg-afghanistan-sects-20101216-story.html.

Economist, The (2007), 'Afghanistan's Hazaras, Coming up from the Bottom'. 15 February 2007. Available at: https://www.economist.com/asia/2007/02/15/coming-up-from-the-bottom.

Giustozzi, A. and Franco, C. (2011), 'The Battle for the Schools: The Taleban and State Education'. Afghanistan Analysts Network, December 2011. Available at: https://www.afghanistan-analysts.org/wp-content/uploads/downloads/2012/10/2011TalebanEducation.pdf.

Ibrahimi, N. (2009), 'The Dissipation of Political Capital among Afghanistan's Hazaras: 2001–2009.' Crisis States Research Centre, Working Paper Series 2 (51), June 2009. Available at: https://www.lse.ac.uk/international-development/Assets/Documents/PDFs/csrc-working-papers-phase-two/wp51.2-dissipation-of-political-capital.pdf.

Ibrahimi, N. (2017), *The Hazaras and the Afghan State: Rebellion, Exclusion and the Struggle for Recognition*. London: Hurst & Co.

Ibrahimi, N. (2023). 'A Violent Nexus: Ethnonationalism, Religious Fundamentalism, and the Taliban'. *The Review of Faith & International Affairs*, 21(3): 22–37. Available at: https://www.tandfonline.com/doi/abs/10.1080/15570274.2023.2235809.

Khalilzad, Z. (2016), *The Envoy: From Kabul to the White House, My Journey through a Turbulent World*. New York: St. Martin's Press.

Osman, B. (2016), 'Descent into Chaos: Why Did Nangarhar turn into an IS Hub?' Afghanistan Analysts Network, 27 September 2016. Available at: https://www.afghanistan-analysts.org/en/reports/war-and-peace/descent-into-chaos-why-did-nangarhar-turn-into-an-is-hub/.

Osman, B. (2020), 'Bourgeois Jihad: Why Young Middle Class Afghans Join the Islamic State'. USIP Peaceworks No. 162. Available at: https://www.usip.org/publications/2020/06/bourgeois-jihad-why-young-middle-class-afghans-join-islamic-state.

Reuters (2010), 'Police Find 11 Beheaded Bodies in Afghan South', 25 June 2010. Available at: https://www.reuters.com/article/us-afghanistan-beheading-idUSTRE65O2ML20100625.

Ruttig, T. (2018), 'Outside, Inside: Afghanistan's Paradoxical Political Party System (2001–16)'. Afghanistan Analysts Network and Konrad Adenauer Stiftung, 6 May 2018. Available at: https://www.afghanistan-analysts.org/en/special-reports/outside-inside-afghanistans-paradoxical-political-party-system-2001-16/.

Semple, M. (2011), 'The Rise of the Hazaras and the Challenge of Pluralism in Afghanistan 1978–2011', Carr Center for Human Rights Policy, Harvard University. Available at: https://cmes.fas.harvard.edu/sites/hwpi.harvard.edu/files/cmes/files/semplepolicysummary.pdf?m=1466457578.

Shahrani, M. N. (2018), 'The Afghan President Has More Powers than a King'. *Al-Jazeera*, 3 January 2018. Available at: https://www.aljazeera.com/opinions/2018/1/3/the-afghan-president-has-more-powers-than-a-king.

Sharan, T. (2011), 'The Dynamics of Elite Networks and Patron–Client Relations in Afghanistan'. *Europe-Asia Studies*, 63(6): 1109–27.

Van Bijlert, M. (2009), 'How to Win an Afghan Election: Perceptions and Practices'. Afghanistan Analysts Network, August 2009. Available at: https://www.afghanistan-analysts.org/wp-content/uploads/downloads/2012/10/2009-AAN-MvB-Afghan-Election.pdf.

16

Minority Games: Intergroup Power Imbalances in a Nation of Competing Identities

Annika Schmeding

The changing of identity is part of the political game.

(2014, Kuchi parliamentarian)

You can't understand any of this if you don't understand questions of land – it's all about land.

(2021, Jogi/peripatetic day labourer)

These two seemingly unrelated sentences, uttered seven years apart by two Afghan nomads – one a parliamentarian, the other a day labourer – allude to several of the core questions tackled in this chapter: How have minority identities been crafted and anchored in the post-2001 state? In which cases is the nomad label of 'Kuchi' revealing of an actual socio-economic constituency and where does it conceal underlying fractures in Afghan society? And how do imaginaries of land, territoriality, belonging and citizenship weave through these conceptualizations and produce real-life consequences?

Based on an ethnographic and historically grounded approach, this chapter examines questions of power and authority by analysing how access to and ownership of land (as well as its attendant connection to citizenship) are crucially linked with imaginaries of territoriality and belonging.[1] The chapter contrasts two diametrically opposed positions within Afghanistan's society that have often been subsumed under one English-language label: nomad. One is represented by the parliamentarian quoted above – a member of a group of leaders who claimed pastoral nomadic ancestry and a shared common Pashtun ethnic identity with those who ruled the Afghan state. The other is represented by the peripatetic nomad who remained marginalized in national discourse, stateless for most of the past twenty years, and denied nomad status and its accompanying rights.

A comparison of the relative rights and socio-economic conditions of these two groups reveals the distinct positionalities from which the different 'nomadic' groups claimed, contested or experienced power and authority. Their respective positions and orientations rested, in large part, on pre-existing economic, societal and political imaginaries of citizenship and belonging. To take these distinctions seriously is to acknowledge land as a multivalent currency of power and belonging that indexes the ability to access a particular status, wealth or political capital.

This chapter explores how, during two decades of post-2001 Afghan statehood, the definition of nomad inscribed an anomaly into law that pretended to support an overarching minority category while actually constructing status for one group at the expense of other nomadic minorities. The term 'Kuchi' (literally meaning 'someone who moves') does indeed denote a nomad, but it encodes two exclusions. First, in Afghanistan it is commonly understood to refer only to pastoral nomads, excluding peripatetics – non-food-producing migratory groups that use strategic movement as a resource. Secondly, even in describing pastoral nomads, the term has been transformed and excludes many pastoralists; the term had been used for particular Pashtun nomadic groups in the past (Hanifi 2008b: 26), but it was not a generic term for all pastoralists in Afghanistan. Historically, pastoralists were known by their profession – *'maldar'* (herder). After 2001, the term 'Kuchi' was reframed through its institutionalization in laws and, in effect, certain Pashtun parliamentarians expanded the category to include their own kin and communities as part of the new constitutional order. In so doing, a particular subset of pastoralists found themselves particularly well-situated to interface with international aid organizations and the government to secure political as well as material resources (Tapper 2008).

The chapter addresses, first, the historic and ethnographic literature on nomadism in Afghanistan, based on research conducted pre-1978, laying a foundational understanding for how the two nomadic categories have been reflected – and challenged – in anthropological writing. The subsequent section tackles the post-2001 literature on the politicization of the category of 'Kuchis' who became identity entrepreneurs in the Afghan government (2001–21) with the ability to claim rights and power at the exclusion of other nomadic groups. Simultaneously, the category of peripatetic nomads surfaced as part of the non-governmental organization (NGO) grey literature on the urban poor in internally displaced person (IDP) camps and temporary settlements, positioning their statelessness as a problem among many in a sea of displacement. The chapter concludes with a discussion of the underlying currency of power – land – and the means by which it interacts with conflict, ethnicity and exclusion. The chapter locates power and authority not solely with particular actors, but rather within discursive narratives about the 'Other' that enable and limit those actors and their groups and map onto the present-day circumstances of their communities.

The Pastoral/Peripatetic Split

The available academic literature on nomadism in Afghanistan can be mapped in several stages. In the nineteenth century, when colonial powers were competing for influence on Afghanistan's borders, scholars, diplomatic emissaries and political agents mentioned nomadic populations in their accounts (Burnes 1973/1834; Caroe 1976;

Elphinstone 1815: 467-1). Pastoral nomads crossed borders and frontiers, connected markets and population centres through their migration, and embodied a population that colonial administrators saw as in need of management. The production of knowledge for the British colonial government about these populations was thus linked to information gathering on the governmentality of the imperial frontier (Hanifi 2019: 46). This early literature focused mainly on pastoral nomads – herders, whom the colonial authorities interacted with and sought to influence or exert control over.

The decades between the 1950s and 1970s represented a fruitful time for research on Afghanistan in general and nomads in particular. The country's opening up to researchers brought a short flowering of ethnographically based accounts, including the 'Carlsberg Nomad Research Project', resulting in a wide variety of published papers and subsequent monographs with visual imageries and extensive research material (Pedersen 1994; Frederiksen 1996; Ferdinand 2006; see also: Dupree 1973: 397–413; Tapper 1973, 1991; Glatzer 1977, 1981, 1983, 1992; Kakar 1979; Barfield 1981). These ethnographic explorations focused on pastoralist caravans and their network of bazaars, genealogies and kinship networks, economic income streams as well as technological change through the introduction of automobiles, buses and trucks.

In the process of studying pastoralists, researchers also started to pay attention to another nomadic group whose livelihoods came not from herding but through craftsmanship, door-to-door sales of cloth and bracelets, performance and begging. Anthropologists called them peripatetic nomads to distinguish them from the pastoralists. These nomads used movement strategically to access different economic resources (Rao 1987b; Rao/Casimir 2003; Rao/Berland 2004). In the specific case of Afghanistan, no studies were conducted on the peripatetics until the 1970s when anthropologists Asta Olesen and Aparna Rao made forays into the field. Both published extensively prior to the Saur Revolution of 1978 (Rao, 1979, 1981, 1982a, 1982b, 1983, 1985, 1986a, 1986b, 1986c, 1987b, 1988, 2003, 2004; Olesen 1982, 1985, 1994).

Peripatetic groups are defined as 'endogamous nomads who are largely non-primary producers or extractors, and whose principal resources are constituted by other human populations' (Rao 1987a: 1). While the degree of spatial mobility can vary – some groups move between provinces in the same general geography, while others might move between urban centres such as Kabul and Jalalabad seasonally – their strategy lies in the combination of mobility and non-subsistence commercialism, focused on 'labor, customers and skills/goods' (Rao 1987a: 3). The people belonging to these groups are neither vagrants nor Roma, Sinti or Travellers, but semi-nomads.[2] The Afghan peripatetics' reasoned and planned mobility has been part of their adaptive strategy to access different markets and customers (Rao 1987a: 4). Furthermore, to lump Afghan peripatetic communities together with Roma, Sinti or Travellers, pejoratively called 'gypsies',[3] would be to mistake a 'clear case of analogy ... for homology' (Rao 2004: 272). Many of these communities in Europe and North America are 'historically and culturally closely related' (Rao 1986a: 280), which is not the case for peripatetic groups in Afghanistan, who do not share the same genealogy with Roma and Sinti. Afghan peripatetics claim different ancestries and ethnicities. Their position in society is, however, an example par excellence of global peripatetism: they have a low, often despised status, residing in a liminality, known to Afghan society but not fully accepted within it.

This position is exemplified through the cognitive category of 'Jat' that is applied to peripatetic groups who reject the term given its pejorative connotations (Rao 2004: 274; Hanifi 2008a). The vague and negative image captured by this derogatory label covers a spectrum of supposed characteristics and activities, from being bad Muslims or non-believers, to being dirty, promiscuous or engaged in prostitution. Those labelled as such are also seen as aggressive and criminal, even participating in child abduction and necrophilia (Rao 2004: 274–82). Additionally, they are associated with a foreign background of Indian or Central Asian origin. Generally, the term 'Jat' is applied as an expletive either directed at peripatetics themselves or used as an insult for non-peripatetic Afghan women whose appearance or behaviour is considered outside the bounds of cultural norms.[4]

This combination of alleged deviant behaviours intersects with the positionality of women within groups identified as 'Jat': most of these peripatetic groups practice a gender division of labour in which women are either the main breadwinners outside of their homes or equally involved in earning an income alongside males. In Afghanistan's post-2001 economy many women were engaged in the workforce, including in positions often associated with men such as pilots, police officers, taxi drivers and office workers in urban areas; however, the markets (*bazaars*) where peripatetic women went to beg or sell bracelets were still, with few exceptions, male-only workspaces. Peripatetic women were considered 'anomalies' and were perceived as demarcating the status of these groups – non-peripatetic interviewees repeatedly pointed out that this characteristic made the peripatetic groups different from anyone else and that no respectable family would allow its women to work in these areas.[5] The presence of women working in the public sphere of the markets, especially as beggars, was interpreted as a mark of 'un-Afghanness'.

While the term 'Jat' is used as a collective term – sometimes as a general description for peripatetics, at other times as an expletive – it is generally rejected by peripatetic groups. Furthermore, like the academic terms 'peripatetic' and 'pastoral', it obfuscates the complex terminological jungle of names and labels used in Afghanistan for different nomads. Aside from pejorative collective terms such as Jat, historically, most groups were referred to by names that indexed their main source of income. Pastoralists were referred to as *pohwenda/powindah/powinda* or *maldar* (livestock tender and livestock owner).[6] Peripatetics had manifold names such as *cheghelbaf, ghalbelbaf* (both 'sieve maker'), *chori-frosh*, (transl.: *choori foroosh*, bracelet sellers; *bangriwal* or *bangudi-forush* in Pashto) or *shadibaz* (monkey players) (Rao 2004: 280, 1986(a): 265–8, 1986(b): 164, 155, 157; Olesen 1994: 206). Names like 'Jogi' are harder to trace, though some groups, such as the *Shaykh Muhammadi* peddlers, were named after their claim of ancestry to 'Sheikh Muhammad, reverently referred to as Sheikh Rohani Baba, the spiritual father' (Olesen 1987: 35).

Until the onset of armed conflict in 1979, both pastoral and peripatetic nomads were primarily researched by anthropologists as part of the general academic endeavour to map populations socially and economically. After the Saur Revolution (1978) and the Soviet invasion (1979) long-term ethnographic research ceased to be an option and most anthropologists shifted their focus to the Afghan refugees in camps in Pakistan and Iran, some of which included nomadic encampments (Pedersen, in: Anderson/Hatch Dupree 1990: 154–9). While most of the research up until this period was largely descriptive, some of it mirrors and reinforces the taxonomic politics that non-nomadic Afghans were engaged in. Some research attempted to coin alternative, more neutral terminology such as the peripatetic nomad. However, this terminology remained within academic writing and did not seem to have influenced the ways in which pastoral, peripatetic and non-nomadic Afghans engaged with each other.

Crafting a Political 'Nomadic' Identity

After the US invasion in 2001, the establishment of the new, internationally backed Afghan government and the influx of international aid and development organizations, nomadic identities resurfaced in newly politicized garb. Frederik Barth, commenting on modern nation-states and their impact on the creation and constitution of groups, remarked how formal legal categories create communities as they 'often generate categorial distinctions within the field of continuous cultural variation' (Barth 1998: 19). This view sees the power and policy-apparatus of the state 'as a specifiable third player in the process of boundary construction between groups' (Barth 1998: 20); after all, states tend to create categories, systems and maps of populations to render them 'legible' and, thus, governable (Scott 1998). The Afghan state was just one player in the administration of state goods in this new, crowded neoliberal landscape (Barnett 2013).

In the site of what Didier Fassin has called the 'humanitarian government' (Fassin 2007: 508), organizations and policy makers showed a strong interest in ameliorating the livelihoods of pastoralists and establishing their rights in the constitution as well as national law. As these minority categories were inscribed through the state and surrounding foreign actors, they also offered opportunities for political identities to be crafted in and around them.[7] On the one hand, peripatetic communities emerged as the new urban poor, a part of the internally displaced population in need of attention from the international aid sector. On the other hand, a particular type of Pashtun pastoral nomad emerged, 'Kuchi' – a newly established quasi-legal neologism – offering adjoining rights and political opportunities. Thus, to be Kuchi theoretically translated into political opportunity and access to resources.

In the post-2001 Afghan state the term 'Kuchi' was used by journalists, NGO workers, government employees and former pastoralists themselves as *the* label to denote (former) pastoral nomads of a particular kind. The political identity and its attendant rights were enshrined in the 2004 constitution, in electoral law, guaranteed parliamentary seats and independent directorates. The delineation of a group as a function of their mobility (versus their ethno-linguistic profile, livelihood or economic circumstance) was novel (Tapper 2008: 98). How did 'Kuchi', a marginal term, which was sometimes even applied with a derogatory tone, take centre stage in nomad-labelling? Part of the answer might lie in the proximity of the Ahmadzai nomads to Kabul as they are 'not only close, physically and politically, to government, but also accessible to journalists and other investigators' (Tapper 2008: 99).

Particular pastoralists such as the Ahmadzai nomads of the Zala Khan Khel have long called themselves *kuchey* (Pedersen 1994: 49ff.). Anthropologist Gorm Pedersen, who researched the group in the 1970s/1980s, observed that the Zala Khan Khel still called themselves *kuchey* even after having given up their migratory lifestyle. They connected this name to a glorious past or considered themselves as 'nomads on the waiting list – nomads who had been temporarily forced out of their occupation, and who hoped for better times *as nomads*' (Pedersen 1994: 97). 'Kuchi' might therefore be the eponym that seized its chance to rise again, this time from a particular group's name to a national category in a moment when the international community was intent on inscribing the rights of marginalized identities into newly crafted laws.

The term, however, was nowhere defined, even though it was used in official documents and legislation. Its meaning was assumed (and assumed to be understood) despite the confusing – even contradictory – multiplicities of usage: 'Kuchi' denoted far more than the odd pastoral nomad in the field; it included recently or even long-settled former pastoral nomads and their descendants, some of whom had never lived a single day as a herder. Furthermore, the term 'Kuchi' was also ethnically implicated given its ties to particular Pashtun nomads.

In the past, pastoral nomads were defined and distinguished by outward physical markers that accompanied their annual treks: escorted by herding dogs, living in tents, such as the black goat hair tent (in Pashto: *khizdei* or *kigdei*; in Dari: *palas* or *ghizdi*), predominantly used by Pashtuns and Baluch, or yurt-type tents, largely used by Uzbek, Turkman, Hazara, Tajik or Aimaq nomads (Dupree 1980/1973: 170; Szabo/Barfield 1991: 29–99; Pedersen 1994: 82). The black goat hair tent became a romantic meme in Afghanistan, featured on postcards and book covers and feeding the Orientalist touristic imagination, even as many nomadic pastoralists had swapped their housing for white (UNHCR) tents, apartments or even houses and villas.[8] Indeed, one semi-nomadic interviewee in Sholgera district in Balkh province, northern Afghanistan, lamented to me the fact that his family hadn't received a UNHCR tent: 'There was a distribution of tents from the government or from an NGO, but we didn't get one, so we still use the old black goat hair tent for summer migration.'[9]

But more than just the tents had changed. Several dynamics that favoured sedentarization had arisen since the 1970s: government policies, droughts, poverty and war forced many to settle down while others chose to do so, having accumulated wealth, access to land or a more diverse income base (Weijer 2005(a): 12, 2007: 12, 31; Wily 2013: 79–80). The array of groups to which the term 'Kuchi' was applied ranged from seasonally migrating pastoral nomads to businessmen who had settled down and were engaged in the transport business, including offering services to foreign armies like ISAF.[10] Others capitalized on the post-2001 reality by transitioning into full-time retail politics, claiming nomadic ancestry through relatives who still lived a nomadic lifestyle. Still others were forced into camps for IDPs after war-time bombardments decimated their herds.

The shifting identities produced conflicting identifications. One woman, whose family used to migrate as pastoralists and now lived in an IDP camp in Abdarra, Kabul, told me: 'In the past they used to call us Kuchi because we were moving. Now we are not moving anymore and they call us camp people. I think this is what we are now.'[11] And, yet, others still identified her as 'Kuchi'. An Afghan government employee, who worked for the National Rural Access Program (NRAP),[12] explained this confusion: 'In our society, when you go to jail and come out after 20 years, the people will still hate you and say that you are a bad person, even if you have had your 20 years in jail. You will still be the person who commits crimes. With the Kuchi it is similar. Even when they settle, they are still called Kuchi.'[13] Acknowledging the fact that being Kuchi, unlike being a criminal, could also be a desirable political identity (even as some evidently saw the two as analogous, if not synonymous), the analogy attests to the durability of 'Kuchi' as a modifier, even extending generationally beyond the point of sedentarization.

And, in fact, this diverse group of now-settled actors has remained loosely connected to the still nomadic pastoralists through their fathers or forefathers who engaged in semi-nomadic pastoralist activities. Some argue that subsequently, 'Kuchi' has come to denote not only a mode of living (nomadic) and a production system (pastoralism) but also a cultural identity. What this 'identity' entails, however, remains vague. Some of my interlocutors insisted that Kuchis had a unique cultural heritage of special clothes, food, language and common traditions [14] to which they felt meaningfully connected. As one settled transport-business manager told me: 'Sometimes we still make 'kuchi food', when we want to feel like Kuchis again. That food has then *krut* [dried buttermilk] in it, which was made by relatives of ours.'[15]

The disparity in definitions shows how different actors tried to claim the cultural label and define their heritage and current status within it. The deliberate vagueness of the term had very real political consequences, as one member of the Independent Election Commission (IEC) pointed out: 'The public outreach campaign from the Electoral Commission was not specific [as to] whether they mean Kuchi as a way of life or as a tribe. Most Kuchi confused these two. The Kuchi parliamentarians are settled, they are "Kuchi as a tribe".[16] The definition's vagueness did not preclude those within the capacious category from making it defined and exclusionary in particular moments of contestation; on the contrary, its flexibility was enabling in this sense.

This tribal definition, furthermore, was inclusive of only some ethnicities. The overwhelming majority of Kuchi parliamentarians were not only ethnic Pashtuns, but Pashtuns from east and south Afghanistan.[17] However, pastoral nomads can be found among Baluch, Aimaq, Turkoman, Kirghiz, Arab, Uzbek, some northern Hazara and Tajiks as well (Kakar 1979: 123,129,130; Pedersen 1994: 81). This observation also resonates with analyses that have compared the political construct of the Kuchi identity to the notion of *qawm* – a flexible and expandable term that refers to kin, village, tribal or ethnic group of solidarity and loyalty (Foschini 2013b: 3). From this short overview it can be concluded that (former) pastoral nomads, now labelled as 'Kuchi', were by no means a homogeneous group, and the definition of who belonged internally to this group was a point of contention and also part of the political game.

The Nomad Label as Political Currency

As an overarching, national category, 'Kuchi' offered political, legal as well as economic opportunities in the post-2001 Afghan government: The 2004 constitution of Afghanistan inscribed category members with rights to education,[18] participation in local councils[19] and, in Article 14, the development of livelihoods.[20] This development mandate was taken up by the Afghan state as well as non-state actors: Ministries had 'Kuchi Focal Points'[21] whose role it was to ensure Kuchis were taken into account in the ministerial planning of projects. While the Ministry of Borders and Tribal Affairs was initially responsible for Kuchi affairs, in 2006 the Independent Directorate of Kuchi Affairs (IDKA) was created to enhance the coordination between Kuchis and state institutions.[22] The directorate established offices in 31 out of 34 provinces[23] and offered access points for Kuchis to contact governmental institutions. Apart from the top level in Kabul, the heads of the provincial offices with whom I interacted were not Kuchis themselves, but they seemed to maintain close contact to Kuchi leaders. The rights of Kuchis and the government's responsibilities towards them were also taken up by non-state actors: NGOs engaged with Kuchis through work in urban poverty programmes, and material distributions, as well as peace and conflict resolution efforts between nomadic and settled communities.[24]

Kuchis received their own specialized ID cards and separate voter cards.[25] The Afghan lower house in parliament reserved ten seats for Kuchi representatives, and in the upper house two Kuchi seats were appointed by the president directly.[26] Initially, the ten seats in the lower house were a single constituency, meaning that Kuchis, who had specific voter cards identifying them as such, could vote anywhere in the country in specific polling stations, and for any Kuchi candidate.[27] This allocation evolved into a constituency divided into seven electoral zones, with one male candidate/seat per zone and three female candidates/seats for the entire country that were not bound to a certain geographical area.[28] This change was directly linked to how the Kuchi label was used (and abused) to obtain political power:

> [T]he 10 seats for the Kuchi became a Pashtun versus non-Pashtun problem. There was a discussion whether they should vanish altogether, and then the compromise was found to have 7 areas, because other ethnicities have Kuchis, too, and not all would be allocated to one tribe.[29]

The accusation that the ten Kuchi seats would be reserved for Pashtuns – and therefore offset the ethnic balance in the parliament – had been raised before. The single constituency Kuchi system had elicited heated discussions earlier in 2009, which were often linked to ethnic debates.[30] Other pastoral nomads in the north argued that they felt left out because they did not have a representative in parliament who could stand up for their needs.[31] Still, not all Kuchis registered as such to vote,[32] and not all parliamentarians with a family background of pastoral nomadism campaigned for a 'Kuchi seat'. The effectiveness of lobbying on behalf of all pastoral nomads remained questionable because of the degree to which ethnic solidarity had come to influence decision-making. Thus, despite their claim to the Kuchi label, non-Pashtun nomadic pastoralists in the north did not feel included in a system that privileged Pashtun pastoralists in the east and south.[33] Furthermore, because of the nature of network politics in Afghanistan (Sharan 2022), which largely determined who would win any given parliamentary seat, influential powerbrokers catered to their own voter banks.

The Peripatetic Reality as Displaced and Stateless

As Pashtun pastoral nomads claimed a central place in crafting nomadic minority labels in the Afghan government after 2001, the socio-economic and political position of peripatetic nomads was relegated to that of an internally displaced population to which the international aid community catered (Hennion/Nicolle 2011). After 2001, in a crucial shift, peripatetic groups were perceived as a part of the general population on the move. According to the Internal Displacement Monitoring Centre, 75 per cent of all Afghans have experienced displacement at least once in their lifetime.[34] According to the UNHCR, Kabul alone had at one point over fifty recognized IDP camps, or 'informal settlements', which were called Kabul Informal Settlements (KIS), with over 30,000 individuals living in tents and temporary housing.[35] Informal settlements were established on a mixture of private- or government-owned land. The people living in these informal settlements were classified as a mixture of IDPs who had fled fighting in their area of residence to major urban areas, or returnees, who had returned from countries where they had fled during earlier decades of conflict. Peripatetic groups surfaced in these camps as one of several groups of people who claimed assistance from international aid organizations such as the UNHCR and NGOs. In twelve camps in the KIS, peripatetic communities (such as Jogi, Jat or Chori Frosh) were registered as either the only ethnicity or being part of the group that lived in the camp (Schmeding 2015).

While peripatetics were registered as part of the general IDP population, they often still considered themselves, or were categorized as, distinctly Jogi/Chori Frosh/peripatetic groups. These two categories were not mutually exclusive. Peripatetic groups often have a place that they consider their home base or to which they frequently return. For instance, the Chori Frosh community I researched in 2013/2014 generally lived in Kabul and registered as part of an IDP camp, but some families from the camp moved to Jalalabad during the winter months. Relatives kept in close contact through mobile phones during that time and visited each other regularly, especially for events like weddings, mourning periods or burials. Opinion on movement and settling was split within the community. Some families in Jalalabad argued that the decision to stay in Kabul during winter was due to the benefits of being 'camp dwellers', which included receiving winterization kits with blankets, clothing and firewood from NGOs working for the KIS taskforce. Other women in Kabul suggested that they had a genuine wish to settle down more permanently.

A 2011 study found that all of the Jogi and Chori Frosh households surveyed in multiple cities described themselves as sedentary and had not moved in the past year. Seasonal migrations still took place but were fewer in number and involved only a few household members (Hennion/Nicolle 2011: 29). Reasons for this adaptation might have included the deterioration of the security situation, increased trucking activity due to modernized infrastructure (i.e. competition to the peripatetics' position as trading intermediaries), as well as a community-driven interest in gaining access to education (Hennion/Nicolle 2011: 38). A sedentarization process seemed to have taken place in which many communities considered one place their permanent home, while only some parts of the family migrated to other places irregularly.[36] Regardless of whether one place was seen as only a temporary base or a more permanent residence, the destruction of their homes or forcible displacement on account of insecurity/fighting could leave peripatetic families with similar struggles to those of an IDP. However, they also had to contend with the strong social stigma of being a peripatetic.

Politics of Belonging and Statelessness

What set the peripatetic communities apart from other populations (including the Kuchis), both in the informal settlements/IDP camps and among other settled and nomadic people, was that they generally were not acknowledged as Afghan citizens by way of the Afghan national identification card (*tazkera*).[37] The Afghan ID-card was first introduced in Afghanistan in 1922 and was required to attend government schools, universities or obtain a passport.[38] It represented the proof of 'a person's identity, which among other things facilitates the realization of its holder's rights to education, ownership of land and property, participation in political processes and other liberties and entitlements under the law'[39] (UNHCR 2005). Furthermore, holders of a *tazkera* were also eligible for the UNHCR land allocation scheme through which many returnees secured resettlement (Hennion/Nicolle 2011: 34).

In theory, every Afghan citizen could obtain a *tazkera* (UNHCR 2005). Many Afghans, however, 'do not have [a] *tazkira* [sic] because they have not gone through the labyrinth of administrative procedures necessary to obtain one' (Hennion/Nicolle 2011: 33). Generally speaking, the procedure seemed simple at first: the submission of an application letter with two recent photographs and 'the *tazkera* of one close relative of the father's side of the family (father, grandfather, brother, uncle, cousin), or for married females with the husband's *tazkera* or that of one of his male relatives'.[40] Problems began, however, when none of the relatives of the applicant possessed an ID card, as most peripatetics had 'never been registered in the national archives and thus have left no bureaucratic trace' (Kuppers 2014: 9). As such, the ownership of officially registered ID cards proved rare or non-existent.

In a survey I conducted for a study on peripatetic Jogi communities in Mazar-e Sharif in 2015, only 9 per cent of male-headed household respondents and 7 per cent of female-headed household respondents stated that their head of household owned an Afghan ID card (Schmeding 2015). These findings were congruent with other reports in which overall 80 per cent of Jogi/Chori Frosh interviewees did not have a *tazkera*[41] (Hennion/Nicolle:5; TLO:13). Oddly, when members of Jogi communities were asked if they themselves, and not the head of the household, possessed a *tazkera*, the respondents showed a surprisingly high prevalence of ownership – 42 per cent among

Jogi men and 27 per cent among women. The wide discrepancy is largely explained by the prevalence of fake ID cards.

Forged *tazkeras* were quite common (TLO:16) and a high number of peripatetics in the survey in Mazar-e Sharif (83 per cent) owned a Kuchi/nomadic *tazkera*. This number was suspiciously high, especially given the procedure of obtaining *tazkeras* for Kuchis, which involved going through the IDKA. Kuchi leaders had to register regionally with IDKA and officials of IDKA were aware, and sometimes even hostile towards, Jogi communities' usage of Kuchi IDs, and attempted to distance the image of Kuchis and Jogis from each other. Jogi elders could not register with IDKA but might have attempted to pass as Kuchis in claiming (fake) Kuchi ID cards.

As the ID cards were non-electronic, the only place to verify them would be the archives. These illegal ID cards, however, did not extend to providing holders with citizenship rights; they were 'just a paper' in the sense that they might help the people who carried them to navigate police checkpoints. Many of the *tazkeras* owned by the Jogi respondents may have been forged, but there were also signs of a change in the policy and policy implementation concerning peripatetic groups. An Afghan Independent Human Rights Commission (AIHRC) official in Kabul stated that the letter sent to then-president Hamid Karzai by the AIHRC about the problem of peripatetic recognition had been answered favourably before Karzai's term ended. However, even if such a statement had been issued, Jogis were still experiencing difficulties, especially in provinces other than Kabul, in obtaining ID cards:

> When Karzai issued a letter to the department of national ID, they [Jogis] were given the ID here in Kabul … [however,] the governments in the provinces are not interested in what Karzai has issued. So they [the peripatetics] face a legal problem. When they go to court they are not helped, because they are not seen as Afghan citizens.
>
> (AIHRC Kabul official)

Far from the administrative centre, officials were often unaware of changes that took place and the bureaucratic procedures needed to accommodate the changes.

Among Jogis, while some were of the opinion that they were not allowed to own *tazkeras*, others reported that it was possible to obtain them in Kabul and Kunduz.[42] These problems were also referenced by the 2014 IDP policy that urged the Ministry of Interior (MoI) to take the lead in a concerted effort to ensure that ID cards were issued to all citizens equally:

> Regarding the *Tazkera* (f) MoI will cooperate with [the Ministry of Women's Affairs] MOWA, [Ministry of Labor, Social Affairs, Martyrs and Disabled] MoLSAMD and [Ministry of Borders and Tribal Affairs] MoBTA to see that assistance is given to separated, unaccompanied or orphaned IDP children to obtain *tazkeras*, and to members of certain groups, notably the Kuchi, Jogi and Chori Frosh, who generally do not have *tazkeras* and who face special difficulties in acquiring them.[43]

The difficulties in obtaining legal identification created a situation that was used by resourceful political entrepreneurs: when I returned to one of the peripatetic IDP camps in Kabul in 2021, I found that a parliamentarian had rented an office close by, equipped with a printer and internet access, in which he helped peripatetics to register for IDs and voter cards – in exchange for their votes in elections and their help to stage demonstrations when it was politically expedient for him. During the comprehensive overhaul of national identity cards into electronic *tazkeras* in 2018, international organizations advocated for the inclusion of peripatetics in the rollout. While this initiative increased the accessibility of ID cards for many peripatetics, they continued to encounter a pervasive atmosphere of hostility and racism at the registration offices. Consequently, a significant number remained hesitant to navigate the entire application process, rendering the parliamentarian's offer all the more appealing.

Owning an ID card was, however, more than a national insignia of belonging, it also regulated access to an important political tool: land ownership.

Land as Dispute, Land as Absence

Across the world, access, use and ownership of land is a crucial asset that indexes the social, political and economic capital that a group possesses. In a historically largely subsistence-based economy – such as Afghanistan – 'wealth is measured in terms of property (land and livestock in particular) rather than money' (Barfield 2010: 57). Even after the economy in Afghanistan partially changed from largely subsistence-based to aid-dependent, land did not cease to play an important role; its use as a currency just changed (e.g. land grabbing and purchasing loyalties from rivals through doling out land parcels) (Sharan 2022). Relative access to land, particularly state-owned, as well as agricultural and pasture land, became a potent political currency in Afghanistan's new republic. Nomadic communities were not immune to the consequences. Indeed, in many ways, they were more affected than others, and the differential allocation of power and authority that the previous parts of the chapter sketched out played a central role in their attempts to access and wield this resource.

For peripatetic communities, land ownership was a major challenge and concern. The absence of property was linked to both the poverty of the communities and the absence of ID card ownership. The nearly complete absence of *tazkera*-ownership until fairly recently made it impossible for peripatetic households to buy or own property. A 52-year-old man from one of the peripatetic Jogi communities in Kabul's Zainuddin camp described his situation as follows: 'If the landlord wants to, he can throw us out any time. It happened several times that we stayed on the street without anything. No home, no nothing.'

Discussions and individual interviews with members of this community explicitly challenged frequent stereotypes about them as enjoying migration without a stable home base. Many described moving from one place to another with the ever-pending threat of expulsion as a general insecurity built into every step of the household's planning, especially with respect to education access. Indeed, while the communities had been peripatetics for generations, some used to have use rights to land that was uncultivated by others (Rao 1986(a): 273). While none of the households that I researched in Kabul, Mazar and Jalalabad owned land, I found in a 2015 survey that more than half of the peripatetic Jogi communities in Mazar-e Sharif (62 per cent) were able to set up rent-arrangements with the landowner and secure their position on the land they stayed on at least for a certain time.

Houses were built by the communities themselves out of *pakhsa* (pressed mud) walls with rent payments measured per room (Schmeding 2015). The rest squatted on the land. These rental arrangements were often part of carefully nurtured social ties to neighbours and surrounding communities that also included economic tie-ins: many peripatetics tended to animals for their neighbours. Jogi families would keep cows, sheep, or horses and were paid monthly until the animals were slaughtered. Peripatetic families also milked cows and were allowed to use a portion themselves or to sell it to shops. These shops functioned as interfaces: most people would not buy dairy from peripatetic communities directly, because they were not considered clean or respectable. However, through the shops, the consumer remained unaware of the origin of the milk and the peripatetics could make a small income. A similar system functioned for the growing of wheat (Schmeding 2015).

As members of a socially marginal group, the individual households benefitted from these carefully nurtured social ties to neighbours and surrounding communities, so much so in fact, that while some households benefitted from seasonal movement, they nevertheless returned to the places they considered their homes and used the established infrastructure and networks. Of course, these ties would be severed when households were forced to abandon their homes for good. Access to land did not necessarily erase migration patterns but was part of interlocking seasonal movement and economic strategies that supported each other. As land became a political currency post-2001, the occupation of land that could be valuable within political manoeuvring became ever more fraught for peripatetic groups who lived on that land. Peripatetics could never be sure that the tenuous agreements they had made would be upheld. The commodification of land and its transformation into a political currency post-2001 meant that, as political actors and economic forces vied for control of these sought-after regions, nomads found themselves at the intersection of power struggles, often lacking the legal or political resources to protect their rights.

While the relationship of peripatetic nomads to land – and arguably many poorer pastoral nomads who became a part of the urban poor as well – was characterized by the absence of ownership (Mielke 2016), the relationship between political pastoral nomadic identities such as the Kuchi and land was more contested. The state-driven and sometimes forced settlement of nomads and their instrumentalization as pawns in political games has served as an enduring pastime for Afghanistan's rulers dating back to the autocratic ruler Abdur Rahman Khan (r. 1880–1901). Abdur Rahman settled nomads in the north of the country and used them as part of his centralization of power: to break the unity among, and independence of, the ethnic Hazaras in the Central Highlands, Abdur Rahman partitioned the Hazarajat into provinces and districts, absorbed friendly Hazara chiefs into his bureaucracy and opened pastureland for Pashtun pastoral nomads (Pedersen 1994: 59; Frederiksen 1996: 45; Emadi 1997: 367f; Monsutti 2005, 2013).[44] These areas remained accessible to nomads until the time of the Russian occupation and the civil war that followed, when Hazaras gradually reclaimed their land (De Weijer 2008b: 14).

Areas that were closed off to pastoral nomads during periods of war were partially re-opened again for Kuchis as pastureland under the Taliban regime of the 1990s (Simonsen 2004: 718; Wily, 2013: 22), which led to changed migration routes for summer pasture and conflict between Kuchi and non-Hazara farmers in parts of Ghazni (Barker 1999: 10). In the post-2001 era, clashes between Hazara farmers and pastoral nomads became so frequent, with major displacements and often deadly consequences for Hazara populations, that a slew of programmes popped up to mediate conflicts and settle land access (Foschini 2010; Sexton 2012; Murtazashvili 2021). These clashes were ongoing as of October 2021, exacerbated by the new Taliban government's quiet acquiescence of Kuchi nomads' land seizures.[45]

Apart from these particular, ethnically coded clashes over pastureland, the question of access to and ownership of land also featured prominently in the electoral-political power struggles, in which Kuchi parliamentarians were involved. Land seizure and redistribution (often colloquially called land grabbing) became an important feature of building relations of patronage and establishing political alliances in post-2001 Afghanistan (Saeed/Parmentier 2017; Sharan 2022; Saeed 2023). With the influx of international aid, the transformation of old houses into accommodations for expatriates and the emergence of new townships for wealthy Afghans returning from abroad, real estate prices skyrocketed in Kabul (also in other urban centres, though to a lesser degree).

Land prices for central neighbourhoods, such as Qala-e Fatullah, increased 'by 1900 per cent from USD 60,000 to 80,000 during the first Taliban regime (1996–2001) to $ 1.2 million in February 2012' (Misza/Monsutti 2014).[46] The appropriation, occupation, redistribution and selling of land translated into capital for new political entrepreneurs, such as the 'nomads' landholding elite' of Kuchi MPs (Foschini 2013b). Several Kuchi MPs – including the former Guantanamo prisoner, Naim Khan Kuchi; the deputy director of the national council of the Ahmadzai, Haji Munjai; and the leader of the Tarakhel and chief of the lower house of parliament's (*wolesi jirga*) Kuchi Affairs Commission, Mullah Tarakhel – were involved in drawn-out battles for land at the fringes of Kabul and Logar (Foschini 2013b; Giustozzi 2018). While their struggles put them at odds with the central government, their acquisitions also assured them loyal voting blocs among their constituency.

Conclusion

In all of the ways detailed, land has surfaced and resurfaced as a multivalent currency of power and belonging in Afghanistan. The inability to acquire land – for example on the part of the peripatetics and poorer pastoral nomads – as well as the violent clashes over access to grazing grounds, made land an arbiter of belonging, wealth and inter-group power politics. For those with access to state land and private real estate – as in the case of Kuchi parliamentarians – land indexed the ability to access wealth or political capital and to wield authority. In these contexts, the status of 'nomad-ness' or 'Kuchi-ness' interacted with the ability to access land (through calling on supporters to violently occupy plots, for example) or the inability to legally own land (as in the case of the peripatetics). Given the vastly distinct means by which the label played itself out in different socio-economic, cultural and political contexts, 'nomad' was not a unified category, but one inflected by particular understandings of who belonged to which (sub)category and what rights and opportunities were intertwined with that particular definition.

Notes

1   Research for this chapter was conducted in several stages. In 2013–14 I conducted six months *in situ* research in Kabul, Parwan, Nangarhar, Ghor and Balkh, which included primarily gathering of documents, qualitative semi-structured interviews, informal conversations and participant observation in nomadic community spaces (Schmeding 2014). Interviews were conducted with Kuchi parliamentarians, officials of IDKA, Kuchi focal points in ministries, NGOs interfacing with nomadic populations, pastoral and peripatetic nomads as well as former, now settled nomads. I also joined political spaces such as the Kabul Informal Settlement (KIS) task force, that catered to IDP camps in which nomads were present, to observe the political interface between NGOs, government and nomadic people. At that time, I also partnered with the Afghan Mobile Mini Circus for Children (MMCC/AECC) and worked with them in IDP camps in Kabul in which many former pastoral and peripatetic nomads were living. I conducted semi-structured interviews among peripatetic as well as pastoral nomads inside as well as outside of IDP camps. In 2015 I returned with the NGO People in Need (PIN) to conduct research on peripatetic communities in Mazar-e Sharif and Kabul, published in a report (Schmeding 2015), which included additional qualitative interviews and a quantitative survey of the communities. In July/August 2021 I returned to conduct additional interviews with Kuchi parliamentarians, non-politically affiliated Kuchis as well as with peripatetic communities that I had known from seven years prior.
2   Various peripatetic groups have lived and migrated in Central Europe, among them the Sinti, the Jenische and the Roma, who belong to the Romani-speaking groups, and who migrated from the fourteenth century onwards from the Balkans into Germany, the UK and Scandinavia. While initially itinerant, many communities have settled in recent decades. The communities were also persecuted as distinct groups during the Holocaust (Margalit/Yaron 2007). 'Travellers' is a term related to peripatetic groups who predominantly live in Ireland and the UK. They are also known as 'Pavees' or 'Minceirs', and while they are predominantly English-speaking, many also speak own languages such as Gammon, Cant or Shelta, which are mixtures of English and Irish Gaelic (Wolniak in Kirkland 2016). Another term that is often applied to these groups, vagrancy, signifies irregular patterns of travel, uncoordinated with social or economic factors, as well as a lack of a place to live, and is therefore not fitting to describe the communities in Afghanistan (Rao 2004: 270).
3   Gypsy has various similar terms in other European languages such as *Calé* (Spanish), *Manouches* (French), *Kalderatsch* (Russian), *Zigeuner* (German), see Bogdal (2011: 15). Olaf Günther subsumes Central Asian peripatetic groups under the label of 'gypsy', arguing that the term of tsiganological relationism (or,

in German 'tsigalonogischer Relationismus') would be better suited to capture the relationship between peripatetic group and settled population in a society. However, apart from trying to reclaim a negatively connoted term, he does not explain sufficiently what would set tsiganologic relations apart from peripatetic ones. See Günther (2008: 71–91).

4   Rao observed in the 1970s that 'Jat' was a frequently used swearword: 'In the Persian (Dari) commonly spoken in Kabul, shrewish women were admonished not to be quarrelsome like the Jat ('Jat na sho!', lit. 'don't be like a Jat!'), children playing about in dirt heaps were mocked at with 'you're like a Jat' ('misl-e Jat asti!') and in orthodox, semi-urban contexts girls who tended to be careless and carefree in speech and dress were also described by disapproving elders as behaving like Jat women' (Rao 2004: 275). This observation was confirmed by non-Jogi interviewees.

5   I have argued this point elsewhere, see Schmeding (2014, 2015).

6   The term *pohwinda* has by some been connected to specifically the fully nomadic Ghilzai Pashtuns although it was in use for both Durrani and Ghilzai Pashtun nomads (see Balland 1991: 205–29; Bruce 1929; Robinson 1978/1935; Kakar 1979: 128). The term *maldar* could also have sub-categories, such as '*watani maldar* (homeland herd-owner), who have strong ties to winter pastures (their *watan*, homeland) and local villages, from the *kuchi maldar* (migrating herd-owner), who have no such ties ... Among these nomads, too, clearly *maldar* was the main self-identity, the term *kuchi* being merely a qualifier' (Tapper 2008: 98). Archival sources that Shah Mahmoud Hanifi analysed delineates three terms (Kochis, Lohanis and Pawendas) as Pashtun 'trading tribes' that transported commodities between Kabul and Peshawar valleys, regions and markets (Hanifi 2008b).

7   Research on the humanitarian sector specifically has pointed out how humanitarian intervention creates categorization of whose life to prioritize. Drawing on the medical concept of triage, these authors show how prioritization is a continuous and highly political process, rather than a one-off exercise to find the best match between needs and programme objectives (Mena/Hilhorst 2022). More than just categorize existing groups of people, humanitarian interventions and governance participated in 'making up' new kinds of people as individuals crafted their selves to fit into the expectations of international agencies and national implementers (Nguyen 2010: 11).

8   This is also evidenced in James Michener's 1963 novel *Caravans*, which demonstrates the extent to which, beyond academia, the Afghan pastoralists captured the western imaginary. See Michener, James. (1963). Caravans. New York: Random House Trade Paperbacks.

9   Interview with Gul Muhammad in Sholgera, 17 November 2013.

10 Interview with Kuchi construction business on the outskirts of Kabul, 6 December 2013.

11 Informal Conversation, Abdarra Camp, Kabul, 2014.

12 NRAP stands for National Rural Access Program. See https://mrrd.gov.af/index.php/node/403 (accessed 22 September 2022).

13 Interview with Ahmad Fawad Fayez, Regional ESM Assistant for NRAP, 10 November 2013 in Mazar-e Sharif.

14 Interview with IDKA director Eng. Ahlam Farooq Obaidy, 10 November 2013, in Mazar-e Sharif.

15 Interview on 6 December 2013 in Kabul with Zabiullah Nasser, trucking manager, part of the Nasseri tribe in Parwan.

16 Interview on 31 October 2013, Zekria Barakzai, in Kabul. Barakzai worked at the time of the interview for Democracy International, but used to work for the IEC.
17 See *Wolesi Jirga* Directory: https://www.ndi.org/files/AFG-2010-2015-Wolesi-Jirga-Directory.pdf (accessed 22 September 2022).
18 Article 44: 'improve education of nomads'.
19 Article 140: 'Participation of nomads in these local councils shall be regulated in accordance with the provisions of the law.'
20 'The state, within its financial means, shall design and implement effective programs to develop agriculture and animal husbandry, improve economic, social and living conditions of farmers [*dehqanan*], herders [*maldaran*] and settlers [*eskan*] as well as the nomads' livelihood [*kuchian*]. The state shall adopt necessary measures for provision of housing and distribution of public estates to deserving citizens in accordance with the provisions of law and within financial possibilities' (Article Fourteen, Afghan constitution, translation additions mine).
21 Ministries with Kuchi focal points were for example: Ministry of Rural Rehabilitation and Development (MRRD), or the Ministry of Agriculture, Irrigation and Livestock (MAIL).
22 Interview with IDKA director in Kabul, 15 December 2013.
23 Excluding Nuristan, Panjshir and Daikundi. Interview with Muhammad Daoud Sherzad in Kabul, 12 December 2013.
24 Organizations such as the Agha Khan Foundation (AKF), Cooperation for Peace And Unity (CPAU) or USAID-funded projects like Rebuilding Agricultural Markets Program (RAMP) or the Pastoral Engagement, Adaption and Capacity Enhancement Programme (PEACE) have engaged Kuchis on security issues, conflict resolution or pasture access. See https://www.acted.org/en/partners/cooperation-for-peace-and-unity-cpau/, http://www.solidarites.org/en/; https://www.usaid.gov/node/51036 and PEACE Report 2011 https://docplayer.net/220606499-Afghanistan-pastoral-engagement-adaptation-and-capacity-enhancement-peace-project.html (accessed 22 September 2022).
25 See http://www.iec.org.af/component/content/article/20-english-uk/for-voters/69-how-where-vote?highlight=WyJrdWNoaSJd (accessed 15 June 2014).
26 See http://www.iec.org.af/pdf/legalframework/law/electorallaw_eng.pdf (accessed 15 June 2014).
27 See http://www.iec.org.af/component/content/article/20-english-uk/for-voters/69-how-where-vote?highlight=WyJrdWNoaSJd (accessed 13 June 2014).
28 See EL art. 23: http://www.iec.org.af/pdf/legalframework/law/electorallaw_eng.pdf and on the process of change: Afghanistan Analyst Network, https://www.afghanistan-analysts.org/en/reports/political-landscape/afghanistans-new-electoral-laws-changes-and-red-flags/, 27 July 2013.
29 Interview with Zekria Barakzai. Kabul, 31 October 2014.
30 'There was a rough ethnic split, with the kuchis and Pashtuns largely in support of the single constituency and most non-Pashtuns in favour of linking the seats to certain regions. The kuchis lost the vote and protested angrily, after which the session was swiftly concluded.' In: https://www.afghanistan-analysts.org/en/reports/political-landscape/who-will-control-the-2014-electoral-process-an-update-on-afghanistans-electoral-laws/; Also: https://www.afghanistan-analysts.org/en/reports/political-landscape/passing-the-electoral-law-four-controversies-down-seven-more-to-go/ (accessed 22 September 2022).

31 Interview in Mazar-e Sharif with Kuchi representatives at IDKA, 13 November 2013. Foschini furthermore remarked that 'Kuchis in the north may be rich, but are, with few exceptions, politically isolated'. See Foschini (2013: 26).
32 Though both has happened: that Kuchis did not vote as 'Kuchi voters' and that other ethnicities, such as Turkmen, were signed up as 'Kuchi'. See Tahir Muhammad, 'Afghan Turkmen Claim They're Being Written Off', Institute for War and Peace Reporting, 27 July 2011, https://iwpr.net/global-voices/afghan-turkmen-claim-theyre-being-written (accessed 22 September 2022).
33 Group interview in Mazar-e Sharif, 13 November 2013.
34 Internal Displacement Monitoring Centre (IDMC), 16 April 2012: https://reliefweb.int/report/afghanistan/durable-solutions-far-reach-amid-escalating-conflict.
35 UNHCR Sub-Office Kabul and DoRR Kabul reference list; UNHCR 'returnees': http://www.unhcr.org/pages/49c3646c1ca.html also: IRIN 2008, AFGHANISTAN: Returnees may become refugees again – ministry: https://www.thenewhumanitarian.org/report/78822/afghanistan-returnees-may-become-refugees-again-ministry; IRIN 2012, AFGHANISTAN: Towards more sustainable solutions for returnees: http://www.irinnews.org/report/94965/afghanistan-towards-more-sustainable-solutions-for-returnees (accessed 22 September 2022).
36 A similar process was perceptible in some pastoral nomadic communities in the north, in which families were split into parts that stayed put and others who moved. This was also part of a process of economic diversification (Schmeding 2014).
37 Hennion/Nicolle:5, 34; UNHCR Universal Periodic Review: Afghanistan, 3, 7; UNHCR-Richtlinien zur Feststellung des internationalen Schutzbedarfs Afghanischer Asylsuchender, 2013:78, see https://www.refworld.org/cgi-bin/texis/vtx/rwmain/opendocpdf.pdf?reldoc=yanddocid=534d34364 (accessed 22 September 2022).
38 http://moi.gov.af/en/page/5747/5749 (accessed 17 May 2014).
39 See UNHCR, 2005: 'Frequently Asked Questions'. A Circular for Afghan Refugees from the United Nations High Commissioner for Refugees (UNHCR) / National Identification Cards (Tazkeras). See http://www.unhcr.org/4497b1c12.pdf (accessed 17 May 2014).
40 UNHCR, 2005: See http://www.unhcr.org/4497b1c12.pdf (accessed 18 May 2014).
41 These numbers stand in comparison with sedentary non-Jogi Afghans, who were found in the same study to have a *tazkera* in over 85 per cent (men) and 60 per cent (women). IDPs were found to have a somewhat lower rate of *tazkera* ownership (77.5 per cent). The data, however, was gathered in Kabul and Paghman (TLO:11).
42 Two male Focus Group Discussions (FGDs) and one female FGD in Kamarband and Zahiruddin, see Schmeding (2015).
43 IBP (International Business Publications) 2017: 127f.
44 Under Abdur Rahman Khan, Hazaras were subject to discrimination, oppression, forced marriages, heavy taxes, enslavement and murder. Hazaras found themselves in the following decades as 'victims of systematic economic and political exclusion' (Monsutti (2013: 189); Emadi (1997)).
45 *Hasht-e Sobh*, 'Kuchis Are Taking Advantage of Hazara Farmlands in Ghazni's Nawur District'. 5 October 2021. See: https://8am.af/eng/kuchis-are-taking-advantage-of-hazara-farmlands-in-ghaznis-nawur-district/
46 Price for a *jerib* of land.

References

Balland, D. (1991), 'Nomadism and Politics: The Case of Afghan Nomads in the Indian Subcontinent'. *Studies in History*, 7(2): 205–29.
Barfield, T. (1981), *The Central Asian Arabs of Afghanistan: Pastoral Nomadism in Transition*. Austin: University of Texas Press.
Barfield, T. (2010), *Afghanistan: A Cultural and Political History*. Princeton: Princeton University Press.
Barker, T. J., Thieme, O., Shah, N. A. and Majok, A. A. (1999), 'Activities of Kuchi Survey Team/ Working Paper No 1/99'. FAO Fiat Panis Livestock Development for Food Security in Afghanistan. Kabul: AREU.
Barnett, M. N. (2013), 'Humanitarian Governance'. *Annual Review of Political Science*, 16(1): 379–98.
Barth, F. (1998), *Ethnic Groups and Boundaries: The Social Organization of Culture Difference*. Prospect Heights, IL: Waveland Press.
Berland, J. C. and Rao, A. (eds.) (2004), *Customary Strangers: New Perspectives on Peripatetic Peoples in the Middle East, Africa, and Asia*. Westport, CT and London: Praeger.
Bogdal, K-M. (2011), *Europa Erfindet Die Zigeuner: Eine Geschichte von Faszination Und Verachtung*. Berlin: Suhrkamp.
Bruce, C. E. (1929), *Notes on Ghilzai and Powindah Tribes*. Peshawar: Govt. Press.
Burnes, A. (1973/1834), *Travels Into Bokhara (1834) Being the Account of a Journey from India to Cabool, Tartary, and Persia*. Karachi, London, New York, Delhi: Oxford in Asia Historical Reprint.
Caroe, O. (1976), *The Pathans, 550 BC–AD 1957*. Oxford: Oxford University Press.
De Weijer, F. (2005a), *Microfinance for Kuchi*. Afghanistan: Microfinance Investment Support Facility for Afghanistan. www.misfa.org.
De Weijer, F. (2005b). *National Multisectoral Assessment of Kuchi (NMAK)*. Afghanistan: Ministry for Rural Rehabilitation and Development. www.mrrd.gov.af?nmak.htm.
De Weijer, F. (2007), 'Afghanistan's Kuchi Pastoralists: Change and Adaptation'. *Nomadic Peoples*, 11(1): 9–37.
Dupree, L. (1980/1973), *Afghanistan*. Princeton, NJ: Princeton University Press.
Elphinstone, M. (1815), *Account of the Kingdom of Caubul, and Its Dependencies in Persia, Tartary, and India: Comprising a View of the Afghaun Nation, and a History of the Dooraunee Monarchy*. Cambridge: Cambridge University Press.
Emadi, H. (1997), 'The Hazaras and Their Role in the Process of Political Transformation in Afghanistan'. *Central Asian Survey*, 16(3): 363–87.
Fassin, D. (2007), 'Humanitarianism as a Politics of Life'. *Public Culture*, 19(3): 499–520.
Ferdinand, K. (2006), *Afghan Nomads: Caravans, Conflicts, and Trade in Afghanistan and British India, 1800–1980*. Copenhagen: Rhodos International Science and Art Publishers.
Foschini, F. (2010), *The Kuchi-Hazara Conflict, Again*. The Afghanistan Analyst Network. 27 May 2010. https://www.afghanistan-analysts.org/en/reports/war-and-peace/the-kuchi-hazara-conflict-again/
Foschini, F. (2013a), 'Rights and Freedoms / Land Grabs (2): Deh Sabz, the New and the Old'. Afghanistan Analysts Network, (2): 1–5. Available at: https://www.afghanistan-analysts.org/en/reports/rights-freedom/land-grabs-2-deh-sabz-the-new-and-the-old/.

Foschini, F. (2013b), 'The Social Wandering of the Afghan Kuchis/Social Patterns, Perceptions and Politics of an Afghan Community'. Afghanistan Analysts Network. Available at: http://www.afghanistan-analysts.org/wp-content/uploads/2013/11/20131125_FFoschini-Kuchis.pdf.

Frederiksen, B. and Nicolaisen, I. (1996), *Caravans and Trade in Afghanistan: The Changing Life of the Nomadic Hazarbuz*. Copenhagen: Thames and Hudson. http://www.getcited.org/pub/103319750.

Giustozzi, A. (2000), *War, Politics and Society in Afghanistan, 1978–1992*. Washington, DC: Georgetown University Press.

Giustozzi, A. (2018). *Typologies of Nomad-Settler Conflict in Afghanistan*. Kabul: AREU.

Glatzer, B. (1977), *Nomaden von Gharjistan : Aspekte d. Wirtschaftl., Sozialen u. Polit. Organisation Nomad. Durrani-Paschtunen in Nordwestafghanistan*. 1. Aufl. Wiesbaden: Steiner.

Glatzer, B. (1981). 'Processes of Nomadization in West Afghanistan', in *Contemporary Nomadic and Pastoral People: Asia and the North*. Williamsburg: College of William and Mary.

Glatzer, B. (1992), 'Pastoral Territoriality in West Afghanistan: An Organization of Flexibility', in *Mobility and Territoriality: Social and Spatial Boundaries among Fishers, Pastoralists and Peripatetics*. New York and Oxford: Berg Publishers Ltd.

Glatzer, B. and Casimir, M. J. (1983), 'Herds and Households among Pashtun Pastoral Nomads: Limits of Growth'. *Ethnology*, (22): 307–25.

Günther, O. (2008), 'Praktizierte Relationen-Das „Zigeunerische" in Ordungsvorstellungen Bei Zigeunergruppen Und Der Mehrheitsbevölkerung Mittelasiens', in *Roma/Zigeuner in Neuen Perspectiven. Roma/Gypsies in New Perspectives*. Leipzig: Leipzig University Press, 71–91.

Hanifi, J. M. (2008a), JĀT. In: Encyclopaedia Iranica. Vol. XIV, Fasc. 6, 589–92.

Hanifi, S. M. (2008b), *Connecting Histories in Afghanistan: Market Relations and State Formation on a Colonial Frontier*. Stanford, CA: Stanford University Press.

Hanifi, S. M. (2019), *Mountstuart Elphinstone in South Asia: Pioneer of British Colonial Rule*. Oxford: Oxford University Press.

Hatch Dupree, N. (1990), 'A Socio-Cultural Dimension: Afghan Women Refugees in Pakistan', in *The Cultural Basis of Afghan Nationalism*. London and New York: Pinter Publishers, University of Oxford, 121–33.

Hennion, C. and Nicolle, H. (2011), 'Jogi and Chori Frosch Out-of-School Children/A Story of Marginalisation'. Samuel Hall Consulting for UNICEF.

IBP International Business Publications (2017), *Afghanistan Immigration Policy, Laws and Regulations Handbook: Strategic Information and Regulations*. Washington, DC: IBP, Inc.

Kakar, H. K. (1979), *Government and Society in Afghanistan: The Reign of Amir 'Abd al-Rahman Khan*. Austin: University of Texas Press.

Kirkland, E. (2016), *Shades of Whiteness*. Oxfordshire: Inter-Disciplinary Press.

Kuppers, M. (2014), 'Stateless in Afghanistan'. *Forced Migration Review*, 46 (May). http://www.fmreview.org/en/afghanistan.pdf.

Margalit, G. and Matras, Y. (2007), 'Gypsies in Germany-German Gypsies? Identity and Politics of Sinti and Roma in Germany', in Stauber, R. and Vago, R. (eds.), *Roma – A Minority in Europe: Historical, Political and Social Perspectives*. Budapest: Central European University Press, 103–16.

Mena, R. and Hilhorst, D. (2022), 'Path Dependency When Prioritising Disaster and Humanitarian Response under High Levels of Conflict: A Qualitative Case Study in South Sudan'. *Journal of International Humanitarian Action*, 7(1): 1–16.

Michener, J. (1963), *Caravans*. New York: Random House Trade Paperbacks.
Mielke, K. (2016), 'Tracing Change: On the Positionality of Traditionally Mobile Groups in Kabul's Camps'. *Internationales Asienforum*, 47(3-4): 245-71.
Miszak, N. and Monsutti, A. (2014), 'Landscapes of Power: Local Struggles and National Stakes at the Rural-Urban Fringe of Kabul, Afghanistan'. *The Journal of Peasant Studies*, 41(2): 183-98.
Monsutti, A. (2005), *War and Migration: Social Networks and Economic Strategies of the Hazaras of Afghanistan*. New York/London: Routledge.
Monsutti, A (2013), 'Anthropologizing Afghanistan: Colonial and Postcolonial Encounters'. *Annual Review of Anthropology*, 42(June): 269-85.
Murtazashvili, J. B. (2021), *Land, the State, and War: Property Institutions and Political Order in Afghanistan*. Cambridge: Cambridge University Press.
Nguyen, V.-K. (2010), *The Republic of Therapy: Triage and Sovereignty in West Africa's Time of AIDS*. Durham [N.C.]: Duke University Press.
Olesen, A. (1982), 'Marriage Norms and Practices in a Rural Community in North Afghanistan'. *Folk. Dansk Ethnografisk Tidsskrift Kobenhavn*, 24: 111-41.
Olesen, A(1985), 'The Sheikh Mohammadi: A Marginal Trading Community in East Afghanistan'. *Folk*, 27(May): 115-46.
Olesen, A. (1994), *Afghan Craftsmen: The Cultures of Three Itinerant Communities*. London and New York: Thames and Hudson.
Pedersen, G. (1990), 'Afghan Nomads in Exile: Patterns of Organization and Reorganization in Pakistan', in *The Cultural Basis of Afghan Nationalism*. London and New York: Pinter Publishers, University of Oxford.
Pedersen, G. (1994), *Afghan Nomads in Transition: Century of Change among the Zala Khan Khel*. London and New York : Thames and Hudson.
Rao, A. (1979), 'Note Préliminaire Sur Les Jat d'Afghanistan'. *Studia Iranica*, 8(1): 141-9.
Rao, A. (1981), 'Qui Sont Les Jat d'Afghanistan?' *Afghanistan Journal Graz*, 8(2): 55-64.
Rao, A. (1982a), *Les Ġorbat d'Afghanistan: aspects économiques d'un groupe itinérant 'Jat.'* Paris: A.D.P.F.
Rao, A. (1982b), 'Non-Food-Producing Nomads and the Problem of Their Classification: The Case of the Ghorbat of Afghanistan'. *Eastern (The) Anthropologist Lucknow*, 35(2): 115-34.
Rao, A. (1983), 'Zigeuneraehnliche Gruppen in West-, Zentral Und Suedasien', in *Zigeuner. Romam, Sinti, Gitanos, Gypsies: Zwischen Verfolgung Und Romantisierung*. Berlin: Ullstein Verlag.
Rao, A. (1985), 'Des Nomades Méconnus: Pour Une Typlogie Des Communautés Péripatétiques'. *L'Homme*, 25(3): 97-119.
Rao, A. (1986a), 'Identité Ethnique Ou Catégorie Économique? Le Nomadism Commercial et La Marginalité Sociale'. *Etudes Tsiganes*, 32(2): 23-8.
Rao, A. (1986b), 'Peripatetic Minorities in Afghanistan – Image and Identity', in *Die Ethnischen Gruppen Afghanistans/Fallstudien Zur Gruppenidentitaet Und Intergruppenbeziehungen*. Reihe B (Geisteswissenschaften) 70. Wiesbaden: Dr. Ludwig Reichert Verlag, 254-83.
Rao, A. (1986c), 'Roles, Status and Niches: A Comparison of Peripatetic and Pastoral Women in Afghanistan'. *Nomadic Peoples*, 21-2: 153-77.
Rao, A. (1987a), 'The Concept of Peripatetics: An Introduction', in *The Other Nomads: Peripatetic Minorities in Cross-Cultural Perspective*. Köln: Bohlau Verlag, 1-32.
Rao, A. (1987b), *The Other Nomads. Peripatetic Minorities in Cross-Cultural Perspective*. Köln: Böhlau-Verlag.

Rao, A. (1988), 'Folk Models and Inter-Ethnic Relations in Afghanistan: A Case Study of Some Peripatetic Communities', in *Le Fait Ethnique En Iran et En Afghanistan*. Paris: Centre National de la Recherche Scientifique, 109–21.

Rao, A. (2004), 'Strangers and Liminal Beings: Some Thoughts on Peripatetics, Insiders, and Outsiders in Southwest Asia', in *Customary Strangers. New Perspectives on Peripatetic Peoples in the Middle East Africa, and Asia*. Westport, CT and London: Praeger, 269–98.

Rao, A. and Casimir, M. J. (2003), *Nomadism in South Asia*. Oxford: Oxford University Press.

Robinson, J. A. (1978/1935), *Notes on Nomad Tribes of Eastern Afghanistan*. 57, Quetta: Nisa Traders.

Saeed, H. (2023), *Transitional Justice and Socio-Economic Harm/Land Grabbing in Afghanistan*. New York: Routledge.

Saeed, H. and Parmentier, S. (2017), 'When Rabbits Are in Charge of Carrots: Land Grabbing, Transitional Justice and Economic-State Crime in Afghanistan'. *State Crime Journal*, 6(1): 13–36.

Schmeding, A. (2014), 'Who's the Real 'Nomad' in Afghanistan? Socio-Political Status, Legal Rights and the Differences between Peripatetic and Pastoral Nomads'. MA Thesis, Leiden: Leiden University.

Schmeding, A. (2015), 'Opportunities at the Margins the Jogi Community in Mazar-e Sharif'. People in Need. https://www.peopleinneed.net/opportunities-at-the-margins-the-jogi-community-in-mazar-e-sharif-911pub.

Scott, J. C. (1998), *Seeing like a State: How Certain Schemes to Improve the Human Condition Have Failed*. New Haven: Yale University Press.

Sexton, R. (2012), 'Natural Resources and Conflict in Afghanistan'. Afghanistan Watch.

Sharan, T. (2011), 'The Dynamics of Elite Networks and Patron–Client Relations in Afghanistan'. *Europe-Asia Studies*, 63(6): 1109–27.

Sharan, T. (2022), *Inside Afghanistan/Political Networks, Informal Order, and State Disruption*. London and New York: Routledge.

Simonsen, S. G. (2004), 'Ethnicising Afghanistan?: Inclusion and Exclusion in Post Bonn Institution Building'. *Third World Quarterly*, 25(4): 707–29.

Szabo, A. and Barfield, T. J. (1991), *Afghanistan: An Atlas of Indigenous Domestic Architecture*. Austin: University of Texas Press.

Tapper, N. (1973), 'The Advent of Pashtun "Maldars" in North-Western Afghanistan'. *Bulletin of the School of Oriental and African Studies*, 34: 55–79.

Tapper, N. (1991), *Bartered Brides / Politics, Gender and Marriage in an Afghan Tribal Society*. Cambridge: Cambridge University Press.

Tapper, R. (2008), 'Who Are the Kuchi? Nomad Self-Identities in Afghanistan'. *Journal of the Royal Anthropological Institute*, 14(1): 97–116.

TLO/UNHCR (2013), 'An Exploratory Study of Afghan Tazkera Ownership'. TLO/UNHCR.

UNHCR. (2005), 'Frequently Asked Questions' A Circular for Afghan Refugees from the United Nations High Commissioner for Refugees (UNHCR) / National Identification Cards (Tazkeras). See: http://www.unhcr.org/4497b1c12.pdf. https://web.archive.org/web/20161005132940/http://www.unhcr.org/4497b1c12.pdf

Wily, L. A. (2013), *Land, People and the State in Afghanistan: 2002–2012*. Kabul: AREU.

Wolniak, M. (2016). 'Travelling through Shades of Whiteness: Irish Travellers as Inferior Whites', in Kirkland, E. (ed.), *Shades of Whiteness*. Oxfordshire: Inter-Disciplinary Press, 119–31.

17

Inheriting Hegemonic Nobility: Urban Elite Lineage and Legitimacy

Adam H. Dehsabzi

Contemporary literature on Afghanistan often depicts a Manichean narrative of ethnic communities that are sharply demarcated and have been engaged in enduring struggles. Upon the US-led intervention in 2001, many international observers digested the Afghan conflict with comparisons to the breakup of Yugoslavia and thus, reduced the complex nuances of the conflict to an ethnic one. This is due, in part, to the complexity of the subject and the need to make it easily comprehensible, but it is also the result of manipulation for political ends by various groups. The central theme of this narrative misrepresents the reigns of hereditary Afghan monarchs as the domination of a single ethnicity collectively subjugating all other ethnic communities. The reiteration of these simplistic ideas has preserved them as an accepted fact within the discourse on the conflict, ultimately dominating the discipline of Afghanistan studies.

Consequently, ethnicity has been highly emphasized and little attention has been given to the multi-layered nature of identity in Afghanistan. A significant form of identity derives from subnational local demonyms that transcend ethnic differences, de-emphasize ethnicity as the fundamental variable of identity and reveal a sense of pluralism amongst Afghans. A multitude of socio-political factors throughout Afghanistan's history led many to identify themselves not by tribal or ethnic affiliation, but by the local demonym of their ancestral village, district, city, province or region. The 'Kabuli' identity is perhaps the most significant of these localized demonyms, epitomizing the complex obscurities of ethnic integration and identity in Afghanistan. As the centre of power, Kabul's cosmopolitan inhabitants were the primary citizens of the state and were much more privileged in comparison to rural Afghans. During the twentieth century, the Kabuli subculture served as the vanguard of ideas and gradual change in Afghan society. An exploration of the Kabuli identity, its legacy and the variables associated with identity challenges the ahistorical narrative that power and authority in Afghanistan were exclusive to a single dominant ethnicity. This widespread fallacy has cultivated a contentious sense of chauvinism for its beneficiaries and resentment for those it alienates, increasingly polarizing Afghans.

In the pages that follow, this chapter seeks to examine the formation of the cosmopolitan Kabuli subcultural identity and its significance for legitimizing power and authority in Afghanistan's contemporary history. The first section provides a historic outline of Kabul's diverse inhabitants and composition. The second section details the socio-political factors that subordinated the varying ethnic origins of Kabulis, and their formation into a distinct cosmopolitan urban collective. It then discusses the classist tendencies of urbanized Kabulis, and the socio-political implications of the city's exclusivist elite subculture. The third section explores the deep-rooted belief in the inherited nature of nobility in Afghan political culture. It underscores the significance of urban elitist lineages for Afghan rulers in the construction of a sense of legitimate authority and the sustenance of power. This valuable lineage is juxtaposed with the struggles of rulers with rural and proletariat lineages and their challenges with political legitimation. The final section concludes with an analysis of the resentment towards Kabul's classist urban elite and explores why this resentment has been reframed in terms of ethnic animosity. Ultimately, the chapter presents a contrarian perspective on power competition in Afghanistan and defies the 'ethnic hegemony' portrait with the counteracting notion of 'Kabuli hegemony'.

The Genesis of Cosmopolitan Kabul

The cherished Kabuli subculture emerged from a cosmopolitan ethos that encouraged urbanites to simply forget their background. Afghans often reminisce about Kabul as the melting pot of Afghanistan that integrated the ethnic diversity of the state like no other Afghan city could. These nostalgic recollections often allude to pre-war Kabul, emblematic of the country's romanticized 'golden era' from 1929 until 1978 (or 1992 for Afghan leftists and their sympathizers). Although many refer to this period to cite the prevalence of miniskirts or discotheques, it was also the pinnacle of the social integration of a diverse plethora of Afghans converging in cities.

Before the terms 'globalization' and 'interculturalism' came into popular use, the Afghan capital was described, as early as the middle of the nineteenth century, as cosmopolitan (Dalrymple 2013). Kabul sits at the intersection of various communities, with the Kohistani Tajik highlands to the north and the Ghilzai Pashtun heartland to the south and east, two mountainous rural regions without a historic urban centre or culture. With a rich history as the capital of Babur's Turco-Mongol Mughal dynasty (Schinasi 2016: 17), the city became the capital of the Pashtun Durrani Empire in 1776 with the support of the Turkic Shia Qizilbash cavalry (Barfield 2010: 105).

Kabul emerged as a modern capital from the ethnically heterogeneous city centre, referred to as Old Kabul. The most established community in Old Kabul was that of the Qizilbash based in the districts of Chindawol, Murad Khani and Bagh-e Ali-e Mardan (Schinasi 2016: 28), an area described as the 'Oxford of Afghanistan' due to its profoundly erudite inhabitants (Hanifi 2015: 1). Due to the royal clans' strong ties with the influential Qizilbash, the kindred of the Pashtun Muhammadzai monarchs and other Durrani aristocrats settled throughout the locality (Schinasi 2016: 32–3).

Old Kabul was also the settlement of the noble Sunni Kurdish tribes, whose district was eponymously named Rika Khana (Schinasi 2016: 34). The famed music quarter, Kharabat, was the district of the Indian Court musicians who were invited by Amir Sher Ali Khan (r. 1863-79) in the 1860s (Baily and Doubleday 1988: 114). Nearby were the districts known as 'Guzar-e Achakzaiha', named after the Kandahari Pashtun clan who inhabited the area (Karimi 2016: 742), and Shor Bazaar, where the influential Mojaddidi clan, of Arab ethnicity, resided (Schinasi 2016: 33). The Andarabi quarter was populated with Kohistani Tajiks originally from the Andarab valley in the northeastern region of Afghanistan (Schinasi 2016: 34).

After the conquest of Kashmir, a province of the Durrani Empire, by Ranjit Singh in 1819, Kabul became the home of Kashmiris fleeing the new Sikh ruler's purge of Durrani loyalists (Kakar 1997: 65). During the reigns of Habibullah Khan (r. 1901-19) and Amanullah Khan (r. 1919-29), Kabul experienced a rush of Ottoman military officers and administrators, as well as Indian Muslim teachers and jurists, who converged on the city to market their expertise to the Afghan kingdom (Ahmad 2013: 1). This was largely a result of the return of Afghan exiles in the early 1900s, such as the Musahiban and Tarzi families. The head of the Iraqi branch of the Qadiriyya Sufi Order and his clansmen also settled in Afghanistan during this time (Crews 2015: 92). After the Soviets defeated the Amirate of Bukhara in 1920, the last Uzbek amir and his aristocratic loyalists settled in Kabul, along with 200,000 other Central Asian Turkic refugees throughout Afghanistan. In this same period, some 30,000 Indian Muslims of the anti-British Khilafat movement were settled in Kabul, Parwan, Jalalabad, Paktia, Ghazni and Kunduz, whilst on their *hijrat* (migration) to protest the British occupation of Istanbul (Reetz 1995: 59).

A 1965 census shows that between 1954 and 1961, a mix of Tajiks, Pashtuns and Hazaras had migrated to Kabul from the provinces closest to Kabul (Dupree 1975: 409), such as Wardak, Parwan, Logar, Laghman, Kapisa, Nangarhar and Ghazni (Jung 1971: 8). Other smaller groups included the Afghan Hindus of Kabul, the Taimani Aimaqs whose settlement later became a suburb eponymously named after them and the Nooristanis who formed a critical part of the military (Katz 1984: 107).

How did these diverse groups assimilate into local populations, deemphasize their differences and, over time and generations, synthesize a uniquely urban Kabuli identity that epitomizes the nostalgic social cohesion of Afghanistan's 'golden era'?

Constructing a Kabuli Collective

The 'golden era' began to take shape in the aftermath of the chaos that ensued from the ousting of Amanullah Khan (r. 1919-29). Inspired by Mustafa Kemal in Turkey, Amanullah's radical and rushed secular reforms outraged the highly conservative population, especially the religious clergy. As king, the country's clergy, who historically bestowed the title of 'Amir-ul Mominin' ('Commander of the Faithful') to Afghan monarchs, legitimized obedience to his authority. His deviation from the ultraorthodox tenets of Islam ultimately provided justification for the clergy to endorse his dethroning. Following Amanullah's flight, Afghanistan experienced nine turbulent months of complete anarchy.

The brief period of instability ceased in October 1929 with the ascent of Nader Shah (r. 1929–33) to the throne, marking the beginning of five decades of peace until the Saur (communist) Revolution. Nader Shah's kingship required the support and appeasement of the very clergy that had discredited Amanullah Khan, most critically the Mojaddidi and Gailani clans who descended from the Arab Sufi Order (Lee 2018: 12). The new king and his government were legitimized by the clergy, who in exchange were granted authority over the interior ministry and justice system. Under Nader Shah, the Ministry of Justice became the domain of the Mojaddidi clan (Nadiri 2017: 102). Their status as non-Pashtun elites descending from a revered Sufi Order symbolized the supremacy of Islamic law, the common religion of all citizens irrespective of ethnic differences and personified the conflation of being Afghan with being a devout Muslim.[1]

For the new king, nothing appears to have been more important than the preservation of internal stability (Barfield 2010: 198). To prevent the lawlessness that preceded the new reign, obedience to the state became synonymous with obedience to Islam. The 1931 constitution formalized the supremacy of Islamic law (Lee 2018: 12). The sixth article stipulated that the king vowed to rule in accordance with Sharia law and for the state to strive for the protection of Islam (Olesen 1995: 176). While Amanullah's 1923 constitution was designed to transform state–society relations, Nader's 1931 constitution reflected the pre-existing distribution of power and reconfirmed the status quo (Olesen 1995: 176) instituted in 1880 by the authoritarian ruler Abdur Rahman Khan (r. 1880–1901) (Tarzi 2017: 134). Nader formed Afghanistan's first modern police force, the ideological 'Amr 'bi'l-Maruf', tasked with enforcing moral (i.e. religious) conduct, eradicating any semblance of Amanullah's unpopular reforms, and any hint of rebellion (Lee 2018: 511).

Nader's Musahiban dynasty went unchallenged and its reign prevailed for several decades, thus allowing Afghanistan to remain stable (Olesen 1995: 176). To prevent the confrontation between the conservative clergy and the ambitious reformists, the state was determined to create a strong military to act as a bulwark for the regime vis-à-vis conflicting segments of society and any other threats to the state. The government's Islamic credentials were critical to creating social cohesion and citizen compliance. Emphasizing the shared Islamic faith of the kingdom's subjects enabled a kind of historical continuity that was critical in obscuring ethnic differences and cultivating cosmopolitan subnational demonyms.

Sharia law was an instrument for the state to suppress any defiance of its authority, labelling dissent as a rejection of God's holy law. The gravity of Islam and the stigma of blasphemy made it invariably difficult for opponents to challenge the new reign. The use of religious sacrality to counteract the risk of anarchy enabled widespread calm and stability for the following five decades. By the early 1950s, this stability allowed the state to focus on economic development that largely advantaged Kabul. Such schemes aimed to transform Afghanistan from a pre-industrial and agricultural economy to a modern industrial and commercial society (Arefi 1975: 2). Along with the construction of asphalt and concrete roads, Kabul saw the development of new modern suburbs, health and educational facilities, and an airport in the city, all of which demanded a labour force of economic migrants from the provinces (Arefi 1975: 3). Throughout this period, the stability and economic opportunities enabled the movement of Afghans to various parts of the country, inducing the migration of new people from a variety of provinces and ethnicities into the cities, especially Kabul. Afghans from various provinces came to coexist in the same mosques, classrooms, bazaars, neighbourhoods and other urban institutions. The establishment of secondary boarding schools in Kabul welcomed selected top-performing graduates of provincial primary schools, as did the Military Academy and the newly established Kabul University (Shahrani 1984: 153–4). Students from a diverse cross-section of Afghan provinces mixed in Kabul's classrooms (Nadiri and Hakimyar 2018: 77).

After a few generations of living in Kabul and intermarrying with other Kabulis, the ethnic identity of the descendants of provincial migrants often became obscured. Identification as a 'Kabuli' whose family originated from a particular province connoted patrilineal descent (Rubin 1992: 79). Ethnic and linguistic identity became subordinate to familial, schooling, occupational, class and neighbourhood ties, generating an environment in which bonding across social categories became unremarkable (Nadiri and Hakimyar 2018: 78). These kinds of linguistic and social integration in Kabul may explain why political groups that were discredited as ethno-centric, such as Afghan Mellat and Sitam-e Milli, resonated little with urbanites (Kakar 1997: 57). Today, many Kabulis of the pre-civil war generations recall fondly the ethnic and provincial heterogeneity of the city's middle- and upper-class neighbourhoods (Sarwari and Ono 2022: 7). This lost social fabric is described in Akram Osman and Rahnaward Zaryab's acclaimed novels set in pre-war Kabul and similarly in Khaled Hosseini's second novel, set on a street in Kabul with diverse residents hailing from the provinces of Ghazni, Parwan, Kandahar and Herat.[2]

A significant by-product of the pluralistic Kabuli subculture was the gradual emergence of a meritocratic elite. By the mid-twentieth century, the government started to recruit younger cohorts based on talent, from the educated new generation graduating from Kabul University and Kabul's prestigious high schools. The most talented graduates received merit-based international scholarships and included recipients from non-elite backgrounds, including many non-Pashtuns and even some Hazaras raised in Kabul (Eberhard 1962: 8). An analysis of application files from the US Overseas Mission shows that almost 70 per cent of the elite sample were born in Kabul. Approximately 30 per cent were the sons of lower- or medium-ranking government employees, of which only 12 per cent were the children of government officials. Up to 45 per cent had received their highest degree at a vocational school, indicating an urban middle-class background (Eberhard 1962: 9). By the 1970s a small university-educated Hazara middle class had emerged in Kabul (Dorronsoro 2007: 13), including individuals such as Dr Sima Samar, Sultan Ali Keshtmand, Wahed Sarabi and Senator Nadir Ali Jaghori.

According to Giustozzi and Isaqzadeh (2011: 9), the Afghan government had become a 'moderate meritocracy' that recruited and promoted based on ability (alongside, of course, loyalty to the regime). Organic meritocracy undoubtedly contributed to the increasingly diverse political elite. Data from the period indicates that by 1963 non-Pashtuns accounted for almost 50 per cent of the Afghan political elite (Rubin 1992: 86). However, the most salient characteristic is that Pashtuns were overrepresented by the Persianized Kabul-based royal clan, while the non-Pashtun populations were overrepresented by Sunni and Farsiwan Kabuli elites (Dorronsoro 2007: 19). In other words, the primary beneficiary of the state was not one ethnic collective, but rather an urban collective of Kabulis who had access to educational and professional opportunities.

Meritocratic practices could be seen in the admission procedures for Kabul University. The university originally admitted students on an open enrolment basis, where formal qualifications were not required. In 1966, the university introduced a standardized general entrance examination that had a momentous impact on the composition and quality of university students (Dupree 1966: 4). In its debut year, the son of the president of the Lower House of the National Assembly and the daughter of the minister of defence failed the exam and were denied admission. Despite 'applied pressure', both decisions remained unchanged (Williams 1981: 247). In 1968, up to 2,000 secondary school students demonstrated because they had failed the exams (Dupree 1974: 5). As Nadiri (2017: 107) argues, the non-reversal of these demonstrated the state's adherence to the standardized examination as well as the value of university admission amongst Kabul's youth.

Although urbanization cultivated a meritocratic elite within the larger socially integrated Kabuli population by the early 1950s, it also advanced a class disparity that polarized urbanites from the rural majority. Historically a rather egalitarian society, the enduring class hierarchy that emerged in Afghanistan during the late nineteenth century centred on Abdur Rahman Khan and the Persianized Kabul branch of his Muhammadzai kindred (Barfield 2010: 157). The royal Muhammadzai clan were made *sharik-e dawlat* (partners of the state), and along with their close network of fellow Kabuli urbanites, became the state's privileged elite class. Since the turn of the twentieth century, it was this elite subset of diverse Kabulis that had embarked on the conceptualization of Afghan nationhood and a shared identity therein. Nascent ideas of Afghan nationalism and constitutional movements originated after the establishment of Lycée Habibia in 1904, the first modern institution for state-elite production. Many of the school's graduates became known as *roshan-fekran,* the Afghan variant of philosophes advocating 'enlightenment' reforms (Rasikh 2010: 3). For these educated Kabulis, nationalism was the path to modernity. For the non-Pashtun elite, nationalism was also a tool to advance their legal status and codify equality (Fazel 2017: 9).

The conceptualization of a national identity was the exclusive prerogative of Kabul's intelligentsia as it was primarily the educated urban elite who were acquainted with western philosophy (Rasikh 2010: 1). This ethnically diverse intelligentsia echoed the revolutionary secular Young Turks movement, calling themselves the 'Young Afghans', or 'Jawanan-e Afghan'. They planted the seeds of a shared national identity congruent with the state's interests (Naim 2023: 96). However, a state-constructed national identity would come to little fruition beyond theoretical design or superficial symbolism. This conceptualization remained unfathomable to many in the illiterate population and was never radically enforced in the ways Reza Khan and Mustafa Kemal pursued in Iran and Turkey. The state lacked such resources, prioritized tangible economic development and feared provoking the clergy with modernizing social change, having observed Amanullah's fate in that regard (Bezhan 2017: 181).

The state-constructed national ideology remained incoherent and weak with little rigorous execution. Instead, the distinguishable elite status of being a Kabuli inadvertently came to form its own Afghan archetype. This was largely due to the city residents' privilege and prestige as the primary citizens of the state. Though Kabul's population was only 1.8 per cent of the entire country in 1959, the city contained 73 per cent of the country's secondary school students (Rubin 1992: 80). Their subcultural urban etiquette morphed into an informal code of ideal Afghan conduct and came to epitomize the ideal Afghan citizenry. Kabulis had become the vanguards of gradual social change. The urban elite was at the forefront of many cautious avant-garde socio-cultural changes in the 'golden era', including the unveiling of women, the public participation of women in civil service, the adoption of western dress, the attainment of modern secular education, the subordination of ethnic identity and the destigmatization of music as a profession (Crews 2015: 190, 214). Efforts to emulate Kabul's powerful and glamorous elite meant that these social initiatives and trends trickled down at a gradual generational pace, shaping the rest of the city's upper- and middle-class families as well as the educated elites of other major cities (Burki 2013: 116).

Legitimizing Authority by Heredity and Descent

Even as colonial discourses have propagated a deceptive narrative about Afghanistan as ruled by a single dominant ethnic collective, the legacy of the Kabuli subculture challenges this unnuanced misconception. A critical examination of contemporary Afghan regimes suggests that legitimate power and authority have been intensely linked to proximity to Kabul's elite classes, rather than just to a particular ethnicity. Critically, in a society where family background was of major importance, belief in the inherited nature of nobility was integral to Afghan political culture (Edwards 2002: 34).

Despite being an ethnic Pashtun of the royal Muhammadzai clan, Nader Shah initially struggled to establish legitimacy for his ascent to the throne in 1930 as he was not a direct descendent of the celebrated king Dost Muhammad Khan (r. 1826–63). Nader's ascent meant that the descendants of Dost Muhammad were being replaced by his brother's offspring. In response to this perceived dynastic change, supporters of the dethroned Amanullah Khan accused Nader of being a treacherous usurper (Barfield 2010: 195). To mitigate this vulnerability, Nader emphasized his Muhammadzai lineage to evoke legitimacy via his clan's status as *sharik-e dawlat* (partners of the state). When Nader's dynastic line was overthrown in the 1978 Saur Revolution, the Afghan Marxists would present it as retribution for Nader's illegitimate usurpation of Amanullah's throne.

In 1963 Zahir Shah (r. 1933–73) began his experiment with constitutional democracy and outlawed members of the royal family from holding government positions. The first non-royal to be appointed as prime minister, succeeding the king's cousin and uncles, was Dr Muhammad Yusuf (Jalali 2006: 92). An ethnic Tajik of non-royal lineage, Dr Yusuf was a Kabul-born urbanite and belonged to the elite classes with close proximity to the monarchy. He was educated in the prestigious Lycée Nejat, had earned a PhD in Physics from Germany and prior to becoming prime minister had served as Professor at Kabul University and in numerous senior government positions (Adamec 2003: 261). His appointment was based on these credentials.

Dr Yusuf's rise as an urbanite Tajik stands in stark contrast to the struggle for legitimacy faced by Noor Muhammad Taraki, the rural and rustic Pashtun leader of the People's Democratic Party of Afghanistan (the PDPA, an Afghan Marxist-Leninist party), which seized power in the April 1978 revolution. Taraki was born in Ghazni province to an impoverished family of Pashtun peasants lacking any noble heritage (Steele 2011: 67), having only received a basic education in a village mosque (Adamec 2003: 368). To stress his humble origins and connection to the impoverished Afghan masses, Taraki's official biography sentimentalized the fact that he did not own any land beyond a modest one-story mud house (Edwards 2002: 43).

During its short-lived rule, Taraki's populist Khalq faction of the PDPA portrayed itself as a 'people's' party leading a proletariat revolution, liberating oppressed peasants from Kabul's profligate bourgeoisie who had ruled over the rural masses with no credential beyond their lineage.[3] Archival propaganda footage in the aftermath of the Saur Revolution explicitly depicted ethnic and religious minorities (namely Sikhs, Hazaras and rural Pashtuns) rallying in support of Taraki, proudly amplifying their provincial customs and sartorial traditions as the beneficiaries of the new Marxist regime. Such rhetoric fatally alienated the PDPA from the urban intelligentsia, compromised their power and undermined their legitimacy (Barfield 2010: 341).

In fact, Taraki's accentuated rural lineage was the subject of widespread clandestine mockery throughout Kabul. Anecdotal jokes spread about his uncouth wife occupying the royal palace, confusing waffle ice cream cones for cups, storing shoes in the shelves of the royal palace's refrigerators and being dumbfounded by the palace's lack of an outdoor clay tandoor. The jibes in this classist ridicule represented an allusion to the nine-month reign of Habibullah Kalakani (r. 1929), an uneducated Kohistani Tajik bandit famous as the only non-Pashtun and non-Durrani king in Afghanistan's history. Accounts of Kalakani's brief rule in 1929 document the villager as overwhelmed by luxurious European commodities in the royal palace, confusing a billiard table for a bed, a water closet for a dining room and a porcelain chamber pot for a soup bowl (Kātib Hazārah 1999: 49). The derisive nickname he is remembered by, 'Bacha-e Saqao', literally translates to 'son of the water carrier' and alludes to his inferior, non-urban, humble parentage. To legitimize him as a monarch and forge his proximity to the elite, there were attempts to arrange Kalakani's marriage into the royal Muhammadzai clan (Barfield 2010: 192).

Kalakani's illegitimacy and dethroning are often exclusively attributed to his non-Pashtun and Kohistani Tajik ethnicity, a conclusion that has cultivated a divisive legacy of chauvinism from his critics and bitter resentment on the part of his sympathizers. However, like the Pashtun Taraki, the Tajik Kalakani was largely undermined on account of his unsophisticated rural lineage and proved unable to attain legitimacy due to deep-rooted classist prejudices among Kabulis. Given the derision Taraki faced, one ought not to presume that Kalakani would have attained legitimacy or sustained power had he been a Pashtun with the same plebeian roots. The comparisons to Kalakani threatened Taraki and the ruling Khalq faction. Just as Kalakani had been overthrown by the exiled Nader Shah in cooperation with the religious Mojaddidi clan, Khalqis feared that Nader's exiled son in Rome, Zahir Shah, could topple the PDPA and regain power once again with the new generation of Mojaddidis in Kabul (Edwards 2002: 75). In early 1979, the overwhelming majority of the Mojaddidi family's adult males were arrested and executed on the orders of PDPA as a pre-emptive measure (Edwards 2002: 81).

A number of examples suggest, in fact, a close correlation between authority and elite patrilineal descent. The 1973 coup technically transformed Afghanistan from a monarchy to a republic, but because it was instigated by the prince-turned-president Daoud Khan, many observers perceived it as a continuation of the Muhammadzai dynasty (Barfield 2010: 211). So much so that the PDPA described Daoud's overthrown Republic in 1978 as 'the last vestige of the cruel monarchy'. Although he allied himself with the controversial Afghan leftists, Daoud's authority was not disputed as his royal *sardar* (ruler) lineage represented a familiar, respected and credible status-quo. Moreover, the lineage of Soviet-backed Babrak Karmal did not generate the same denigration as Taraki's lineage had done. Karmal was an urbanite Kabuli with Kashmiri ancestry, categorizing him as Tajik (Kakar 1997: 65). Being *general-zada* (the son of an army general) with connections to the monarchy, a popular law student at Kabul University in the 1950s, renowned for exceptional oration, Karmal belonged to the city's intelligentsia and bureaucratic elite (Steele 2011: 68). While his non-Pashtun ethnicity did arouse curiosity, it was not the source of his fragile legitimacy. It is, in fact, worth noting that a multitude of texts incorrectly describe Karmal as a Persianized Pashtun, due to his ethnically obscure Kabuli identity.[4] Ultimately, it was Karmal's installation by the invading Soviet forces that tarnished his legitimacy, and, to a lesser degree, his notoriety amongst Kabulis as an infamous atheist, drinker and womanizer. In fact, Karmal's opponents compared him to Shah Shuja (r. 1839–42), the hated nineteenth-century Sadozai Pashtun king who was installed by and dependent on the invading British troops (Barfield 2010: 237).

Karmal's successor, Dr Najibullah, was also weakened by the stigma of Soviet backing, communism and especially his notoriety as the brutal head of the PDPA's feared secret police. This was despite Najib being a privileged Pashtun born in Kabul, the son of a well-connected civil servant, the grandson of a renowned war veteran, a graduate from the elite Lycée Habibia and Kabul Medical School and the husband of a member of the royal clan (Adamec 2003: 273). In his quest for national reconciliation after the Soviet withdrawal, Dr Najibullah appealed to several influential Afghans in exile, such as former king Zahir Shah and former prime minister Yusuf (Khybari 2021: 103), and appointed a few renowned politically neutral intellectuals as cabinet ministers (Hyman 1992: 274). Alongside his engagement with rural Afghans in the provinces as a form of public diplomacy, this was an attempt to project a reformed image, to dilute the communist repute of his government and to legitimize it by way of well-respected non-leftist figures.[5] The common denominator amongst these high-profile figures was not their ethnicity, rather it was that they were all from the urban intelligentsia. Dr Najibullah appeared to consider it prudent to engage with these former elites in the service of saving his regime given its near-total estrangement from the war-weary population.

Following the overthrow of the PDPA in 1992, neither the Pashtun Gulbuddin Hekmatyar nor the Tajik Burhanuddin Rabbani had significant nationwide legitimacy, beyond their small constituencies, to establish respect for central authority in the new post-PDPA Islamic government (Edwards 2002: 282). Despite being of two sizable ethnic categories, both Hekmatyar and Rabbani were of rural stock with insignificant lineages and little connection to the urban elite (Edwards 2002: 265). Their families were not socially connected, well-known or distinguished. Hekmatyar and Rabbani were the first generation of their families to relocate from the provinces to the city. As provincial boarding students at Kabul University, their rural backgrounds were automatically accentuated and demarcated them from local Kabuli students (Sands and Qazizai 2019: 40, 75). Before the PDPA's collapse, a 1987 survey found that 70 per cent of Afghan refugees preferred the return of Zahir Shah as king to lead Afghanistan after the Soviet withdrawal rather than any major mujahidin faction (Sands and Qazizai 2019: 227).

It would be the Kabul-born Sibghatullah Mojaddidi, leading a relatively small monarchist faction, who would win the most support and be deemed an appropriate president of the post-PDPA interim government (Sands and Qazizai 2019: 240). Despite his membership in the much smaller ethnic Arab minority, Mojaddidi's advantage arguably came from his urban elitist clan's close affiliation to the royal family. His family's renowned role in generating the influential clergymen whose endorsement had long been critical in legitimizing Afghan monarchs would have been of particular help. Mojaddidi, in contrast to the other factional leaders, represented the most neutral contender deemed to have much more nationwide acceptance. Like Daoud in 1973, Mojaddidi's lineage evoked a sense of continuity vis-à-vis a familiar status quo.

The cosmopolitanism of the Kabuli identity was once again evident during the Bonn Conference of 2001. The Rome Group was a monarchist delegation of exiled Kabuli elites representing Zahir Shah (Barfield 2010: 283). The group included Dr Sima Samar, a Kabul-raised Hazara physician, and Rona Yusuf Mansuri, the daughter of Prime Minister Dr Yusuf. Despite his weak rule, there was an initial appetite for the restoration of Zahir Shah as a symbolically unifying head of state to defuse the ethnic tensions of the 1990s (Barfield 2010: 291). The Rome Group later selected Dr Abdul Satar Sirat, a Kabuli Uzbek jurist, as its proposed president for the new republic (Steele 2011: 260). Instead, the United States opted for Hamid Karzai as a Pashtun figurehead for a Northern Alliance-dominated government. The selection of Karzai accommodated the Rome Group not because of his ethnicity, but his proximity to the elite through his credentials as Mojaddidi's trusted political advisor and the spokesman of his pro-monarchy mujahidin party.

In retrospect, these examples from recent history challenge the common conception that manufacturing legitimacy to rule Afghanistan is largely contingent upon ethnic identity. Rather, there appears to be a salient trend amongst Afghan leaders, irrespective of their ethnicity, to establish their political credibility via their ancestral affiliation, membership or proximity to Kabul's elite classes and urban intelligentsia. This trend undermines the prevalent notion of ethnic hegemony in Afghanistan as *the* defining variable in power politics.

Fermenting Separate Ethno-Political Consciousnesses

Given the classist inflections of the Kabuli elite identity described above, Marxism would tap into the vast socio-economic disparities between urban and rural Afghans and the social hierarchy imposed by the heritability of nobility. In particular, the ideal of a classless society promised distinction on the basis of merit rather than ancestry. After all, the Kabuli subculture largely excluded ethnic Hazaras and emanated a pomposity that stigmatized features of rural identity, such as speaking Pashto or not speaking Farsi in a Kabuli accent. Much of Afghanistan's enduring provincial stereotypes and ethnic insults reflect a Kabuli orientation with respect to non-Kabulis rooted primarily in urban classism with indirect undertones of ethnic prejudice.

Leftist movements nurtured rural resentment, as their political ambitions depended on support from these marginalized communities (Misdaq 2008: 236). For rural Pashtuns who only spoke Pashto, the leftist rhetoric depicted the royals and Kabul's political elite as treacherous Persianized Pashtuns who discriminated against them linguistically and limited opportunities in favour of Persian speakers. For rural non-Pashtuns, the left portrayed the monarchy and Kabuli elites as dominated exclusively by Pashtuns who had oppressed ethnic minorities for centuries. Although successive Afghan kings were patrilineally ethnic Pashtuns, their mother tongue and administrative court language was Persian (Nawid 2012: 34). The emergence of modern centralized states and economic modernization made upward social mobility contingent upon adopting the culture of the dominant group (Fearon and Laitin 2003: 78). Language served as an instrument of domination as Afghan monarchs' established political and economic power structures were articulated in Persian. They privileged access to these structures largely through Persian rather than their ancestral Pashto (Hanifi 2004: 308). The complexity of Kabul's urbanite subculture simultaneously validated multiple conflicting narratives that actually sustained power: Kabul could be justifiably described as either a Pashtun city, a Persian city, a Persian-speaking city ruled by Pashtuns or a city where Persianized Pashtuns ruled (Hanifi 2022: 4–5). Perhaps these concurrent, competing and contradictory truths about Kabul's obscure identity epitomize Afghanistan's broader complexities.

The Soviet occupation brought a more systematic emphasis on ethnicity. The Soviets considered northern Afghanistan to be within their sphere of influence due to common ethnic kin on both sides of the Soviet-Afghan border (Lee 2018: 556). In order to secure their supply route from their border to Kabul, the Soviets and their client regime exploited the underlying insecurities of non-Pashtuns in northern Afghanistan (Kakar 1997: 182). The Ministry of Tribal Affairs and Nationalities was established to portray the PDPA as an emancipatory pro-minority government (Kakar 1997: 181). This was an attempt to gain the northern non-Pashtun population's support for the regime and to replicate in Afghanistan the superficial nationality models at play in

Central Asia (Kakar 1997: 274). The Soviets also sought a security buffer in the north, fearing a victory that would empower Gulbuddin Hekmatyar, the leader of the largest and most fundamentalist mujahidin faction. Such a win would risk inspiring Central Asia's disenfranchised Muslims to revolt and establish Islamist regimes (Sands and Qazizai 2019: 236).

Similarly, the mujahidin factions themselves also loosely recruited along ethnic lines. This was influenced by the Pakistani intelligence that organized the influx of Afghan refugees along ethnic lines and designated their management to mujahidin factions that represented the simplistic categories (Kakar 1997: 276). Having supported the Jordanian Armed Forces against the Palestine Liberation Organization (PLO) in 1970, the Pakistani government feared the demographic threat a large refugee population could pose and feared an informal Afghan state emerging within its territory. To mitigate this threat, the Zia-ul Haq regime distributed differently coloured ID cards to Afghan refugees based on their ethnicity in an effort to prevent the emergence of a single united constituency (Alimia 2019: 399, 417).

During the Soviet occupation, Kabul became a haven for refugees fleeing the mujahidin warfare and Soviet aerial bombardments in the rural provinces (Barfield 2010: 242). By the onset of the civil war, a considerable proportion of the city's cosmopolitan middle and upper classes had fled, and many of the last of them were likely part of the estimated 500,000 to 700,000 people (Nadiri and Hakimyar 2018: 82; Tarzi 1993: 165) who escaped the city by 1993 (Dorronsoro 2007: 12). The mujahidin's territorial ethnic violence in Kabul obliterated the city's cosmopolitan fabric and superficially sharpened ethnic differences. The factional violence forced residents to evacuate districts controlled by non-co-ethnic mujahidin militias, dividing the city along ethnic cleavages – a tragedy resembling ethnic cleansing and urbicide. Although much of the violence during the civil war was ethnically motivated, reducing it to a conflict between domineering Pashtuns and defiant non-Pashtuns does a disservice to its complexity (Rubin 1994: 187). For much of the four-year civil war, the largely Pashtun militia, Ittehad, was allied with the largely Kohistani Tajik militia, Jamiat (Sands and Qazizai 2019: 324). These two factions fiercely fought against the triple alliance composed of the Hazara militia Wahdat, the Uzbek militia Junbish and the largely Pashtun militia Hizb-e Islami (Sands and Qazizai 2019: 347).

Meanwhile, other Pashtun factions (such as those led by Yunus Khalis and Jalaluddin Haqqani) remained neutral and pledged allegiance to Jamiat's government, whilst Hizb-e Islami's Tajik deputy did not defect to Jamiat in ethnic solidarity (Sands and Qazizai 2019: 322). A closer examination of the civil war's factional dynamics reveals that many of the mujahidin commanders recruited their co-provincials or native districts locals into their militias (Dorronsoro 2007: 15). This highlights the enduring significance of local identities and ties, in contrast to ethnic affinity (Christia 2012). Ultimately, the civil war was a series of clashes between a conglomerate of rural Afghans, all of whom were historically marginalized in the periphery of Kabul's powerful elite.

Later, the Taliban's repressive regime exacerbated the ethnic animosities inflamed by the mujahidin. Like Nader Shah and the Mojaddidi family in 1930, the Taliban's emphasis on Islamic law's supremacy was a mechanism to enforce stability, end the anarchic civil war, assert themselves as an undisputed authority and conflate opposition to their rule with a blasphemous disobedience to Islam. Not only was the Taliban's clergy-led government unprecedented in Afghanistan's entire history, so too was a regime exclusively dominated by parochial rural Pashtuns in the country's twentieth-century history. The violence and insecurity that Afghanistan had endured since 1978 prevented the free movement of Afghans, limiting interactions with others across the country and therefore largely alienated the new generations from one another. Due to the insecurity caused by war, the disconnection between Afghanistan's regions helps to explain why rural communities were vulnerable to Taliban propaganda.

Although they had monopolized power, the Taliban's peasant roots deprived them of legitimacy. The Taliban perceived most non-Pashtuns as conspiring with the ousted ethnic factions of the mujahidin, with whom they were fighting in a new civil war. Meanwhile, Jamiat interpreted its ousting in 1996 by the Pashtun Taliban as a repeat of fellow Kohistani Tajik Kalakani's dethroning in 1929. This belief was validated by the few Pashtun intellectuals exiled in the West who welcomed their ascent, if not for ideological reasons but as an opportunity to reinstate the (Pashtun) monarchy (Crews and Tarzi 2008: 25, 27). For isolated communities that had gone years without interacting across ethnicity due to violence and insecurity, the Taliban's cruel and unjust rule reinvigorated their prejudices.

In the aftermath of 9/11 and the Taliban's collapse, western media and policy makers viewed Afghanistan's ethnic puzzle as the main source of its instability. As a consequence, the international community's strategy to resolve an ostensibly ethnic conflict was to ensure a well-balanced representation of ethnicities in the country's new political architecture (Schetter 2016: 465). Throughout the Republic's two decades, the effective imposition of ethnic quotas turned ethnicity into a tool for political mobilization and made democratic elections increasingly look like an ethnic competition (Schetter 2005a: 11). This was a far cry from the emergent meritocracy of the pre-war era. However, the ethnicization of national politics enabled former mujahidin warlords to assert that they were the representatives of their ethnic communities. While outwardly portraying their political parties as Islamic and trans-ethnic, the exonerated warlords regularly reframed any criticism of their actions as an attack on their entire ethnic group. Highly discredited for their brutality during the civil war, the political survival of mujahidin warlords depended on the mobilization and sustenance of ethno-nationalist identity politics. This institutionalized ethnocentrism inflamed the resentment many already harboured towards the mujahidin: these leaders had escaped justice for their war crimes and now ruled with impunity with the support of the West (Karimi 2016: 739).

Following Karzai's second term, the 2014 presidential elections caused ethnic dissatisfactions to resurface. The two primary nominees subtly capitalized on grievances as part of their campaign strategy, thus turning the election into an ethnic power competition (Barfield 2022: 347). Abdullah Abdullah's rhetoric drew upon Kohistani Tajiks who saw Karzai's installation – at the expense of the previous president, Burhanuddin Rabbani – as evidence of Pashtun hegemony. Similarly, Ashraf Ghani's messaging exploited disillusioned Pashtuns who viewed Karzai as a facade for a Tajik-dominated Northern Alliance regime that systematically discriminated against

Pashtuns. After disputed results and allegations of electoral fraud, the United States mediated a power-sharing agreement that formed an extra-constitutional National Unity Government (NUG). The triumphant Ghani largely appointed technocrats from the Afghan diaspora who had been in exile for decades and a new generation of hyphenated Afghans raised in the West (Barfield 2022: 349). This diaspora network played an enormous role in weaponizing ethnicity to undermine or sideline other ethnically motivated power bases within the NUG,[6] leading to accusations of Ghani discriminating against non-Pashtuns and southern Durrani Pashtuns in favour of his own eastern Ghilzai Pashtun loyalists (Barfield 2022: 362).

The emergence of ethnicity as the predominant form of socio-political stratification and heterogeneity in Afghanistan is reflected in the contrasting references to social diversity in constitutions before and after the 1978 revolution (Sharma 2017: 18). The 1964 constitution, drafted during Zahir Shah's parliamentary monarchy in the pre-war era, ambiguously recognized diversity within the Afghan state without specifying its various forms. The 1987 constitution, drafted by the Soviet-backed PDPA prior to their withdrawal, based this diversity on ethnic and tribal terms. The 2004 constitution of the US-backed Republic recognized diversity strictly along ethnic lines, explicitly listing fourteen ethnic categories (Sharma 2017: 19). The Republic's constitution went a step further by stipulating that all fourteen ethnicities had to be mentioned in the national anthem's lyrics. The notion of diversity transformed from being an ambiguous and multi-layered concept by urban elites during the pre-war era, to being exclusively defined by ethnicity during foreign occupations. This development reflects the foreign influence on the codification of ethnic stratification, an effort not unrelated to divide and conquer tactics long associated with imperial encounters the world over.

The systematic measures under both the Soviet- and American-backed regimes, as well as the ethnic fragmentation and politicization during the 1990s interval between the two foreign occupations, not only mainstreamed the use of ethnonyms but also heightened a greater sense of awareness to ethnic identity (Misdaq 2008: 22). The new bureaucratic elite and urban middle class frequently came to think of their political interests through the prism of ethnicity. But for the Afghan laymen who were seldom beneficiaries of these corrupt puppet regimes, ethnonationalism was often associated with unpopular invading militaries and their despised Afghan oligarchs.

Conclusion

The decades of stability that Afghanistan experienced before 1978 induced a diverse cross-section of Afghans to migrate to various urban and provincial centres, where coexistence in civic amenities led to assimilation and integration over time. The increased diversity heightened identities that transcended and de-emphasized difference. In the process, subnational demonyms and regional subcultures obscured major ethnic identities. This was especially prevalent in the city of Kabul, where the cosmopolitan dynamics of urban living in this timeframe fostered a collectivist 'Kabuli' subculture and subordinated ethnic differences among its diverse residents.

As the centre of power, intellectual pursuit, opportunity and social advancement in Afghanistan, the Kabuli subculture possessed a degree of soft power to spread certain norms and influence gradual change throughout the country. The obsolescence of ethnonyms and the prevalence of local demonyms was one such influence. Consequently, till today many Afghans beyond Kabul identify themselves not by tribal or ethnic affiliation, but by the demonym of their ancestral village, district, city, province or region. An overemphasis on ethnicity or even an inquiry into ancestral background continues to be taboo in many contexts. Rather, subnational demonyms such as Herati, Kandahari, Logari, Mazari, Jalalabadi or Shamali have endured as a prime form of identity, especially in an apolitical context. Due to the persistence of inter-ethnic marriage throughout the generations, many Afghans remain uncertain of their precise ethnic composition. One analyst recalled from his travels to Afghanistan in 1997 that 'it was usual among Afghans to name the province when explaining one's origins and not to refer to one's ethnicity' (Schetter 2005b: 75). Many Afghans feel a closer affinity with those from the same city, province or village, irrespective of their ethnic differences, than with their co-ethnics across the country.

A critical re-examination of Afghanistan's recent past challenges many of the prevalent beliefs about social cohesion, identity and power. It reveals that the emphases on religion, political stability, urbanization and socio-economic opportunities in the pre-war era allowed Afghans of diverse backgrounds to interact and coexist. Over time, new subnational demonyms and regional subcultures often transcended different ethnic origins. Nowhere was this more evident than in the capital, Kabul. The legacy of Kabul's diverse and integrated identity challenges the fallacy that Afghanistan can only be ruled by a single ethnicity. A scrutiny of contemporary Afghan political figures underscores a salient trend of legitimacy as contingent upon proximity to Kabul's urban elite, irrespective of ethnicity. Kabul's diverse, distinguished and romanticized identity may even serve as a testament to the potential for a cohesive and pluralist Afghanistan.

More critically, and contrary to mainstream discourse, the conflict in Afghanistan was not instigated by a struggle between eternally demarcated and hostile ethnic groups. Rather, four decades of ceaseless violence and foreign interference crystallized ethnic identities, a rupture from the past where such differences were not at the fore and coexisted with multiple other layers of Afghan identity. Rather than discotheques and miniskirts, perhaps discourse on Afghanistan's pre-war era should attend more to the ethno-linguistic integration and cohesion that emerged in various parts of the country, starting with the paradigmatic case of Kabul. In contrast to an emphasis on reductive ethnic categories as a source of opportunity, power and legitimacy, a distinct orientation towards geographic space and place as a binding social agent reveals the means by which trans-ethnic bonds emerged between Afghans.

Notes

1   Among the seven anti-Soviet mujahidin parties, two out of the three pro-monarchy factions were led by ethnic Arabs of the Mojaddidi and Gailani families.

2. See Khaled Hosseini's (2007) novel *A Thousand Splendid Suns*, Akram Osman's novel *Our Street* (Persian: کوچه ما, transliterated to *Kochaye Mā*) and Rahnaward Zaryab's (1980) short story 'The Purple Bangles'.
3. The front page of the *Kabul Times* newspaper after the Saur Revolution announcing Taraki's cabinet, composed largely of Afghan leftists with rural and working-class origins: https://www.marxist.com/images/stories/afghanistan/1978.jpg.
4. A multitude of texts mistake Babrak Karmal's ethnicity as a Persianzed Pashtun. For the Afghan laymen, it was difficult to decipher his ethnicity and hence, either claim was credible. According to Kakar (1997: 103), Karmal himself would take advantage of his obscure ethnic origins to broaden his appeal. However, among Kabul's intelligentsia, it was widely known that he had Kashmiri roots (paternally) and was categorized as Tajik.
5. In the lead up to the Soviet withdrawal, President Najibullah appointed prominent urban intellectuals as cabinet ministers who were not members of the PDPA. Among them were Hamidullah Tarzi (of the royal clan), Dr Mehr M. Ejazi (a French-educated professor of medicine) and Saleha Faruq-Etemadi (of the royal clan and former parliamentarian under Zahir Shah).
6. See 2017 Reuters article reporting accusations of ethnic bias in the Afghan government under Ashraf Ghani's leadership: https://www.reuters.com/article/us-afghanistanpolitics/leaked-memo-fuels-accusations-of-ethnic-bias-in-afghan-government-idUSKCN1BW15U/.

References

Adamec, L. W. (2003), *Historical Dictionary of Afghanistan*. 3rd edition. Lanham, MD: Scarecrow Press.

Ahmed, F. (2013), 'Rule of Law Experts in Afghanistan: A Socio-Legal History of the First Afghan Constitution and the Indo-Ottoman Nexus in Kabul, 1860–1923'. PhD dissertation, University of California, Berkeley.

Alimia, S. (2019), 'Performing the Afghanistan–Pakistan Border through Refugee ID Cards'. *Geopolitics*, 24(2): 391–425.

Arefi, A. G. (1975), 'Urban Policies, Planning and Implementation in Kabul, Afghanistan'. PhD dissertation, Indiana University.

Baily, J. and Doubleday, V. (1988), 'Modèles d'imprégnation Musicale En Afghanistan', in *Cahiers de Musiques Traditionnelles*, 112–24. https://journals.openedition.org/ethnomusicologie/2301

Barfield, T. (2010), *Afghanistan: A Cultural and Political History*. 1st edition Princeton, NJ: Princeton University Press.

Barfield, T. (2022), *Afghanistan: A Cultural and Political History*. 2nd edition. Princeton, NJ: Princeton University Press.

Bezhan, F. (2017), 'Nationalism, Not Islam: The "Awaken Youth" Party and Pashtun Nationalism', in Green, N. (ed.), *Afghanistan's Islam: From Conversion to the Taliban*. Oakland, CA: University of California Press, 163–86.

Burki, S. (2013), *The Politics of State Intervention: Gender Politics in Pakistan, Afghanistan, and Iran*. Lanham, MD: Lexington Books.

Christia, F. (2012), *Alliance Formation in Civil Wars*. New York, NY: Cambridge University Press.

Crews, R. D. and Tarzi, A. (2008), *The Taliban and the Crisis of Afghanistan*. Cambridge, MA: Harvard University Press.

Crews, R. D. (2015), *Afghan Modern: The History of a Global Nation*. Cambridge, MA: The Belknap Press of Harvard University Press.

Dalrymple, W. (2013), *The Return of a King: The Battle for Afghanistan*. London: Bloomsbury.

Dorronsoro, G. (2007), 'Kabul at War (1992–1996): State, Ethnicity and Social Classes'. *South Asia Multidisciplinary Academic Journal* [Online], Free-Standing Articles, Online since 14 October 2007.

Dupree, L. (1966), 'Afghanistan, 1966: Comments on a Comparatively Calm State of Affairs with Reference to the Turbulence of Late 1965'. American Universities Field Staff (AUFS) Report.

Dupree, L. (1974), 'The Emergence of Technocrats in Modern Afghanistan'. American Universities Field Staff (AUFS) Report.

Dupree, L. (1975), 'Settlement and Migration Patterns in Afghanistan: A Tentative Statement'. *Modern Asian Studies*, 9(3): 397–413.

Eberhard, W. (1962), 'Afghanistan's Young Elite'. *Asian Survey*, 1(12): 3–22.

Edwards, D. B. (2002), *Before Taliban: Genealogies of the Afghan Jihad*. Berkeley, CA: University of California Press.

Fazel, S. M. (2017), 'Ethnohistory of the Qizilbash in Kabul: Migration, State, and a Shi'a Minority'. PhD dissertation, Indiana University.

Fearon, J. D. and Laitin, D. D. (2003), 'Ethnicity, Insurgency, and Civil War'. *The American Political Science Review*, 97(1): 75–90.

Giustozzi, A. and Isaqzadeh, M. (2011), 'Afghanistan's Para-Military Policing in Context: The Risks of Expediency'. *Afghanistan Analysts Network*.

Hanifi, M. J. (2004), 'Editing the Past: Colonial Production of Hegemony through the "Loya Jerga" in Afghanistan'. *Iranian Studies*, 37(2): 295–322.

Hanifi, S. M. (2015), 'Making Space for Shi'ism in Afghanistan's Public Sphere and State Structure'. *Perspectives on History*, 1 July 2015, https://www.historians.org/research-and-publications/perspectives-on-history/summer-2015/making-space-for-shiism-in-afghanistans-public-sphere-and-state-structure.

Hanifi, S. M. (2022), 'Deciphering the History of Modern Afghanistan', in *Oxford Research Encyclopedia of Asian History*. Oxford: Oxford University Press.

Hyman, A. (1992), *Afghanistan under Soviet Domination, 1964–91*. 3rd edition. London: Palgrave Macmillan.

Jalali, B. (2006), 'Afghanistan: 1963–1973'. PhD dissertation, University of California, Berkeley.

Jung, C. L. (1971), 'Observations on the Patterns and Procedures of Rural-Urban Migrations to Kabul'. The Afghanistan Council of the Asia Society, Occasional Paper 2.

Kakar, M. H. (1997), *Afghanistan: The Soviet Invasion and the Afghan Response, 1979–1982*. Berkeley, CA: University of California Press.

Karimi, A. (2016), 'Street Fights: The Commodification of Place Names in Post-Taliban Kabul City'. *Annals of the American Association of Geographers*, 106(3): 738–53.

Kateb-Hazara, F. M. [1930] (1999), *Kabul Under Siege: Fayz Muhammad's Account of the 1929 Uprising*. 1st edition. Princeton, NJ: Markus Wiener Publishers.

Katz, D. J. (1984), 'Responses to Central Authority in Nuristan', in Canfield, R. L. and Shahrani, M. N. (eds.), *Revolutions and Rebellions in Afghanistan: Anthropological Perspectives*. Bloomington, IN: Indiana University Press, 94–118.

Khybari, M. (2021), 'The Specter of Overture', in Rasikh, J-S. (ed.), *In Search of Peace for Afghanistan*. Kabul AF: Kakar History Foundation Press, 102–13.

Lee, J. L. (2018), *Afghanistan: A History from 1260 to the Present*. London, UK: Reaktion Books.

Misdaq, N. (2008), *Afghanistan Political Frailty and External Interference*. New York: Routledge.

Nadiri, K. H. (2017), 'Brokers, Bureaucrats, and the Quality of Government: Understanding Development and Decay in Afghanistan and Beyond'. PhD dissertation, Johns Hopkins University.

Nadiri, K. H. and Hakimyar, M. F. (2018), 'Lineages of the Urban State: Locating Continuity and Change in Post-2001 Kabul', in Shahrani, M. N. (ed.), *Afghanistan: Assessing the Impact of 35 Years of Wars and Violence on Social Institutions*. Bloomington, IN: Indiana University Press, 77–101.

Naim, H. (2023), 'The Genesis of the Afghan Mashrūtah Movement'. *Afghanistan*, 6(1): 73–101.

Nawid, S. (2012), 'Language Policy in Afghanistan: Linguistic Diversity and National Unity', in Schiffman H. F. (ed.), *Language Policy and Language Conflict in Afghanistan and Its Neighbors: The Changing Politics of Language Choice*. Leiden: Brill, 31–52.

Olesen, A. (1995), *Islam & Politics in Afghanistan*. 1st edition. Richmond, UK: Curzon Press.

Rakish, J. S. (2010), 'Nationalism in Afghanistan – A Descriptive Analysis'. Middle Eastern Communities and Migration Student Research Paper Series 01, Building Knowledge in and of Afghanistan, 1–10.

Reetz, D. (1995), *Hijrat: The Flight of the Faithful. A British File on the Exodus of Muslim Peasants from North India to Afghanistan in 1920*. Berlin: de Gruyter.

Rubin, B. (1992), 'Political Elites in Afghanistan: Rentier State Building, Rentier State Wrecking'. *International Journal of Middle East Studies*, 24(1): 77–99.

Rubin, B. (1994), 'Afghanistan in 1993: Abandoned but Surviving'. *Asian Survey*, 34(2): 185–90.

Sands, C. and Qazizai, F. (2019), *Night Letters: Gulbuddin Hekmatyar and the Afghan Islamists Who Changed the World*. London: Hurst & Company.

Sarwari, F. and Ono, H. (2022), 'An Analysis of Urban Ethnic Inclusion of Master Plans – In the Case of Kabul City, Afghanistan'. *Urban Science*, 7(1): 1–17.

Schetter, C. (2005a), 'Ethnicity and the Political Reconstruction in Afghanistan'. ZEF Working Paper, 3.

Schetter, C. (2005b), 'Ethnoscapes, National Territorialisation, and the Afghan War'. *Geopolitics*, 10(1): 50–75.

Schetter, C. (2016), 'Playing the Ethnic Card: On the Ethnicization of Afghan Politics', *Studies in Ethnicity and Nationalism*, 16(3): 460–77.

Schinasi, M. (2016), *Kabul: A History 1773–1948*. Translated by R. D. McChesney. London: Leiden: Brill.

Shahrani, M. N. (1984), 'Causes and Context of Responses to the Saur Revolution in Badakhshan', in Canfield, R. L. and Shahrani, M. N. (eds.), *Revolutions and Rebellions in Afghanistan: Anthropological Perspectives*. Bloomington, IN: Indiana University Press, 139–69.

Sharma, R. (2017), *Nation, Ethnicity, and the Conflict in Afghanistan: Political Islam and the Rise of Ethno-Politics 1992-1996*. New York: Routledge.

Steele, J. (2011), *Ghosts of Afghanistan: The Haunted Battleground*. London: Portobello.

Tarzi, A. (2017), 'Islam, Shari'a, and State Building under 'Abd al-Rahman Khan', in Green, N. (ed.), *Afghanistan's Islam: From Conversion to the Taliban*. Oakland, CA: University of California Press, 129–44.

Tarzi, S. M. (1993), 'Afghanistan in 1992: A Hobbesian State of Nature', *Asian Survey*, 33(2): 165–74.

Williams, R. F. (1981), 'Legal Education in Afghanistan Prior to the Soviet Occupation'. *Suffolk Transnational Law Journal*, 6(2): 247–76.

18

Failed Democracy in Afghanistan: Rethinking Deliberation and Pluralism

Omar Sadr

Afghanistan's third republic, founded in 2001, lasted only twenty years. By 2021, the fall of the democratic order and the reappearance of the Taliban brought a full-scale return to the totalitarian regime that the group had presided over in the late 1990s. This chapter argues that a key factor in the failure of democracy was the inability of the democratic framework to adjust to and accommodate cultural diversity and moral disagreements. While diversity should have been a factor in strengthening the system, it turned into a catalyst for its failure.

In my book, *Negotiating Cultural Diversity in Afghanistan* (2020), I analysed the politics of intercultural dialogue in Afghanistan as a fragile society. Based on comparative political theory and empirical cases, I concluded that, beyond the recognition of moral and cultural diversity, the establishment of a stable and pluralistic society necessitates the possibility of open, respectful, meaningful and effective intercultural dialogue and participation. Having concluded that the Afghan state failed to accommodate intercultural dialogue, in this chapter, I aim to explore how the failure of liberal democracy in Afghanistan is related to the failure of intercultural dialogue over moral disagreements, in particular.

The main purpose of this chapter is to focus on how contentious disagreements including moral conflicts led to the failure of the democratic order and its public sphere in Afghanistan. Moral conflict centres on questions of 'values, how they are to be interpreted and priorities established; about the nature of the good society, the values it should exhibit and the extent to which particular institutions exemplify

---

This chapter is based on research undertaken while holding a fellowship at the University of Pittsburgh's Center for Governance and Markets (April–December 2023). The author is grateful to Dr Anna Larson, Dr Dipali Mukhopadhyay, Dr Michael Mackenzie and Munnaza Ebtikar. A short version of this paper was presented at the University of Pittsburgh's Center for Governance and Markets and US Institute of Peace (USIP) conference titled 'Negotiating Pluralism and Difference in the Way Ahead' in April 2023 and an early draft was presented at Cornell University's South Asia Center conference titled Learning from the Past to Build the Future of Afghanistan on 9 September 2023 and Association for the Studies of Middle East and Africa (ASMEA), Washington DC, in November 2023.

them' (Horton 1993: 109). The conflict emerges as these values are deemed to be both incompatible and incommensurable (Dzur 1998: 377).

In the coming pages, I first examine how deliberative democrats might explain the failure of democracy in Afghanistan and how a deliberative model of democracy might have provided an institutional framework more resilient to disagreement and debate. I then interrogate this idea further by employing Nancy Fraser and Chantal Mouffe's concept of critical democracy: namely that moral differences can never be resolved through deliberation and that deliberation will always be pervaded by existing power dynamics and imbalances within a given community. Finally, I explore Mouffe's contention that 'agonistic pluralism' and Fraser's de-centred public sphere are ways to mitigate conflict in a polarized society, and conclude that, in Afghanistan, this model could have prevented the catastrophic collapse of democratic institutions.

Why Democracies Fail

A review of the literature on democratic backsliding reveals several factors that contribute to the fall of democracies. The global trends of democratic failure changed since the end of the Cold War. Military coups as the traditional model of retreat of democracy during the Cold War were replaced with non-military means of revising democracy. In our time, democracies are failing more subtly and slowly, eroded by demagogic elected leaders who abuse or misuse their constitutional authorities and prerogatives even as they showcase 'a veneer of legality' (Levitsky and Ziblatt 2018: 77). President Ashraf Ghani's (2014–21) demagoguery and abusive practices of power fit the second pattern. Although the Taliban victory was not a military coup, the task of forceful takeover of Kabul was made easier for the insurgents by the US withdrawal. Yet, the failure of democracy in Afghanistan cannot simply be attributed to the failure of a military strategy, the abrupt US withdrawal from Afghanistan, or the crisis of good governance and excessive corruption, even though all of these played critical, interconnected roles. Beyond, in between, and underneath these factors, one must also ask if there was something wrong with the democratic arrangement, per se, and its underlying philosophy. Afghanistan's fate also cannot be explained as a case of democratic backsliding. Similar to some Eastern European countries where democracy was only installed institutionally and long-lasting communist culture slowed down democratic consolidation (Pejovich 2003; Hanley, Dawson, and Cianetti 2018), Afghanistan was far from a consolidated democracy.

Political science scholarship and discourse on Afghanistan over the last two decades have included analyses of electoral processes (Vendrell 2011; Jochem, Murtazashvili, and Murtazashvili 2015; Schmeidl 2016; Johnson and Barnhart 2020); the tension between democracy promotion and state building (Nixon and Ponzio 2007; Hill 2010; Coburn and Larson 2014; Gomes 2018); political parties and movements (Emadi 2001; Larson 2009; Loyn 2019); and the political economy of democracy (Goodhand, Suhrke, and Bose 2016; Coyne 2008). Given the persistence of armed conflict along with the democratic order in Afghanistan between 2001 and 2021, some have also recognized the coexistence of democratization and violent conflict (Larson 2021). Others have argued that democratization and social change cannot be enforced by a military intervention unless there is a shift in the underlying preferences of people or pre-existing conducive and compatible social norms for democracy already exist (Coyne 2008). Tensions existed in Afghanistan, as elsewhere, between establishing order and freedom and between building democratic institutions and the quest for stabilization (Diamond 2006).

What has been missing from this literature is a substantial exploration of the moral and value disagreements in Afghanistan and the inability of a democratic system to accommodate them by embracing value pluralism. In sum, no volume of the existing literature stands out as a seminal work on the interconnection between the root causes of democratic failure and pluralism in Afghanistan.

What happened in Afghanistan negates the fundamental theoretical logic of democracy as a minimal institutional setting to allow peaceful resolution of conflict in a society. As Alfred Stepan argues, 'democracy is a system of conflict regulation that allows open competition over the values and goals that citizens want to advance' (Stepan 2000: 39). However, instead of democracy creating space for conflict resolution, in Afghanistan, conflict dissolved democracy. This challenge, at some level, stems from the inherent paradoxes of democracy. Democracies, for example, must find a balance between conflict and consensus. Democracy necessitates conflict in the form of political competition, albeit in moderation. It must be constrained within well-defined and universally acknowledged parameters. However, consensus is essential in moderating the display of cleavage (Diamond 1990: 49).

The deliberative model of democracy is a response, explored by a number of scholars in the 1990s, as to how democracy should deal with a diverse society and moral disagreement (Benhabib 1996):

> Deliberative democracy is grounded in an ideal in which people come together, on the basis of equal status and mutual respect, to discuss the political issues they face and, based on those discussions, decide on the policies that will then affect their lives.
>
> (Bächtiger, Dryzek, Mansbridge, and Warren 2018: 2)

As Chantal Mouffe (2000) explains, deliberative democracy as a new paradigm of democracy is also a response to the 'aggregative model' theorized by Joseph Schumpeter in his seminal work *Capitalism, Socialism and Democracy*. Deliberation can take place not only in state institutions such as parliament, courts and juries but also through civil society and the public sphere (Bächtiger, Dryzek, Mansbridge, and Warren 2018: 11). This chapter is interested in deliberation within the public sphere.

The science of deliberative democracy suggests that the crises that democracy faces, such as polarization and uncivil behaviour, could be addressed through increased political participation at the local level. Deliberative democracy suggests that the decline in the citizen's political participation originates from a political situation where the content of the message becomes less important than partisan cues. In response, deliberative democracy arranges the opportunity for a citizen to directly get involved in the decision-making process which, in turn, should prevent a form of elite manipulation. Tools to enable deliberation include access to information, support from a facilitator and the involvement of experts (Dryzek et al. 2019).

It is important to note that the deliberative model is not a model exclusively for advanced liberal democracies. The promises of deliberation can contribute to the course of democratization and provide a pathway for a society that aims to transition from armed conflict (Curato and Steiner 2018: 491). Dryzek (2009: 1391) argues, 'To the extent that new democracies develop deliberative capacity, they become able to cope with the dangers identified by social choice theory: arbitrariness, instability, civil conflict, and a lapse into dictatorship.'

For instance, Colombia's Office of the High Commissioner for Reintegration used deliberation as a model of collective reflection on the past and possibilities for peace (Curato and Steiner 2018: 494). Moreover, non-electoral local participation such as *consulta popular* (a Colombian constitutional arrangement in the form of local referendum at the municipality level to allow people to decide crucial issues related to their lands) enabled citizens to actively mobilize and decide on crucial issues such as mining at the local level (Shenk 2022).

Ian O'Flynn and Didier Caluwaerts (2018: 750) argue that inter-group deliberation plays a positive transformational role in divided societies. Not just political elites but also common people have the capacity to engage in deliberation across pre-existing group divisions. The authors confirm Moffue's assumption that deliberation works not just with respect to non-contentious issues but also contentious ones such as divergent understandings of justice or visions for the future. Nonetheless, the authors agree that the question remains as to whether 'the organization of deliberative mini-publics in high-conflict settings produce[s] ripple effects across the wider public sphere'.

The Case for Deliberative Democracy in Afghanistan

The underlying cause of the failure of democracy in Afghanistan was inherent in the liberal model of democratization as implemented. This model could not generate legitimacy because it reduced democracy to the aggregated preference of citizens in elections in a way that prioritized the state over society. Most analyses of democracy in Afghanistan also limited themselves to state-centric frameworks which neglect the public sphere (Nixon and Ponzio 2007; Hill 2010; Vendrell 2011; Jochem, Murtazashvili, and Murtazashvili 2015; Goodhand, Suhrke, and Bose 2016; Schmeidl 2016; Gomes 2018; Johnson and Barnhart 2020).

In Afghanistan, many observers contend that democracy failed because the system was not democratic enough. For instance, arguing from an aggregative democracy standpoint, Jennifer Murtazashvili states that '[r]epresentative democracy was never given a chance to demonstrate its ability to solve problems, aggregate citizen preferences, and hold politicians accountable' (Murtazashvili 2021: 22). This approach came from the philosophical foundation that considers 'practical rationality' embedded in the institutions of liberal democracy.

To use Habermas' words, the efforts of democratization in Afghanistan were to 'view society as centred in the state – be it as the guardian of a market society or the state as the self-conscious institutionalization of an ethical community' (1996: 26). This effort failed to create fair procedures to facilitate deliberation and discursive politics at the local level and in informal institutions and spaces. The intense focus on building formal institutions controlled by the state in the capital practically disempowered the masses. The institutions of democracy modelled on aggregative assumptions essentially circumvented participation and deliberation in political discourse. In the absence of institutions that could nurture reasonable deliberation, democracy in Afghanistan, in the words of deliberative democrats, experienced a 'descent into personality clashes, celebrity politics, sound-bite "debates" and naked pursuit of personal gain and ambitions' (Held 2008: 232). Coburn and Larson (2014) found that elections have been a destabilizing force in a conflict-affected context like Afghanistan's, where they reinforced illicit political elite, corruption and patronage.

An alternative model of democracy that Habermas called discursive theory forms the basis of 'deliberative democracy', which is based on the institutionalization of common procedures and processes at the local level. Deliberation is not limited to formal bodies at the macro level such as parliamentary institutions. Rather, it also encompasses local informal institutions (Habermas 1996: 28). Deliberative democracy can overcome the deficiency of representative democracy in two major ways. First, it puts the question of legitimacy at the centre of the democratic project. The deliberative theory of democracy assumes that legitimacy can be constructed and maintained in a fair process of public deliberation among equal individuals. Political institutions are supposed to represent the interests of all in an impartial way. Meanwhile, the legitimacy of a decision is dependent on the possibility of an open deliberation among equal citizens about the same decision (Benhabib 1996: 69).

In Afghanistan, it was assumed that participation in elections would automatically generate legitimacy, as elections aggregate the 'predetermined will of individuals' (Held 2008: 232). Yet, as Coburn and Larson argue, these assumptions would soon prove to be unfounded:

> The greater problem is when elections promise to deliver participation but fail to allow individuals to shape meaningfully the way power is distributed, or worse, allow certain powerful figures in the ruling elite to further consolidate their power in ways that close political processes to the average voter.
> (Coburn and Larson 2014: 224)

Coburn and Larson, in interviews with voters across the country, found that elections were not considered as necessarily connected to democracy in Afghanistan. In other words, people did not automatically consider elected officials to be their representatives. Instead, elections were considered a process where political and economic opportunities were distributed. The authors argue that, for many in Afghanistan, 'elections and democracy were separate subjects that had relatively little connection to one another' (Coburn and Larson 2014: 14).

This conclusion is further affirmed by the recent studies of democracy in Afghanistan from a political economy perspective (Sharan 2023). In an atmosphere of patronage, corruption and ethnocentrism, elections deviated from their original mandate and could be instrumentalized as a mechanism for bargaining among corrupt political elites. Evidence from Afghanistan's three electoral cycles over twenty years shows that elections were marked by intimidation, coercion, the instrumentalization of identity-based divisions, opportunism and fraud. Instead of democratization, elections served the interests of incumbents and those aligned with them. Central democratic institutions, such as parliament, turned into a marketplace and 'network building arena[s]' that connected elites of different political and social levels with each other and allowed them to distribute resources to each other (Sharan 2023). As Sharan argues, 'instead of producing the hoped-for democratic plurality, Afghanistan's first parliamentary elections set the stage for conflict and contest between competing networks for the control of the state and constituencies' (Sharan 2023: 219).

Afghanistan's democratization experience, paradoxically, did not account for the people's agency and capacity to be deliberative and part of the decision-making process.[1] The elites and international interlocutors who aimed to design democracy made sure to limit the public engagement of the people in the political process as much as they could. For instance, the process of crafting the constitution and discussion over the nature of the state, political system and role of Islam took place through a highly elite 'political bargaining between the Islamists and the international community, particularly the US, rather than a nationwide deliberation' (Sadr 2021: 42). The public consultation phase was limited to two months between May and June 2002 (Secretariat of the Constitutional Review Commission 2003), making the entire process performative. Not only was the draft constitution not made public, but the Review Commission also failed to incorporate public views in the final version of the draft constitution (Pasarlay 2016: 206). This failure was based on a lack of trust in the demos. The demos were assumed fragmented, tribal and traditional. Instead of trusting people with power and providing them with the tools to take part in decision-making, they were deprived of it. President Ashraf Ghani further increased bureaucratization and centralization of policy making, creating layers of corruption and further reducing public deliberation and participation (Sadr 2021).

According to its proponents, in a deliberative democracy, legitimacy is attained when each political decision is open to public deliberation. Seyla Behabib presents at least three criteria for a deliberative process: (1) right to equal access to deliberation, (2) right to question the topic of discussion and (3) right to question the rules and procedures.[2]

These principles of deliberation would have been well-suited to Afghanistan given the country's history and culture of deliberation. Historically, Afghanistan has been characterized by a polycentric system of governance. This includes a multiplicity of institutional frameworks beyond the state. In other words, Afghanistan's society has organized itself at the community level through voluntary civic associations. Despite the state's attempts to circumvent *de facto* polycentrism in favour of a more state-centric and centralized form of governance, it is evident that non-state institutions and community-based governance regimes have exhibited peculiar resilience.

Consequently, a network of informal institutional structures and governance mechanisms that has historically evolved operates across Afghanistan, ensuring not only survival but also managing common pool resources, delivering public goods, mitigating risks, sustaining basic economic activities and finding alternative avenues for accessing resources and markets. Appreciation for and recognition of these institutions had great potential for the establishment of a deliberative democracy. The state tried to use and project the grand *Jirga* (assembly), in the words of Benhabib as 'a general deliberation assembly in which the united people express their will' (1996: 74). However, it disregarded various decisions and consultations with local bodies that people initiated. Instead of serious deliberative bodies, the government tried to organize various forms of gatherings in which the president or high-ranking officials were delivering speeches. Hence, people felt discredited and disempowered. This, in return, negatively impacted the integrity of civil society and its role in the public sphere.

Moral Differences, Power Imbalances and the Limits of Deliberation

A key advantage of deliberative democracy is its acknowledgement of value pluralism and the fact that moral and ethical disagreements are a key feature of society and everyday politics. It assumes that disagreement should be accommodated 'through the deployment of various discursive practices' (Held 2008: 254). In other words, the public sphere presents a set of institutional arrangements where political preference would be shaped, justifiable stances discussed and legitimacy constructed. On the one hand, it encourages various forms of association and civil society groups to form; and, on the other, it encourages accountability through the cultivation of a civil society based on the public sphere (Calhoun 2011).

However, critical democrats such as Mouffe highlight two critical flaws of deliberative democracy with respect to pluralism. First, deliberative democrats such as Habermas distinguish ethics from politics and morality and exclude ethics – questions concerning the good life – from rational public debate. In other words, ethical issues are seen as a domain where consensus is not possible and, hence, is precluded from the implications of value pluralism. Second, deliberative democracy ignores the antagonistic dimension of pluralism. It does so by overlooking the power dynamic in the public sphere and pushing for a rational consensus. According to Mouffe, 'If we accept that relations of power are constitutive of the social, then the main question for democratic politics is not how to eliminate power but how to constitute forms of power more compatible with democratic values' (Mouffe 2000: 14).

A call for inclusivity and openness is far from formal recognition of equality. The liberal public sphere in theory grants each gender, race and ethnic group the opportunity for political participation. However, what matters is the pattern of discursive interaction in a public arena. So, a question persists: To what extent do power, social status and other characteristics impact equal access to the public sphere? And, to what degree is social equality a prerequisite for an open public sphere and democracy? Charles Tilly

(2007), who looked at the intersection of democracy, equality and inequality in South Africa, argued that under two conditions inequality hampers democracy: first, if day-to-day differences or continuous differences are translated into categorical differences such as religion, ethnicity, race or gender; second, if this crystallization is transformed into politics. Hence, the health of democracy is related to the extent politics is safe from categorical inequalities. Tilly's main proposition was to insulate politics from inequality. By insulating against inequality, he did not mean eliminating inequality; rather he contended that 'politics does not divide sharply at the boundaries of unequal categories'. In other words, if inequality exists in society but does not inscribe itself into politics, its effects can be mitigated. In this sense, Tilly agreed with radical theorists of democracy such as Mouffe and Fraser that social inequality based on gender, class or ethnicity could have a deleterious effect on the quality of the public sphere and democracy.

Since power is embedded in social relations, it will never fade away through any sort of rational deliberation. Having said, that any sort of consensus that is manufactured through the exercise of power will always create exclusions. In such a scenario, deliberation 'serves as a mask for domination' (Fraser 1990: 64). Similar to radical democrat theorists, critical deliberative democrats also believe that no deliberation is free of power relations and hence impartial deliberation is not possible (Held 2008). In other words, there is no consensus without exclusion. As Mouffe argues, 'By postulating the availability of a non-exclusive public sphere of deliberation where a rational consensus could be obtained, they [deliberative democrats] negate the inherently conflictual nature of modern pluralism' (Mouffe 2000: 17).

Given that power cannot be eliminated from the public sphere and pluralism of values is irreducible, the task of democratic politics is to transform antagonism between 'us vs them' into a kind of workable coexistence. The 'them' should no longer be seen as an enemy to be eliminated from the political scene, but conceived, instead, as an adversary with a legitimate divergent irreconcilable idea or value. Arrival at this stage would be called 'agonistic pluralism'. For this reason, Mouffe considers democracy not as a form of government but as a 'mode of being'. Democracy is not simply a set of institutions or a regime but a 'symbolic ordering of social relations' (Mouffe 1996: 245). Finally, Mouffe argues that the solution does not lie in replacing the 'aggregative rationality' of liberals with the 'communicative rationality' of deliberative democrats; rather, the solution resides in 'the constitution of an ensemble of practices that make the constitution of democratic citizens possible', which 'can only be made possible by multiplying the institutions, the discourses, the forms of life that foster identification with democratic values' (Mouffe 2000: 11).

Exclusion and Lack of Participatory Parity in Afghanistan

In the springs of 2019 and 2021, I spoke in two televised public debates hosted and broadcasted by *TOLOnews* on the peace process in Afghanistan. The first brought together Nazar Muhammad Mutmeen, who later became the Taliban's head of Sports and Physical Education; Orzala Nemat, a policy analyst; Iqbal Khayber, the head of the People's Peace Movement (Junbish Soleh Mardumi); and myself.[3] In the second debate, I was joined by four peace activists from Balkh, Kapisa, Kunar and Kandahar.[4] It was the first televised public debate for the four peace activists. This personal account is the tale of the public sphere in the third republic of Afghanistan (2004–21).

These were not decision-making deliberative forums by the citizens; however, political debates in the media functioned 'as a forum for civic debates' (Maia 2018: 350). They helped citizens to form their public opinion through everyday political talk based on which they would take political action (Conover and Miller 2018: 387). At face value, this practice had two features that distinguished it as a model of the democratic, pluralistic public sphere: openness and deliberation. The debate was open, both in terms of audience and inclusivity of people participating in it. A Taliban member, a woman, an activist from a rural area, voices from provinces, an analyst, an academic, and over two dozen participants who did not know each other engaged in a live televised public debate over a public issue. As Craig Calhoun has argued, the ideal of the public sphere is its openness: 'The public sphere is public first and foremost because it is open to all, not only in the sense that all can see and hear but also that all can participate and have a voice' (2011: 13). Second, the debate featured a form of political participation through talk and deliberation. In other words, it served as an arena of public discourse that operated as distinct from the state and the market.

If one takes the above scenario as a best-case practice of an open and pluralistic public sphere in Afghanistan, then the questions that merit asking are: why did the pluralistic public sphere not sustain itself, and, instead, collapse catastrophically? And, more fundamentally, was the post-2001 public sphere ever truly pluralistic? To address these questions, one must understand the limits of the liberal and deliberative public sphere as well as the nature of society in Afghanistan. The third republic of Afghanistan featured three salient characteristics in the post-2001 order. It was culturally diverse: there existed a plurality of ways of life, values and identities. It was segmented: it upheld gender and racial hierarchies and divisions. It was polarized over the question of fundamental values should define and shape the promises of politics, society and culture. This polarization could be marked, at least in one sense, by the divide between liberal and conservative values over human rights, democracy and diversity. A society that is culturally diverse, socially and structurally segmented, and politically polarized is best suited, I would contend, to models of democracy that can accommodate these traits – one example being what Mouffe calls agonistic pluralism.

In post-2001 Afghanistan, a number of structural inequalities undermined inclusion and pluralism, and as Mouffe (2000: 16), predicted 'democratic confrontation' was displaced by identity politics. This eventually hastened the demise of democracy. Ethnic and gender inequality were reproduced in Afghanistan with systematic discrimination against subordinated ethnic groups and women. Agonistic democracy would not distribute power based on ethnic categories as this would intensify the antagonism and power politics. In the world of Tilly, discussed in the previous section, ethnic quotas will shape politics based on categorical difference. In fact, the pattern of power sharing during the republic was based on ethnic categories whereby a Pashtun was elected as president and a Tajik and a Hazara as the two vice-presidents, projecting categorical ethnic difference into the realm of politics.

Agonistic pluralism, instead, requires a new discourse to provide an opportunity for inclusion. To transform existing ethnocentric antagonistic identity politics into legitimate pluralistic agonism in Afghanistan, Mujib Rahimi (2017: 246) suggests Changiz Pahlavan's 'common civilizational sphere discourse' as a framework with the potential to create coexistence between various ethnic groups and bridge the gap between conflicting discourses. The common civilizational discourse acknowledges the shared historical and cultural heritage rooted in Iranian-Islamic civilization without denying the socio-ethnic diversity in Afghanistan. Consequently, it transforms us vs them 'antagonistic' relations from enmity to an 'agonistic' position where all sides consider each other as legitimate adversaries in Afghanistan.

Moreover, the political economy of military intervention created a cycle of corruption which 'produced a new class of Afghan predatory entrepreneurs, local strongmen-turned-businessmen, contractors, bankers and others who made their fortunes because of their association with, and hoarding of, international security and aid assistance' (Sharan 2023: 239). Many of these figures came to behave like cartel members, purchasing votes at the elections. The best example of this was the contest in 2019 between a few wealthy businesspeople over the leadership of the lower house in the third legislature which turned the elections of leadership into an auction.

As one would expect, the impact of inequality transcended the political domain and shaped the nature of the cultural domain. In other words, the public sphere was not immune to cultural biases and exclusions. For instance, most of the powerful strongmen and business elites owned their own media houses and thus were able to influence popular debate and behaviour. The civil society organizations that emerged in the democratic order of post-2001 were more accountable to their donors than the public. For instance, a report by the Afghanistan Research and Evaluation Unit (AREU) in 2016 found that 'while these activists [civil society] build strong relations with donors and government officials, their relations with the population in general and with their own constituencies, in particular, are very weak or non-existent in most cases' (Nemat and Werner 2016: 26). The report concluded that civil society actors lacked legitimacy and suffered from patronage politics and corruption. In this way, they were neither democratic nor committed to the public good.

The CEOs of most NGOs and civil society organizations amassed a lavish lifestyle in a matter of years. Some research organizations became private clubs that were only open to their members. Most importantly, the allegedly corrupt politicians with murky legacies established their own civil society organizations while working with the government. They used public positions to channel public funds and resources to their NGOs. Such organizations also served as a retreat for politicians once they left the government. The lack of oversight on civic associations is rooted in the Rawlsian view as it only understands the state and its institutions to comprise the public sphere. On the contrary, for deliberative democrats like Benhabib, public scrutiny may be applied to civil society organizations (Benhabib 1996: 76). In other words, associations and corporations should not only be accountable to their members but also the public.

It is clear that the political process failed to bracket social inequality from politics. With the limited availability of an inclusive public sphere, most of the civil society organizations in Afghanistan were only accountable to their donors. As Craig Calhoun argued, civil society served specific interests and turned into exclusive enclaves by using private security services. The solution lies in the intersection of radical democracy's agonistic pluralism with the critical deliberative model. Their consideration of civil society as part of the public sphere and their acknowledgement of exclusion as being rooted in the disparities of power that structure social relations are equally important – as the following sections will demonstrate.

Polarization and Identity Politics

Post-2001, society in Afghanistan was fragmented along various axes. These included progressives vs conservatives, and technocrats vs warlords. Moreover, religious fundamentalism challenged the democratic order which was defined based on mingled liberal and Islamic values. Identity politics became more salient over time. Efforts at democratization were mediated through wartime social forces such as non-state armed groups and strongmen, the diaspora and international military intervention. These social forces restrained the space for a democratic interface between different individuals within society. Interestingly, besides the wartime social forces, new cultural forces such as a class of technocrats, a new generation of educated youth, and an emergent middle class also emerged, exerting influence through cross-cutting social ties. These new cultural and social forces attempted to transform post-conflict society through social activism and an expansion of the public sphere.

A communitarian notion of politics became stronger over two decades in Afghanistan, consequently, as Habermas argues in other contexts, essentially constricting political discourse along ethical lines (Habermas 1996: 23) and solidifying an essentialist understanding of community culture (Sadr 2020).[5] Under Ashraf Ghani, this form of politics was epitomized in the notion of *Afghaniat* (Afghanness). Ghani even adopted traditional clothes as an epitome of Afghanness.

Both discursive theorists of radical democracy and deliberative democrats believe that the idea of communitarianism goes against diversity. For exponents of deliberative democracy, there are two problems with such a communitarian approach. First, for a law to be legitimate, it should resonate beyond the ethical tenets of a particular community and appeal to universal moral claims. A deliberative democracy should not be based on a substantive form of ethical type; rather it is based on creating a fair regulated bargaining process between multiple forms of argumentation and 'the multiplicity of communicative forms of rational political will-formation' (Habermas 1996: 25).

Second, in a situation of diversity and socio-cultural pluralism, the common solution does not emerge through ethical discourses; rather it comes through compromises made on interests. The outcome of this process would be what Habermas calls an 'intersubjectively shared form of life' (Habermas 1996: 26). In other words, communitarianism contradicts pluralism. Similarly, radical democrat Mouffe argues:

> [A] substantive idea of the common good which is found in some communitarians is antithetical to the pluralism that defines liberal democracy as a new political form of society. Radical democrats agree on the need to recover such ideas as 'common good', 'civic virtue' and 'political community', but they believe that they must be reformulated in a way that makes them compatible with the recognition of conflict, division, and antagonism.
>
> (Mouffe 1992: 12)

In Afghanistan, state policies did not prevent such bad politics; rather, state policies aided and abetted bad politics. A key policy of the state that pushed for further ethnicization of politics was the controversial national identity card with pejorative and predetermined ethnic categories. The Ministry of Ethnicity and Tribal Affairs deliberately created a list of the ethnic groups – most of which were clearly flagged for further division of non-Pashtuns into smaller communities. In a country where resources and power were designed to be shared by ethnic blocs, every small community demanded to be recognized as a distinct group entitled to political group rights. Consequently, it reinforced uber-communitarianism. In theory, a pluralistic approach would have been more sustainable in terms of preserving diversity while preventing any form of essentialist communalism.

Lack of Shared Religious Values

Afghanistan's third republic's democracy came with a set of value baggage that was contested. Cultural contestation ensued with respect to norms around gender, the role of Islam, democracy, alternate notions of liberty, and more along a diverse spectrum of Islamists and secularists. Kamran Bokhari and Farid Senzai (2013: 27–30) provide a useful typology of how various Muslims encounter democracy (Figure 18.1). Their typology resonates with the various parties of cultural contestation in Afghanistan. It presents nine categories namely militant secularist, radical secularist, liberal secularist,

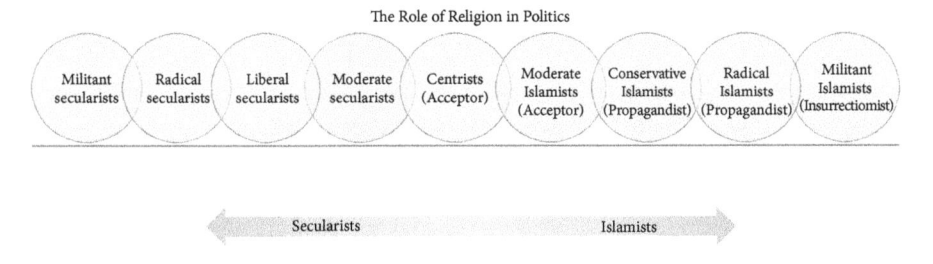

Figure 18.1 The Islamist-secularist spectrum.

Source: Bokhari and Senzai 2013: 29.

moderate secularist, centrist, moderate Islamist, conservative Islamist, radical Islamist and finally militant Islamist.

The Taliban epitomized the 'militant Islamists' constituency, violently rejecting the constitutional set of rights and democratic framework. Beyond the Taliban, Hizb al-Tahrir was the 'radical Islamist' that propagated radical ideology but refrained from the use of violence. The conservative forces within the systems such as the Council of Islamic Clergy (Shura Ulema) who could be considered as 'conservative Islamists' were also uncomfortable with the new emerging values. In other words, there were deep ethical and moral disagreements. In fact, some scholars argue that democracy itself was a site of contestation over values in Afghanistan. Terms such as democracy and elections were understood not as value-neutral but as concepts with a certain 'political agenda' (Coburn and Larson 2014: 15). To Mouffe's point 'given the ineradicable pluralism of value, there is no rational resolution of the conflict, hence its antagonistic dimension' (Mouffe 2000: 15).

The 'common civilizational sphere discourse' of Pahlavan addresses the above challenge. It conceives of Islam as the shared heritage and denominator of Iranian civilization with its roots in Sufi and Persian culture. Such a reading of Islam provides distinct outcomes that can help mitigate the perils associated with Sharia-related legal disparities and contention within Islamic sects (Rahimi 2017: 252). Unfortunately, as anthropologist Annika Schmeding found, Afghanistan's third republic's policy towards religious institutions particularly Sufis was a combination of indifference, ambiguity and failure. The government failed to protect Sufis and define moderate understanding of Islam (Schmeding 2023: 72).

Agonistic Pluralism and the Possibilities for Plurality of Public Spheres

If a stratified society suffers from a lack of participation parity, then what sort of institutional arrangement would address the challenge? The solution, according to Fraser, rests in the plurality of the public sphere. She argues that 'arrangements that accommodate contestation among a plurality of competing publics better promote the ideal of participatory parity than does a single, comprehensive, overarching public' (Fraser 1990: 66). Since the subordinated groups are barred from participating in the mainstream public sphere, they will constitute a counter-public sphere. In a diverse and pluralistic society, the comprehensive single public sphere not only imposes one discursive idea but also frames people's identities. A single public sphere is not a culture-free zone, but rather privileges one culture over others.

Amidst the disarray in Afghanistan, a thriving public sphere emerged after 2001, allowing oppressed groups to express themselves free of state intervention. To counter the masculinist, homogenizing and conservative public sphere, many women, marginalized ethno-linguistic groups and secular organizations created their 'counterpublics'. In the following, I discuss five cases of the de-centred model of the public sphere.

A key counterpublic was constituted by Farsi media outlets against the homogenizing mainstream public sphere. Equality of all languages was recognized by the constitution; however, discursive interaction mandated the usage of Pashtu vocabulary as a national terminology.[6] While the 2004 constitution did not specify a predefined list of national terminology, right-wing Afghan nationalists considered Pashtu terminologies as national terminology (*mutalihat mili*) that should be incorporated into Farsi and other minor languages in Afghanistan. National Radio and Television of Afghanistan (RTA) as well as other mainstream media such as Ariana TV and Pahjwok News adopted the same terminology.

One of the key terms on which contestation took place was the term *pohantoon* (Pashtu: university). The debate over a plurality of national terminology was challenged by the right-ethno-majoritarians. The efforts to rectify the higher education bill through legislation that would have recognized Persian terminology as official along with Pashtu official terminologies did not succeed; right-wing Afghan nationalists blocked the ratification process. What was impossible through the democratic process of the legislature became possible through the creation of counterpublics. Alternative media such as Tolo TV and *TOLOnews* provided the space to resist the state's cultural dominations by continuing to use Persian terms. Appearing in the newspapers, on television or speaking through radio and social media, Persian intellectuals contributed to the creation of the 'counterpublic'. Novelist Rahnavard Zaryab, poet Sami Hamid, movie director Roya Sadat, and singer and music director Wahid Qasimi amongst many others contributed to the Persian counterpublic through *TOLOnews* and Tolo.

Over the course of the Third Republic, the media became an arena of contestation over cultural and ideological issues, human rights and democracy.[7] When the Council of Islamic Clergy under the leadership of Enayatullah Baleq[8] took several stances against women's music, Indian soap operas and many progressive issues covered by the new media in 2008 (Paikan 2020), in most cases, the media outlets resisted pressure from the conservative Islamists or strongmen, or the court ruled in their favour. For instance, when President Karzai, under pressure from the Council of Clergies, messaged *Hasht-e Sobh* newspaper on 1 June 2011, to refrain from publishing materials that were deemed to be contrary to Islam and the interest of the state, the court ruled in favour of the newspaper arguing that the newspaper only published the findings of human rights organizations. Even as the court does not represent a counterpublic, its ruling paved the way for the accommodation of plurality within the public sphere. The liberal media continued to publish on human rights issues while functioning alongside the media that refrained from doing so. Similarly, Killid Group, a network of radio and magazines, produced 125 episodes about war crimes in spite of backlash from local strongmen.

Intellectuals also used cultural icons to mobilize people against Taliban fundamentalism. Nawroz became a political activity for these young activists whose performativity challenged the authorities of conservative groups. For instance, an anti-Nawroz online campaign in 2018 used a poster showing a Muslim man in traditional Arabic attire and beard and a woman in black hijab proposing to cancel the Nawroz celebration, depicting it as 'a Zoroastrian festival' and *haram* (forbidden) in Islam (Figures 18.2 and 18.3, respectively) To counter this Islamist cancel culture,

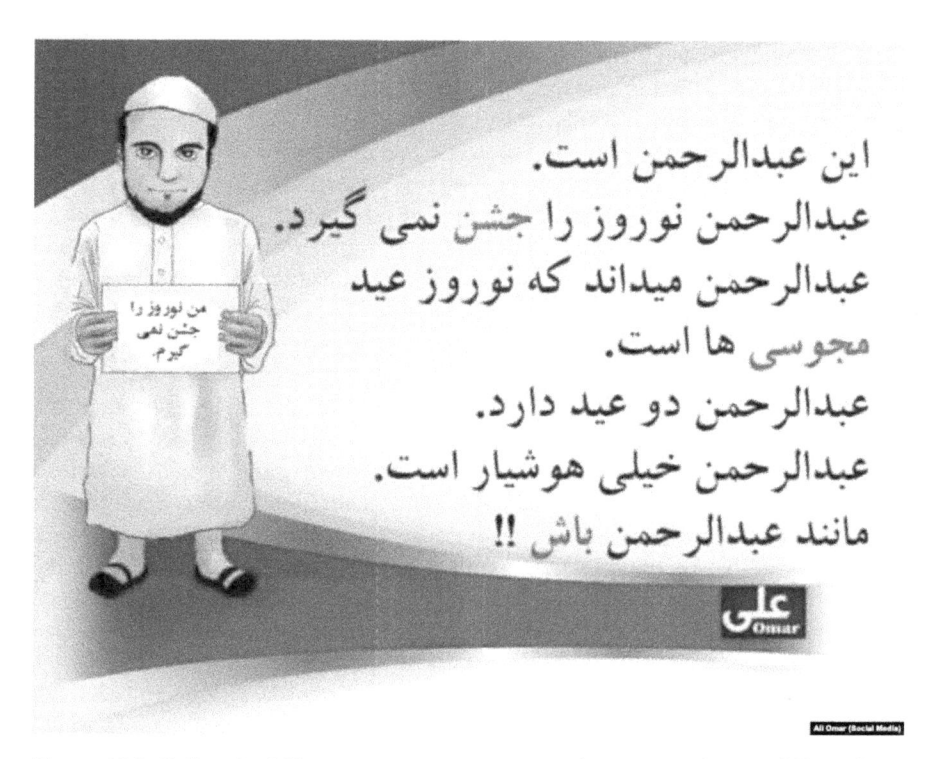

Figure 18.2 Online Anti-Nawroz campaign picture 1. The text translates as follows: 'This is Abdur Rahman Khan. Abdur Rahman Khan does not celebrate Nawroz. He knows that Nawroz is the Eid of Magus (Zoroastrians). Abdur Rahman has only two *Eids* (festivals). Abdur Rahman is very smart. Be like Abdur Rahman' (translated by the author).

Source: LoveAfghanistan Facebook page, 9 March 2018 https://www.facebook.com/10150126008305294/posts/10160329036540294/

counterpublics reasserted the significance of Nawroz as a festival that is not anti-Islamic but, rather, rooted in the country's culture and Persian heritage. The Pen Association of Afghanistan and Khorasanian Association were among these counterpublics. Mujib Rahimi (2017: 252) who proposes Pahlavan's common civilizational approach as an alternative discourse suggests that Nawroz should not present an exclusive heritage of one group, instead it should be highlighted as a shared heritage of all.

Women's counterpublic spheres not only presented alternative publics for some women to have a voice but also redefined what was traditionally considered private. For instance, 1 TV produced a debate show called *Niqab* (Mask) in which a woman (whose identity was kept confidential) appeared to discuss her experience as the victim of domestic violence (1TV 2013). Meanwhile, artists employed graffiti and other media to demonstrate the desire for peace and an end to the conflict. Murals highlighted issues related to corruption, women's rights violations, war and militarism. One artist, Aman Mojaddidi, stated that 'cultural changes are not about evolving but are about shifting, absorbing, and merging' (Recchia 2014). He used his art to criticize warlordism in Afghanistan and raise public awareness regarding political rights.

Figure 18.3 Online Anti-Nawroz campaign picture 2. The text translates as follows: 'This is Fatima. In addition to not celebrating Nawroz herself, Fatima also hinders other Muslim sisters because she knows that celebrating Nawroz is both heresy and a Zoroastrian practice. Fatima is cautious about following Sharia. Be like Fatima (translated by the author).

Source: LoveAfghanistan Facebook page, 9 March 2018 https://www.facebook.com/10150126008305294/posts/10160329036540294/

In 2018, after the National Unity Government made a peace deal with the notorious warlord Gulbuddin Hekmatyar, also famous as the 'Butcher of Kabul', a group of street artists including students from the American University of Afghanistan painted the portrait of the late Hamida Barmarki, a law professor and member of human rights commission, on the American University of Afghanistan (AUAF)'s blast wall in front of Hekmatyar's house. Though the artists were warned by affiliates of Hekmatyar not to paint, the mural was completed – but then eventually erased. The mural's emergence and erasure contributed to public debate over the legacy of terrorists and warlords. The AUAF administration had also warned the students not to paint contentious murals on the university's walls. Yet, these artistic expressions enabled common citizens and students to create a counterpublic of their own, one that went against the interests of *both* the AUAF administration and warlords such as those of Hekmatyar and the Taliban.

The above-mentioned plurality of publics should have provided the possibility of conversations and exchanges amongst individuals of different publics – in other words, plurality demands that different publics interact with one another. But this requires commitment to pluralism, a shared set of values to enable deliberation and reasoning, namely a kind of 'multicultural literacy' (Fraser 1990: 69). This kind of understanding requires reform of the education system. Otherwise, the inability to communicate and comprehend across different publics ends in polarization, thereby converting publics into enclaves of the kind that crystallized in Afghanistan as the years went on.

Conclusion

This chapter investigated the relationships between democracy, the public sphere and pluralism in the third republic of Afghanistan (2001–21). It demonstrated how democratic failure in Afghanistan can be explicated through a normative understanding of democracy as rooted in a liberalism that does not attend to the predicament of pluralism and, thus, should be reimagined. The democratic project in Afghanistan was unable to accommodate diversity and moral differences. Even if the classic liberal theory does have some deliberation built in, it is under-theorized and underdeveloped in ways that end up mattering in practical terms.

The chapter tried to develop a theory of pluralistic democracy using the case of Afghanistan. Agonistic pluralism conceives politics in a discursive way to formulate unity in diversity and transform 'us/them' relations in terms compatible with pluralism. Moreover, agonistic pluralism as the normative foundation of a pluralist democracy embraces the conflictual nature of pluralism. Knowing that a rational consensus comes at the cost of exclusion, a pluralist democracy refrains from imposing rational consensus. Instead, it promotes a decentred model of the public sphere that facilitates coexistence of counterpublics and accommodates moral disagreements. In post-2001 Afghanistan, diversity made itself manifest in identity politics, majoritarianism, polarization and structural inequality, all of which rendered the success of the pluralistic public sphere impossible. Anxiety about rapid social change underpinned attacks on the plurality of publics. This, in turn, prevented the possibility of a pluralistic democracy. For a complex and diverse society, a decentred model of the public sphere – one that would have allowed for different modes of civil society – would have facilitated both legitimacy formation and accommodation of diversity.

Most importantly, this multiplicity of publics might have come to function, not as a collection of enclaves, but rather as engaged in an intercultural dialogue amongst themselves. Of course, this decentred model of the public sphere would have had a number of institutional requirements. What would these institutions have looked like if they were properly informed by agonistic democracy? And can counter-publics be institutionalized as a democratic force of diversity without being neutered in the process? Does institutionalization negate their 'counter' quality? What is required of us is to figure out how to institutionalize the politics of difference without pulling society apart. Further research and theorizing are imperative to consider the right balance so as to hold society together without homogenizing it along the way.

Notes

1. O'Flynn and Caluwaerts (2018: 743) confirm that the comparative literature also does not pay attention to the feasibility of meaningful deliberation amongst ordinary citizens in a divided society which is why it has focused on elite bargaining, institutions and parties.

2   These criteria are similar to the republican theorist Phillips Pettit's (2002) three criteria of contestatory democracy.
3   TOLOnews. 2019. Debate: Afghanistan Youth Role in Peace Process. Available at: https://www.youtube.com/watch?v=cQI-MB_KErYandt=378s.
4   TOLOnews. 2021. Mehwar: Role of Afghanistan Youth in Peace. https://www.youtube.com/watch?v=2aIzehDMwXI.
5   For more on how the communitarianism notion of culture and identity was strengthened in Afghanistan, see Sadr, O. (2020).
6   For a detailed discussion of language politics in Afghanistan and how Pashtu words were made mandatory for usage in Farsi and other languages in Afghanistan, see Sadr, O. (2020).
7   For more, see Osman, W. (2020) and Afghanistan Analysts Network (2015).
8   Enayatullah Baligh was a member of the Islamic Clergy Council and Professor of Islamic theology at Kabul University. Baligh has been closely associated with Abdul Rab Rasul Sayyaf. Baligh joined the Taliban during their first rule in 1996 as a deputy minister of promoting virtue and prohibiting vice. However, he left the group later. During the talks between the Islamic Republic of Afghanistan and the Taliban in 2021, Baligh was appointed to the Republics' negotiating team.

References

Afghanistan Analysts Network (2015), 'The Difficult Path of Freedom of Speech and Journalism in Afghanistan'. Available at: https://www.afghanistan-analysts.org/dari-pashto/reports.

Afghanistan Independent Elections Commission (2004), *Afghanistan Presidential Elections Results – 2004*. Kabul: IEC.

Bächtiger, A., Dryzek, J. S., Mansbridge, J. and Warren M. E. (eds.) (2018), *The Oxford Handbook of Deliberative Democracy*. Oxford: Oxford University Press.

Benhabib, S. (1996), *Democracy and Difference*. New York: Princeton University Press.

Bokhari, K. and Senzai, F. (2013), *Political Islam in the Age of Democratization*. New York: Palgrave and Macmillan.

Calhoun, C. (2011), 'Civil Society and the Public Sphere', in Edwards, M. (ed.), *The Oxford Handbook of Civil Society*. New York: Oxford University Press, 311–23.

Coburn, N. and Larson, A. (2014), *Derailing Democracy in Afghanistan: Elections in an Unstable Political Landscape*. New York: Columbia University Press.

Conover, P. J. and Miller, P. R. (2018), 'Taking Everyday Political Talk Seriously', in Bächtiger, A., Dryzek, J. S., Mansbridge, J. and Warren M. E. (eds.), (2018), *The Oxford Handbook of Deliberative Democracy*. Oxford: Oxford University Press.

Coyne, C. J. (2008), *After War: The Political Economy of Exporting Democracy*. Stanford, CA: Stanford Economics and Finance.

Curato, N. and Steiner, J. (2018), 'Deliberative Democracy and Comparative Democratization Studies', in Bächtiger, A., Dryzek, J. S., Mansbridge, J. and Warren, M. E. (eds.), (2018), *The Oxford Handbook of Deliberative Democracy*. Oxford: Oxford University Press.

Dahl, R. (1998), *On Democracy*. New Haven: Yale University Press.

Diamond, L. (1990), 'Three Paradoxes of Democracy'. *Journal of Democracy*, 1(3): 48–60.

Diamond, L. (2006), 'Promoting Democracy in Post-Conflict and Failed States Lessons and Challenges'. *Taiwan Journal of Democracy*, 2(2): 93–115.

Dryzek, J. S. (2009), 'Democratization as Deliberative Capacity Building'. *Comparative Political Studies*, 42: 1379–402.
Dryzek, J. S, Bächtiger, A., Chambers, S., Cohen, J., Druckman, J. N., Felicetti, A., Fishkin, J. S., Farrell, D. M., Fung, A., Gutmann, A., Landemore, H., Mansbridge, J., Marien, S., Neblo, M. A., Niemeyer, S., Setälä, M., Slothuus, R., Suiter, J., Thompson, D. and Warren, M. E. (2019), 'The Crisis of Democracy and Science of Deliberation: Citizen Can Avoid Polarization and Make Sound Decisions'. *Insights Policy Forum*, 363(6432): 1144–6.
Dzur, A. W. (1998), 'Values Pluralism vs Political Liberalism'. *Social Theory and Practice*, 24(3): 375–93.
Emadi, H. (2001), 'Radical Political Movements in Afghanistan and Their Politics of Peoples' Empowerment and Liberation'. *Central Asian Survey*, 20(4): 427–50.
Fraser, N. (1990), 'Rethinking the Public Sphere: A Contribution to the Critique of Actually Existing Democracy'. *Social Text* 25/26.
Gomes, A. (2018), 'Hybrid Democracy: Electoral Rules and Political Competition in Afghanistan'. *Revista Brasileira de Política Internacional*, 61(1): e007.
Goodhand, J., Suhrke, A. and Bose, S. (2016), 'Flooding the Lake? International Democracy Promotion and the Political Economy of the 2014 Presidential Election in Afghanistan'. *Conflict, Security and Development*, 16(6): 481–500.
Habermas, J. (1989), *The Structural Transformation of the Public Sphere: An Inquiry into a Category of Bourgeois Society*. Boston, MA: MIT Press.
Habermas, J. (1996), 'Three Normative Models of Democracy', in Benhabib, S. (ed.), *Democracy and Difference*. New York: Princeton University Press.
Hamid, S. (2022), *The Problem of Democracy*. New York: Oxford University Press.
Hanley, S. L., Dawson, J. and Cianetti, L. (2018), 'Rethinking "Democratic Backsliding" in Central and Eastern Europe – Looking beyond Hungary and Poland'. *East European Politics*, 34(3): 243–56.
Held, D. (2008), *Models of Democracy*. London: Polity Press.
Hill, M. A. (2010), 'Exploring USAID's Democracy Promotion in Bosnia and Afghanistan: A "Cookie-Cutter Approach"?' *Democratization*, 17(1): 98–124.
Horton, J. (1993), 'Moral Conflict and Political Commitment'. *Utilitas*, 5(1): 109–20.
Jochem, T., Murtazashvili, I. and Murtazashvili, J. (2015), 'Social Identity and Voting in Afghanistan: Evidence from a Survey Experiment'. *Journal of Experimental Political Science*, 2(1): 47–62.
Johnson, T. H. and Barnhart, R. J. (2020), 'An Examination of Afghanistan's 2018 Wolesi Jirga Elections: Chaos, Confusion and Fraud'. *Journal of Asian Security and International Affairs*, 7(1): 57–100.
Larson, A. (2009), 'Afghanistan's New Democratic Parties: A Means to Organize Democratisation?' Kabul: Afghanistan Research and Evaluation Unit. March 2009. Available at: https://www.refworld.org/docid/49c254a02.html (Accessed: 19 September 2023).
Larson, A. (2021), 'Democracy in Afghanistan: Amid and Beyond Conflict'. Washington, DC: United States Institute for Peace.
Levitsky, S. and Ziblatt, D. (2018), *How Democracies Die*. London: Penguin UK.
LoveAfghanistan Facebook, 9 March 2018: https://www.facebook.com/10150126008305294/posts/10160329036540294/.
Loyn, D. (2019), 'Politics without Parties: Afghanistan's Long Road to Democracy'. *Asian Affairs*, 50(1): 40–59.

Maia, R. (2018), 'Deliberative Media', in Bächtiger, A., Dryzek, J. S., Mansbridge, J. and Warren, M. E. (eds.), (2018), *The Oxford Handbook of Deliberative Democracy*. Oxford: Oxford University Press.

Maley, W. (2009), 'Democracy and Legitimation: Challenges in the Reconstitution of Political Processes in Afghanistan', in Bowden, B., Charlesworth, H. and Farrall, J. (eds.), *The Role of International Law in Rebuilding Societies after Conflict: Great Expectations*. Cambridge: Cambridge University Press, 111–33.

Maley, W. (2011), 'Challenges of Political Development in Afghanistan: Mass, Elite and Institutional Dimensions'. *International Studies*, 48(1): 21–41.

Mask (2013), 'Female Victims of Social or Sexual Violence Are Interviewed while Wearing Masks'. *YouTube* Video, Posted by 1 TV, 19 Videos, 2013, https://www.youtube.com/playlist?list=PLoKOy73atHGbc5KR-JP0XP66sYYkW0i82.

Mouffe, C. (1992), *Dimensions of Radical Democracy*. London: Verso.

Mouffe, C. (1996), 'Democracy, Power and "the Political"', in Benhabib, S. (ed.), *Democracy and Difference*. New York: Princeton University Press.

Mouffe, C. (2000), *Deliberative Democracy or Agonistic Pluralism* (Reihe Politikwissenschaft/Institut für Höhere Studien, Abt. Politikwissenschaft, 72). Wien: Institut für Höhere Studien (IHS), Wien. https://nbn-resolving.org/urn:nbn:de:0168-ssoar-246548.

Murray, E. (2020), *How Art Helped Propel Sudan's Revolution*. Washington DC: USIP. 12 November 2020. Available at: https://www.usip.org/blog/2020/11/how-art-helped-propel-sudans-revolution.

Murtazashvili, J. (2021), *Democracy Denied: The False Promise of Afghanistan's Constitutional Order*. Kabul: Afghanistan Institute for Strategic Studies (AISS).

Nemat, O. A. and Werner, K. (2016), *The Role of Civil Society in Promoting Good Governance in Afghanistan'*. Kabul: AREU.

Nixon, H. and Ponzio, R. (2007), 'Building Democracy in Afghanistan: The Statebuilding Agenda and International Engagement', in *International Peacekeeping*, 14(1): 26–40.

O'Flynn, I. and Caluwaerts, D. (2018), 'Deliberation in Deeply Divided Societies', in Bächtiger, A., Dryzek, J. S., Mansbridge, J. and Warren, M. E. (eds.), (2018), *The Oxford Handbook of Deliberative Democracy*. Oxford: Oxford University Press.

Osman, W. (2020), *Television and the Afghan Cultural Wars: Brought to You by Foreigners, Warlords, and Activists*. Chicago: University of Illinois Press.

Paikan, W. (2020), 'Mawlawi Baligh; Sheikh of Afghanistan Negotiating Team [Mawlawi Baligh; Sheikh Hayiat Muzakra kunenda Afghanistan]'. *Independent Persian*. Available at: https://www.independentpersian.com (Accessed: June 2023).

Pasarlay, S. (2016), 'Making the 2004 Constitution of Afghanistan: A History and Analysis through the Lens of Coordination and Deferral Theory'. University of Washington Electronic Theses and Dissertation. Available at: https://digital.lib.washington.edu/researchworks/bitstream/handle/1773/36735/Pasarlay_washington_0250E_16099.pdf?sequence=1andisAllowed=y.

Pejovich, S. (2003), 'Understanding the Transaction Costs of Transition: It's the Culture, Stupid'. *The Review of Austrian Economics*, 16(4): 347–61.

Pettit, P. (2002), *Republicanism: A Theory of Freedom and Government*. Oxford: Oxford University Press.

Rahimi, M. al-R. (2017), *State Formation in Afghanistan: A Theoretical and Political History*. New York: I.B. Tauris.

Recchia, F. (2014), 'Nationality, Identity, and Art'. *Himal*, 27(1): 72–82.

Sadr, O. (2020), *Negotiating Cultural Diversity in Afghanistan*. London: Routledge.

Sadr, O. (2021), *The Republic and Its Enemies: The Status of Republic in Afghanistan*. Kabul: Afghanistan Institute for Strategic Studies (AISS).

Schmeding, A. (2023), *Sufi Civilities: Religious Authority and Political Change in Afghanistan*. Stanford, CA: Stanford University Press.

Schmeidl, S. (2016), 'The Contradictions of Democracy in Afghanistan: Elites, Elections and "People's Rule" Post-2001'. *Conflict, Security and Development*, 16(6): 575–94.

Secretariat of the Constitutional Review Commission (2003), 'Analytical Report of People's Views and Recommendations for the Drafting of a New Constitution'. Kabul, Transitional Islamic State of Afghanistan.

Sharan, T. (2023), *Inside Afghanistan: Political Network and Informal Order and State Disruption*. London: Routledge.

Shenk, J. (2022), 'Does Conflict Experience Affect Participatory Democracy after War? Evidence from Colombia'. *Journal of Peace Research*, 60(6): 1–17.

Stepan, A. C. (2000), 'Religion, Democracy, and the "Twin Tolerations"'. *Journal of Democracy*, 11(4): 37–57.

Tickner, A. (2003), 'Seeing IR Differently: Notes from the Third World'. *Millennium: Journal of International Studies*, 32(2): 295–324.

Tilly, C. (2007), *Democracy*. Cambridge: Cambridge University Press.

Vendrell, F. (2011), 'Elections and the Future of Afghanistan', in Gillies, D. (ed.), *Elections in Dangerous Places: Democracy and the Paradoxes of Peacebuliding*. Montreal and Kingston: McGill-Queen's University Press, 21–31.

19

Mujahidin Memory and the Legacies of Wartime Governance in Afghanistan

Munazza Ebtikar

We have 22 bases (qarâgah-hâ) which remain from the beginning of the period of jihad [the Soviet-Afghan war]. A legacy that has been left behind by the national hero [Commander Ahmad Shah Massoud]. They have been left untouched. And the bases (qarâgah-hâ) have been kept intact.

These remarks are from an unidentified individual, his face concealed by the camera lens, amidst an assembly of similarly concealed figures, located in a remote mountainous region of Panjshir, Afghanistan. This scene was shot by *Arte*, a European public broadcast service, as part of a documentary chronicling the resistance in Afghanistan in the spring of 2022. The man alludes to the military bases established in the north and northeastern regions of Afghanistan during the Soviet-Afghan war in the 1980s and the subsequent wars of the 1990s. Mujahidin fighters from the area, under the leadership of Ahmad Shah Massoud, constructed these bases.[1] These strategic fronts have assumed newfound significance in the contemporary struggle against the Taliban. They have undergone a renaissance, resurrected not only in physical presence but also by way of the historical and mnemonic resonances they embody.

Contemporary scholarship on governance in Afghanistan has predominantly centred on post-2001 state building efforts, overlooking the diverse governance models that existed during the wartime periods of the 1980s and 1990s and their enduring influence on the current socio-political order. Such analyses consider Afghanistan as a 'post-conflict' blank slate or tabula rasa after 2001 (Murtazashvili 2016: 99), characterizing the preceding decades as chaotic, marked by the destruction of political order. Some studies have looked at informal or traditional forms of local governance outside the formal state apparatus (Murtazashvili 2016), while others have focused on non-state actors such as the Taliban and their governance practices, both during their rule in the 1990s and in the post-2021 context (Terpstra 2020; Williams 2022). These conceptualizations preclude the emergence of a range of

---

The transliteration system for this chapter follows a modified version of Encyclopaedia Iranica for both spoken and written Persian in Afghanistan.

opposition groups and their methods of governance in diverse jurisdictions across Afghanistan during past conflicts, as well as the endurance of their governing institutions today. Although scholars have attended to the emergence of political institutions and order, with some important exceptions (Roy 1995; Roy 2001; Rubin 2002; Dorronsoro 2005), they have not engaged with what Zachariah Mampilly (2011) would call 'microlevel processes'. These processes are essential for a better understanding of the relationship between civilians and governance structures shaped by violent conflict.

In this chapter, I consider the historical formations and mechanisms that continue to contribute to the institutionalization of power and authority in contemporary Afghanistan. More specifically, I discuss how local forms of governance and systems of administration created in Afghanistan under wartime conditions in the 1980s and 1990s persisted in the socio-political order under the Islamic Republic of Afghanistan (2001–21). My examination is particularly centred on Kabul and the northeastern regions of the country. Diverse opposition groups that defended, resisted and fought against the Kabul-based central state apparatus and the Soviet military presence practised local forms of governance and established related structures during the Soviet-Afghan war between 1979 and 1989. Many of these groups subsequently fought against one another in the early 1990s and in opposition to the Taliban in the mid- to-late 1990s. To gain a better understanding of the relationship between civilians and local forms of governance shaped by wars and conflict, as well as their continuity within Afghanistan's current socio-political order, I adopt memory as an analytical framework to understand how inhabitants and prominent wartime figures recalled, invoked and instrumentalized the wartime past, especially during times of heightened socio-political anxiety. This analysis extends to the resurgence of the Taliban in mid-2021 and to the emergence of the political opposition front (*jabha*) by the name of the National Resistance Front, also referred to as the 'second resistance' (*muqâwumat-e duwwum*).

The central theme of this chapter is that local governance practices created during the Soviet-Afghan war retain resilience and legitimacy for communities in Afghanistan. I investigate how recollections of the past – individual and collective – are reproduced in the present through symbols (such as flags), embodied practices (such as clothing) and visual culture (such as images and iconography of martyrs and political personalities). The memories conveyed by these symbols have normative value as they create communities and identity and, in so doing, legitimize present-day resistance and subversion vis-à-vis the current Taliban *de facto* authorities. They have also become a source of community debate over meaning in conversations amongst my interlocutors. As there are important contributions to local governance in Afghanistan in the presence and/or absence of the state, approaching the interplay of memory and governance represents a pertinent point of departure.

I try to understand how historical events permeate and shape identities, institutions, governance structures and political dynamics within communities in Afghanistan. In line with the work of sociologist and historian Maurice Halbwachs, and later pioneers such as Pierre Nora and Paul Connerton, an individual's memories function within a sociocultural environment, and memory in the collective sense contributes to shared versions of the past. In a similar vein, I understand memory as a social phenomenon that allows for the persistence of the past in the present. Collective memory, more specifically, constitutes narratives of the past constructed by specific groups, serving as meaningful forms of identification that are subject to negotiation and reassessment (Krawatzek 2020). Collective memory, alongside the institutions and practices that uphold it, plays a vital role in creating, sustaining and reproducing what Benedict Anderson referred to as 'imagined communities' (Anderson 1983). These communities provide individuals with a sense of history, place and belonging.

In studies of political memory, mnemonic actors invoke myths and symbols of the collective past in order to 'shape and delimit their societies' identities, legitimize their power, mobilize electoral support and exchange power resources. This usually resonates with the population, creating 'a dialectical connection between the elites' efforts to manipulate the past and the configuration of myths and beliefs shared by the society' (Malinova 2021). As such, I discuss the ways in which my interlocutors from Panjshir, as well as prominent wartime political figures in Afghanistan, invoke the past in their everyday lives, during the time of the Republic until today, as well as in *lieux de mémoire* (sites of memory) (Nora 1989), to weigh in on the present and the possible future.

Collective historical memory has practical continuity as well as presentist aspects; the past is being kept alive but, at times, reconstructed in light of the present (Halbwachs 1980). As there is a relational nature between individual and collective memory, I use a mixed-methods approach that relies on historical and anthropological tools including ethnography and semi-structured elite interviews. In addition, oral histories with women from their mid-20s to late 40s in Panjshir offer gendered interpretations. My argument speaks largely to, and from, the data I collected from Kabul to the northeastern regions of the country, including Panjshir, Parwan, Kapisa and Baghlan between 2018 and 2019. These regions are mostly composed of Persian-speaking (*fârsi zabân*) inhabitants who identify as Tajik. During the 1980s and 1990s (the war decades), they fell under the jurisdiction of the Jamiat-e Islami (henceforth Jamiat) political faction. This chapter is also based on interviews and ethnographic research I conducted since the end of my physical fieldwork, after the fall of the Islamic Republic of Afghanistan, the usurpation of power by the Taliban and the creation of new political resistance fronts.

I start by centring the discussions my female interlocutors have in gatherings of mourning in Panjshir that offer links with local practices of remembering in the everyday and living with the past in the present and possible future. This provides a gendered representation of the past that intersects with collective memory-making amidst acute socio-political anxieties heightened by political violence and the unmaking of the state in the late 2010s. In the second section, I look at memory in its collective sense to tie the history of local governance during the 1980s and 1990s wars in the north and northeastern regions and their legacies during the Republic in the third section. In the last section, I bring my discussion to the post-2021 socio-political order with the emergence of the National Resistance Front and discuss its relationship with the past.

Memory and Mourning in Panjshir

During my fieldwork in Panjshir between 2018 and 2019, I visited families that had lost their men – sons, husbands, brothers and other relatives. Most of these men were in their 20s and 30s, killed while serving in the Afghan National Defense and Security Forces (ANDSF). Visits with grieving families and the paying of respects represent local customary practices. Accompanied by my mother and aunt, visitations were as much of a necessity as they were a formality for locals. From the standpoint of my interlocutors, the men of the families that we visited had achieved martyrdom (*shahâdat*). During these visits, mourning women – and at times men – were consoled by visitors who made reference to the martyrdom of the men in previous wars, including men who were prominent and well-known fighters, close relatives or from the area (*ahl-e manteqa*). They expressed grief for this loss, but also that their loved ones' deaths were dignified as they were martyred during the periods of 'jihad' (the local term for the era during the Soviet-Afghan war) and *muqâwumat* (the local term to refer to the wars against the Taliban from 1996 to 2001). Martyrdom during this twenty-year period – the 1980s and 1990s – is commonly understood as a sacrifice for a multifaceted cause: religion (*din*), the people (*mardum*) and the homeland (*watan*).[2]

The memory and heroism of the martyrs in the past were systematically linked to those who sacrificed in the present. Memories of past death and martyrdom gave meaning to the contemporary deaths of ANDSF members and the experiences of their families. Gatherings entailed more than just mourning – long discussions about the present socio-political crisis faced in Afghanistan would follow. On one occasion, we visited Nargis, the mother of a martyr. During this visit, another visitor, Mariam, narrated a conversation she had had with her friend, Asma, to Nargis, as a form of consolation (*dildāre*). Asma's husband, an ANDSF soldier, was to return in four or five months from fighting in Helmand, a southern province that was the location of prolonged intense warfare, to Panjshir, and Mariam described that the conversation went as follows:

> Mariam (to Asma): if he comes [home to Panjshir], is he allowed to not return [to Helmand]? It's dangerous there, they will kill him. You have three children, look how young you are!
> Asma: Yes, he can choose not to return [to Helmand].
> Mariam: Why don't you tell him? Your husband [who] is in Helmand, you don't know when they will bring his casket to you?'.
> Asma: We tell him many times, many times, just do the most basic task here [i.e., take the most menial of jobs here at home], but just do not go [back]. Because not only [is it] your life, but also your income, and expectations from you are unknown. To which he says, 'I have children, I have a father and mother, what am I to do?'

These conversations took place in 2019, a period of heightened political tensions and violence, during the parliamentary and presidential elections as well as the ongoing negotiations between the Taliban and the United States. Mariam recalled that she had advised Asma to stop her husband from serving in the ANDSF because the fight had become unclear (*nâ ma'lum*), illegitimate (*nâ mashro'*) and she was likely to lose him. The idea that there was a danger that these soldiers faced for an unclear, now illegitimate, fight emerged as a recurring sentiment in these gatherings. The government was perceived to be corrupt (*fesâde*) and ungodly (*be imân*) for several reasons, the most significant of which was that it was cowering to the United States in releasing the same Taliban prisoners against whom many ANDSF were losing their lives on the battlefield. And, so, it seemed to women like Mariam and Asma that the fight in which their men were taking part was no longer for a religious, collective or nationalist purpose. Instead, suggestions to not send their men to serve in the ANDSF became commonplace, 'Why doesn't Ashraf Ghani send his son to fight? Why does it have to be our poor son (*bache-ye gharîb-e mâ*)?'

Alternative prescriptions, which invoked the place of the individual and the collective in the previous wartime past, would follow. In one instance, in another gathering, a woman expresses:

> Let's build it [what existed from the past] again, let's keep our honor, let's keep our daughter, let's keep our son. Let's come and start from nothing. Do you remember what had happened during the jabha, it was us against the Soviets? The Soviets had said, 'if you destroy their [the inhabitants'] homes, they will build another, if you destroy their school, they will build another, if you kill one of their sons, they will have another'. We can do that again.

In these moments, mourning for martyrs shaped and renewed a sense of community. It also demonstrated how wives and mothers conveyed normative or moral sentiments about the meaning of war, including through an invocation of the idealized past war as a means of critiquing the one unfolding at present. For my interlocutors, the past was invoked and valorized to give meaning to the present. The difference between the two eras was that the fight in the past was by the people for the people. Now it was the fight by the people for the government. Conversations on the future were charged with uncertainty given the precarious present. This remembrance of the past wars in everyday conversations was tied to a kind of collective remembrance of the war and the time when a *jabha* (front) existed in Panjshir. The invocation of this past – and the contrast it provoked with the present – was made not only by my interlocutors in a gathering like this one. Prominent wartime political figures in the region also invoked the wartime past as a means of diagnosing the present and prescribing the future, especially in times of heightened socio-political anxiety.

Collective Memory and Commemorative Practices

As I rode the Kabul-Salang highway from northwest Kabul to Panjshir during the 2019 presidential campaigns, I found the landscape dotted with green, white and black mujahidin flags (flags of those who fought against the Soviets and the People's Democratic Party of Afghanistan [PDPA] government and later, the Taliban in the 1990s), frequently in lieu of the national flags of Afghanistan. These flags also appeared on the campaign posters of the presidential candidates who were sporting the Palestinian *keffiyeh* (locally termed as *destmâl*), *pakôl* hats and military-style clothing. The slogans on these posters contained words like '*muqâwumat*' (resistance), '*jihad*' and '*shahīd*' (martyr). This visual culture and mnemonic practices were connected to Afghanistan's wartime pasts and invoked by prominent wartime and political figures, as well as the women whom I visited in gatherings of mourning in Panjshir.

This collective memory is based on the 'symbolic processes' of the 1980s and 1990s, a time when the governance structure of the region had 'communal motifs, national signs, and ideologies' to 'promote solidarity and social cohesion among a diverse population while imbuing it with a sense of moral unity' (Mampilly 2011; Mampilly 2015: 78). Alongside symbolic elements, 'rebel governance' during the previous wartime periods unique to these regions had a strong material relationship with the local community. An established political order operated with its own security force while providing key public goods, including legal services, healthcare, education systems and forms of taxation (Rubin 2002).

In February 2020, when the presidential election results were officially announced with Ashraf Ghani as the winner, his main opponent, Abdullah Abdullah, accused him of vote-rigging. Abdullah held a parallel inaugural ceremony in March 2020, also declaring himself as the winner. Abdullah's inaugural ceremony had similar visual material to what I had seen on the Kabul-Salang highway, with similar points of reference. A few weeks prior to the ceremony, Abdullah opposed the Ghani-appointed new governors in the country's northern provinces. He had received the most votes in these provinces, namely Sar-e Pul, Jawzjan, Samangan and Baghlan. Even the Ghani-appointed governor in Panjshir openly expressed his support for Abdullah. Abdullah had some roots in Panjshir and had served as the assistant and advisor to the late anti-Soviet and anti-Taliban resistance leader, Ahmad Shah Massoud, in the previous war decades. This background had secured him a degree of political legitimacy in the northern regions. Moreover, he had held the position of chief executive officer (CEO) of Afghanistan from 2014 to 2020, giving him and his supporters an important role in the state institutions of the Republic (Ruttig 2015).

Political and wartime figures such as Abdullah Abdullah were striving to obtain legitimacy by curating a particular version of the past, choosing which events were highlighted, leaving some as forgotten, and rearranging events to conform to the chosen social narrative of the moment.

For the inhabitants of the region, as well as prominent wartime figures, the memory of the previous wars was recuperated and strengthened during important commemorative events, such as Martyr's Day (*rôz-e shahîd*) and Martyr's Week (*hafta-ye shahîd*). Established in the early 2000s, these commemorative events act as *lieux de mémoire* to honour the martyrdom of those who fought in the wars of the 1980s and 1990s. Memory is also manifested in visual form: the mujahidin flags and attire – the Palestinian *keffiyeh*, *pakôl* hats and military-style clothing – are all indicative of the twenty-year wars when this was the uniform of mujahidin fighters in these regions used to distinguish them from the civilian population. References to *jihad* and *muqâwumat* act as an invocation of memory of the collective past in the present, as well as a way to contest and respond to the political order at the time.

The mujahidin flags that I saw on the Kabul-Salang highway were the flags of a pre-2001 Afghanistan, when mujahidin factions, headed by Jamiat, had created an interim government, the Islamic State of Afghanistan, after the fall of the central government in 1992. Jamiat had claimed the northern regions of the country under its control, including the regions from the north of Kabul to Panjshir. The faction had grown increasingly prominent during the Soviet-Afghan war and continued to play an integral role in the subsequent civil war, the war against the Taliban in the late 1990s and the post-2001 US-led campaign that ousted the Taliban regime. As such, the presence of mujahidin flags, at times in lieu of the national flags of Afghanistan in late 2018 and 2019, illustrated a legacy of the past in the present. This urban landscape had been largely under the jurisdiction of Jamiat when it operated as a fighting force and later as the key stakeholder in the 1990s government that nominally controlled these northern regions of Afghanistan, even as it contested the Taliban's later grip on the majority of the country.

The symbolic connotation of a past government flag also served as a political claim, one that not only challenges the legitimacy of the state but also provides alternative paths and possible calls for political autonomy. Continuities from the previous wars into the time of the post-2001 Republic are usually understood through the role of strongmen in state building processes (Giustozzi 2009; Mukhopadhyay 2014) or through political networks (Sharan 2023) that provide governance and services. By adopting collective memory as an analytical framework, we see how the past penetrates and develops identities, institutions and forms of governance, and political processes among communities into the future.

Legacies of Wartime Governance and Systems of Administration

Diverse political organizations and socio-political and military fronts formed and developed during the wars that functioned outside, and mostly, against the government. In the 1980s, political factions across Afghanistan were established and united in their opposition to the Soviet military forces as well as the Soviet-backed Kabul government. The Soviets exercised their largest control in the capital, while the majority of the country fell under the control of these political factions. In the absence of state control over most parts of the country, new governance structures and diverse forms of local governance established security and resistance against the Soviet army, the government and other factions. These factions were headed by local military leaders or local notables, organized along tribal, regional, clan, family, ethnic or sectarian lines, and largely received support among the local population (Shahrani and Leroy 1984).

During the 1980s, Jamiat was active across the country, but more concentrated in the northern regions of Afghanistan with several high-ranking commanders, including Ahmad Shah Massoud, as a military and political leader (*âmir*) of the Panjshir front.[3]

Although the Panjshir front was a stronghold, it expanded into the south of the Salang, the Shamali plains and neighbouring Andarab district, among other areas. A front (*jabha*) was usually composed of several bases (*qarârgâh-hâ*), most of which were located among the local population and usually composed of members therein (Mansour 1990; Roy 1995; Roy 2001; Rubin 2002). The stronger Jamiat was in a region, the more bases it had. Panjshir, for example, had twenty-two bases at one time all affiliated with Jamiat. Every base had control of several villages, for example the bases in Parandeh, Jangalak, Bazarak, Astana, Rahmankhel until Rukha on one side of the Panjshir River, were all affiliated with the base in Parandeh.[4] Bases served as military and political structures; they performed acts of governance and served as checkpoints to control population movement (Mansour 1990).

Each base had a commander, doctor, financial officer and so on. These bases had a judge (*qâzi*) who dealt with the legal matters of the local population as well as a treasury, usually to collect taxes or finance supplies for the front. Educational systems (commonly taught in mosques) and healthcare systems for fighters and civilians also existed. Among all bases there were general committees. For example, in Panjshir there was one general committee that headed the health committees in all the bases, and the head of all committees was Massoud himself, a system Sandy Gall described as 'embryonic ministries'. Each base had a different number of members, for example the base in Rukha had around 500 at one time.

The well-trained fighters in the bases were called *mutaharek* (mobile units composed of thirty-two fighters). The task of the *mutaharek* was to engage in guerrilla operations outside Panjshir. Another force was the *zarbate*, composed of around 30 to 40 fighters. This group functioned inside and outside Panjshir and was equipped with light and heavy weapons. The last group was *mahale*, this group was made up of the local population, who assisted fighters, tended to the wounded, provided logistical support and gathered information on the enemy's movements in the neighbouring regions (Ariya 2020). Based on these structures, Massoud later created the *shurâ-ye nizâr* (supervisory council) in the mid-1980s, a proto-state structure that acted as a civilian shadow government in northeastern Afghanistan (Malejacq 2020). The *shurâ-ye nizâr* united the commanders of the geographically connected northern fronts and had state-like institutions and committees (military, political, judicial, health, education, cultural, reconstruction, etc.) to provide services to the population while receiving funding from NGOs and international organizations.[5] These northern networks were largely based on *qawm*, a concept designating a 'solidarity group' often based on kinship ties (Jochem and Murtazashvili and Murtazashvili 2015). The leaders of a *qawm* held significant influence over the local population.

Three years after the Soviet withdrawal from Afghanistan in 1989, the communist regime in Kabul fell. On 25 April 1992, the Islamic State of Afghanistan was formed by some of these mujahidin factions, even as a struggle for power among them continued. The leaders and commanders of these factions emerged as 'strongmen' with their own networks as different regions were controlled with separate state administrations and bureaucracies (Sharan 2023). The day-to-day politics of the wars were 'marked by continuities as well as disruption' (Arjona et al. 2015: 10). When the Taliban took control of Kabul from 1996 to 2001, they were met with organized military opposition from a coalition of some mujahidin factions from the northern and central parts of Afghanistan. This coalition was called the National United Islamic Front (UIF) for the Salvation of Afghanistan and was headed by Massoud and Jamiat until 2001. The Taliban regime fell in 2001 when the US-led coalition forces allied with the UIF and intervened in Afghanistan. After the intervention of the US-led coalition forces, the Republic was established with a new legal framework in the early 2000s. The Republic was created on the basis of power-sharing between different groups. One of these groups included the leaders of the mujahidin factions and prominent figures, such as Atta Muhammad Noor and Abdul Rashid Dostum, the majority of whom were from Jamiat and other factions within the UIF.

These figures became part of a new centralized state structure to strengthen government institutions and prevent hostility while also holding on to their existing subnational networks which remained from the wartime past. These figures not only maintained inherited networks of supporters and systems of administration from the war periods, but they also held additional forms of power and influence within this new state structure (Malejacq 2020). As we have seen quite consistently in post-2001 Afghanistan, these prominent figures largely believed in, worked for and with the government of the Republic. As such, when Abdullah stood in opposition to Ghani during the 2020 presidential elections, and accused him of fraudulent electoral activity, he appointed governors from the regions of Afghanistan within which he held support. That support dated to the 1980s and 1990s, when most of the northern regions were under the jurisdiction of Jamiat. As Ghani, once announced the winner, made clear his plans to disband the office of the CEO, Abdullah gathered supporters from prominent figures of the war decades and invoked the memory of the periods of *jihad* and *muqâwumat* to contest the results. Once the Taliban took power in Kabul in August 2021, a new political resistance group emerged from these regions, composed, or supported by these figures who made reference to pasts and relied on previous networks, governance structures and systems of administrations.

The Inception of Anti-Taliban Front and Their Relationship to the Past

When the Taliban captured Kabul militarily on 15 August 2021, on the same day, the son of Ahmad Shah Massoud, Ahmad Massoud, took a helicopter to Panjshir. He saw Panjshir and its surrounding regions as a safe haven from the time of his father's politico-military activities. As the majority of the Republic's leadership fled the country, Massoud's decision to fly to Panjshir, alongside a group of local and military personnel from the Republic, including Vice President Amrullah Saleh, coupled with the support of the local commanders in the region including commanders in districts of Baghlan province, laid the ground for what became the first politico-military front against the Taliban in 2021 called the National Resistance Front. This new front has continued its military activities mostly in the north and northeastern regions of the country, including Panjshir, Baghlan, Parwan, Kapisa and Badakhshan, among others, alongside other allied politico-military groups, such as the Andarab Resistance Front, or the Afghanistan Freedom Front created in 2022 composed of Special Forces commanders of the Republic. The National Resistance Front is grounded in, and evokes, the wartime past in the present. Even before the Taliban takeover of Kabul, when the international forces announced their withdrawal and major cities began to fall, former mujahidin leaders such as Ismail Khan, Atta Muhammad Noor and Abdul Rashid Dostum – all of whom were integral to the Republic – held meetings and publicly discussed forming a strong defence against the Taliban. In those assemblies, they discussed their resistance in the past as a lesson for their planned resistance in the precarious present.

With the Taliban in Kabul and Massoud in Panjshir, in consultation with Panjshir's local religious authorities (*ulema*), the resistance vied for an unsuccessful peace deal with the Taliban in late August. The Taliban's victorious euphoria, combined with its inability to access Panjshir (on account of the resistance presence), left the group uninterested in peace negotiations. Instead, following a centralization of power in the capital, the Taliban demanded surrender and an oath of allegiance and sought to take the province militarily. In late August 2021, they started to engage in small erosive attacks in Paryan, on the northern most border of Panjshir, a valley that only has two major ways in and out. Their strategy was to tire the best fighters and launch a major attack. The Taliban also attacked from surrounding regions including Kapisa, Baghlan and Badakhshan. Eventually, they broke into Panjshir (Giustozzi 2021). The Resistance continued to defend itself, some of their tactics based on memories of the wars against the Soviets in the 1980s such as blocking incoming Taliban columns, similar to Soviet ones, by blowing up the surrounding mountainside (Giustozzi 2021). Meanwhile, Massoud and the local religious authorities remained hopeful for a successful peace negotiation. But, by 28 August, the Taliban cut telecommunication lines and by 29 August, blockaded the province.

The blockade, the lack of telecommunications and the withdrawal of all international forces from Afghanistan by the end of August left this newly formed resistance group in a tenuous position. During the time of the Republic, Panjshir had been demilitarized and was perceived as a relatively safe region by inhabitants, under government control and without an immediate Taliban threat. Prominent anti-Taliban figures had been integrated into Afghanistan's defence and security sectors but, by the end of Ghani's tenure, local and prominent anti-Taliban governors were being sidelined and removed from power. Neither individuals nor institutions remained in place to effectively repel future Taliban advances (Mobasher and Qadam Shah 2022). As such, the military front that had existed in the 1980s and 1990s under Jamiat, for whatever remnants remained, could not recreate itself in time to meet the threat. Vice President Amrullah Saleh had been sending weapons to Panjshir from Kabul, and there were weapons caches preserved in Panjshir dating from the time of the 1980s wars. But the Taliban gained ground fast, precluding a robust resistance similar in strength to that before 2001.

The Resistance was unprepared for and vastly outnumbered by the Taliban's onslaught in early September 2021. The Pakistani intelligence chief, Faiz Hameed, visited Kabul on 4 September, and the next day, Panjshir was subjected to indiscriminate aerial and ground attacks with the assistance of the Pakistani Special Forces. Anyone suspected of being part of or sympathetic towards the Resistance was detained or killed. Meanwhile, a manhunt against Amrullah Saleh left behind a trail of massacres in the side-valleys of Panjshir. The Taliban's assassination of well-known national journalist and spokesperson of the Resistance, Fahim Dashty, shocked the Resistance and its supporters. On 6 September, Massoud released a public recording stating, 'Dear compatriots! Wherever you are, whether inside or outside the country, we appeal to you to rise up in resistance for the dignity, integrity and freedom of our country. Whatever means at your disposal, rise up against a crippling humiliation brought on us today by foreigners' (Massoud 2021). This message galvanized protests, most notably, in neighbourhoods with predominant Tajik and Hazara residents in Khair Khana and Dasht-e Barchi in Kabul, and across the world. The leadership of the Resistance, including Massoud and Saleh, left for Dushanbe, where they created their political office. The Resistance adopted the green, white and black mujahidin flags alongside the red, black and green flag of the Republic to demonstrate their relationship to the past. These flags invoked anti-Taliban sentiment and the memories of the wars against the Taliban.

As the Taliban took control of the majority of the country and Panjshir remained in the Resistance's grip, videos surfaced on social media capturing caravans of young men in motorcycles and cars driving on the main road of Panjshir, parading the green, white and black mujahidin flags. The expressed goal of the Resistance remains to recapture the capital and the northern regions of the country through both unconventional and conventional means, employing lessons from the first Resistance (*muqâwumat-e awwal*) (Wasielewski 2022). The Taliban's recruitment area is not large in these geographical areas, as they recruit mostly from the southern regions and rely on districts where they have long maintained a presence. The Resistance is not driven by an ambition for geographical control so much as by attempts to engage in small erosive guerrilla attacks that exhaust the Taliban. They aim to capture small regions and then move on to larger and more strategic areas. Regions in the north, including Panjshir and the Andarab district of Baghlan among others, where the Resistance has been fighting, are connected on a socio-topographic level. These regions are mountainous and understood by the fighters and the local population. Many in the Resistance were fighters – even commanders – during the 1980s and 1990s wars, and many were soldiers or commanders in the post-2001 National Defense and Security Forces. Their past experiences have become, once again, relevant during this second period of Taliban rule.

Since the 1980s, the geo-strategic location of Panjshir, as well as its adjacent regions, has made it a key stronghold for resistance. It is a valley surrounded by mountains, a landscape that allows for guerrilla fighting with a rich socio-political legacy and inhabitants who have long held a memory of anti-Taliban sentiments. These sentiments remain rooted in the collective memories, grievances and sentiments of this recent past, before the American military presence when the UIF led the fight against the Taliban. That legacy carried on during the time of the Republic, when the ANDSF fought alongside NATO against the Taliban. This is also a place where governance structures, systems of administration, and networks were built and developed in a wartime context that extended deep into local communities and persisted, through the lifetime of the Republic and into the once-again resistant present.

Conclusion

An examination of pre-2001 forms of governance and administration through the lens of collective memory enables us to move beyond conceptualizations that centre the relationship between prominent figures of the past and the state, as evidenced in most work on governance in Afghanistan. Instead, we can begin to investigate the memories, grievances, and sentiments that ordinary citizens and their leaders continue to carry in ongoing contexts and how these recollections inform their day-to-day views on the present in the face of political upheaval. My interlocutors, as well as prominent wartime figures from the north of Kabul to Panjshir, invoked the memory of the 1980s and 1990s wars when diverse forms of governance and systems of administration were created. These historical legacies – and the collective memory that carries them – remain visible and influential in Afghanistan, impacting everyday life, especially in times of heightened tension and insecurity. Collective memories from that period have been constructed and reconstructed over the years for, and by, my interlocutors as well as prominent wartime figures to make sense of the precarious present and uncertain future.

As the Taliban demonstrate their determination to establish a totalitarian form of governance following their second takeover of Kabul (Sakhi 2022), an examination of collective memory, grievances and subnational governance sheds light on the calls for a decentralized system (*ghair-e mutamarkez*). This call for decentralization is closely connected with the social and political history of particular territories, regions and places in Afghanistan (Shahrani 2001; Murtazashvili 2014; Shahrani 2018a; Shahrani 2018b; Balkhi 2022; Mobasher and Qadam Shah 2022). Future research can extend beyond a given region, such as Panjshir, or organized military groups, like the National Resistance Front. It can consider how diverse spatial and power dynamics exist and operate beyond traditional, territorial and state-centric analyses to gain a more comprehensive understanding of the enduring impact of the past on the present. Foregrounding a bottom-up approach, which does not just privilege prominent male actors – and, in fact, democratizes knowledge production in meaningful new terms – might allow us to better understand the relationships between civilian populations and the systems of governance and administration as well as social networks in their midst. This approach has the potential to offer a critical and nuanced examination of power and authority in twenty-first-century Afghanistan (and beyond).

Notes

1   In the context of Afghanistan, the term 'mujahidin' (translated as those engaged in jihad) refers to various opposition groups from Afghanistan from the late 1970s until today. They mainly opposed the Soviet-backed Kabul government since 1978 and the Soviet invasion in 1979. However, the term itself is always changing in meaning: today, it is also used by the Taliban, human rights activists, women's rights organizations, and former combatants and community-militia commanders in the

country, see Bhatia (2007). Here, I adopt the local meaning among my interlocutors, which refers to people engaged in the fight against the Soviet Union militarily and non-militarily, against opposing political factions during the 1990s, and against the Taliban. Specifically, it is a reference to those largely affiliated with Jamiat.
2   For an ethnographic elaboration on martyrdom in Islam, see Khalili (2009) and Deeb (2006).
3   Serves as a political and military leader and understood to be the governor of a faction in a particular region.
4   Author interview with Muhammad Yahya Massoud, former diplomat and the elder brother of Ahmad Shah Massoud, 17 April 2019.
5   For an ethnographic and oral history account of the mujahidin in northeastern provinces of Afghanistan during the late 1980s and early 1990s, see Walwaji (1999).

References

Afghan, H. (2021), 'Humayoun Afghan Has Reached Panjshir'. *YouTube*. Available at: https://www.youtube.com/watch?v=8r3EC7pJFYsandt=1s.
Anderson, B. (1983), *Imagined Communities*. London and New York: Verso.
Ariya, Z. (2020), 'Massoud: Istratejeke Nezami [Massoud: Military Strategist]'. *Hasht-e Subh*. Online. Available at: https://8am.media/fa/masoud-military-strategist/.
Arjona, A., Kasfir, N., and Mampilly, Z. (2015), *Rebel Governance in Civil War*. Cambridge: Cambridge University Press.
Arte TV (2022). 'The Afghan Resistance'. *Arte TV*, 20 May 2022. Available at: https://www.arte.tv/en/videos/108011-000-A/arte-reportage/.
Azoy, W. (2003), 'Masood's Parade: Iconography, Revitalization, and Ethnicity in Afghanistan'. *Penn Museum*, 45(1): 39–45.
Balkhi, M. (2022), 'To Achieve Inclusivity, Afghanistan Needs Decentralization', in *The National Interest*. The Center for the National Interest. https://nationalinterest.org/blog/middle-east-watch/achieve-inclusivity-afghanistan-needs-decentralization-204242
Bergholz, M. (2017), *Violence as a Generative Force: Identity, Nationalism, and Memory in a Balkan Community*. Ithaca, NY: Cornell University Press.
Bhatia, M. (2007), 'The Future of the Mujahidin'. *International Peacekeeping*, 14(1): 90–107.
CABAR.asia (2022), 'Afghanistan One Year Later under the Taliban. Interview with Dr. Omar Sadr'. *CABAR.asia*, 2 September 2022. Available at: https://cabar.asia/en/afghanistan-one-year-later-under-the-taliban-interview-with-dr-omar-sadr.
Centlivres, P. and Centlivres-Demont, M. (2010), *Afghanistan on the Threshold of the 21st Century: Three Essays on Culture and Society*. Princeton, NJ: Markus Wiener Publishers.
Crews, R. D. (2020), 'Mourning Imam Husayn in Karbala and Kabul: The Political Meanings of Ashura in Afghanistan'. *Afghanistan*, 3(2): 202–36.
Deeb, L. (2006), *An Enchanted Modern: Gender and Public Piety in Shi'i Lebanon*. Princeton: University Press.
Dorronsoro, G. (2005), *Revolution Unending: Afghanistan, 1979 to the Present*. Paris: Columbia University Press in association with the Centre d'Études et de Recherches Internationales.

Gall, S. (2022), *Afghan Napoleon: The Life of Ahmed Shah Massoud*. London: Haus Publishing Ltd.
Giustozzi, A. (2009), *Empires of Mud: War and Warlords in Afghanistan*. London: Hurst.
Giustozzi, A. (2021), *The Lessons Not Learned: Afghanistan after the Fall of Panjshir*. London: Royal United Services Institute.
Halbwachs, M. (1980), *The Collective Memory*. New York: Harper and Row.
Hobsbawm, E. J. and Ranger, T. O. (1983), *The Invention of Tradition*. Cambridge: Cambridge University Press.
Jochem, T., Murtazashvili, I. and Murtazashvili, J. (2015), 'Social Identity and Voting in Afghanistan: Evidence from a Survey Experiment'. *Journal of Experimental Political Science*, 2(1): 47–62.
Khalili, L. (2009), *Heroes and Martyrs of Palestine: The Politics of National Commemoration*. Cambridge: Cambridge University Press.
Krawatzek, F. (2020), 'Collective Memory'. Oxford Bibliographies (Online). Available at: https://www.oxfordbibliographies.com/display/document/obo-9780199756223/obo-9780199756223-0301.xml.
Malejacq, R. (2020), *Warlord Survival: The Delusion of State Building in Afghanistan*. Ithaca, NY: Cornell University Press.
Malinova, O. (2021), 'Politics of Memory and Nationalism'. *Nationalities Papers*, 49(6): 997–1007.
Mampilly, Z. (2011), *Rebel Rulers: Insurgent Governance and Civilian Life during War*. Ithaca, NY: Cornell University Press.
Mampilly, Z. (2015), 'Performing the Nation-State: Rebel Governance and Symbolic Processes', in Arjona, A., Kasfir, N. and Mampilly, Z. (eds.), *Rebel Governance in Civil War*. Cambridge: Cambridge University Press, 74–97.
Mansour, A. H. (1990), *Panjshîr dar dawran-e jihâd* [Panjshir during the Era of Jihad]. Edited by A. Ata and S. F. Farouq. 1st edition. Tehran: Ketâbkhane wa markaz-e asnâd-e bonyâd-e iran shenâsi.
Massoud, A. (2021), 'Ahmad Massoud's Message to the World.' *YouTube* Video, available at https://www.youtube.com/watch?v=gznGZzNUTSw
Mobasher, M. B. and Qadam Shah, M. (2022), 'Deproblematizing the Federal–Unitary Dichotomy: Insights from a Public Opinion Survey about Approaches to Designing a Political System in Afghanistan'. *Publius: The Journal of Federalism*, 52(2): 225–53.
Mukhopadhyay, D. (2014), *Warlords, Strongman Governors, and the State in Afghanistan*. Cambridge: Cambridge University Press.
Murtazashvili, J. B. (2014), 'Informal Federalism: Self-Governance and Power Sharing in Afghanistan'. *Publius: The Journal of Federalism*, 44(2): 324–43.
Murtazashvili, J. B. (2016), *Informal Order and the State in Afghanistan*. Cambridge: Cambridge University Press.
Nora, P. (1989), 'Between Memory and History: Les Lieux de Mémoire'. *Representations*, 26: 7–24.
Olick, J K and Robbins, J. (1998), 'Social Memory Studies: From "Collective Memory" to the Historical Sociology of Mnemonic Practices'. *Annual Review of Sociology*, 24: 105–40.
Roy, O. (1995), *Afghanistan: From Holy War to Civil War*. Sundridge, Kent, UK: Darwin Press.
Roy, O. (2001), *Islam and Resistance in Afghanistan*. 2nd ed. Cambridge: Cambridge University.

Rubin, B. R. (2002), *The Fragmentation of Afghanistan: State Formation and Collapse in the International System*. 2nd ed. New Haven, CT: Yale University Press.

Ruttig, T. (2015), 'The President's CEO Decree: Managing Rather than Executive Powers (now with Full Translation of the Document)'. Afghan Analysts Network. Available at: https://www.afghanistan-analysts.org/en/reports/political-landscape/the-presidents-ceo-decree-managing-rather-then-executive-powers/.

Sakhi, N. (2022), 'The Taliban Takeover in Afghanistan and Security Paradox'. *Journal of Asian Security and International Affairs*, 9(3): 383–401.

Shahrani, M. N. (2001), 'Not "Who?" but "How?": Governing Afghanistan after the Conflict'. *Federations*. Available at: www.forumfed.org/libdocs/Federations/V1afgh-af-Shahrani.pdf.

Shahrani, M. N. (2018), 'The State and Community Self-Governance: Paths to Stability and Human Security in Post-2014 Afghanistan', in Bose, S., Motwani, N. and Maley, W. (eds.), *Afghanistan – Challenges and Prospects*. New York: Routledge, 43–62.

Shahrani, N. (2018), 'The Afghan President Has More Powers than a King'. *Al Jazeera*, 3 January 2018. www.aljazeera.com/opinions/2018/1/3/the-afghan-president-has-more-powers-than-a-king/.

Shahrani, N. M. and Canfield, R. L. (1984), *Revolutions and Rebellions in Afghanistan: Anthropological Perspectives*. Berkeley, CA: Institute of International Studies, University of California.

Sharan, T. (2023), *Inside Afghanistan: Political Networks, Informal Order, and State Disruption*. Abingdon, UK: Routledge.

Tarzi, A. (2013), 'The Maturation of Afghan Historiography'. *International Journal of Middle East Studies*, 45(1): 129–31.

Terpstra, N. (2020), 'Rebel Governance, Rebel Legitimacy, and External Intervention: Assessing Three Phases of Taliban Rule in Afghanistan'. *Small Wars and Insurgencies*, 31(6): 1143–73.

Walwaji, A. (1999), *Dar Safahât-e Shamâl-e Afghânistan Che Mêguzasht?* [What Was Happening in Northern Afghanistan?]. Part Two. 1st edition. Tehran: Markaz-e inteshârât wa ketâbforôshi al-azhar (Mohammad Ebrahim Mohseni).

Wasielewski, P. (2022), 'The Afghan National Resistance Front Outlines Its Strategy: Implications for US Foreign Policy'. Foreign Policy Research Institute, 21 November 2022. Available at: https://www.fpri.org/article/2022/11/the-afghan-national-resistance-front-outlines-its-strategy-implications-for-us-foreign-policy/.

Williams, P. (2022), 'US Intervention in Afghanistan and the Failure of Governance'. *Small Wars and Insurgencies*, 33(7): 1130–51.

Afterword

Dipali Mukhopadhyay

We began work on this volume in the summer of 2021, on the cusp of a cataclysmic transition in contemporary Afghan history. As the Taliban swept back into power, their victory heralded the collapse of the country's latest experiment with republicanism as well as the ignominious end of America's longest war. For one of our editors, Omar Sharifi, this moment spelled a particularly personal form of devastation with the loss of his homeland; for the other two, Anna Larson and myself, profoundly shaped by our sustained encounters with Afghanistan, the despair was also acute. We redoubled our commitment to this collection, determined to ensure that 2021 did not mark the end of scholarly attention to and reflection on this country, its peoples and their ongoing entanglements with the world around them. On the contrary, we recognized an opportunity to provide a platform for the plurality of voices, epistemic traditions and methodological approaches that we had encountered over the last two decades. The body of work that this plurality has produced – much of it conducted by young indigenous scholars and researchers – has the potential to revise, expand, and sustain knowledge production in and on Afghanistan.

In compiling the volume we were also interested in bringing these new perspectives into conversation with more established ones; to this end we offered a number of senior scholars an opportunity to revisit and reflect on their own understandings as they had evolved over time. We hope readers take note of the several striking continuities that emerge across the chapters as well as a number of productive disruptions and departures that arise. We also hope they find fodder for their own research pursuits and, in so doing, ensure that the study of Afghanistan persists in new incarnations even as the challenges of in-country research remain formidable.

In reflecting on the volume as a whole, there are a few contributions we wish especially to underscore. In the popular western imagination, Afghanistan has long served as a kind of empty signifier into which much has been deposited. It has served as a crucible for blame, vengeance, competition and aspiration. It was the 'graveyard of empires', and, then, a 'safe haven' for terror, but also a fertile garden in which the West could plant the seeds of a new kind of imperial ambition. It was a place to be both conquered and liberated. One marked by centrifugal tribal divisions and warlordism but also a blank slate on which to paint neoliberal fantasies of good governance, free markets and democratic rule. As Nivi Manchanda put it, 'an "idea" of Afghanistan as a strategically organized ensemble of historico-political knowledges' has existed and evolved in terms that have especially lent themselves to its classification as a sui generis case.[1] In the academy, the vagaries of colonialism and postcolonial geopolitics left Afghanistan orphaned in contemporary area studies, a status that was only exacerbated after the attacks on 11 September 2001.

But, in fact, Afghanistan's encounters with empire, the fluid complexities of its centre–periphery relations, and the tensions between structure and agency that mark its politics are hardly unique.[2] One of the most gratifying contributions of this volume is an inclination on the part of many authors to speak (back) to larger empirical developments and theoretical debates that bring Afghanistan as a site of study into a wider set of conversations. Here and elsewhere, a new generation of scholars has taken up capacious subjects like Islamist politics, rebel governance, civil–military relations, neopatrimonialism and western military intervention – to name a few – while entering into dialogue with a variety of theoretical traditions related to democracy, postcolonialism, critical feminism and so on. It is our hope that the themes, logics and arguments many of them have surfaced in the process will travel productively to other parts of the world even as they enrich our understanding of Afghanistan.

On the concepts of power and authority in particular, our contributors have innovated in a number of important ways. Some bring new and critical focus to the material dimensions of these concepts, pushing us to rethink conventional wisdoms across several arenas, including the security sector, the marketplace, land tenure and foreign aid. Several also attend to the more symbolic, ideational, and discursive features of power and authority. In so doing, they deconstruct some of the long-held myths and memes that have animated common understandings of Afghanistan (Manchanda 2020). Reflection, for example, on the multiplicity of female perspectives and experiences on a given issue – whether it be access to education or the politics of insurgency – takes the reader beyond the common one-dimensional portrait of 'the Afghan woman'. Meanwhile, attention to metropolitan (and, more generally, geographical) identity formation counteracts the ubiquitous assumption by scholars (and interveners) that ethnicity is *the* determinative variable in Afghan politics. Similarly, labels like 'nomad' and 'Islamist' are revealed to be chapeaus for a number of different – even contradictory – meanings whose distinctions and complexities can only be unpacked through careful consideration. These scholarly moves bring new insight into state–society relations in Afghanistan and also have relevance for students of comparative politics in other parts of the world.

A number of authors in this volume apply a critical lens to the 2001 to 2021 international intervention, exposing the ways in which foreign myopia, dysfunction, and prejudice shaped relations of power and authority in profound ways. International actors brought with them a set of theoretical assumptions, including that electoral democracy, formal institution-building and aid-driven service delivery would produce authoritative governance. Several chapters bring these assumptions – and the hypocrisies attendant in their pursuit – under the microscope. Presumptions about the nature of the Taliban as an object of both war-fighting and diplomacy are also the object of closer inquiry. Authors note the persistence of concepts and frameworks that remained largely divorced from realities on the ground and yet continued to dominate and drive the western imaginary, dictating key decisions over twenty years. They also point to the ways in which foreign governments, militaries and non-governmental actors ignored or failed to understand the import of performance, symbolism, ideology and memory to governance, whether on the part of the Afghan government, the insurgency that challenged it or the many actors that operated in the spaces between. Here, again, students of international relations – particularly those concerned with counterterrorism, democracy promotion and counterinsurgency – have much to learn from the evolving ways in which students of intervention in Afghanistan have come to understand how events unfolded there after 2001.

At the same time, our authors' critical considerations of interveners and their efforts do not come at the cost of acknowledging indigenous agency in the many forms it made itself manifest after 2001. On the contrary, each author in this volume does the work of centring Afghan actors, institutions and processes, many of which remained largely invisible to their foreign counterparts even as they affected foreign efforts in significant ways. Several chapters explore the nature of regime politics, reflecting on the choices made by key leaders and their very real effects on the trajectory of state building and war-fighting. Others draw our attention to those less easy to characterize – communities organized around mujahidin politics, for example, whose associations and allegiances transcended facile categories like 'state' or 'non-state'; businessmen whose networks and methods enabled them to survive, even thrive, by routinely transgressing the 'government' versus 'insurgent' divide; or minority populations whose historic marginalizations took on new inflections as their members rose to prominence after 2001. Many open the aperture of time, urging readers to reject 2001 as a start date and, instead, to consider the continuities – of republicanism, feminism, resistance, traditionalism and so on – that mirror a range of abiding indigenous agencies, ideas and authorities over many decades, even centuries.

Ultimately, this collection reflects Afghanistan as a site of study that offers up an exquisite collection of paradoxes that we anticipate (and hope) will continue to attract careful scholarly attention no matter which ways the geopolitical winds blow. This is, after all, a nation never colonized but also a state perpetually dependent on the patronage of outsiders. It is a collective of innumerable, sometimes clashing ethnicities, sects, tribes and clans; and, yet, not one has ever pushed for formal independence.[3] A vibrant political periphery has long made those at the margins undeniably central to negotiations of rule and governance. And, even as some have silenced and oppressed in the name of religion, deep faith-based traditions have proved unusually syncretic, flexible and resilient to ideology and tumult. Meanwhile, feminist, modernist, and democratic impulses have existed and evolved for more than a century, even as they are so often glossed as novel to the 'post-2001' period. Our authors do not engage these features as part of an exoticizing exercise that isolates the Afghan case from others; instead, they expose and probe them as abiding tensions that have long shaped – and will continue to shape – relations of power and modes of authority.

Notes

1   For more on the relationship between imperial encounter and knowledge production in/on Afghanistan, see Manchanda (2020). And with thanks to Haroun Rahimi for pointing my attention to the idea of Afghanistan as an 'n of 1'.
2   For example, I place Afghan state–society relations – and palace politics, in particular – into conversation with scholarship on the Arab state in Mukhopadhyay (2024).
3   On this point and the larger question of nationhood and belonging, see Sharifi (2019).

References

Manchanda, N. (2020), *Imagining Afghanistan: The History and Politics of Imperial Knowledge*. Cambridge: Cambridge University Press.
Mukhopadhyay, D. (2024), 'Palace Politics as Precarious Rule: Weak Statehood in Afghanistan', in Heydemann, S. and Lynch, M. (eds), *Making Sense of the Arab State*. Ann Arbor, MI: University of Michigan Press.
Sharifi, O. (2019), 'The Nauroz Festival as a Social Site: Understanding Faith, Ethnicity, and Nation-ness in Afghanistan'. PhD diss, Boston University.

Index

Abdul Ali Mazari 87
Abdul Rashid Dostum 87, 149, 279–80
Abdullah Abdullah 147, 276
Abdur Rahman Khan 4, 85, 127, 140, 221, 234, 236. *See also* 'Abd al-Rahman Khan, or Amir 'Abd al-Rahman 181–5, 193
accountability 4, 7, 83, 90, 92, 94, 110, 113, 256
activist 123, 258, 58, 61, 63
Afghan Mellat 58, 235
Afghan National Defense and Security Forces 9, 81, 85, 166, 274. *See also* ANDSF 81–3, 85–94, 149, 166, 274–5, 281
Afghan Republic 51, 130, 157–8, 166. *See also* Islamic Republic of Afghanistan 5, 23, 81–2, 94, 149, 258, 266, 272–3. *See also* Government of the Islamic Republic of Afghanistan 81
Ahmad Shah Abdali 3. *See also* Ahmad Shah Durrani 3–4, 29, 172, 192. *See also* Ahmad Khan Saddozai 172
aid (economy) 6, 10, 109, 142, 147, 220, 259
   agencies 7, 45, 102, 210, 213, 217
   and interference 7
   bilateral 75–8, 108–9, 113, 165, 178
   budgetary authority over 113–14
   budgets 106–7, 110, 147
   flows 151, 159
   humanitarian 109, 159
   influx of 152, 222
   international aid community 146, 217
   military 18
   oversight of 113
   power, authority and 287
   programmes 7
   reliance on 7, 109, 147, 220
   service delivery and 41, 287
   Taliban-distributed 41
   undelivered 114
   worker 153
Al Qaeda 29–30, 32, 59, 141, 164
Amanullah Khan 17–18, 27, 29, 40, 52, 57, 59, 74, 85, 103–4, 121, 140, 233–4, 237. *See also* Aman-Allah (Khan) 192
Amir Habibullah 140. *See also* Habibullah Khan, 233. *See also* Habib-Allah (Khan) 185–6, 188–93
Amir Habibullah Kalakani 17. *See also* Habibullah Kalakani 17, 140, 238. *See also* Kalakani 18, 239, 243
Amir-ul Mominin 62, 66, 233
Ashraf Ghani 17, 52, 77, 82–3, 86–94, 113, 146–7, 150, 154, 157, 166, 244, 255, 260, 275–6, 279. *See also* President Ghani 17, 52, 77, 82–3, 86–94, 113, 146–7, 150, 154, 157, 166, 244, 255, 260, 275–6, 279
authoritarian 1, 9, 28–9, 188, 234
authority 4–5, 21, 139–40, 154, 209, 220, 232, 282, 287–8
   as linked to descent/lineage 237, 239
   breadth and depth of 8
   budgetary 107, 110, 113
   charismatic 29
   decision-making 86, 89–90, 92, 201, 234
   definitions of 5, 8, 139, 142
   dissolution of international 106
   epistemic 124
   epistemological 118, 125, 129, 130
   local forms of 152, 154, 158
   narratives of 210, 231, 237
   obedience to 188, 191, 233–4
   of liberation discourse 126
   of mujahideen strongmen 77, 149, 152
   of the amir/head of state 64, 72, 77, 92, 188, 239
   patriarchal 104
   peripheral 171

political 71, 103, 113, 172–3, 203–4
public displays of 26, 30, 36
religious 29, 243
securing 10, 232, 272
state 6–7, 87, 111, 152, 172–3, 184, 193, 234, 240
substantive 10
through land ownership 222, 231
through reliance on foreign troops 23
traditional 103, 127
vague 139
autocracy 65, 188
autocratic 84, 188, 221

Barakzai (dynasty or clan of) 4, 140, 172, 174, 179, 182, 192
Bonn Agreement 88, 110–1, 114, 146
border 18, 34, 50, 56, 59–60, 109, 153, 172, 180, 185, 187, 190–1, 193, 241, 280
border thinking 59
brokers 150, 152–5, 158–60
bureaucracy 150, 221
Burhanuddin Rabbani 38, 59, 87, 240, 243

capital 146, 154, 220, 222
economic 27, 104, 109–10, 112
human 83, 112
land as 222
political 153, 210
Central Intelligence Agency 125, 141, 202. *See also* CIA 125, 141, 202
centralization 65–6, 83, 90, 94, 181, 221, 255, 280. *See also* decentralization 76, 173, 282
CIA (*See also* Central Intelligence Agency) 125, 141, 202
citizen 218, 234, 252–3
citizens 6–7, 29, 66, 109–10, 115, 130, 142, 151, 174, 177, 184, 200, 218–19, 231, 234, 237, 252–4, 257–8, 265, 282
citizenship 118, 127, 209–10, 219
civic associations 255, 259
civil society 27, 56, 110, 171–2, 193, 252, 256, 259–60, 266
civil war 5, 17, 50, 90, 106, 109, 123, 145, 154, 222, 235, 242–3, 277
clergy 4, 10, 56, 171–4, 177–8, 180–5, 187–8, 192–3, 23–4, 237, 243, 262–3

clerics 22, 29, 36, 45, 49. *See also ulema* 22, 36, 39, 49–50, 52, 56, 280. *See also* ulama 171, 173–5, 178–93
Cold War 9, 49–50, 75, 108–9, 127, 141, 251
Colonial
architecture 119
authorities/rule 57, 61, 108, 121, 210–1
circumstances 139
difference 59
discourses 57–8, 120, 122, 130, 237
empires 140
encounters 120, 127
eras/periods 119, 147
ethnography 121
expansion 6
feminism 122
interventions 73
legacies 10
logics of engagement 130
occupation 73
outsiders 143
roots 2
state 61
See also colonizers 10, colonialism 287, 71, 119–21, neo-colonialism 147 anti-colonial 1, 122, 140, quasi-colonial 9, 74, 120–1 crypto-colonial 9, 104, neocolonial 9, postcolonial 8, 55–7, 59–60, 72, 101, 108–9, 117, 119–21, 141, 287
colonization 120. *See also* decolonization 56, 108
commanders 38, 62, 84, 86, 90–1, 94, 111, 152, 202, 242, 277–81
communist 4, 19, 21–3, 32, 38, 49, 51, 71, 85, 87, 141, 143, 157, 234, 239, 251, 278
communist party factions 19
consensus 56, 64–5, 109, 129, 252, 256–7, 266
constitution 4, 18, 51, 65, 76, 90, 103, 114, 119, 121–2, 126, 151, 201, 203, 213, 216, 234, 244, 255, 257, 263
constructivist 6, 165
contractors 81, 150, 155–6, 160, 259
corruption 21, 74, 77, 82–3, 113, 128, 142, 146, 155, 157, 251, 254–5, 259, 264
counterinsurgency 128, 160, 288
countermodernity 25, 28, 38, 45

coup 9, 20, 22-3, 27, 49, 75, 83-9, 92, 94, 141, 239, 251
    Coup-proofing 83-94
critical juncture 4, 75

Daoud Khan 17-18, 20-2, 49, 75, 239
decolonization 56, 108. *See also* colonization, colonialism
defence 82, 87-8, 112, 166, 177, 202
deliberation 250-8, 265-6
democracy 11, 51, 53, 57, 106, 110, 114, 129-30, 146, 151, 159, 237, 250-62, 266, 287-8
    liberal democracy 11, 114, 129, 250, 253, 261
    parliamentary democracy 18
democratization 72, 77, 111, 151, 154, 252-5, 260
Deobandi 55, 59, 61, 66. *See also* neo-Deobandi 39, 55
Dependency 139, 142-3
diaspora 27, 244, 260
discourse 10, 28, 40, 60-1, 64, 67, 101-2, 117-30, 146, 163, 209, 231, 245, 251, 254, 258-60, 262, 264
discrimination 142, 199, 202-3, 258
dissent 8, 64-5, 204, 234
donors 110-1, 113, 115, 146, 154, 259-60
Dost Muhammad Khan 4, 237. *See also* Dust Muhammad Khan 173, 177-80
Durand Line 49, 109, 184, 186, 190

education 9, 27, 38-9, 42, 51, 56, 65-7, 85, 101-2, 112, 140, 141-3, 146, 159, 174, 188-9, 199-200, 216, 218, 220, 237-8, 258, 263, 265, 276, 278, 287; women's education 9, 27, 38-9, 42, 65-7, 101-4
elders 151, 156-7, 160, 219
elections 4-5, 29, 50-1, 65, 72, 77, 82, 111-2, 114-15, 139, 143, 146-7, 151, 200-2, 204, 220, 243, 253-5, 259, 262, 274, 279
electoral process 5, 204
elites 8, 10-1, 49, 72, 77, 103, 126, 139, 142, 151, 160, 234, 236-7, 240-1, 244, 253, 255, 259, 273

ethnicity 87, 127, 156, 210, 217, 231, 233, 237-45, 257, 261, 287
exclusion 10-1, 45, 142, 203-4, 210, 257, 260, 266

faction 23, 45, 111, 141, 238-40, 242, 273, 277
    Factions 19, 50, 59-61, 75-6, 111, 123, 145, 187, 201, 242-3, 277-9
failed state(s) 17, 109, 111
feminist 6, 26, 28, 56, 101, 128, 288
First World War 186, 189
Foucault, Michel 5, 31, 36, 117-18, 121-2
Fragile state(s) 7-8. *See also* Fragility (State) 7-8
fragility (State) 7-8. *See also* fragile state(s) 7-8
framing 118, 165-6
fundamentalism 28, 44, 57, 60, 67, 203, 260, 263
    fundamentalisms 55, 58
    fundamentalist(s) 9, 28, 45, 55-60, 62, 66-8, 242

GDP 81, 85, 112, 147
gender 26-7, 38, 46, 67, 101, 103, 114, 125, 212, 256-8, 261
Global South 57, 124
governance (structures of) 3, 10, 17, 51, 73-5, 118, 128, 131, 158, 277
    authoritative 4
    centralized system of 142, 255
    customary/local 126, 130, 158, 271-3, 276-8, 281-2
    externally imposed structures of 9, 71-3, 75
    global 108
    good 2, 127-8, 146, 251, 255, 286
    hybrid 75
    informal 72, 75, 256
    neopatrimonial 72, 74
    of international funds 113
    participatory 142
    past structures of 279, 282
    projects/programmes 141, 146, 159-60
    rebel 11, 276, 287-8
    stable 4, 18
    Taliban 9, 64-6, 68, 271, 282

transitional 114–15
wartime 271, 277, 281–2
Government of the Islamic Republic of Afghanistan, 81. *See also* Islamic Republic of Afghanistan 5, 23, 81–2, 94, 149, 258, 266, 272–3. *See also* Afghan Republic 51, 130, 157–8, 166
governmentality 118–19, 129–30, 211
Gulbuddin Hekmatyar 59, 87, 145, 200, 240, 242, 265

Habib-Allah (Khan) 185–6, 188–93. *See also* Habibullah Khan, 233. *See also* Amir Habibullah 140
Habibullah Kalakani 17, 140, 238. *See also* Amir Habibullah Kalakani 17. *See also* Kalakani 18, 239, 243
Habibullah Khan 233. *See also* Habib-Allah (Khan) Amir Habibullah 140
Hamid Karzai 46, 50, 76, 115, 146, 201, 219, 240. *See also* Karzai 52, 73, 77, 219, 240, 243, 263
hegemony 50, 55, 68, 120, 165, 232, 241, 243
Hijab 67, 263. *See also* veiling 18, 38, 41, 45–6, 67
Hizb-e Islami 51, 59, 61, 87, 165, 200, 242
Hizb-e Wahdat-e Islami Afghanistan 201
human rights 40, 42–3, 51, 65, 68, 89, 102, 111, 114, 117, 126, 146, 150, 219, 258, 263, 265

identity 11, 51, 58, 60–1, 87, 126–7, 130, 148, 209–10, 213, 215, 218, 220, 231–3, 235–7, 239–41, 243–5, 255, 258–61, 264, 266, 272, 287
IDP (Internally Displaced Person) 210, 215, 217–20
imperialism (European) 6, 45, 61, 107–8, 119–22, 125–6, 131, 159
incentives 76, 111, 153, 202
independence 6, 17, 104, 108, 115, 121, 140, 157, 174, 182, 185, 189–90, 192–3, 221, 288
instability 4, 6, 23, 151, 172, 234, 243, 253
institutions 8, 11, 72, 106, 115, 235, 250, 256–7, 262, 272–3, 277–8, 280, 288

bureaucratic 71, 73
democratic 251–5
educational 19, 199
financial 112, 114
formal 21, 72, 74, 76, 87, 254
informal 71–3, 254
international 107
military 85–6
non-state 51, 255, 278
parliamentary 254
political 71, 73, 254
rational legal 72, 74
religious 185, 262
security 88, 90, 109, 114–15
state 83, 108, 151–2, 216, 252, 259, 276, 279
insurgency 5, 22–3, 55–6, 59–60, 63, 65, 67, 91, 114, 146, 203, 287–8
international intervention 1, 71, 77, 124, 153, 160, 287
International Security Assistance Forces 110, 125. *See also* ISAF 110–2, 125, 214
interventionism 119, 130, 160
ISAF 110–12, 125, 214. *See also* International Security Assistance Forces 110, 125
Islam 1, 9, 22–3, 25, 32, 34, 36, 40, 45, 49–50, 52–3, 55–68, 102, 140, 143, 146, 177, 184, 187, 189, 192–3, 233–4, 243, 255, 261–3
Islamic Emirate 53, 65–6, 117, 145, 203
Islamic Republic of Afghanistan 5, 23, 81–2, 94, 149, 258, 266, 272–3. *See also* Government of the Islamic Republic of Afghanistan, 81 Afghan Republic 51, 130, 157–8, 166
Islamism 28, 49
Islamist 21–2, 38, 40, 44, 46, 49, 51, 53, 57, 60, 71, 75, 152, 242, 261–3, 287
pan Islamism 57–8, 172, 185, 189, 192–3
ISI 143, 60
ISIS 59, 85, 164, 201
ISKP (Islamic State Khorasan Province) 201

Jamiat 242–3, 273, 277–80. *See also* Jamiat-e Islami 19, 59, 61, 87, 273

Jamiat-e Islami 19, 59, 61, 87, 273. *See also* Jamiat 242–3, 273, 277–80
jihad 50, 61, 86, 141, 171–2, 176–81, 184–7, 190–3, 271, 274, 276, 279
jirgas 186, 191. *See also* loya Jirga 18, 38, 114, 172, 256. *See also* wolesi jirga 5, 222
Junbish 242. *See also* Junbish-e Milli Islami 87
Junbish-e Milli Islami 87. *See also* Junbish 242
Justice 18, 31, 56, 140, 146, 188, 234, 243, 253
   Afghanistan's former chiefs of 46, 50
   informal 126–8
   local 151
   National Sector Strategy 126
   Taliban Chief, 65–6, 203
   Taliban forms of 43
   Taliban minister of 65–6

Kabul University 59, 235–6, 238–40
Karzai 52, 73, 77, 219, 240, 243, 263. *See also* Hamid Karzai 46, 50, 76, 115, 146, 201, 219, 240
Khalq 19, 58, 75, 141, 238–9
   Khalqi 76
   Khalqis 239
Kuchi 11, 209–10, 214–16, 219, 221–3

land
   access to 214, 220–3
   as a currency of power 210, 220
   grants 74, 185
   imaginaries of 209
   ownership 76, 174, 209, 217–18, 220–3, 238, 287
   prices 222
   (reforms) 61, 103, 175–6
   seizure 222
   UNHCR allocation of 218
leadership 7, 9, 21, 50, 59, 81–3, 85, 88, 94, 150, 180, 192, 263, 271, 279, 281
   Afghan military 81, 91–3
   appointments 89–90
   concept of 172, 175
   foreign 147
   local structures of 143, 152
   parliamentary 259

Taliban 62, 65
legitimacy 6, 8, 10, 23, 30–2, 52–3, 77, 83, 102–3, 109, 113–15, 139, 142–3, 145–7, 152, 171–2, 179, 193, 231, 237–40, 243, 245, 253–4, 256, 259, 266, 272, 276–7 deficit 10, 73, 109
legitimation 1, 7–8, 112, 124, 232
liberation 118, 123–6, 129–31, 242
logics of rule 2, 8–9
Loya Jirga 18, 38, 114, 172, 256

madrasa 61, 143, 174, 176, 184, 187–9. *See also* madrasas 154. *See also* madrasa 61, 143, 174, 176, 184, 187–9
Mahmud Tarzi 57–8, 189, 191
Marxist 27, 58, 165, 238
media 1, 28, 31, 37, 51, 67, 88, 125, 151, 200, 258–9, 263–4
   social 68, 163, 203, 263, 281
   western 243
militia 6, 29, 40, 60, 76, 154, 242
minority 209–10, 213, 217, 240–1, 288
modernism 25, 28, 57–8
   modernist 34, 40, 55–6, 58–60, 64, 67, 288
modernity 25–9, 32–3, 36, 40, 56–9, 66, 118, 120, 129, 236
modernization 18, 56–7, 76, 241
Mojadiddi 233–4, 239–40, 242, 264. *See also* Mujaddidi 173, 176, 183, 189, 191, Mujaddidis 182, 185
monarchy 20–1, 31, 50, 74, 172, 193, 238–41, 243–4
moral 23, 26, 33, 36, 44, 49, 52–3, 64, 234, 250–2, 256, 260, 262, 266, 275–6
morale 81–3, 90, 93, 166, 203
mosque 29–30, 33, 42, 173–4, 238
   mosques 31, 33, 35, 44, 123, 174, 178, 180, 191, 235, 278
Muhammad Mohaqeq 200
Muhammadzai 140, 172–3, 179, 232, 236–9
Mujaddidi 173, 176, 183, 189, 191
   Mujaddidis 182, 185
See also Mojadiddi 233–4, 239–40, 242, 264
mujahidin 49–52, 59–63, 66, 77, 87, 111, 141, 145, 165, 240, 242–3, 271, 275–81, 288

Mullah Haibatullah Akhundzada 65
Mullah Muhammad Omar 29, 61. *See also*
    Mullah Omar 29–31, 35–7, 40, 42,
    44–5, 61–2, 64–6
Musahiban, (dynasty of) 4, 8, 17–19, 21,
    23–4, 57, 71, 73–5, 77, 140, 233–4
Muslim Brotherhood 19, 22, 50
Muslim Youth Organization 21, 59, 75

Nader Khan 17, 87, 140. *See also* Nader
    Shah 18, 85, 140, 234, 237, 239, 242
Nader Shah 18, 85, 140, 234, 237, 239, 242.
    See also Nader Khan 17, 87, 140
(Dr) Najibullah 32, 76, 87, 145, 239–40
nation-state 63–6, 107, 110, 127, 139
National Unity Government (NUG) 244,
    265
nationalist 1, 21, 52–3, 57–8, 60, 87, 115,
    148, 192, 243, 275
    nationalism 49, 52, 57, 87, 140, 146–7,
    172, 185, 187–9, 193, 236
nativism 40, 56
NATO 81–2, 85–6, 92–3, 101, 107, 141,
    143, 147, 166, 202, 281
neo-colonialism 147
neo-Deobandi 39, 55. *See also* Deobandi
    55, 59, 61, 66
neoliberal 124, 213, 286
neopatrimonial 9, 71–3, 77–8
networks 72–7, 112, 150, 154–6, 158, 160,
    211, 221, 255, 277–9, 281–2, 288
NGO (Non-Governmental Organization)
    5, 210, 213–14
    NGOs 51, 110, 113, 126, 155, 157,
    216–17, 259, 278
nobility 231–2, 237, 241
nomad 209–11, 213–14, 216, 222–3, 287
    nomads 200, 209–17, 222
Northern Alliance 29, 46, 88, 111, 240, 243

opposition 8, 18, 20–1, 26, 29, 58, 63, 103,
    123, 125, 177–8, 182, 188, 210, 202,
    243, 272, 277–9
Osama Bin Laden 29, 141

Pakistan 21, 27, 34, 38, 42, 49–50, 52, 66,
    101–2, 107, 141, 143, 145, 163, 166,
    200, 213
    Pakistani 34, 36, 49, 60, 142, 243, 280

Pan-Islamism 57–8, 172, 185, 189, 192–3
Parcham 19, 21, 58, 75, 141
    Parchami 22, 76
parliament 5, 21, 90, 92, 157, 192, 201,
    216, 252, 255
    parliamentarian 209, 220
    parliamentarians 155, 210, 215–16, 222
    parliamentary 5, 18, 82, 146, 157,
    200–1, 213, 217, 244, 254–5, 274
Pashtunistan 49, 52
Pashtūn-wāli 172. *See also* Pashtunwali
    126
Pashtunwali 126. *See also pashtūn-wāli* 172
patriarchal 26–7, 104
    patriarchy 28, 44, 125
patrimonial 71, 74–8
    patrimonialism 71–8
See also neopatrimonial 9, 71–3, 77
patronage 9, 72–4, 76–7, 112, 114, 185,
    199, 201–2, 204, 222, 254–5, 259,
    288
PDPA. *See also* People's Democratic
    Party of Afghanistan 23, 63, 75–6,
    238–41, 244, 275
peace 17, 23–4, 38, 50, 62, 106–7, 109, 117,
    127, 140, 145–6, 181, 216, 134, 253,
    258, 264
    negotiations/talks 102, 164, 203–4,
    280
    peace process 257
    settlement 179, 265, 280
peace building 10, 106–7, 109
People's Democratic Party of Afghanistan.
    See also PDPA 23, 63, 75–6, 238–41,
    244, 275
performativity 64, 145–6, 263
    performative 145, 255
peripatetic 209–13, 217–21, 223
    peripatetics 210–2, 217–23
periphery 107–8, 192, 242, 287–8
persecution 22, 200
piety 27, 32, 36, 173, 175–6, 179, 182, 184
Pir Gilani 30
pluralism 130, 146, 231, 250–2, 256–62,
    265–6
poetry 3, 57, 62
political culture 139–40, 142–3, 232, 237
political economy 8, 10, 49, 139, 142,
    152–4, 159–60, 251, 255, 259

political parties 49, 51, 58, 75, 152, 157, 159, 201, 243, 251. *See also* political party 66, 201
populist 17, 51, 113, 238
postcolonial 8, 55–7, 59–60, 72, 101, 108–9, 117, 119–21, 141, 287
power 1–11, 18–20, 22, 25–6, 28–9, 32, 37–8, 44–5, 49–53, 55–6, 59–68, 72–4, 76, 82–3, 86–90, 92, 103–4, 109, 112–14, 117, 121–3, 126, 130–1, 140–2, 150–1, 154, 158, 160, 165, 172–3, 175–6, 183, 185, 188, 193, 199, 202–4, 209–10, 216, 220, 222, 231, 234, 237–39, 241, 243, 245, 251, 254–58, 260–1, 272–3, 278–80, 282, 286, 288
   American 119, 123–4, 129–130, 147
   centralization of 66, 181, 221, 280
   de facto 51
   definitions/concepts of 1–11, 151, 165–6, 209–10, 213, 287
   economic 173–4, 241
   imperial 118, 120–2, 131, 177
   leased 10, 139–42
   power by spectacle 8, 25, 28–9, 31–2, 37, 43, 44
   power-knowledge 119–21
   power-sharing 111, 243, 258, 279
   productive 118–19, 121–2, 130–1
   religious 171–2, 181, 183, 185
   struggles 61, 172, 178–9, 192, 221–2, 243
   symbolic 32, 147
powerbrokers 10, 76, 176, 201, 217
private sphere 25–6, 37, 45
propaganda 55, 62, 238, 243
public sphere 25–8, 32, 37, 45, 212, 250–3, 256–63, 266
punishment 32, 36, 43–4, 67, 124

Qawm 215, 278
Quetta Shura 65–6

reconstruction 10, 85, 92, 106–7, 110, 114, 131, 152, 199, 278
refugee 27, 60, 242
   refugees 38, 40, 154, 213, 233, 240, 242
religion 3, 26, 28, 33, 39, 44–5, 58, 64, 102, 146, 171, 234, 245, 257, 274, 288

rentier economy 10
rentier state 7
representation 26, 28, 32, 36, 118, 157, 201–1, 243, 273
republican 78, 85, 93, 163, 179
resistance 2, 8, 10–1, 53, 59–63, 68, 76, 87, 112, 125, 127, 141, 149–50, 157, 165, 177–8, 182, 190, 193, 203–4, 271–3, 276–7, 279–82, 288
Revolutionary Association of Afghan Women (RAWA) 28, 42
ritual 26, 30, 32, 45, 64
royalty 4, 49–50, 5

Sadduzai 172–3, 177–8, 192. *See also* Sadozai, 4, 239
Sadozai 4, 239. *See also* Sadduzai 172–3, 177–8, 192
Salafist 55, 201
schools 9, 38–41, 101–2, 112, 123, 154, 174, 188, 199–200, 203, 218, 235
Second World War 18, 28, 75, 108, 140
security 5, 8, 10, 73, 82, 86, 88–90, 94, 106–14, 127, 142, 145–6, 204, 218, 242
   assistance 82–3, 94, 109–10, 112, 159, 259
   contractors 156, 159, 260
   expenditure 85
   forces 9, 81, 85, 90–2, 110–2, 155, 166, 274, 281
   global security agenda 115
   human security 146
   institutions 88, 109, 114–15
   local 276–7
   National Directorate of Security 202
   National Security Council 86, 92
   national strategy 82
   officers/officials 87, 89–90, 202
   sector 83, 85–6, 110, 280, 287
   Security Sector Reform 94, 110
   Taliban security 160
   UN Security Council 108, 110
   US security 107–8
Sharia 28–9, 31–3, 35, 37–9, 43, 52, 61, 65–6, 172, 174, 179, 183, 188, 191, 203–4, 234, 262, 265
Shia 50, 202–3, 232
Sitam-e Mili 58, 235

socialism 23, 75, 252
   socialist 57, 60, 75, 141, 151
sovereignty 10, 74–5, 106–8, 113–15, 118, 122, 127–8, 130–1, 177
Soviet Union 9, 18–19, 26, 49, 75, 149
stability 4–5, 7–8, 17, 23, 62, 73–4, 77, 106, 109, 128, 140, 146, 234–5, 242, 244–45
state building 1, 7, 10, 57, 63, 74, 76–7, 82, 103, 106–12, 114–15, 127–8, 145, 147, 160, 251, 271, 277, 288
state capacity 4, 6–8, 112
statehood 2, 7, 65, 127, 210
succession (lines of) 3, 140, 171–3, 181
suffrage 4, 114
Sufi 49, 56, 59, 62, 173–6, 183–4, 187, 190, 233–4, 262
Sunni 50, 172, 189, 203, 233, 236
surveillance 37, 44, 191

taxation 9, 103, 143, 276
taxes 34, 75, 140, 142, 156, 183, 278
technocrats 51–2, 244, 260
territoriality 209
   territorial 7, 171, 177, 242, 282
terrorist 55, 164
   terrorists 112, 124, 164–6, 265
tribal affairs 4, 191, 216, 219, 241, 261
tribalism 40, 49, 106, 117–19, 125–31

ulama 171, 173–4, 178–93. *See also ulema* 22, 36, 39, 49–50, 52, 56, 280. *See also* clerics 22, 29, 36, 45, 49
ulema 22, 36, 39, 49–50, 52, 56, 280. *See also* ulama 171, 173–5, 178–93. *See also* clerics 22, 29, 36, 45, 49
UN 87, 106–12, 114–15, 154–5. *See also* United Nations 106
United Nations, 106. *See also* UN 87, 106–12, 114–15, 154–5
United States 5, 6, 9, 18, 44, 49, 50, 73, 75, 77, 81–2, 85–6, 88–9, 93, 107–15, 118–19, 123–8, 131, 141–2, 152, 154, 158–9, 163–6, 199, 202, 204, 231, 240, 244, 274–5, 277, 279. *See also* US 10, 21, 37, 50, 77, 81–2,

85–6, 88, 90, 92–4, 101–2, 104, 107–8, 110–2, 115, 117–19, 122–5, 127–9, 131, 141–2, 147, 152, 153, 155–6, 159–60, 163, 165–7, 202, 213, 235, 251, 255
urbanization 51, 236, 245
US 10, 21, 37, 50, 77, 81–2, 85–6, 88, 90, 92–4, 101–2, 104, 107–8, 110–2, 115, 117–19, 122–5, 127–9, 131, 141–2, 147, 152–3, 155–6, 159–60, 163, 165–7, 202, 213, 235, 251, 255. *See also* United States 5, 6, 9, 18, 44, 49–50, 73, 75, 77, 81–2, 85–6, 88–9, 93, 107–15, 118–19, 123–8, 131, 141–2, 152, 154, 158–9, 163–6, 199, 202, 204, 231, 240, 244, 274–5, 277, 279

veiling 18, 38, 41, 45–6, 67. *See also* hijab 67, 263
violence 5, 8, 83, 101–2, 111–2, 130, 146–7, 151, 153, 159, 163, 165, 200, 204, 242–43, 245, 262
   domestic 264
   epistemic 67
   imposition of 146, 159
   monopoly of 4, 6
   non-violence 61
   political 273–4
   spectacles of 8
   Taliban 32

Wahdat 87–8, 201, 242
war on terror 50, 56, 63, 68, 101, 109–10
Weber, Max 6, 72, 139
withdrawal (international troop) 1, 9, 10, 81–2, 86, 93, 102, 104, 117–19, 128–9, 131, 164–7, 181, 251, 280
   British 182
   soviet 61, 239–40, 244, 278
Wolesi Jirga 5, 222

Young Afghans 57–8, 236

Zahir Shah 17–21, 30, 65, 74, 237, 239–40